THE *HISTORY* OF
THEOPHYLACT SIMOCATTA

The *History* of Theophylact Simocatta

An English Translation with Introduction and Notes

MICHAEL

AND

MARY WHITBY

CLARENDON PRESS · OXFORD

Oxford University Press, Walton Street, Oxford OX2 6DP

Oxford New York Toronto
Delhi Bombay Calcutta Madras Karachi
Petaling Jaya Singapore Hong Kong Tokyo
Nairobi Dar es Salaam Cape Town
Melbourne Auckland

and associated companies in
Berlin Ibadan

Oxford is a trade mark of Oxford University Press

Published in the United States
by Oxford University Press, New York

First published 1986
Reprinted 1988

British Library Cataloguing in Publication Data

Theophylact, Simocatta
The History of Theophylact Simocatta: an English
translation with introduction and notes.
1. Byzantine Empire—Politics and
government—527–1081
I. Title II. Whitby, Michael III. Whitby, Mary
949.5'01   DF571
ISBN 0–19–822799–X

Library of Congress Cataloging in Publication Data

Simocatta, Theophylactus.
The History of Theophylact Simocatta.
Translation of: Historiae.
Bibliography: p.
Includes index.
1. Byzantine Empire—History—Maurice, 582–602.
I. Whitby, Michael. II. Whitby, Mary. III. Title.
DF573.5.S513 1986   949.5'01   85–18840
ISBN 0–19–822799–X

Printed in Great Britain by
Antony Rowe Ltd,
Chippenham

. . . καὶ τὰν μάλουριν, τὰν ἔτρεμε θηρία μικκά.

Preface

THE publication of the first English translation of Theophylact Simocatta's *History* requires no justification. The work is an important
source for the history of the Roman empire in the late sixth century,
but the style of Theophylact's Greek is such that few people are likely
to read the text in the original, while the Latin translation by I. Bekker
in the Bonn Corpus edition (Bonn, 1834), to which readers are most
likely to turn for assistance, is based on a poor text and is often more
obscure than the original. There is also an early French translation
(without notes) by L. Cousin (*Histoire de Constantinople*, iii, Paris, 1685),
but this is not widely available; in any case Cousin used the inaccurate
text of Fabrottus (Paris, 1648), and tended to paraphrase rather than
translate Theophylact's obscurities. The only modern translation of
the *History* is the Russian version, with brief notes, by N. Pigulevskaja
(Moscow, 1957).

This project arose from a study of the *History* of Theophylact which
led to an Oxford D.Phil. thesis by Michael Whitby. We decided to
undertake this translation in collaboration in the hope that two heads
would be better able than one to resolve the complexities of Theophylact's Greek, and the translation of the text has been a joint enterprise throughout. The notes and introduction are derived from the
D.Phil. thesis, which provides fuller discussion of the various problems presented by the text; the thesis is to be published as an Oxford
Historical Monograph under the title 'The Emperor Maurice and his
Historian'.

This publication has been generously assisted by grants from the
Last/Atkinson Funds administered by the Society for the Promotion
of Roman Studies, the Derby Scholarship Fund on the recommendation of the Craven Committee of Oxford University, and the Oxford
Inter-Faculty Committee for Slavonic and East European Studies.
We are most grateful for these grants, and to those who assisted us in
obtaining them, particularly Professor C. A. Mango, Dr J. F. Mat-
thews, and Professor Sir Dimitri Obolensky. Especial mention should
be made of the long-standing encouragement and assistance of Dr
J. D. Howard-Johnston, who supervised the D.Phil. thesis which

preceded the translation. We are much indebted to David Moncur, whose assistance at a critical time revived spirits that were flagging under the weight of Theophylactean rhetoric, and whose acute perception of the nuances of Greek and English improved the translation at many points. Most of the work on the translation was carried out during the period of a Junior Research Fellowship at Merton College, to whose generosity we are grateful.

The task of translating a major text has revealed to us the difficulties of producing an acceptable version. There are undoubtedly imperfections in our translation, and its style will not suit the tastes of all, but we take comfort in the fact that even Theophylact was prepared to admit his inadequacies (*Proem* 16). We shall be satisfied if the appearance of this translation stimulates greater interest in a neglected historian.

Contents

Maps

List of Abbreviations

AB	*Analecta Bollandia*
BMGS	*Byzantine and Modern Greek Studies*
BNJ	*Byzantinische-neugriechische Jahrbücher*
BZ	*Byzantinische Zeitschrift*
CSCO	*Corpus Scriptorum Christianorum Orientalium*
CSHB	*Corpus Scriptorum Historiae Byzantinae*
FHG	*Fragmenta Historicorum Graecorum*
JRGS	*Journal of the Royal Geographic Society*
MGH	*Monumenta Germaniae Historica*
PG	*Patrologia Graeca*
PO	*Patrologia Orientalis*

Introduction

THEOPHYLACT SIMOCATTA, who wrote in the early seventh century during the reign of Heraclius (610-41), was the last in the succession of secular classicizing historians of late antiquity, writers who undertook to provide a narrative devoted mainly to the military, diplomatic, and political (but not religious) history of the Roman empire, in self-conscious imitation of classical historians such as Herodotus, Thucydides, Diodorus Siculus, or Arrian. He was the continuator of the histories of Procopius, Agathias, and Menander Protector, who had recorded most of Roman (i.e. east Roman) history from the accession of Justin I in 518 to the death of Tiberius in 582. His own history of the reign of the emperor Maurice (582-602) was not continued until the late eighth or early ninth century, when the Patriarch Nicephorus produced a brief account of the seventh and eighth centuries that was designed to follow on from Theophylact's narrative.

Life and writings

Relatively little is known about Theophylact. His surname or nickname Simocatta appears to mean 'snub-nosed cat', and presumably refers to his appearance. In contrast to Agathias and Menander, whose prefaces contain numerous personal details, Theophylact declined to present such information to his audience directly, and it is only incidentally that he remarks that he came from Egypt (vii. 16. 10),[1] where one of his relatives had occupied the post of *Augustalis* at the end of Maurice's reign (viii. 13. 12). His date of birth is unknown, but it was probably towards the end of the 580s. He no doubt received his early education at Alexandria, where he would have been given a general rhetorical training of a literary and philosophical character that served as a basis for later specialist studies in the law. He may have attended the University of Alexandria, where at the end of the sixth century the traditions of Aristotelian scholarship were maintained by the philosopher Stephen, to whom there may be an allusion in Theophylact's introductory Dialogue (§ 6 with n. 7). At about the age of twenty, perhaps towards the end of the first decade of the seventh century,

---

[1] All references are to Theophylact's *History* unless otherwise stated.

xiii

Theophylact moved to Constantinople to pursue a legal education. At any rate, Theophylact had arrived in Constantinople by, or shortly after, the overthrow of the tyrant Phocas and the start of Heraclius' reign in 610, since he was on hand to deliver a panegyric to commemorate Maurice and his family (viii. 12. 3-7) when Heraclius belatedly organized a funeral for his murdered predecessor. This grandiloquent speech may well have furthered his legal and administrative career, which, to judge from his rank of *ex-praefectus* and *antigrapheus* recorded in the title to the *History* (preserved by Photius), was highly successful. This career may well have been crowned by appointment to the specialized post of sacred judge, since an *ex-praefectus* named Theophylact is attested in that post by an inscription from Aphrodisias, which should probably be dated to 641.[2] Like the two lawyer historians of the late sixth century, the cousins John of Epiphania and Evagrius, who were employed in the service of Gregory, the Patriarch of Antioch, it is possible that Theophylact's legal career was pursued in the employment of the Patriarch of Constantinople, Sergius: the introductory Dialogue (§§ 8-12) alludes to Sergius as the man who had encouraged the composition of history and who had perhaps provided some sort of position for Theophylact ('an advantageously sited rostrum', § 10 with n. 11).[3]

In addition to the *History*, there are three surviving minor works by Theophylact. Two of these are secular, the *Quaestiones Physicae* and the *Ethical Epistles*. The *Quaestiones Physicae*, or *Problems of Natural History*, is in the form of a Platonic dialogue and deals with some of the supposed wonders of nature such as why ravens do not drink in summer; it is scarcely a serious work of scholarship, but merely a brief example, intended to entertain, of the paradoxographic genre of pseudo-scientific literature which discussed such matters (cf. e.g.

---

[2] H. Grégoire, *Recueil des inscriptions grecques chrétiennes d'Asie Mineure*, i (Paris, 1922), 88, no. 247.

[3] This reconstruction of Theophylact's life differs from that recently advanced by Olajos, 'La carrière de Théophylacte', who revived the suggestion of Haussig, 'Exkurs' 292-3, that Theophylact was employed at some stage in the service of Probus, bishop of Chalcedon (from 592). The evidence is not convincing. Theophylact has information about Probus' diplomatic mission to Chosroes II (v. 15. 8-11, with n. 82 for the date, probably after 595), and retails a story about the miracles of St Euphemia of Chalcedon (viii. 14. 1-9, but note that the bishop involved is not named). Both these reports are likely to have gained currency after Maurice's death (see book v n. 83, and vii n. 86), and would have been known to people outside the immediate entourage of the bishop of Chalcedon. There is no sign in the *History*, not even in the account of Maurice's death at Chalcedon, that Theophylact himself was in the vicinity of Constantinople during Maurice's reign.

Aelian, *de Natura Animalium*). The eighty-five *Ethical Epistles* present a fictitious correspondence, divided into the categories of ethical, rustic, and amatory, between various historical and mythical characters on a range of moral topics. They belong to the genre of fictitious epistolography (cf. e.g. the letters of Alciphron) and, like the *Quaestiones Physicae*, are intended for the entertainment of their readers. Neither work is particularly substantial, and it is probably correct to regard the *Quaestiones Physicae*, and perhaps also the *Ethical Epistles*, as *juvenilia*, literary exercises that displayed Theophylact's cultural attainment and his familiarity with some of the topics of secular education.

Theophylact's third minor work is a discussion entitled *On Predestined Terms of Life*, which deals with the theological question of whether the lengths of human lives are predetermined. The discussion consists of balanced speeches by two opposing speakers (Theognostus and Theophrastus), followed by a third set speech in which two adjudicators (Evangelus and Theopemptus) pronounce their verdict. In form, *Predestined Terms* reflects the pattern of the *controversiae* (a speech and counter-speech that might be followed by a concluding evaluation or judgement) which constituted a standard element in the rhetorical education that Theophylact received in his youth. In terms of subject, however, it is hard to find antecedents for this work. Garton and Westerink, the editors of the text, suggest that the topic was probably a matter for discussion in contemporary theological circles; they point to a mention of the question of 'the terms of life' in the fourth-century Church Father Basil,[4] but there is no extant full-scale discussion of the theme before Theophylact, so that Theophylact may actually have collected for himself the numerous biblical references which provide the backbone for the various arguments in the debate.[5] In *Predestined Terms* Theophylact (in the persons of the adjudicators) cautiously adopted a middle course between predestined and random fate, and placed emphasis on the limitations of human knowledge: in the face of man's inability to reach certainty, human life must be governed by moderation and caution (*Predestined Terms*, p. 30). This conclusion to the work is relevant to Theophylact's judgement of events in his *History*: cautious moderation in both good and bad fortune is praised, while immoderate reactions of triumph and despair are naturally criticized. *Predestined Terms* demonstrates Theophylact's interest in religious

---

[4] Basil, *Homil. quod deus non est auctor malorum* 9. 3 (*PG* 31. 333b).
[5] *Predestined Terms*, Introduction x–xi.

questions, his knowledge of the Bible, and his familiarity with the idiosyncratic Greek style of the Septuagint. The Christian interests of *Predestined Terms* are reflected in the *History*, both in Theophylact's biblical knowledge (the sermon of Bishop Domitianus at iv. 16 is, like *Predestined Terms*, replete with biblical allusions) and in his choice of vocabulary, which combines Septuagint and classical language. Although the *History* is placed in the tradition of secular historiography, it is more clearly a work of Christian history than the works of Procopius and Agathias had been: they had managed to preserve, to a significant extent, a careful façade of intellectual detachment towards religious matters, whereas Theophylact was content to introduce Christian terminology and to display his interest in religious questions and his liking for hagiographical stories. Theophylact was well educated in both secular and Christian culture, a joint training that is reflected both in his minor works and in the *History*.

None of Theophylact's literary works can be precisely dated. The three minor works contain no datable references, and it is no more than an assumption that these lesser works were composed before the major *History*. Broad *termini* for the *History* can be established: from the introductory Dialogue it appears that it was begun after the death of Phocas in 610 (§§ 3-7), but before that of the Patriarch Sergius in 638 (§§ 11-12); the latest event that is clearly mentioned in the *History* is the death of Chosroes II in 628 (viii. 12. 13), but Heraclius' triumph over the Persians in the same year is also foreshadowed in Chosroes' astrological prophecy (v. 15. 3-7 with nn.), and the mood of this triumph is reflected in Domitianus' speech at Martyropolis (iv. 16). It is probable that the whole work was composed towards the end of the 620s, when the defeat of Persia encouraged the Patriarch Sergius to believe that the tradition of secular historiography, which had stopped at the end of Menander's history with the death of Tiberius, should be brought down to the present day. At the very same time, a second historical work, the *Chronicon Paschale*, was being produced, in order to extend the *Chronicle* of Malalas down to 630 and Heraclius' triumphant restoration of Roman affairs; this too was probably composed under the patronage of Sergius. Secular history was never in fact brought up to date: although Theophylact proclaimed his intention of describing the events of Phocas' reign (viii. 12. 14, 14. 10), and very probably intended to cover Heraclius' victories over the Persians, these parts of the *History* were not completed, so that the work terminates, somewhat abruptly, with the overtures to the renewal of war between Rome and Persia in 602. The reasons for Theophylact's failure to complete the work are unknown, but if the revival of history had been inspired by Heraclius' victories against Persia it is possible that this inspiration was quenched when the Arab invasions of the 630s rapidly invalidated these victories.

The History

The period covered by Theophylact's *History* is the twenty-year reign of Maurice, within which two major topics dominate the historical narrative: warfare in the Balkans against the Slavs and Avars and on the eastern frontier against the Persians. Throughout the sixth century the Roman provinces in the Balkans had been subjected to repeated attacks by different bands of tribesmen, principally the Slavs and Bulgars, but during the 570s two factors had combined to make the situation markedly worse: the Romans had been forced to devote all available money and manpower to the war against Persia, which they had provoked in 572, so that the Balkan defences were inevitably weakened; meanwhile, to the north of the Danube the Avars, recent arrivals from Central Asia, had managed to impose their control over many of the disparate tribal groups whose internal feuding the Romans had previously manipulated to their own advantage. As a result, the Avars were sufficiently powerful to demand concessions from the Romans, and if these were denied they could wrest them by force, as in the case of the city of Sirmium which they captured in 581/2 after a three-year siege (i. 3. 3-5 with n. 15). At the same time the expansion of Avar power impelled other tribes who were reluctant to fall under their suzerainty to migrate: most of the Lombards, the former allies of the Avars, had moved to Italy in 568, and in the 570s the Slav tribes along the lower Danube began to seek safety by crossing the river to invade Roman territory. By the end of Tiberius' reign, Avar might was symbolized by the humiliating treaty which they imposed on the Romans (i. 3. 3-7), while Roman weakness was revealed by the growing tendency of Slav raiders to settle inside the empire on the deserted lands which had been abandoned as the result of their ravaging.

In the first half of Maurice's reign, until the conclusion of the Persian war in 591, there was relatively little that the emperor could do to improve the position. The Slavs were pushed back from the environs of Constantinople (i. 7. 1-6), but the limited forces available to the Romans were insufficient to oppose the Avars (ii. 10. 8-17. 13; vi.

3. 9-5. 16). Numerous cities along the Danube were sacked by the Avars, while Slav raids and migrations were directed towards the parts of the Balkans remote from Constantinople, particularly towards Greece, where Thessalonica was besieged and Athens and Corinth sacked. The conclusion of the Persian war (591) and the transfer of good troops from the eastern front changed affairs, and the second half of Maurice's reign is the story of the gradual reassertion of Roman authority in the region south of the Danube and of the aggressive strikes to the north of that river which were intended to thwart further invasions. The Roman recovery was slow and not without setbacks, as when the Avars caught the disorganized Roman armies by surprise (vii. 13. 1-15. 14), but the Avars were no longer the irresistible force which they had been in the 580s, whereas the Romans obtained regular successes against the Slavs. The defence of the Danube frontier required constant vigilance by the Romans. Experience taught the Romans the best tactics for dealing with the different military threats of the Avars and Slavs, tactics which are enshrined in the contemporary military handbook known as the *Strategicon* of Maurice (particularly xi. 2, 4); this important work was composed by an officer who had experience of these Balkan campaigns and who was probably writing towards the end of Maurice's reign. Success against the Slavs could best be achieved by campaigns in winter as well as in summer, but this year-round activity strained the allegiance of the Roman armies, who were accustomed to the rhythm of summer campaigning and winter rest. Maurice's insistence on winter campaigning (viii. 6. 2-7. 7), coupled with recurrent financial shortages that made him appear miserly, provoked unrest in the armies, who elected the officer Phocas as leader of their mutiny; the success of the mutiny placed Phocas on the imperial throne.

On the eastern frontier, the fifty-year peace which had been negotiated between Justinian and Chosroes I lasted only ten years before it was broken by Justin II, who refused to continue the annual payments to the Persians stipulated in the treaty. Various pretexts could be advanced to cloak his bellicosity (iii. 9. 6-8), but the principle inducement to war was probably the apparent disarray of the Persian empire, which was troubled by serious disaffection among its Christian subjects in Armenia and by the threat of an invasion across its northeast frontier by the Turks, who had promised to co-ordinate their attack with Justin II. The events of the first decade of the war are briefly narrated by Theophylact in a digression (iii. 9. 1-18. 4). Affairs proceeded disastrously for the Romans. After minor initial successes that were achieved because the Persians were unprepared, the Roman lack of proper military preparations was starkly exposed when in 573 the Persian king Chosroes I attacked and captured the major frontier fortress of Dara (iii. 11. 2); this had been regarded as an impregnable bastion of the Roman empire and constituted a perpetual irritation to the Persians ever since its construction by Anastasius in the first decade of the sixth century. News of the disaster unhinged Justin II's mind, and the Romans were forced to purchase truces, which terminated the fighting in Mesopotamia and restricted hostilities to Armenia. In December 574, the appointment of Tiberius as Caesar began a gradual recovery by the Romans; troops were recruited and trained (iii. 12. 4-8), and an over-ambitious expedition into Armenia by Chosroes ended in humiliation (iii. 12. 11-14. 11), even though the great Roman victory in pitched battle that Theophylact describes probably never took place; from 578 onwards, under the leadership of Maurice, the Romans were on the whole able to maintain the strategic initiative in the war by encroaching on Arzanene (iii. 15. 14-15), ravaging Mesopotamia (iii. 16. 1-2, 17. 3-4), and defeating Persian invasions (iii. 18. 1-2). After the accession of Maurice, this general pattern of Roman success continued, with further attacks on Arzanene, widespread ravaging of the territory on both sides of the Tigris, and victories in pitched battles. On the Persian side the only major success came when the Roman frontier city of Martyropolis was captured by treachery. The war ended suddenly. A revolt in the Persian army led to the overthrow and death of King Hormisdas in February 590, and the flight of his successor Chosroes II to the Romans for assistance. With Roman help, the usurper Baram was defeated and Chosroes reinstated in 591, with the result that peace was made on terms favourable to the Romans.

In addition to these two main theatres of warfare, the Romans were engaged in military or diplomatic activity in Africa, Italy, France, and Spain during Maurice's reign, but events in the western Mediterranean are scarcely mentioned by Theophylact, who clearly had little interest in researching or recording such distant affairs. The defeats of Moorish attacks on Africa are twice noted (iii. 4. 8; vii. 6. 6-7), but no details are provided of the considerable successes achieved by Gennadius the governor. Lombard attacks on the city of Rome are mentioned once (iii. 4. 8), but there is no narrative of the fluctuations of Lombard power in northern and central Italy or of the various attempts by Maurice to organize a Frankish attack on the Lombards in conjunction with a Roman offensive from Ravenna. An embassy from one of the Frankish kings is reported (vi. 3. 6-8), but there is no mention of Maurice's support for the Merovingian pretender Gundovald, which aimed to install a Roman client as king of part of France, and no reference to the fighting and diplomacy between Franks and Avars, although this had some bearing on events in the Balkans. There is no mention at all in Theophylact of Spain, where the limited Roman possessions in the south of the peninsula were gradually reconquered by the Visigoths. Africa, Italy, and France had been areas which attracted the attentions of Theophylact's predecessors Procopius and Agathias; Theophylact's lack of interest in western events reflects the contraction of the mental horizons of the east Roman world in the first quarter of the seventh century.[6]

Apart from the dominant themes of Balkan and eastern warfare, Theophylact provides a limited amount of information on affairs in the capital, particularly during the first and last years of Maurice's reign. Most of this information is connected with the imperial family, Maurice's marriage (i. 10), his consulship (i. 12. 12-13), his son's marriage (viii. 4. 10-5. 4), as well as the long account of the disturbances connected with his overthrow (viii. 7. 8-11. 6). In addition there are occasional notices of natural phenomena or disasters (i. 11. 1-2, 12. 8-11; vii. 6. 8-9), and of major events such as the death of the Patriarch (vii. 6. 1-5). This Constantinopolitan information would not have been out of place in a chronicle, and it is not surprising to discover that most of these events are reported, independently of Theophylact, in the Byzantine chronicle tradition represented by Theophanes, Georgius Monachus, and Leo Grammaticus.[7] Besides this chronicle information, there is a group of stories of a markedly religious nature, of which many are intended to display Maurice in a saintly light or to provide a prediction or explanation for his overthrow by Phocas (e.g. i. 2. 1-2; v. 16. 7-vi. 3. 4; viii. 13. 7-15). These stories may well have been culled by Theophylact from a hagiography of Maurice, a work that would have been useful to Heraclius when his rebellion against Phocas cast him into the role of avenger of Maurice.[8]

[6] For a narrative of western affairs during Maurice's reign, see Goubert, *Byzance avant l'Islam* ii (1), (2).

[7] On this, see further L. M. Whitby, 'Theophanes' Chronicle Source for the Reigns of Justin II, Tiberius and Maurice (A.D. 565-602)', *Byzantion* 53 (1983), 312-45.

[8] On this, see further Whitby, art. cit., esp. 335-44. A short hagiography of Maurice survives in Syriac (ed. and tr. L. Leroy and F. Nau, *PO* 5 (1910), 773-8), which illustrates in outline how such a hagiography might have been constructed.

Sources

Theophylact's *History* is our major source for the events of Maurice's reign, but this importance reflects the lack of any other comprehensive treatment of the whole reign rather than any particular quality in the *History*. Readers are likely to be disappointed by the selectivity of Theophylact's narrative, which can only partly be rectified by reference to other ancient sources, and to be frustrated by the obscurity of much of what Theophylact did choose to relate. An investigation of the sources of information used by Theophylact helps to elucidate his narrative. Unlike Procopius, Theophylact was not describing actions that he had witnessed himself. At the time when he began composition, the events of his *History* were already between thirty and sixty years in the past, so that it would have been difficult, if not impossible, to find eye-witnesses who could be cross-examined to construct a historical narrative purely from oral sources. It is likely that people remembered and transmitted interesting anecdotes and stories rather than sober and accurate detail of historical events. For much of his *History*, Theophylact had to rely on written sources and, although it is not possible to establish with certainty the precise source for every section of the *History*, certain broad categories of information can be identified.

It is convenient to begin this analysis of sources with the narrative of the Persian wars, since the accidental preservation of a few pages from the opening of John of Epiphania's *History* reveals that this was the major source on which Theophylact relied for his eastern narrative; ancient historians rarely refer to their main sources, and Theophylact does not mention John. John was a lawyer employed in the service of Gregory, Patriarch of Antioch, and at some date in the 590s he had also served on an embassy to Persia. John proudly states that he had conversed with numerous important persons, and as a result was well placed to narrate the history of the greatest events of his lifetime, the flight of Chosroes II to the Roman empire and his subsequent restoration with the assistance of Maurice; as a prelude to this detailed narrative, John undertook to provide a brief account of the earlier course of the war from its outbreak in 572. The proportions of John's narrative largely determined those of Theophylact's, because for the first ten years of the war (572-82) before Maurice's accession, Theophylact only wished to provide a summary account in his digression on these events (iii. 9. 1-18. 4), and so did not make use of the much fuller information provided by Menander Protector. On the other hand, for the latter half of the war (582-91), when Theophylact might have wished to present a more detailed narrative, no supplementary Greek source was available. John's full-scale account most probably began with Baram's defeat in Suania in 589, since Theophylact's own narrative noticeably increases in scale at this point (iii. 6. 6), and the subsequent progress of Baram's revolt (including the transcripts of diplomatic correspondence which Theophylact presents verbatim, iv. 7. 7-11, 8. 5-8, 11. 1-11) were no doubt recorded by John. For the earlier years of the war (572-89), on those occasions where Theophylact's narrative becomes relatively full or discursive, there is often reason to suspect that he has invented information or had access to a second source, so that he could expand the brief account offered by John.

An example of possible invention is Theophylact's complicated account of the Roman victory in a pitched battle against Chosroes I in Armenia (iii. 12. 12-14. 10): in all probability, the pitched battle never occurred (cf. book iii n. 65), and it is likely that Theophylact has grossly expanded what had, in John, been a mention of Chosroes' reverse and a limited Roman success. Theophylact's elaborately contorted language and the pre-battle harangue by the general Justinian help to create the illusion of a Roman triumph, but the whole narrative is merely a literary setpiece: in Theophylact, grandiloquent language and bombastic imagery are often an indication of a lack of factual substance. Another example of invention by Theophylact is likely to be the disparaging comments which he makes about Chosroes II (e.g. iv. 13. 1, 15. 9; v. 3. 4). John of Epiphania, writing in the latter part of Maurice's reign, is unlikely to have emphasized details that were unfavourable to Chosroes, who was still in general on good terms with the Romans; on the other hand, it was natural for an author writing during the reign of Heraclius to take every opportunity to denigrate the arrogant and aggressive Chosroes, whose invasions had nearly overthrown the Roman empire.

The probable influence of a second source can be detected in the accounts of the campaigns in which Heraclius, the father of the emperor, plays a prominent role, where it appears that Heraclius' actions have been exalted at the expense of those of his commanding officer. Such emphasis on Heraclius is unlikely to have been introduced into the narrative by a historian writing during Maurice's reign. A clear example of this is in the account of Comentiolus' victory at Sisarbanon in 589, where Theophylact's account (iii. 6. 1-4) of a single-handed triumph by Heraclius after the cowardly flight of Comentiolus can be compared with that in Evagrius (vi. 15, p. 233. 5-10), according to which Comentiolus was nearly killed in fierce fighting after his horse had been slain, but was saved by an unnamed member of his bodyguard: in Evagrius, there is nothing cowardly about Comentiolus' action and there is no named hero; in Theophylact, Comentiolus flees in panic and Heraclius wins the battle. It is probable that there has been similar reshaping of the narrative in some of the earlier campaigns in which Heraclius participates, particularly in the campaign of 586, which Theophylact narrates at very considerable length (i. 15. 1-ii. 10. 5), and in which Heraclius again receives more credit than his general, Philippicus (e.g. ii. 10. 4-5). The elder Heraclius was perhaps also the source for the anecdotal stories that adorn the eastern campaign narratives, the wounded hero of Solachon whom Heraclius meets (ii. 5. 10-6. 9), and the brave soldier Sapeir (ii. 18. 15-25): such extended anecdotes are unlikely to have been included in John of Epiphania's summary account of events. This 'Heraclius source' might have been a written panegyric celebrating the achievements of the imperial family, or it might have been a member of the family who passed on information orally to Theophylact: the precise nature of the source is of less importance than the recognition of the distorting effect that it has had on Theophylact's narrative.

With regard to Theophylact's Balkan narrative, the influence of a similar distorting source can be observed. It is noticeable that there is a certain unity of detail and approach underlying the narrative of campaigns between 586/7 and 602 (i. 8. 1 onwards), apart from the intrusive account of Maurice's expedition to Anchialus (v. 16. 7-vi. 3. 8, see below): the principal events are narrated from the viewpoint of the main Roman army in the Balkans; the narrative concentrates on action, the advance of the army to the frontier, the skirmishes and battles, which are narrated with details of days and place-names, but it tends to overlook the intervals between these important events, so that the account is inclined to disintegrate into a patchwork of detailed reports of individual incidents deprived of their strategic context.

This narrative is united by a consistency of bias, which favours the general Priscus at the expense of Comentiolus and Peter, the two other Balkan commanders appointed by Maurice. Priscus' victories are extolled and his failures minimized, while his rivals appear lazy and incompetent. For example, in the 599 campaign Priscus wins a series of sweeping victories over the Avars, while Comentiolus remains idly in camp (viii. 1. 11-4. 3). Priscus is not blamed for his failures in the 588 campaign (vi. 3. 9-6.1), which was in fact as disastrous as any conducted by Comentiolus, since the Avars ravaged as far as the Sea of Marmara. Comentiolus and Peter are frequently idle through laziness or illness (ii. 11. 1-3; vii. 2. 12-13; viii. 2. 5-7), their most energetic interest is hunting (vii. 2. 11, 14. 5), their campaigns are full of mistakes and disasters (e.g. vii. 3. 1-10, 13. 9-14. 11; viii. 4. 3-7), and any successes are the work of their subordinates (vii. 2. 1-9; viii. 5. 10-12). Even the emperor Maurice is not spared criticism for his handling of the armies: his insistence that the armies winter north of the Danube is ascribed to avarice (viii. 6. 10-7. 3), he is tricked by the Avar Chagan into returning prisoners that Priscus had captured (viii. 4. 1-2), and he unjustly rebukes Priscus for appeasing the Chagan on one occasion (vi. 11. 18-21). The bias in Theophylact's Balkan narrative can be identified by reference to the advice on fighting the Slavs which is contained in the *Strategicon* of Maurice (xi. 4), a work that records the ideas on tactics and strategy which were current during Maurice's reign. Most notably the *Strategicon* provides the correct explanation for the winter campaigns, that of military advantage rather than imperial avarice, and it helps to explain Comentiolus' and Peter's interest in hunting and the tendency for their subordinates to reap the credit for military successes (cf. books vi n. 54, vii nn. 8-10, viii nn. 8-9). The biased campaign-narrative which Theophylact used must have been produced during the reign of Phocas: Peter and Comentiolus were both executed in 602 during Phocas' coup, whereas Priscus prospered under Phocas, being appointed *comes excubitorum* and marrying Phocas' daughter Domentzia (Theophanes 294. 11-13). The exact nature of this 'Priscus source' is not known, but it was perhaps a work of modest literary level, a memorandum rather than a full-scale classicizing history, composed by an officer in the Balkan army who wished to ingratiate himself with the important men in the new regime. These officers (e.g. Alexander, cf. book viii n. 59, and Bonosus, book viii n. 25) were Phocas' closest supporters, and it was natural for them to denigrate Maurice's supporters and to praise Priscus. Priscus fell from favour shortly after the accession of Heraclius, and this provides a *terminus ante quem* for the composition of this source. Later, when Theophylact came to write his *History*, his ignorance of military matters and of geography prevented him from penetrating the bias of this source, with the result that his Balkan narrative accidentally preserves the prejudiced judgements of the reign of Phocas.

In addition to this 'Priscus source', two other sources provided Theophylact with information on Balkan military affairs. These were the Constantinopolitan chronicle and the collection of hagiographical stories connected with the emperor Maurice, both of which Theophylact also used for information on events at Constantinople.[9] The Constantinople chronicle provided Theophylact with brief reports of some major military events in the vicinity of the capital, in particular the accounts of Comentiolus' victories over the Slavs (i. 7. 1-6) in which there is no hint of the anti-Comentiolus bias of the 'Priscus source', a brief notice of Maurice's expedition to Anchialus (v. 16. 1-6) and some stories (ii. 15. 5-12, 16. 1-11). The hagiographical collection provided most of the account of Maurice's expedition, with the various portents that foreshadowed his doom (v. 16. 7-vi. 3. 8); to this source precise military details and exact chronology were of less importance than the underlying significance of events. Thus the bulk of Theophylact's *History* was compiled from five sources: John of Epiphania, the 'Heraclius source', the 'Priscus source', the Constantinople chronicle, and the hagiography of Maurice.[10]

Compilation of the History

The quality of Theophylact's historical narrative was determined by two factors, the quality of the information available to him and his own skill at assessing and combining this information into a comprehensive narrative. As has been seen above, some of Theophylact's information was distorted by serious biases, which he reproduced in his narrative. This suggests that Theophylact's ability or willingness to criticize and cross-check his information was limited. His campaign narratives are sometimes obscure and confusing, and it appears that he did not have the necessary military or geographical knowledge to understand the events described in his sources. As a result he could not clarify or explain the information which he retailed. It is always necessary to follow his campaign narratives on a map, and to be cautious of any personal 'explanatory' comments that he might have added to the factual reports of his sources (e.g. i. 4. 1 with n., about the

[9] Cf. Whitby, art. cit. n. 7 above.

[10] Some specific passages were derived from other sources: for example, the analysis of the Nile flooding (vii. 17) is paraphrased from Diodorus Siculus, i. 37 ff., and the account of Kabades' exile (iv. 6. 6-11) is probably based on Procopius, *Wars* i. 5-6; the digression on central Asian affairs (vii. 7. 6-9. 12) must ultimately have been derived from a diplomatic memorandum, although it cannot be certain that Theophylact consulted such an official source directly.

lack of military preparation at Singidunum; iv. 2. 1 with n., about Baram's advance towards Media; vii. 15. 13, about Roman responsibility for war with the Avars).

The combination of information from different sources presented particular problems. Theophylact's approach to questions of dating and arranging the narrative in logical order is sometimes bizarre: thus, for no apparent reason, he reports certain events four years after they had occurred, or so he claims (vii. 6. 1-9 with nn.), and records a prophecy from Maurice's nineteenth year (vii. 12. 10-11) a considerable time before the main narrative reaches this point (viii. 4. 9). Such dislocations do not inspire confidence in Theophylact's competence in chronological matters, but fortunately it is probable that he had to make relatively few decisions on how to combine disparate material. John of Epiphania provided a chronological framework for the whole account of Persian warfare, and the only errors in Theophylact are the omission of two separate years in his digression on the events of Justin II's and Tiberius' reigns (iii. 12. 10-11, 17. 2-3 with nn.): in each case there was no major military action, and most of the year was occupied by negotiations and embassies whose duration might not have been stated specifically by John.

Balkan chronology is more problematical. Information from the chronicles would have been dated, but it is probable that the 'Priscus source', which provided most information, was much less specific: its campaigns were narrated in the correct sequence, but the precise intervals between campaigns may not always have been clearly noted. As a result, one year that was probably taken up by embassies and military preparations has been omitted (book viii n. 6), and one campaign, that of Priscus' first Balkan command (vi. 3. 9-6. 1), appears to have been separated from its immediately preceding campaign (the 587 campaign led by Comentiolus, ii. 10. 8-17. 13), and instead been connected with Priscus' second campaign in 593 (vi. 6. 2-11. 21; see book vi nn. 17, 35); between Priscus' two campaigns, the general had fallen into disfavour with Maurice (Gregory, *Register* iii. 51), quite possibly as a result of the disasters of his first campaign. This dislocation of Priscus' first campaign is connected with the major chronological crux of Theophylact's narrative, the date of Maurice's expedition to Anchialus (v. 16. 1-vi. 3. 8). Theophylact's information on this expedition was not derived from the 'Priscus source', and so its placing in the sequence of campaigns was determined by Theophylact's own notions of chronology, rather than by his source. His

narrative of the expedition contains certain chronological incon-
sistencies, and it is very likely that Theophylact himself incorrectly
combined two separate reports of actions by Maurice: a brief
chronicle notice of an expedition to Anchialus in autumn 590, and a
sequence of stories from the hagiography laden with portents of
Maurice's doom, which originally had been connected with the events
of 598 (see books v n. 86, vii n. 73).

Theophylact's construction of his narrative tends to be mechanical.
Transitions from one source to another and from the eastern front to
the Balkans are often signalled by bombastic periphrases which interrupt the narrative (e.g. i. 9. 1-3, 11. 1; v. 15. 12-16. 1). Books i and ii are
particularly disjointed, since Theophylact has attempted to produce a
composite narration of events in the Balkans, Constantinople, and the
east. The effect is unsatisfactory, since Theophylact managed both to
obscure the chronology and to disrupt the flow of the military campaigns. On the other hand, when one of his sources provided him with
a substantial narrative of a long sequence of events (for example,
Chosroes II's exile and restoration, or Maurice's overthrow), Theophylact was content to preserve the narrative flow and he provides a
relatively clear and attractive portrayal of events.

Style

If deficiencies in Theophylact's organization have on occasion
obscured his account, a much more serious obstacle to the use of the
History as a historical source is constituted by the style and language in
which he chose to clothe his information. As a classicizing historio-
grapher, Theophylact was undoubtedly more interested in the artistic
packaging than in the factual content of his narrative, but his stylistic
ideals, self-conscious rhetoric, and reluctance to use clear or simple
expressions are distasteful to modern readers, and did not find much
favour even among his Byzantine audience. It is apposite to quote
Photius' judgement: 'His expressions have some grace, except that the
excessive use of metaphorical words and allegorical concepts leads to
a certain frigidity and juvenile lack of taste. In addition the inopportune introduction of sententious language reflects an officious and
excessive conceit.'[11] This judgement has been described as '. . . still
too lenient for one of the most affected and stilted of all Byzantine
writers'.[12] Such are Theophylact's linguistic excesses that the editors

---

[11] Photius, *Bibliotheca*, cod. 65.
[12] N. G. Wilson, *Scholars of Byzantium* (London, 1983), 105.

of his religious treatise *On Predestined Terms of Life* suggested that, by his intricate style, he might 'even have been parodying the elaborate rhetoric of contemporary ecclesiastical controversies'.[13] Theophylact's use of a similar ornate style for the most rhetorical passages of the *History* indicates that he was not parodying, but imitating, Christian rhetoric, which provided a stylistic ideal to be set alongside the Greek of classical writers. Photius and later critics have drawn attention to the very stylistic features in which Theophylact would have taken the greatest pride, the extravagant metaphors, sententious artistry, and ornate rhetoric.

It would, however, be incorrect to suggest that the whole of the *History* is composed at the same elaborate stylistic level. There is a noticeable change in the nature of Theophylact's Greek at about the end of book ii: in the first two books, Theophylact was clearly taking great pains to compose in a high literary style throughout and to imitate the practice of classical Greek, for example in the use of particles; thereafter the narrative is generally less elevated and easier to understand, although the repetitive use of a restricted range of particles becomes tedious. Theophylact's determination to write complex Greek and to reflect classical usage appears to have waned. As a result large parts of the military narrative are presented in quite straightforward terms, and in these passages the occasional flash of metaphorical exuberance or rhetorical cleverness is tolerable. Overall, Theophylact did not deploy his rhetoric to the full without some purpose: it is naturally used in speeches, where ornament sometimes obscures meaning, it serves to highlight transitional sections (e.g. iii. 8. 9; v. 15. 12-16. 1), and it decorates brief descriptive passages or *ecphrases* (e.g. ii. 11. 4-8; iv. 3. 7-8); it is regularly used to elevate information that can be ascribed to Theophylact's chronicle source, which suggests that Theophylact felt the need to improve the literary level of such material (e.g. i. 11. 1-2, 12. 8-11; vii. 6. 8-9); it also serves to adorn many of the stories which Theophylact included in his narrative, the miraculous tales about Paulinus (i. 11. 3-21) and St Euphemia (viii. 14. 1-9), or the military stories of the Solachon hero (ii. 5. 10-6. 9) and Sapeir (ii. 18. 15-25). Changes in the rhetorical level of Theophylact's narrative are worth noting for the light they may cast on the compilation of the *History*.

[13] *Predestined Terms*, Introduction xi-xii.

The Translation

Theophylact's style presents difficulties for the translator. We have deliberately chosen to produce a fairly literal rendering of Theophylact's phraseology. A more mellifluous but less exact version could perhaps have evaded the problems of some of the passages where Theophylact's rhetoric merges into verbose inanity, but such an approach would have seriously distorted Theophylact's presentation. Self-consciously elaborate rhetoric was for Theophylact a central element of historiography, and so some attempt must be made to convey the bombast of the speeches and the constant reminders of affected artistry, the deliberate rhetorical excesses that are only highlighted by qualifications such as 'as it were', 'I suppose', or 'like some sort of', and the periphrastic or apologetic references such as 'the thing known as' or 'as it is called'. Although such qualifications were a standard element in the vocabulary of classicizing writers, it is worth making clear how often Theophylact chose to use them, and what terms or phrases required apology in his opinion: his use of these terms is frequently mere affectation, a tendency which is particularly noticeable in his account of Maurice's overthrow (e.g. viii. 10. 1-3). Theophylact's language would have struck the Greek reader as excessive, and so it would be wrong to mitigate it deliberately in a translation. We are aware that Theophylact's rhetoric does not always read elegantly in English. There are perhaps some passages where we have failed to reproduce the full scale of Theophylactean bombast, but we hope that the translation conveys some of the flavour of the original. We have translated Wirth's revised version of de Boor's Teubner text, apart from a very few departures which are recorded in the notes.

In any translation proper names present a problem. Although it might appear ideal to transcribe the Greek forms, this would introduce confusion in cases where two or three slightly different forms are used for the same name, and would raise problems where there is uncertainty about the exact form of the name in the text. We have Anglicized personal names where appropriate (i.e. Maurice rather than Maurikios), Latinized the names of other Romans (i.e. Philippicus rather than Philippikos), and accepted the standard transliterations for names of foreigners such as Chosroes or Hormisdas. For place-names, we have adopted forms that seemed unambiguous, yet remained close to the Greek. Anyone who is interested in the precise form of a particular name used by Theophylact must consult the Greek text and apparatus criticus.

The notes are intended to elucidate the narrative on matters such as chronology, military strategy, and literary allusions, and to provide cross-references to accounts of events in other sources that are worth comparing with Theophylact. For the Persian wars, the most important of these sources are the fragments of the histories of Menander Protector and John of Epiphania, the ecclesiastical histories in Greek and Syriac respectively of Evagrius and John of Ephesus (all four authors wrote during Maurice's reign), and various later eastern sources: the mid-seventh-century *Anon. Guidi* (a Syriac chronicle written in lower Mesopotamia), the Armenian *History* of Sebeos (a work probably of the eighth century), and the later compilations by Michael the Syrian (Syriac) and Tabari (Arabic) which respectively reflect earlier Syriac and Persian traditions. For the Balkan wars, the most important sources are the *Strategicon* of Maurice, the collection of Pope Gregory I's letters which cover the years 590 to 604, and Paul the Deacon's *History of the Lombards*, a compilation of the eighth century; there is also useful information in Menander, Evagrius, and John of Ephesus. Other important sources are the ninth-century *Chronicle* of Theophanes and the seventh-century Coptic *Chronicle* of John of Nikiu. All references to these and other texts are to the editions cited in the bibliography.

A chronological table, gazetteer, and index of names are also provided. The maps aim to facilitate the comprehension of the military narratives; it would be advisable for any reader seriously interested in such matters to consult in addition a large-scale relief map.

THE *HISTORY* OF
THEOPHYLACT SIMOCATTA

Dialogue

The Characters of the Dialogue:
PHILOSOPHY AND HISTORY.[1]
PHILOSOPHY *speaks first.*

(1) WHAT is this, daughter? Come now, resolve this dilemma for me, since I am eager to learn, with the clarity that like a thread traverses a labyrinth which is not mythical.[2] For I find the preliminaries of the investigation difficult to approach and hard to pursue.

(2) *History.* O Philosophy, queen of all–if indeed it is proper to learn from me and for you to be taught–I will answer to the best of my understanding, for 'may I keep nothing fair unknown': this is my opinion as well as the Cyrenian's.[3]

(3) *Philosophy.* Gladly would I ask, daughter, by what means and how it was that only the other day you returned to life. But the great seductiveness of disbelief checks us from speech again and, as if with a bridle, restrains us to silence, lest perchance an apparition of wonders should be beguiling us. (4) For, my child, you were long dead,[4] ever since the steel-encircled Calydonian tyrant entered the royal court, a barbarian mongrel of the Cyclopean breed, the Centaur, who most brutally ravaged the chaste purple, for whom monarchy was a feat of wine-swilling:[5] I will keep silent about the rest, out of respect for my

---

[1] The following dialogue is suffused with literary allusions that are intended to lend an intellectual tone to the opening pages of the *History*. The circumstances of the composition of the *History* emerge obliquely through these allusions. Other late Roman historians (for example Agathias, *History*, proem, and Menander, fr. 1) convey this information to their readers directly. There is no parallel for Theophylact's use of such a dialogue between Philosophy and History, although in philosophical and religious works conversations between Philosophy and the author are not unknown (e.g. Boethius, *Consolation of Philosophy*).

[2] An allusion to Theseus' escape from the Cretan labyrinth through the guidance of Ariadne's thread.

[3] A reference to the 3rd-c. BC scholar and poet Callimachus, who came from Cyrene in North Africa. Theophylact quoted the same tag (Callimachus, fr. 620 Pf.) at *Quaestiones Physicae* 1, p. 19. 2-3 Massa Positano.

[4] i.e. the writing of history had been impossible.

[5] Cf. viii. 10. 4 for similar abuse of Phocas the usurper (602-10). The Erymanthian boar (not the Calydonian boar, to which Theophylact alludes) and the Centaurs were monsters conquered by Heracles, and so are apt parallels for the 'monstrous' Phocas, who was overthrown by Heraclius. Similar imagery was used by George of Pisidia (e.g.

own decorum and for the dignity of the audience. (5) I too, my daughter, was ostracized then from the royal colonnade, and could not enter Attica at the time when that Thracian Anytus destroyed Socrates my king.[6] (6) But subsequently the Heraclidae saved and restored the state, exorcized the pollution from the palaces, and indeed settled in the royal precincts.[7] (7) I celebrate the royal courts and compose these antique Attic hymns.[8] For me indeed this is the source of prosperity; but as for you, my daughter, who was your saviour and how were you saved?

(8) *History*. My queen, do you not know the great high priest and prelate of the universal inhabited world?[9]

Philosophy. Certainly I do, my daughter; this man is my oldest friend and most familiar treasure.

(9) *History*. Assuredly, my queen, you have at hand the godsend you were seeking. That man brought me to life, raising me up, as it were, from a tomb of neglect, as though he were resurrecting an Alcestis with the strength of an evil-averting Heracles.[10] He generously adopted me, clad me in gleaming raiment, and adorned me with a gold necklace. (10) This chignon of mine—look, a golden grasshopper is

Heraclias ii. 34-40, *In Herac. ex Africa red.* 14-23); see further J. Trilling, 'Myth and Metaphor at the Byzantine Court', *Byzantion* 48 (1978), 249-63. Olajos, 'La carrière de Théophylacte' 46, used these references to Phocas as proof that Theophylact composed this Dialogue immediately after Phocas' overthrow in 610, considerably in advance of the main body of the *History*. The implausibility of this hypothesis is revealed by the comparable language of George of Pisidia, *Heraclias* ii, a poem composed after the defeat of Chosroes II in 628. The Dialogue is likely to have been written after the rest of the *History*, whose composition had brought History back to life.

[6] Theophylact uses ostracism, a form of exile from classical Athens, to claim that philosophy had been impossible under the 'Thracian' Phocas, who is represented as Anytus, the accuser of Socrates (i.e. Maurice), and hence an archetype for opponents of knowledge.
[7] The Heraclidae were the mythical descendants of Heracles who led the Dorian invasions of Greece in the post-Mycenaean period to re-establish legitimate Greek control of the Peloponnese and other areas of Greece. Thus they are an appropriate mythical image for Heraclius, who came to Constantinople to oust the usurper Phocas and establish 'legitimate' rule. The return of Philosophy may refer to the establishment of the philosopher Stephen of Alexandria as a teacher at Constantinople; on Stephen, see H. Usener, *De Stephano Alexandrino Commentatio* (Bonn, 1880).
[8] Cf. *Quaestiones Physicae*, Introduction, p. 15. 10-11. Philosophy claims that she phrases her literary productions in the approved literary style, that of Attic Greek (or what contemporaries accepted as Attic).
[9] The Ecumenical Patriarch Sergius (610-38), who was also the patron of George of Pisidia.
[10] The parallelism between Heraclius and Heracles, who restored Alcestis to life after fighting with Death, is here extended to incorporate Sergius; for the application of this parallel to Heraclius, see George of Pisidia, *Heraclias* i. 71 f.

sitting upon it[11]–was glorified and made resplendent in the present congregation by this holy man, who provided an advantageously sited rostrum and unthreatened freedom of speech.[12]

(11) *Philosophy*. My daughter, I admire the hierophant for his magnanimity, and for the great ascent of good deeds he has mounted; he sits on the lofty summit of divine wisdom and makes his abode on the peak of the virtues.[13] He clings to terrestrial excellence, and the all-perfect words are life to him, for he does not wish even the earthly order to remain disordered.[14] (12) May I thus profit my devotees. Either he lives as an incorporeal philosopher on earth, or he is the incarnation of contemplation dwelling as a man among men.

(13) *History*. My queen, excellently indeed have you woven the garland of praises. But, if you agree, sit awhile by this plane here; for the tree is wide-spreading, and the height and shade of the chaste willow are most attractive.[15]

(14) *Philosophy*. Lead on then, my child, and insert a proem like a starting-line to your account for your attentive audience. I will fix my mind on you, just like an Ithacan, with unstopped ears, and I will listen to Sirens' tales.[16]

(15) *History*. Accordingly, I will obey your command, my queen, and will stir the lyre of history. May you be for me a most musical plectrum, for you are an Ocean of knowledge and a Tethys of words, and in you is every grace, like an island in the garland of a boundless sea.[17]

---

[11] This precious language is a learned reference to Thucydides i. 6. 3.

[12] Wilson, *Scholars of Byzantium* 59–60, interprets the allusion to 'an advantageously sited rostrum' as an indication that Sergius created a teaching post for Theophylact.

[13] A reference to Hesiod, *Op*. 289 ff., a much-quoted passage in antiquity.

[14] For panegyric of Sergius, cf. George of Pisidia, *Hexaemeron* 1 ff., 1869 ff.

[15] The shady tree is derived from Plato, *Phaedrus* 230 B, where it provides a suitable place for intellectual conversation. Theophylact also used the allusion at *Quaestiones Physicae* 5, p. 23. 7–8.

[16] The story of Homer, *Odyssey* xii. 165 ff.

[17] Adapted from ibid. x. 195. Tethys was the sister-wife of Ocean.

Table of Contents

Book One of the Universal History of Theophylact,
ex-praefectus *and* antigrapheus[1]

[1] Theophylact's titles indicate that he had pursued a successful administrative career. The *antigrapheus* or *magister scriniorum* was a high-ranking bureaucrat; the title *ex-praefectus* might have been honorary, but it is more likely, in view of Theophylact's education and legal training, that he had served as city prefect: cf. Introduction, p. xiv, and Haussig, 'Exkurs' 292 n. 7.

The authorship of the table of contents is uncertain. Ecclesiastical historians (e.g. Evagrius and John of Ephesus) prefaced their works with such lists, and Theophylact might have copied their example. The language of the table is rather pompous, which might support Theophylact's authorship. There are some factual discrepancies between the table of contents and the text (e.g. vi. 18, where the history of Conimundus at vi. 10. 7-13 is wrongly described as a digression), which might be regarded as evidence to the contrary; however, as Dr Holford-Strevens has kindly pointed out, Gellius' list of chapter-headings to the *Attic Nights* contains inaccuracies but is certainly by Gellius himself. On the other hand, some names (e.g. Kardaregan) appear in a different form from that in Theophylact's text.

The subdivisions of the table do not correspond to the chapter-numbers of editions of Theophylact.

Book Two of the Universal History

Book Three of the Universal History

TABLE OF CONTENTS

Book Five of the Universal History

Book Six of the Universal History

Book Seven of the Universal History

Book Eight of the Universal History

BOOK ONE OF
THE UNIVERSAL HISTORY

Proem

(1) IT is right that man should be adorned not only by the benefits of nature but also by his own discoveries, for he possesses reason, a thing which is divine and admirable. Through this, he has learned both to revere and worship God and to see the image of his individual nature; and he is not ignorant of the arrangement of his own formation.[1] (2) Therefore through reason men have focused on themselves as well, wheeling round the mind from external contemplation towards itself, and have unfolded the mysteries concerning their own creation. (3) Now, many are the benefits that this has given to men, and it is an excellent collaborator with nature. (4) For what the latter left unfinished reason has brought to completion most excellently, beautifying some things to sight, while sweetening others to taste, stiffening or softening some things to touch, making others tuneful to hearing, bewitching the soul and enticing it to listen by the charm of its resonance. (5) And is not this a most compelling expert in crafts as well? From wool it has woven a robe of fine thread, from wood it has fabricated a plough-handle for farmers, for sailors an oar, and for the soldier a shield and buckler to ward off dangers of war. (6) And, most remarkable of all, it has set out the extensive experience of history, a delight for the ear, but educational for the soul; for in souls eager for learning there is nothing more seductive than history. (7) Sufficient proof for anyone is a story from the Homeric poem. The son of Laertes, recently cast ashore upon the dry land from the sea's surge, was entertained at the court of Alcinous the king, and great hospitality was poured upon Odysseus. (8) For there was ready for him, naked and physically exhausted by the disaster of shipwreck, a bright garment to fasten on, and he also had the honour to share the king's table. And so the stranger was granted liberty of speech and freedom

---

[1] Praise of reason is a common theme in prologues of literary works; for antecedents, see T. Nissen, 'Das Prooemium zu Theophylakts Historien und die Sophistik', *BNJ* 15 (1939), 3-13.

for exposition of tales.[2] (9) The history so delighted the Phaeacians that, bidding farewell to drinking, they regarded the banquet as a theatre, pricked up their ears, gaped as they watched the man, and were not wearied in the slightest by the length of the description. (10) And yet many of the stories kept their countenance downcast: for experience of greatest perils spread through the gathering, since their ear was inquisitive and insatiable, as it feasted on an amazing account.

(11) Hence indeed it is possible to see how the poets were the first to have achieved a reputation for education: for these took over men's souls which longed for knowledge, were constantly eager for learning and thirsty for strange tales; they constructed mythical narrative for them, clothed speech with fiction, painted the falsehood with rhythm, and beautified the conjuring trick with metre, as if with charming embroideries. (12) So great was the power of their entertainment that it was even believed that they were theologians, and that the gods came among them, and by the tongues of those men disclosed to mankind their personal affairs and whatever success or misfortune had ever occurred in their own life.

(13) Therefore one should regard the common history of all mankind as a teacher, which advises what should be undertaken and what should be ignored as disadvantageous. It can be seen that generals are most prudent by means of her, since she knows how to arrange forces and how the enemy should be deceived by ambushes. (14) Through the disasters of others she makes these men more provident, guiding them by means of the earlier mistakes of others. Then again by successes she renders them more fortunate, causing great peaks of virtue to grow from small beginnings. (15) For the aged she is a guide and staff, for the young a most excellent and sagacious tutor, by wide experience lending grey hairs, as it were, to youth and anticipating the gradual lessons of time.[3] (16) For my part, I am about to make an attempt on her, even though the undertaking is greater than my resources because of the ignobility of the diction, the feebleness of the ideas, the ugliness of the arrangement of the language, and the ineptitude of the organization.[4] But if any of the things expounded should appear felicitous to anyone, let him attribute it to chance; for knowledge is not the cause.

[2] Homer, *Odyssey* vii. 167 ff.

[3] §§ 13-15 are paraphrased from Diodorus Siculus i. 1. 1-5.

[4] An apology for the writer's inadequacy is traditional; cf. e.g. Menander, fr. 2, Agathias, *History*, pr. 12-13, although Theophylact's description of his own failings is more extreme.

(i. i) When it was necessary for the emperor Tiberius to pass on at last from the present sphere and to yield to the universal law of nature, since black bile, as children of physicians are accustomed to call it, was aggravating his disease, Maurice was proclaimed, was magnified with imperial rank and, a newcomer to the purple, was granted a share in the great power of the emperors.[5] (2) For the emperor Tiberius was carried on a litter to the open-air palace courtyard which adjoins the many-couched hall of the royal mansion, a far-famed vestibule and most glorious porch.[6] He summoned the president of the high-priestly throne (at that time John steered the rudders of the church),[7] and convened the congregation of the priestly dignitaries, the bodyguards, guards, all those arrayed in imperial office, and furthermore the more distinguished members of the people as well.[8] (3) He himself did not address the meeting at all, but designated as imperial mouthpiece John, a skilled orator and expert in Roman laws, who through the clarity of his eloquence ennobled the imperial commands in a manner worthy of royal majesty; in their native utterance Romans call this man *quaestor*.[9] (4) So the emperor attended the royal investiture together with his daughter Constantina, whom he made partner of Maurice's destiny and of his life; before the actual proclamation he presented the following words to the congregation:

(5) 'Romans, the name which is far-famed and honoured among the nations, the name which because of its glory is clothed with honour on many lips, great and final now are the travails of anxiety which surround us, some compelling us to make a proper disposition of mortal affairs, others confounding us at the dissolution of death and urging us to present to the Creator the account of our mortal life. (6) And today my former freedom and impunity cause me great fear: for those who possess abundance of power are likely also to be

---

[5] On 5 Aug. 582, Maurice was raised to the rank of Caesar and betrothed to Tiberius' daughter, Constantina. On 13 Aug., the day before Tiberius' death, Maurice was proclaimed as successor; cf. *Chron. Pasch.* 690. 8-9, Theophanes 252. 1-13. Tiberius' illness was caused by eating a dish of mulberries.

[6] Theophylact locates the scene at the Tribunal adjoining the Hall of the Nineteen Couches, a common setting for important imperial ceremonies. However, since Tiberius died in the suburb of the Hebdomon (*Chron. Pasch.* 690. 12-16), it is perhaps more likely that the meeting assembled at the Campus Tribunalis at the Hebdomon, and that Theophylact confused two ceremonial locations known as the Tribunal.

[7] i.e. John Nesteutes (i.e. the Faster), Patriarch of Constantinople 582-95.

[8] Probably the leaders or officials of the circus factions (cf. viii. 7. 10).

[9] i.e. *quaestor sacri palatii*, who, in addition to performing important administrative and judicial functions, was responsible for drafting imperial constitutions (Jones, *LRE* 504-5).

attended by more numerous faults. (7) But all the same our travails concerning the kingdom are keener and predominate–not how to resign it as quickly as possible but how it may be properly disposed, since I did not undertake this for the luxury of power and for physical gratification. But I see that nature too, as well as fate, is wearing us down. (8) For kingdom and children and wife are likewise burdens, the one seeking a wise leader, the next a most capable and dutiful guardian for widowhood, my daughters men to lead them by the hand because of their immature youth and the greater weakness of female nature. (9) Often, because of the disease, I disregard nature, shirk her bond, and forget my children, and my wife is overlooked, as I imagine that I am already dead and have obtained freedom from this preoccupation. (10) But at once inexorable anxiety about the sceptre bursts in: for the struggle is not only to preserve the power that has been entrusted, but also to pass on the inheritance to others in the proper manner. (11) For successors must be better than preceding leaders, so that they may introduce their personal correction for earlier errors, or else, in short, the entire dominion must slip away, when a weaker foundation supports the kingdom.

(12) 'While these considerations are preying on our mind, Providence the craftswoman assists us in our toils, together with us producing a single plan, and designating the man who will rule and ascend to power–Maurice here, a man of greatest benefits, who has stored up many great toils for the Roman realm and has deposited these in advance like sureties for his future providence for the dominion. (13) Today you will see this man as emperor. Such is the confidence that I have in this most momentous enterprise (and my mental activities are not crippled) that I have also entrusted this man with my daughter as well as with the kingdom. Reassuring you with this great bond of nature, I will carry away this consolation for my journey to that distant exile.

(14) 'As a result of your experiences while we held the reins of power and this man rode beside us with the utmost prudence, I have you as worthy witnesses to this excellent arrangement. (15) But you pray, Maurice, make your reign a most glorious epitaph for us. Adorn my tomb with your virtues, do not shame the hopes of those who have trusted you, do not abuse your virtues or shun the nobility of your spirit.[10] (16) Rein authority with reason; steer power with wisdom.

[10] The following advice on kingship is comparable to that in Justin II's speech to Tiberius (iii. 11. 8-11 and John of Ephesus iii. 5); both imperial speeches are greatly

Kingship is an exalted and lofty matter, which elevates on high its rider and puffs him up in his reasoning. Reckon that you do not surpass all men in degree of intellect, even though you have achieved heights of fortune beyond all. (17) Seek from your subjects goodwill rather than fear, instead of flattery honour reproof as an excellent teacher; for authority does not accept advice or tolerate instruction. Before your eyes let there be Justice as an assessor, regulating punishment for offenders. (18) Like a philosopher, regard the purple as some cheap rag to dress in, and the crown to be no different at all from the pebbles on the seashores. The brilliance of the purple is detestable, and my advice is to recommend kings to be moderate in their good fortune and not to be exuberant over, and exult in, this sorrowful garb of monarchy; for the sceptre of kingship professes to pursue not authority for intemperance, but glorious servitude. (19) Let clemency guide anger, but let fear guide prudence:[11] for nature has assigned leaders even for the bees, and has fortified the ruling bee with a sting, as if grafting on to it, as it were, an automatic power, so that it can also strike the man who does not correctly obey. (20) But the sting is not tyrannical in the bee; rather it is a public benefit and just. Therefore we shall be imitators of the bee, unless, that is, reason has managed to grant greater examples as well.

'This is my parental advice. But you will have as arbiter of your judgement the impartial authority which honours virtues and despises evil.'

(21) Then, after the emperor's discourse was concluded, much weeping surged up among the spectators; some, those who were richer in goodwill, were grieving at the suffering, while others through sympathy were charmed to pity; for disaster is accustomed to share the suffering with the spectator as well. (22) The emperor took up the crown and the double cloak of purple, and put them on the Caesar. A great cry poured from the subjects in acclamation: for some, admiring the emperor for his good counsel, marvelled at their leader, others at the man who had been proclaimed and who presented himself as worthy of such great command, but all marvelled at God, who was responsible for all these things and had arranged this happy conjunction.

influenced by the *Ecthesis* of Agapetus Diaconus, a collection of brief moral advice on kingship that had been addressed to Justinian in the early years of his reign.

[11] At first sight, the notion that fear should guide prudence is strange; the sense is that, although an emperor must be clement, he should avoid an excess of clemency which might otherwise lead him to pardon offenders whose punishment was thoroughly deserved and was to the benefit of the state.

(23)　After this great and final objective of the emperor had been fully accomplished, and when the rites of proclamation had been completed in accordance with the royal decrees, the emperor Tiberius returned to his own bed.

(2. 1) There is also a story that, shortly before his illness, the emperor Tiberius was instructed by a divine voice: for in his sleep a man seemed to stand beside him, most fair in appearance, wearing a likeness of a divine beauty, indescribable in word, yet inimitable in painting. The youth had white raiment which illumined the place and the onlooker with the gleams of its radiance. (2) He spoke to the Caesar,[12] complementing his speech in the gesture of his hand: 'Tiberius, the Thrice-Holy says this to you: the tyrant years of impiety will not come during your reign.' Then the emperor woke in alarm at the apparition, rose at daybreak, and recounted to his entourage the visions of his dreams.

(3) On the next day (for I am returning to my account)[13] Tiberius submitted to the universal law of nature, even though he happened to be a king, departed this life, and unloosed the soul's tent, as it were, this burdensome mortal cloak of ours. Extensive lamentation surged up in the city; for a stream opened from many eyes and breached ducts of tears, and great grief invaded the people's spirits. (4) Bright clothing was rent asunder and garments of gloom took its place. The report convened all men to that hateful spectacle. The masses entered the royal court; the vestibule did not have guards at the many curtains which reluctantly bestow entry on dignitaries.[14] There was night-long melancholy hymnody, which presented a gloomy aspect to the illuminating torches. (5) Next, after daybreak, as the sun cast forth its rays and sped across the heavenly hemisphere, everyone escorted the dead emperor, and their weeping showered down, together with acclamation. There was copious funerary panegyric, one theme pouring forth from many mouths, just as a river is divided into many sources, or as

[12] i.e. to Tiberius, who was Augustus rather than Caesar; Theophylact's use of technical and official terminology is usually imprecise.

[13] The story of Tiberius' vision, which foreshadows Maurice's overthrow by the tyrant Phocas, is treated by Theophylact as a digression, which strongly suggests that it had originated in a different source from the surrounding narrative. The story was probably part of the collection of hagiographic and marvellous anecdotes which gathered around the figure of Maurice; see further Introduction, p. xxv, books vii n. 73, viii nn. 64-5.

[14] For door-curtains and their guards in imperial ceremonial, cf. Constantine Porphyrogenitus, *de Caer.* i. 1 (p. 4. 10), *al.*, and for brief discussion of curtains see Averil Cameron on Corippus, *In laudem Iustini Augusti minoris* (London 1976), 188-9.

a lofty and leafy tree is separated into many offshoots of mighty branches. (6) For subjects are accustomed to show great grief at the untimely decease of those who have ascended to power, at any rate if they began their rule in a winning and popular manner. (7) When the tomb of the emperors had received him,[15] everyone turned towards the emperor Maurice as guardian, and on that very day there was an end to weeping: for recollection of past events has less effect on men than the eager concern for the present.

(3. 1) Now, as I begin to weave the web of history and make a record of barbarian wars, I will first mention the action against the Avars, because of the close proximity of the events and of the appropriateness of the arrangement.[16] (2) Numerous, then, were the violent deeds which they impetuously ventured at that time. These people are Huns, who dwell beside the Ister, a most untrustworthy and insatiable nation among those who live as nomads.[17] (3) These people sent an embassy to the emperor Maurice, not least because they had come into possession of the greatest township; this was named Sirmium and was a most famous city, of great renown and repute among the Romans who inhabit Europe. (4) This had been captured only very shortly before the emperor Maurice was seated on the Caesar's throne,[18] when he donned the cares of the Romans together with the purple. (5) The circumstances were clearly declared by the famous Menander; on this subject I have not the time to expound in greater detail those lengthy accounts, to relate again what has already been clearly reported, or to waste time in

---

[15] According to *Chron. Pasch.* 690. 14-16, Tiberius was buried in the Church of the Holy Apostles, after his body had been brought from the Hebdomon to Constantinople by boat. Tiberius had been a popular emperor, and the grief at his death was sufficiently remarkable to be noted even by Latin chroniclers (e.g. Paul the Deacon iii. 15).

[16] Theophylact presumably means that events in the Balkans were physically closer to Constantinople than were operations against the Persians. In terms of chronology, it would have been more appropriate to start with eastern events, since the Romans fought the Persians in autumn 582 (i. 9. 4-11), whereas this Avar campaign began in 583 (i. 3. 13-4. 1).

[17] For the Avar reputation for greed and deceit, cf. Maurice, *Strategicon* xi. 2. 16-20. The Avars were not Huns, as Theophylact should have known from his discussion of their origins (vii. 7. 13-8. 5). Literary authors like Theophylact self-consciously disregarded precise designations, and tended to call all nomads by classical names such as Getae (iii. 4. 7, of the Slavs) or Scyths (iv. 10. 1, of the Turks), or by the more recent but still respectable general term of Huns (cf. i. 8. 5, of the Turks).

[18] Sirmium, located between the rivers Sava and Danube, had been one of the greatest cities of the Roman empire in the 3rd and 4th cc. Throughout much of the 6th c. the city was in barbarian hands. Justin II recaptured it from the Gepids in 567, but it was lost to the Avars after a long siege in late 581 or early 582.

contrived criticism.[19] (6) After the city had come into the hands of the Huns, a treaty ensued, so that warfare might welcome peace and pursue quiet. (7) The terms were most disgraceful to the Romans: for after such a monumental disaster, like a panel of judges in session, they gave the barbarians glorious gifts, as if a prize for excellence, and agreed to deposit with the barbarians each year eighty thousand gold coins in the form of merchandise of silver and of embroidered cloth.[20] (8) The treaty did not last longer than two years: for the Chagan of the Huns, as he is known, behaved arrogantly towards the Romans. Before the destruction of the peace, a certain rumour had circulated in his presence that creatures of most remarkable size and physique were nurtured among the Romans. Wherefore he demanded from the emperor that he come to a sight of these. (9) And the emperor quickly assuaged the love of enquiry, and granted that he come to contemplation of elephants by sending him the most outstanding of the beasts bred by him. (10) But when the Chagan saw an elephant, the Indian creature, he at once terminated the display, and commanded that the beast return to the Caesar, whether in terror or scorn of the marvel, I cannot say: for I would not keep it secret. (11) He pestered the Caesar to fashion a gold couch and to send that to him as well, for the peak of his current good fortune had raised him so high; the emperor had the gift made and royally conveyed it. (12) But he arrogantly assumed even haughtier airs, as if he had been besmirched by the unworthiness of the gift, and he sent back to the emperor the ostentatious gold couch as though it were something cheap and common. (13) Furthermore he demanded that, in addition to eighty thousand gold coins, he be paid by the Romans another twenty thousand annually as well,[21] and indeed when the emperor angrily refused, he spurned the agreements and threw his oaths to the winds. (4. 1) At once, raising the trumpet dear to war, he collected his forces, and captured by surprise the city of Singidunum, which was ungarrisoned and bereft of military equipment because of the great peacetime indolence which had spread throughout Thrace: for peace is not watchful and does not tolerate forethought.[22] (2) He encountered the majority of the city's

---

[19] Menander's narrative survives only in fragments (frr. 63-6), and the longest extant account is in John of Ephesus vi. 30-2.

[20] These were the same terms as the Avars had imposed before the attack on Sirmium, but the Romans were also forced to concede the payments which they had refused to make during the three years' war over Sirmium (Menander, fr. 66).

[21] Theophanes 252. 31 records that the demand was made in May (sc. 583).

[22] Singidunum (the modern Belgrade) was, following the loss of Sirmium, the Roman

inhabitants encamped in the fields, since the harvest constrained them to do this; for it was the summer season and they were gathering in their subsistence. (3) But the barbarian did not capture the city without a struggle: for a very fierce engagement took place at the city gates, which resulted in many Avars being killed, and, as the saying goes, a Cadmean victory was won.[23] The Chagan ravaged many other neighbouring cities, easily and without effort in these cases, since the evil was unforeseen and contrary to expectations. (4) After destroying Augustae and Viminacium (these are illustrious cities in the tax district of Illyricum), he immediately encamped and blockaded Anchialus, and laid waste the surrounding villages;[24] (5) it is said that he did not disturb the hot-water baths:[25] a story has reached us that here the Chagan's harem cleansed themselves, and that as reward for their pleasure they asked him not to demolish the bathhouses. It is said that these waters are beneficial for bathers and conducive to their health. (6) After three months had passed, the Romans sent an embassy to the Chagan and asked for an end to the war. As ambassador they dispatched Elpidius, a man who had been elevated to the senate, been governor of Sicily, and ascended the praetor's tribunal; this office is not without distinction among Romans.[26] (7) They paired with him Comentiolus, a man prominent among the emperor's bodyguards, whom in the Latin utterance Romans call *scribo*.[27] So the two then came to the Chagan at Anchialus, and asked about a treaty, as they had been ordered. (8) The Chagan did not act moderately in his crimes, but even added more wilful threats that he would destroy the Long Walls, as they are called.[28]

base furthest upstream on the Danube. Theophylact's assertion that the city was ungarrisoned is surprising, and was perhaps a mistaken inference occasioned by his desire to introduce the comment about the improvidence of peace; since the Avars met stiff opposition (i. 4. 3), it is likely that there were soldiers in the city.

[23] i.e. a prohibitively expensive victory.

[24] The Chagan's campaign had swept him through the Danube cities of Viminacium and Augustae to Anchialus on the Black Sea coast. From Augustae it was a journey of about 250 miles, involving the crossing of the Haemus mountains (Stara Planina) to Anchialus; Theophylact was clearly unaware of the distances involved.

[25] On the baths near Anchialus, see Procopius, *Buildings* iii. 7. 19-23.

[26] In the 6th c., following the Justinianic reconquest, Sicily was administered by a praetor (Jones, *LRE* 283); it is probable that Elpidius had held the post of *praetor Siciliae*, and not two distinct offices as Theophylact's description might suggest.

[27] The *scribones* were a select element in the imperial guard who were most commonly used on special missions (Jones, *LRE* 658-9); for a similar periphrastic reference to *scribo*, cf. vii. 3. 8.

[28] The Long Walls, constructed in the 5th c. as the outer defence of Constantinople, crossed the Thracian peninsula about 40 miles west of Constantinople, from near Selymbria on the Sea of Marmara to the Black Sea, a distance of almost 30 miles.

While Elpidius yielded to his words, though without pandering to his swollen arrogance, (9) Comentiolus proudly demonstrated the nobility of his tongue, espousing Roman freedom unsullied like a chaste matron, and not corrupting it with whorish flattery. In the presence of the leading Avars, as well as the Chagan, he employed the following phrases:

(5. 1) 'Chagan, the Romans thought that you would worship your ancestral gods, respect the guarantees of oaths, and in no way repudiate pledges and agreements, that the chariot of peace would not be overthrown by you, and in truth that you would remember both many royal gifts and Roman kindness, that you would never have become forgetful of their benefaction, in other words their hospitality, to your ancestors, and that you would never suffer other people under your command to injure Romans. (2) For it is fitting for leaders to be more prudent than their subjects, both in fact as well as in name, so that their superiority in power is also matched by their distinction in virtue. (3) Accordingly, because of their peaceable benevolence, the Romans ignore your previous outrages, have become forgetful of your many crimes and, since they are distinguished from all nations by their humanity, they have not mobilized arms in a desire for retaliation. (4) For they had valued future quiet more highly than crimes wilfully perpetrated in the past, having bid farewell to recompense. (5) But since you have disregarded every aspect of good conduct, since the eye of Justice is blind and the feet of Providence lame and unable to weigh out a just return for offenders, and since your god is your will, which is moved whithersoever it wishes, the Romans will not forget their own excellence, but will organize an exceedingly great war against you and will inflict great slaughter. (6) For war is more congenial to them than peace, unless the enemy should welcome tranquillity. For what nation on earth has ever contended more gloriously than Romans for freedom, honour, fatherland, and children? For if there is fierce battle and frenzied confrontation among the most insignificant of birds, so that each may avoid defeat and the one not yield to the other, what indeed do you think men do, especially Romans, a most warlike nation and most renowned kingdom? It is not easily despised, except perhaps only at the very outset. (7) Then do not brag over what you have wickedly and faithlessly arranged today: for it is perhaps laudable to take pride in right achievements, but it is fitting that boasting over wickedness be designated in the category of arrogance, not as glory. (8) Great are your recent feats of haughtiness, but very great also is the

power of the Romans, the diligence of the Caesar, the support of the tributary nations, the weight of their resources, and their religion, which is most pious beyond all the nations of the inhabited world, and for that reason most efficacious as well. (9) You wished only to campaign against them, but the consequences you disregarded. What sort of reputation for honour will you win even among your neighbouring tribes now that you have abused Romans? Or what guarantee of trust has been left for you in future? (10) Your gods have been outraged by you; oaths are violated, agreements are broken, benefactors suffer harm from you; gifts with their hallowed power do not prevail. Leave us in peace. Do not change your prosperity into evil gossip by trying to outrage those who have committed no offence except that of being your neighbours. (11) Show greater respect to this Roman territory of ours than to your own head: this has been your salvation, it embraced you when you were a migrant, and gave you a home when you were a foreigner and stranger, after your splintered segment had broken away from its ancestral tribe in the east.[29] (12) Do not break the fair bond of hospitality; let not men disparage charity; do not teach your audience to loath piety as a cause of evils. If you desire money as well, this has already been fulfilled for you by the Romans: for the nation is generous and its treasury is magnificent and munificent. (13) You have a land that is broad, and is additionally endowed with great length, so that the inhabitants are never overcrowded and incomers never lack a subdivision.

(14) 'Go back, then, to your own land, which indeed the Romans have lavished on you,[30] and do not divert your power beyond your borders. (15) Even though the winds attack furiously, they will do no harm to the strong tall tree, which has abundant leafage, stout trunk, thriving roots and wide-spreading shade, and which is nurtured by the seasons and by moisture, that either irrigates it through channels or inundates and enriches it by rains from heaven. (16) Those who extend an intemperate foot beyond their own property, will become

[29] The Avars entered Roman diplomatic horizons in 558 as a group of refugees from the expanding power of the Turkic federation in central Asia. They soon defeated the tribes bordering the Black Sea, and extended their control westwards along the Danube (see Bury *HLRE* (1) ii. 115-16).

[30] The Avars had asked Justinian to be allowed to settle in Roman territory, and they had been offered Pannonia Secunda (Menander, fr. 9), which had formerly been a Roman province, but was then occupied by Lombards, Gepids, and Heruls. The Avars took over Pannonia by conquest, after helping the Lombards to defeat the Gepids, and thereby frightening the Lombards into migrating to Italy.

wise belatedly at the time of their just punishment, being unable to endure the shame which is more grievous than their afflictions.'

(6. 1) When this great man had terminated his spoken rebuke, boiling blood whipped up great passion in the Chagan, his whole face grew crimson with anger, while his eyes gleamed golden-bright with the flame of wrath and demonstrated through their whole aspect that he would not spare the ambassadors. His eyebrows shot up and almost threatened to fly off his forehead, and the gravest danger hovered over Comentiolus as a result of his speech. (2) For the barbarian destroyed the sanctity of the ambassadors, dishonoured Comentiolus with chains, crushed his feet in the clamp of wooden stocks, tore apart the ambassador's tent, and hence, according to a native custom, threatened the death-penalty. (3) On the following day his passion became calm, and the most powerful of the Avars soothed their leader with persuasive arguments, gradually persuading him not to pronounce the death-penalty against Comentiolus, and convinced him that the fetters would be sufficient injury for the ambassadors. So the Chagan agreed, and dispatched them to the emperor in dishonour, granting an unexpected reprieve to the men themselves.

(4) In the following year,[31] Elpidius was again appointed and sent out on the same mission. When he reached the Chagan, he asked that an ambassador should come with him to the emperor, so that he might reanimate the treaty and they should permit the addition of a further twenty thousand gold coins to the agreement. (5) The Chagan adopted the proposal and sent Targitius, a respected man in the tribe of the Avars,[32] to the Caesar with Elpidius. They both came to the emperor, and a covenant and accord was reached, namely that the Romans should pay out twenty thousand gold coins in addition to the eighty thousand, or be repaid with war if they neglected this. (6) Therefore the agreement seemed to have been somewhat revived, and warfare accepted an armistice. After a brief moment of time the well-being of the peace was adulterated, and once again the tribe of the Avars attacked the Romans, not openly, however, but in a rather knavish and crafty manner. (7. 1) For the Avars let loose the nation of the Sclavenes,[33] who ravaged very many areas of the Roman territory,

---

[31] i.e. 584.

[32] Targitius was the name of the Avar ambassador to Constantinople in 568/9 and 580 (Menander, frr. 28-9, 63); Haussig, 'Exkurs' 358-9, suggested that the name was the title of the Chagan's deputy.

[33] Theophylact has probably exaggerated the extent of Avar control over the Slavs (Sclavenes), the collective name for the primitive forest- and riverside-dwellers who

suddenly invaded like lightning as far as the Walls named Long, and wrought great slaughter on their captives. (2) Wherefore, in fear, the emperor both garrisoned the Long Walls and led out from the city his personal body of soldiers, instantly devising a most distinguished defence, as it were, around the city.[34]

(3) Then indeed, then Comentiolus was entrusted with a not insignificant command; he moved into Thrace, drove back the hordes of the Sclavenes, reached the river Erginia, as it is named, suddenly confronted the Sclavenes, boldly attacked, and improvised great destruction for the barbarians.[35] (4) It was for this reason that he was again appointed general by the emperor and sent out, adorned with Roman titles and bearing the military honour of command called by Romans *praesentalis*.[36] (5) Next, when the summer came around,[37] he collected the Roman forces, moved to Adrianopolis, and encountered Ardagastus, who had in train great hordes of Sclavenes with a most distinguished haul of prisoners and splendid booty. After passing the night, at daybreak he approached the fort of Ansinon and courageously engaged the barbarians. (6) The enemy backed off, were thrust into flight, and were driven right out of the Astike, while the Roman success raised a bright day for the prisoners. The general sang a victory hymn and set up a trophy.[38]

(8. 1) At the beginning of autumn,[39] the barbarians again dissolved

had spread along most of the Danube frontier by the mid-6th c. The Slavs along the upper Danube, in the vicinity of the Avar homeland of Pannonia, were probably under Avar control, but along the lower Danube the Slavs were still much more independent, and might indeed have invaded the Roman empire in order to escape from the encroaching threat of Avar control. John of Ephesus, vi. 25, records that the Slavs had ravaged much of the Balkans from 578 onwards, and had by 584 started to settle in the deserted countryside.

[34] The guard is 'distinguished' because it was composed of men of distinguished rank. Theophanes 254. 7 records, probably correctly, that Maurice also led out the circus factions to defend the Long Walls.

[35] The battle was probably fought in the vicinity of the Long Walls of Constantinople, to which according to John of Ephesus, vi. 25, the Slav raids extended. The river Erginia (modern Ergene), a tributary of the Marica, drains the hinterland of Heracleia, just beyond the Long Walls.

[36] i.e. *magister militum praesentalis*, the commander of the troops stationed in the vicinity of the capital.

[37] Presumably in the following year, i.e. 585.

[38] Comentiolus' counter-offensive against the Slavs had already driven them back from the vicinity of the Long Walls (i. 7. 3 and n.), and he now clears them from the Astike, the fertile Thracian plain.

[39] Although Theophylact has not recorded the arrival of a new year, this must be autumn 586, because of the subsequent synchronism with events on the eastern front (ii. 10. 8).

the agreement and openly abased the compact. I will reveal the cause and not deny it. (2) A Scythian man who bore the surname Booko-labra (if you should have any desire to learn the clarification of his appellation, I will immediately translate the name into the Greek utterance: (3) magus, that is to say priest, is the interpretation we reach by transforming the Scythian into the noble utterance), at that time this man performed a foolhardy venture. (4) For he slept with one of the Chagan's wives and, enticed by brief pleasure, he was caught in the strong snares of death. Suspecting that perchance his crime might be discovered and that he would feel the pangs of the well-known cross-examination, he suborned seven of the subject Gepids[40] and made his flight towards his ancestral tribe. (5) These are Huns, who dwell in the east as neighbours of the Persians and whom it is more familiar for the many to call Turks.[41] (6) Therefore, after traversing the Ister and coming to the city of Libidina, he was captured by one of the Roman commanders posted to guard the Ister,[42] and disclosed his race, his former abode, and the pleasure which drove him from there. (7) Since the account of his misfortune seemed plausible, he was sent on by the commander to the emperor. Hence the Roman treaty was thought to be severed,[43] and the war was laid bare, while Targitius was still present at the royal city in the role of ambassador, harvesting from the Romans the annual wealth which the agreements nurtured each year for the Chagan. (8) This not unnaturally provoked the emperor to anger, since he considered that he was being thoroughly swindled by the Avars, with one Avar demanding their annual wealth and the revenues of peace, while the other was not remaining quiet but was ravaging Europe and laying waste cities. (9) So Targitius was banished to the island of Chalcitis and passed six months in hardship:[44] this was the limit to which the

---

[40] During Justinian's reign, the Gepids had disputed the mastery of Pannonia with the Lombards. At the start of Justin II's reign, the Gepids briefly achieved supremacy, but they were crushed by an alliance of Lombards and Avars and subsequently remained a subject member of the Avar federation.

[41] Cf. i. 3. 2 with n., for the use of the term Huns, and iii. 6. 9 and iv. 6. 10 for similar periphrastic references to Turks.

[42] Libidina (or Ibida/Libida) was situated near the Black Sea coast; if the Bookolabra had seduced the Chagan's wife in Pannonia, he had managed to travel a very considerable distance before being arrested by the Romans.

[43] Menander, fr. 66 records that in 581/2 the Avars asked Tiberius to find and return a fugitive seducer of one of the Chagan's wives; the request had perhaps been repeated in the treaty made with Maurice in 584.

[44] One of the Princes' Islands in the Sea of Marmara, which were used as a place for relatively comfortable imprisonment.

emperor's passion was inflamed, for there were threats that the death-penalty would even be pronounced against the ambassador. (10) The Chagan's men ravaged all the environs of Scythia and Mysia, and captured many cities, Rateria, Bononia, Aquis, Dorostolon, Zaldapa, Pannasa, Marcianopolis, and Tropaion.[45] (11) The enterprise provided him with considerable labour: for he did not reduce these cities without sweat and trouble, even though he was helped along by a strong following wind in the suddenness of the invasion, which was particularly effective because of the irresistible evil of indolence. The emperor elevated Comentiolus as general and placed him in charge of the whole command.

(9. 1) But, since the prelude of my history has been concerned with the Huns who live beside the Ister, come now, come and let us bestir the Persian actions on the lyre of narrative. For I will return to the proclamation of the emperor Maurice, now that I am about to record the Median war. (2) Let no one be angered at me on the grounds that I am now regressing to earlier events, since we are not returning to the same actions even though we are going back in turn to the same times; (3) for the continuity of the previous narrative did not tolerate a bridle, lest by the intermediate insertion of different narratives confusion might be brought upon events.[46]

(4) It was still during the course of the first year of the reign of the emperor Maurice, after that glorious Persian campaign in which Tamchosro was at that time leader of the Median armies;[47] the emperor transferred John (the hairiness of his upper lip provided a surname for him, and Romans in fact called him Mystacon) from the camps in Armenia to the Roman eastern forces. (5) Then, when the general was newly invested with the eastern cares, he camped where the river Nymphius is united with the waters of the Tigris; in this

---

[45] This record of destruction charts the Chagan's advance, via the Timok valley where Aquis was situated, eastwards along the Danube past Bononia (Vidin), Ratiaria (Arčar) and Dorostolon (Silistra) to Tropaion, and then southwards through Zaldapa and Marcianopolis (Devnja) to Pannasa in the Haemus mountains. Theophylact has not listed these cities in the probable order of their capture, and he is unlikely to have known their relative locations.

[46] This elaborate formula of transition, together with references to 'the continuity of the narrative' and 'intermediate insertion' is a strong indication that Theophylact is changing sources and stitching together their different narratives (cf. e.g. iii. 5. 1, v. 15. 12-16. 1, vii. 16. 12, viii. 14. 10). In this case, Theophylact has switched from his Balkan source to John of Epiphania.

[47] The battle of Constantina (iii. 18. 1-2) fought in June 582, in which Tamchosro was killed.

very place a battle was prepared,[48] the Roman force being commanded by John and the Persian by the Kardarigan. (6) This is a Parthian title;[49] the Persians like to be called by their titles, as if they consider it unworthy to bear their birth-names: for, regarding their own appellation, they have greater admiration for fortune's benefaction than for parental custom which grows up with them when they have newly emerged from their mothers' wombs.

(7) And so John marshalled the whole body of his force in three parts; he himself took over the centre of the army, the second-in-command Curs the right wing, and Ariulph the left. The three groups were arranged roughly like this, and the Persians were also drawn up in the same way. (8) When the trumpets sounded for war and the intervening gap was narrowed, the battle made its entry. Accordingly, the Romans attacked with two sections, John in the centre and Ariulph on the left, and indeed overcame the opposing forces. (9) Curs did not join battle, since he begrudged John success on the grounds that he was contending for greatest glory.[50] Therefore the Persians turned back, since they feared that the opposition might perhaps press the assault more heavily. (10) When the Romans saw that Curs and his force were not engaging, they showed their backs to the barbarians and retreated towards the higher ground. (11) The Persians made a counterattack when they saw that the Roman cavalry was exhausted by the exertion of the chase and by the difficulty of the retreat to their steeply sited fort; they bravely attacked, slaughtered most of the Romans, and the barbarians scarcely allowed the Romans to return to their camp. At this the war was terminated, and the autumn season gradually crept in.[51]

(10. 1) The emperor gave his father Paul, who had recently arrived in the city of Constantine, a splendid and distinguished welcome to the royal court, and on the next day the emperor was escorted as bridegroom. (2) For he summoned to the palace John, the leader of the high-priestly thrones;[52] in the great chamber, which is adjacent to

---

[48] The Nymphius (Batman) river was the border between the Roman district of Sophanene and Persian Arzanene. Theophylact does not record on which side of the river the battle was fought, but in view of the Roman victory earlier in the year it is probable that the Romans were on the offensive and were invading Arzanene.

[49] The name means Black Falcon (Justi, *Iranisches Namenbuch* 156).

[50] Curs and John had formerly been colleagues in Armenia (John of Ephesus vi. 28), so that Curs was now jealous of John's promotion.

[51] Autumn 582.

[52] The Patriarch John Nesteutes; see Evagrius vi. 1 for another extravagant description of this marriage.

the largest court of the palace (this in fact is named that of Augustus),[53] he begged to be granted the Almighty's approval through the priest's intercession with God, so that the undertaking of the marriage might turn out favourably for the emperor. (3) The priest attended to the royal wish with supplication to God, took the royal pair's hands, joined them to each other, and blessed the emperor's marriage with salutations of prayer. And indeed he set the crowns on the royal heads and shared with them the incarnate mysteries, according to the custom for those who practice this most holy and authentic faith. (4) Next, after that, those who were distinguished with the topmost titles entered the royal bridal chamber; the emperor did not consider these men unworthy to be called parents,[53a] rather than offspring, as if they had engendered goodwill. (5) At the entrance to the palace these men, who formed the emperor's escort, begged with acclamations that the bridegroom and Caesar should appear enthroned before the armies and bestow marriage-gifts on his subjects. (6) The royal bridal chamber had been magnificently arrayed within the circuit of the first great precinct of the palace,[54] adorned with gold and princely stones, and furthermore empurpled with crimson hangings of priceless deep-tinged Tyrian dye. (7) The daughter of Tiberius, the virgin bride, preceded the emperor to the bridal throne, as though in hiding, shortly to be seen by the people when the fine curtains were suddenly thrown apart as if at an agreed signal. At once the emperor arrived at the bridal chamber, magnificently escorted by many white-robed men. (8) And so he entered within the lofty curtains to escort the queen to the presence of the onlookers and to embrace her. The emperor's bridal attendant was present; this man was an imperial eunuch,

---

[53] The Augusteus ('the great chamber') was the principal stateroom of the palace of Daphne, the oldest part of the Great Palace; on the west, it was flanked by the Octagon, a withdrawing-room for emperors on state occasions, and beyond the Octagon was located the Church of St Stephen, which was a traditional place for imperial marriages: see Janin, *Constantinople* 113. Constantine Porphyrogenitus, *de Caer*. i. 48 (39) and 50 (41), preserves detailed records of the ceremonial for the marriage, and the marriage and coronation, of an empress in this suite of rooms: this description combines elements of the marriage ceremonial from specific occasions in the 8th and 10th cc. (see J. B. Bury, 'The Ceremonial Book of Constantine Porphyrogennetos', *English Hist. Rev.* 22 (1907), 209-27, 417-39, at 429-31), and at some points it is at variance with Theophylact's account of the 6th-c. ceremonial.   [53a] i.e. they were patricians.

[54] In the ceremony described in *de Caer*. the principal bridal chamber is located in the Magnaura (pp. 20-2); but it also seems that a secondary bridal chamber was situated near the Hall of the Nineteen Couches (p. 21. 3-7; cf. 9. 1-3), to which the bridal pair proceeded from the Magnaura. Theophylact's description probably refers to this latter bridal chamber.

Margarites by name, a distinguished man in the royal household. (9) The queen rose from her throne to honour her bridegroom the emperor, while the factions chanted the bridal hymn. In full view of the people, the bride's attendant saluted the bridal pair with a cup, for it was not right to put on crowns, since they were not in fact private individuals who were being married: for this action had already been anticipated by their royal title.[55]

(10) These indeed were the events of the first day, but the city celebrated for seven days and was garlanded with silver vessels: for there were deep platters, basins, cups, bowls, plates, and baskets: Roman wealth was poured forth, and a luxuriance of golden adornment, the mysteries of the household, provided a spectacle to feast the eyes of all who wished. (11) Flutes, pipes, and lyres sounded, carefree and at the same time seductive; all day long numerous conjurors paraded their individual diversions before the eager spectators; (12) actors who abuse whoever they wish presented their humorous plays with keenest rivalry as though in some serious business; chariot-races were performed, and the emperor entertained men of rank in the royal dwelling. In this manner that illustrious marriage was brought to a conclusion.

(11. 1) Since it is for the man who writes history to set forth the notable events publicly and clearly to everyone, come now, come, let us also mix the less happy fortunes with the more glorious. At the beginning of spring, in the Forum, as it is called (this is an illustrious place in the city), raging flames of fire ignited the beauty of the city, and it was impossible to control the wrath of the all-consuming fire.[56] (2) Nevertheless the citizens gradually mitigated the fire's golden streams, subduing, as it were, its harshness. For the force of the wind happened to be strong, so that almost the whole of the city shared the smoke.

(3) In this very year, a certain Paulinus, a man not undistinguished in the city, who had received an excellent education, was discovered to have thrust his soul down into the abyss of witchcraft. The manner of his conviction is an unusual miracle-story, and I will record this since

---

[55] The different acclamations at the various stages of the ceremony are recorded in the *de Caer*. (esp. pp. 7-10), which also states (p. 20. 14-5) that the emperor did receive a nuptial crown even though he was already crowned.

[56] The fire broke out in Apr. 583 (Theophanes 252. 27). The imperial fora were located along the Mese, the main street of Constantinople; it is not known in which forum the fire started. There is a comparable periphrastic reference to a forum at vii. 12. 10.

it is certainly wonderful.[57] (4) The wizard owned a silver basin, in which he used to collect the streams of blood whenever he communed with the apostate powers. This silver basin he sold to some merchants. (5) And so the merchants paid Paulinus the price of the basin, tried to dispose of the vessel in turn, and placed it before the doors of their own shop, providing an opportunity for purchase to anyone who wished. (6) Then it was fated that the bishop of the city of Heracleia, which the ancients once named Perinthus,[58] was at that time staying in Byzantium, and saw the wizard's basin hung up for sale; he joyfully purchased it, left the city, and returned to his own seat. (7) Since a bronze basin used to receive the divine aromatics of the martyr Glyceria, out of respect for the relic, the bishop exchanged the vessels; he removed the bronze one from that most holy service but proffered the silver receptacle for the divine flow of aromatics. (8) Hence the river of miracles ceased, and the fountain of grace was hidden. The martyr did not publicize her powers, she withdrew her benefaction, removed her gift, and ordained that the aromatic should not well forth on account of the pollution; for in truth it is not right for the pure to touch the impure, so as to insert into my narrations an appropriate element of secular learning as well.[59] (9) When this had in fact happened for many days and the misfortune had become known in the city, the priest was turned to grief: he bemoaned the affair, mourned the interruption of the miracles, summoned back the benefaction, was unable to bear the loss, sought the cause, and could not endure the shame: life for him was lifeless, since the church was bereft of the miracle. (10) For this reason fasts and prayers were deposited, tears conscripted, lamentations made allies, all-night supplications marshalled, and everything assembled that can change God's grief to mercy. (11) Then, after God had properly both shunned the pollution and justly pitied the ignorance, the abominations connected with the basin were revealed in a dream to the bishop of the city. (12) And so at once the priest removed from the shrine the basin which had been purchased, brought out in public the bronze one, and placed it before the relic

[57] The story is also recorded by John of Nikiu xcviii, and there is a similar contemporary tale of polluted silver being used for sacred purposes in the *Life* of Theodore of Syceon, 42.

[58] Cf. vi. 1. 1, 5. 8, for similar periphrastic references to Heracleia on the Sea of Marmara. In John of Nikiu it is the abbot of an unnamed monastery who purchases the bowl as a receptacle for holy water.

[59] The moral tag is adapted from Plato, *Phaedo* 67 b.

as a pure and venerable servant, like a maiden untainted by abominable witchcraft. (13) Next the miracle was at once manifest again and aromatic showered down: the benefaction gushed forth, the gift welled up, weeping was dispatched, grief checked, gloom dispelled, the abomination publicized, and once more the city donned its own glory. For God is ready to pity when he is piously implored.

(14) And so when the priest had come to the royal city and had ascertained from the merchants who it was who had sold the basin, he approached the high priest John and revealed all that had occurred. (15) And so John was distressed by the narratives and, unable to endure the story, he immediately went to the palace, and shared with the emperor the tale which had been narrated to him. (16) Now Maurice was somewhat reluctant to contemplate the execution of the miscreants, since he preferred to heal those who had gone astray with repentance rather than punishment. (17) But the chief priest overruled the objection and urged in accordance with the Apostles that those who have renounced the faith should be consigned to fire;[60] he brought to his lips the words of Paul, speaking as follows, word for word:[61] (18) 'It is impossible to restore again to repentance those who were once enlightened, and tasted of the heavenly gift, and became partakers of the Holy Spirit, and tasted the good word of God and the powers of the life to come, and have gone astray, since they have in themselves crucified the Son of God anew and made a mockery of him. (19) For the earth which drinks the rain which often comes upon it, and produces a fitting crop for those even by whom it is tilled, partakes of blessing from God; but if it produces thistles and tares, it is reviled and all but accursed, and its end is to be burnt.' (20) Then the royal wish was less powerful and John prevailed by his arguments; on the next day a court was convened, the wizards were examined and, ensnared by inescapable condemnation, were handed over for punishment. (21) And so Paulinus was impaled on a stout pole whose summit gaped upwards; in the attachment of this he was hung by the vertebrae in his neck together with his throat, and he was throttled.[62] So he terminated his impious

---

[60] John Nesteutes was, however, known for his tolerant attitude towards Monophysite Christians (John of Ephesus v. 21).   [61] Heb. 6: 4-8.

[62] Theophylact is probably describing the form of execution known as *apotympanismos*, a variant on crucifixion in which the victim was hung from a vertical plank by iron bands around his neck, wrists, and ankles; he was then killed by the gradual tightening of the neck collar. The description, however, is confused, since it also suggests that he was impaled on a pole (for impalement as a punishment, cf. vi. 9. 15); John of Nikiu records, perhaps correctly, that Paulinus was burnt to death.

life, having first witnessed the execution of his son: for he had shared
with his son the abominable and impious sorcery of the wizards.

(12. 1) The satrap of the Median force invested and attempted to
capture the fort of Aphumon. When the Roman brigadier learned of
this, he approached the Nymphius and tried to capture Akbas.[63]
(2) This stronghold is difficult to capture and is impregnable by siege:
the fort is placed on the neck of a mountain, there are sheer drops on
both sides, and its rear side is hollowed out by deep ravines, so that in
consequence the sole approach is at the front, which is fortified by a
construction of close-fitted stone. (3) When the general attacked
those in the fort, the besieged lit signal-fires on the parapet of the
fortification, indicating the magnitude of the danger to the Kardarigan's men who were striving to reduce Aphumon; for the Persian
general had established such an agreement with the men in Akbas.
(4) At the first hour, as day grew bright, the Persians stood in array
against the Romans; the barbarians dismounted from their horses,
began the battle, and by their continuous bombardment defeated the
Romans. (5) For they confused their opponents' vision by their discharges of missiles: for they are a nation of archers and their might is
this winged dart.[64] (6) The Romans were hemmed in and close-
pressed on a part of the mountain, since the assault was, as it were,
squashing them. Many of the soldiers jumped off the cliff that fronted
the river Nymphius, for the descent was not raised above an unattainable depth; some were captured by the barbarians; (7) but others
made their way down through the foothills of the mountain, escaped
the danger, were unexpectedly saved, and after crossing the river
Nymphius encamped with the Roman contingent.

(8) When the spring of the past year was in its prime and covering
the earth with green growth, on the anniversary day for the dedication
of the city (this was the first year of the emperor's reign), a terrestrial
affliction arose, and a very great earthquake persisted, as if the earth
were leaping from its very foundations.[65] (9) I will not discuss its

[63] The transition to the eastern campaign of 583 is abrupt, and no indication of
chronology is in fact given. The Romans and Persians are again operating in Arzanene,
with the Persians trying to recapture Aphumon in central Arzanene, which they had lost
to the Romans in 578 (iii. 15. 14), while the Romans attacked Akbas, a fort sited further
to the west on the east bank of the Nymphius opposite Martyropolis.

[64] Cf. Maurice, *Strategicon* xi. 1, 15-17, 41-53, for the Persian superiority at archery
and the tactics needed to counter it.

[65] According to Theophanes 252. 29, the earthquake struck on 10 May; this was the
day before the anniversary of the city's foundation, which was usually celebrated on 11 May.

cause, since the Stagirite has devoted considerable thought to this subject; if his account appears plausible to anyone, let him be praised for his cleverness, but if not, let the doctrine be returned to its father for fostering.[66] (10) Accordingly, as day was waning, the earth's axis was shaken and there was extraordinary panic, so that even the racing fanatics were suddenly converted by fear to prudence, just like children playing at dice on the surprise appearance of their teacher, (11) and the banner outside the arena for the equestrian contests, which was in fact a signal for rejoicing, was removed on account of the unexpected danger;[67] and it came about that all men, in terror of death, took sanctuary in the holy precincts.

(12) This was the second year of Maurice's rule, and in the season of winter the emperor was proclaimed consul.[68] His procession in the royal chariot was most spectacular: it was not horses or mules or elephants which drew the emperor, but men indeed, the most honourable being and appellation.[69] (13) When he had mounted the chariot, he made his subjects partners in his own treasuries; the citizens shared the royal good fortune and sang the Caesar's praises with hymns, as the golden feast illumined them, as it were, and made them sparkle.

(13. 1) In this current year,[70] John was relieved of the reins of generalship, since the Persians had proved irresistible and had been granted the balance of advantage in the war. (2) But Philippicus was nominated instead and proclaimed as general by the emperor; he was a man of talent and was most closely connected with the royal family: for he had in fact married the emperor's sister Gordia.[71] (3) And so, following his appointment, the general came to Monocarton, pitched camp near the mountain known as Aïsouma, and collected men for military service. At the beginning of autumn he camped by the Tigris;

---

[66] 'The Stagirite' is a pompous allusion to Aristotle; cf. vii. 6. 8-9 for another grandiloquent reference to theories about the causation of natural phenomena. Byzantine views on the causation of earthquakes are discussed by G. Dagron, 'Quand la terre tremble . . .', *Travaux et mémoires* 8 (1981), 87-103.

[67] The anniversary games, the Genethliaca, were naturally postponed because the earthquake had struck the evening before. For the flag as the customary signal that chariot-races would be held, cf. Malalas 474. 21.

[68] On 25 Dec. 583, according to Theophanes 253. 24-5.

[69] In the story of Sesostris (vi. 11. 11) Theophylact presents a different view of a ruler's chariot being drawn by men.

[70] The current year must be the second year of Maurice's reign (i. 12. 12), so that the following eastern campaign belongs to 584.

[71] Philippicus was appointed *comes excubitorum*, the position which Tiberius and Maurice had held before being raised to the rank of Caesar.

(4) and after many camps he reached a place named Carcharoman. While he was, as if, residing there, he learned that the Kardarigan was about to move on Mount Izala by way of the strong points of Maïacariri. (5) It was for this reason that the general set out from that place, approached the plain adjacent to Nisibis, camped on the high ground, and then suddenly swooped down upon Persia and won massive booty.[72] (6) Not long afterwards a farmer disclosed the Roman incursion to the Kardarigan; what he said was this, that he, on the one hand, was wandering in the mountains, borne along by mere hopes, while the Romans were ravaging the Median land. (7) Then, after the Kardarigan came back and was making some attempt to lay an ambush for the Romans, the general gathered his forces, moved camp to Mount Izala, because the region provides security to those who approach it, and assigned the booty to a most watchful guard. (8) After this he came to the river Nymphius,[73] having accomplished a not inglorious prelude to his command.

Once again Philippicus was emboldened to attack the Median land, and he ravaged the areas by Bearbaës. When the Persians heard of this, they spurred on their cavalry, for which reason indeed the greater portion of the cavalry perished. (9) Report has it that the Romans, in amazement at the enthusiasm of the barbarian approach, withdrew from the Median land, after dividing the whole contingent in two. (10) The men with the general came to Sisarbanon, and next to Rhabdion, while the other section strayed apart and unprofitably toiled along the road to Theodosiopolis. That land, as we know by hearsay, is waterless and parched as far as the river called Aboras.[74] (11) So

---

[72] Theophylact's description of Philippicus' moves is not completely clear. After camping at Monocarton near Constantina, to the south of Mount Aïsouma (Karaca Dağ), he must then have marched north-east to the Tigris, and then south-west across the Tur Abdin plateau (Mount Izala) in a circular move that allowed him to attack the vicinity of Nisibis as soon as the Persian army moved from Nisibis. The Kardarigan had lost track of Philippicus' moves and must have believed that he was still north of the Tur Abdin, hence the Persian decision to campaign westwards from Nisibis towards Maïacariri, which was located on the main route from the Mesopotamian plain across the Tur Abdin (between Mardin and Amida/Diyarbakır).

[73] Philippicus had retreated north across the Tur Abdin plateau, probably following the same route as his earlier advance.

[74] The description of this second raid resembles the immediately preceding expedition, with Philippicus crossing the Tur Abdin to ravage Bearbaës (Beth Arabaye), the vicinity of Nisibis, and then retreating north into the Tur Abdin. The only difference is the retreat of the second Roman detachment south-east across the parched Mesopotamian plain to Theodosiopolis on the Khabour river. The reference to 'hearsay' is odd, and might indicate that Theophylact's account of the second raid was not derived from John of Epiphania but from a participant (possibly the elder Heraclius, who is

inexorable danger befell the Romans, for they were exceedingly short of water: what could be more serious than this for an army? However, they formulated a very harsh decree against the captives, and slaughtered all the men and women; (12) they spared the children, out of pity for their immature youth. Nevertheless, not long afterwards, the shortage of water destroyed these as well; after encountering great troubles, the Romans entered Theodosiopolis.

(14. 1) In the following year,[75] Philippicus proudly planted his spear in the region of Arzanene and captured a glittering and most distinguished booty. (2) A story was current that the general, who was very fond of learning and who drew his military knowledge from the experts of the past, had acquired this aptitude for wise strategy from the shrewdness of Scipio, the perfect general. (3) For, according to the reports of those who have set down the histories in writing like sacred statues in the precinct of memory, when Hannibal the Carthaginian general was ravaging the European territory of the Romans, the elder Scipio committed the war at home to deferment, attacked the Carthaginian land, and drove the enemy to serious trouble; (4) when Hannibal heard about the fortunes of the Carthaginians, he retreated to his own land, being taught the mutability of affairs from the adversities which had befallen himself. This seemed to be an account parallel to that of Philippicus, and his plan did not miss the mark.[76] (5) It chanced that the general was afflicted in body, since he was struck by a severe illness; therefore he came to Martyropolis, after he had entrusted the army to the brigadier Stephen (this man had been bodyguard of the emperor Tiberius), and appointed Apsich the Hun as second-in-command of all the companies. (6) And so the general was thus a non-combatant because of disease, but the Kardarigan took his whole force and attacked the city which had recently been designated Tiberiopolis, but which had formerly been named Monocarton. In the previous year the general had strengthened its aged walls and fortified it in foresight of the future. (7) The Persian general attacked the city but was unable to reduce it; therefore he entered the environs

prominent in the subsequent campaigns). If this suggestion about two separate sources is correct, then the second raid should probably be regarded as a doublet of the first.

[75] i.e. 585.

[76] The application of the analogy of Scipio Africanus to Philippicus is odd, since there has been no reference to a Persian attack that Philippicus was trying to disrupt. The example of Scipio was, however, more appropriately used as a parallel for the emperor Heraclius (George of Pisidia, *Heraclias* i. 97-8), and this might have influenced Theophylact in this passage.

of Martyropolis and burnt down the church of the prophet John, which was situated about twelve miles from the city towards the western horizon.[77] (8) Here indeed there happened to be an academy of men who spend their lives in thought: these men are in fact called monks, and their task is to anticipate departure from the body, to be dead while living, and to transmigrate to higher things through a sort of prudent madness. The barbarian also razed this place to the foundations. (9) On the next day he set out from there and came to the place Zorbandon, where he ordered his followers not to leave the rampart on any account. On the eighth day he returned to his own country.[78] (10) His own intention perhaps was to enter Roman territory on further brigandage and to carry off the same glory as the Romans. But the general shook off his illness and broke camp (for the season of winter had apparently already arrived), and returned to Byzantium to salute the emperor.

(15. 1) When spring emerged again and warmth spread over the earth,[79] Philippicus set out from the royal city. When he entered Amida, the Persians sent an embassy to settle the war in some glorious manner: for they sent the satrap Mebodes to the general and instructed him to secure a treaty at Roman expense. (2) Therefore the Persian Mebodes arrived among the Romans, and the general convened an assembly, summoning to his presence the brigadiers, captains, bodyguards, and the more distinguished of the fighting force. When the meeting was fully gathered, the Persian began with these words:

(3) 'Enemies (may the prelude of the embassy not upset the audience: for if you change your minds, I too will alter the salutation), dismiss war and array peace, let spear and sword take leave as obsolete, and enlist a flute that sounds a melody at once gentle and pastoral. (4) The Persian king is a lover of peace and takes pride in being the first to cast off war:[80] for the cultivation of peace is regal, just as belligerence is characteristic of tyrants. (5) You men who share the same sufferings as us, let war, which alone of all things is insatiate, be

---

[77] Theophylact's narrative conceals a considerable jump in the theatre of military operations, from Monocarton in the plains south of the Tur Abdin to the vicinity of Martyropolis, north of the Tigris. It is possible that, unknown to Theophylact, Martyropolis was attacked by a separate Persian army and general operating from Persian Armenia, not by the Kardarigan, who was based on Nisibis.

[78] The Persians have probably retreated to Persian Armenia, via the Illyrisis pass across the Taurus to the north-west of Martyropolis.

[79] i.e. spring 586.

[80] Contrast the description of Hormisdas at iii. 16. 8-13.

stayed. We have enriched the earth with blood and have often observed death, for war is death's artist in my opinion, its archetype, the founder and self-taught teacher of human troubles.

(6) 'Is there anyone who loves money? But we have become a sport for wealth and poverty, sometimes conquering, sometimes being conquered; we participate in the fluctuations of war, and eternally reap a harvest of change, so to speak. Is there a warrior who preens himself at gold? He has acquired mistrust as well as pleasure: (7) for what is less trustworthy in war than money, which is immediately transferred to another and again from that man to another, so that the man who possessed it looks at a dream on waking, or remembers on the morrow a recent drinking bout?

(8) 'You, Romans, have in the past given free rein to war; you too become disciples of peace; at the invitation of the Persians, cast off the lamentable war; for it is fitting that those who initiated a wrong should also repent in its rectification.[81] (9) Do not let yourselves be emboldened by these benevolent words: for the Persian king is not renouncing the conflict because he was terrified only the other day when the Romans outraged the land of Media, since he commands that the Romans purchase peace with much gold and glorious gifts. (10) For it is not right for the transgressors to settle the war with impunity. For the payment must be sufficient both to soothe Persian anger and to repress Roman boldness, which reaches for the trumpet of war.'

(11) Then, while the speech was still in progress, the Romans condemned the ambassador, hissing and creating uproar by shouting, as if they were distressed by the barbarian's words: for the Romans saw fit to take pride in recent events, whereby they had invaded the Persian state, won booty, and deceived the Kardarigan. (12) The general dismissed the assembly, and the Persian did not bring his words to completion. Then, after a few days had elapsed, the chief luminary in the priestly ranks of Nisibis[82] came to the general and made public the same proposals as Mebodes. (13) Accordingly, at this point the general conveyed the Persian words to the emperor by courier, but when the emperor had examined the general's message, he at once responded with royal injunctions, commanding Philippicus to reject

---

[81] Although the Romans had been aggressors in 572, they had subsequently made strenuous efforts to secure peace and been thwarted by Persian reluctance to make peace on equal terms (iii. 15. 5-10; 17. 2). The devious rhetoric of this speech is intended to illustrate Persian dishonesty.

[82] i.e. the bishop of Nisibis, who was at this time Simon (573-c. 595).

this disgraceful agreement as incompatible with Roman majesty. (14) However, when the general had folded up the imperial missive, he moved camp to Mambrathon. (15) And so the war thus blossomed forth. But the general assembled the army and enquired whether they were advancing to battle with hearts inspired by manly desire. When the forces assented and reinforced their aspirations with sworn agreements, the general moved from there and came to Bibas, where the river Arzamon flows by.[83]

[83] The Romans had advanced south from Amida on the Tigris to Bibas (Tel Beş) and the river Arzamon (Zergan) in the Mesopotamian plain immediately south of Mardin and the Tur Abdin plateau.

BOOK TWO

(1. 1) ON the next day he moved camp towards the uplands adjacent to the plain, in the foothills of the mountain, putting Mount Izala on his left.[1] Mount Izala is very fertile, for it produces wine and bears countless other varieties of fruits. The mountain is densely populated, and its inhabitants are fine men; the mountain is particularly exposed to attack, and is a subject of dispute, since the enemy do not live far away. (2) You could not persuade these people to leave their contentious land either by threats or promises, even though the neighbouring Persians frequently encroach on and plunder their territory. (3) This particular mountain of Izala is adjacent to another mountain whose appellation is Aïsouma: Aïsouma is like a ridge, it stretches up to a very great height, and from its summit two spurs reach downwards. (4) From these Izala proceeds: it begins to rise from a lowly position, next it gradually rears up its head, and, progressively stretching out its neck, it extends as far as the river Tigris. And it would even link with the Eastern or the Caucasian range, if some solicitude of the Creator had not established the division.

(5) Here the general stationed his army, reckoning that there was no water between the river Bouron in Persian territory and the Arzamon,[2] and that the enemy would be compelled to choose one of two alternatives: (6) for they would either remain inactive, content to defend their own territory, or otherwise, if they attempted to attack the Latins, they would be weakened by exertion and thirst; their cavalry would very soon perish, since the Roman force would not allow the barbarians to draw water from the river Arzamon.

(7) On the third day, the Persian contingent learned that the Romans were waiting at the Arzamon. (2. 1) The Kardarigan had reached such a degree of insolence that he roundly poured scorn on

---

[1] The text is uncertain at this point. We have translated ἐν ἀριστερᾷ τοῦ Ἴζαλὰ ⟨τὸ⟩ ὄρος πεποιηκώς, as opposed to de Boor's conjecture (ὄρους for ὄρος) which would have given the following sense '. . . and sited it [the camp] in the foothills on the left of Izala'. Philippicus sited his camp so that Mount Izala protected his left flank as he faced east against the Persians.

[2] The Bouron is most probably the Dara river, the most westerly supply of water in Persian hands at that time, a distance of about 20 miles from the Arzamon.

44

his informants, as if it were a piece of idle gossip, but as the substance of the report buzzed among the Persians more clearly, the enemy were infuriated. (2) The satrap questioned the disciples of sorcery, demanded from the magi to learn the steps of prophecy, and from those women inspired by the Pytho's breath, who appeared to be impregnated by the error of the devil, he demanded a prediction of the future.[3] (3) Those possessed by the demons said that victory would accompany the Medes, and that in the course of the expedition Persians would carry off Romans and at the same time change Persian luck.[4] And so the Persians, as if in exultation, were fortified by the prophecies. (4) Then they set out from the river Bouron and moved towards the Romans. Next they loaded up herds of camels with a heavy burden of water-skins, so that the Romans should not conquer them easily because of their shortage of the watery element. They were so firmly possessed by their hopes of success that they also carried with them fetters, some made of wood, others of iron, and in very great quantity.

(5) The general instructed the Romans not to touch the farmers' labours, enjoining this in order to spare the countryside. So, on the next day he equipped selected men to reconnoitre the enemy, and entrusted them to the captain Sergius, by whom the protection of Mardes had been undertaken, along with Ogyrus and Zogomus; these were tribal chiefs of the force of Roman allies, whom Latins are accustomed to call Saracens.[5] (6) And so the men sent out by the general hunted down some of the barbarian throng and, after torturing them, found out about the Kardarigan's current and earlier camps.

This was in fact the seventh day in the cyclical progress of the week; this was named the sabbath by the high priest Moses.[6] (7) When these events were announced to the Roman contingent, a suspicion came to the general that the enemy would attempt an attack on the following day, on the grounds that the Romans honoured the day as a rest from labour out of respect for its sanctity. The next morning the scouts

---

[3] The Kardarigan's consultation of the magi is grandiloquently described in language derived from the practices of the Delphic oracle, where divine responses were given by the Pythian priestess in a state of frenzy.

[4] In Greek the prophecy is ambiguously phrased, and could equally mean '. . . Romans would carry off Persians . . .'.

[5] i.e. the Ghassanid Arabs; Ogyrus and Zogomus are not otherwise known, but were presumably the leaders of some of the fifteen princedoms into which the Ghassanid federation had disintegrated following the arrest by Maurice of their phylarch Naman (John of Ephesus iii. 42).

[6] i.e. Saturday, so that Sunday, the day of rest, followed.

came and announced to the general that the armies were approaching. (3. 1) And so Philippicus arranged the Romans and marshalled the army in three divisions: the left wing he entrusted to Eilifreda (this man was governor of Emesa); furthermore Apsich the Hun also assumed the same force; the brigadier Vitalius took that on the right, (2) while the general, that is to say Heraclius, the father of the emperor Heraclius,[7] took over the central section. (3) The Persians were also drawn up as follows: on the right flank was Mebodes the Persian, on the left flank Aphraates, who was said to be a nephew of Kardarigan the satrap, and the Kardarigan himself was allotted the central portion.

(4) When the enemy came into view and the dust was thick, Philippicus displayed the image of God Incarnate, which tradition from ancient times even to the present day proclaims was shaped by divine wisdom, not fashioned by a weaver's hands nor embellished by a painter's pigment.[8] (5) It was for this reason that it is celebrated among the Romans even as 'not made by human hand', and is thought worthy of divine privileges: for the Romans worship its archetype to an ineffable degree. (6) The general stripped this of its sacred coverings and paraded through the ranks, thereby inspiring the army with a greater and irresistible courage. Next, when he reached the middle of the throng, pouring out an unquenchable flood of tears over the wastage of the conflict, he employed phrases of exhortation to.the army. (7) The character of his words was sufficient both to heighten the efforts of the eager and to arouse the enthusiasm of the indolent and slothful. Now indeed the trumpets echoed the call to attention and when they sounded forth whetted the forces for battle. (8) The general conveyed that image of the Lord to Mardes, to Symeon who occupied the priestly throne of Amida; for it happened that the man was staying in the fortress at that time.[9] (9) Those in the fort besought

[7] The elder Heraclius plays a prominent part in this and the following eastern campaigns, and his actions tend to be praised, whereas those of his commanding general are denigrated (e.g. ii. 7. 11-8. 5, 10. 1-5; iii. 6. 1-5). It is probable that some of Theophylact's information on these events was provided by a member of the Heraclius family, or by a source which was eager to praise the family's actions; see Introduction, pp. xxii-xxiii.

[8] This image was probably one of the two famous 'divinely created' images of Christ which came to prominence in the second half of the 6th c., either the Camuliana image, which had been transferred to Constantinople from Syria in 574, or the image of Edessa. The importance of proper religious preparations before military action is stressed in Maurice's *Strategicon*, e.g. preface 36 ff., viii. 2. 1, etc.

[9] The fort of Mardes, the modern Mardin, was perched on a peak of the Tur Abdin that commands an extensive view over the Mesopotamian plain and the site of the battle.

and propitiated the Divinity on that day, and with an abundance of tears made supplications that the Romans might gain the victory in the contest. (10) The captains and the front ranks of the forces, or rather the tribunes, assembled and entreated the general to move to the rear of the force; for they feared that the fighting might at some stage become more dangerous for them if they were allocated the general as a colleague in their labours. (11) 'For fighting', they said, 'does not have clear movements, since it loves variety and takes many forms; for its nature is to be habitually changing and it is reliable only in its unreliability. Hence chance misfortune has infinitely exceeded successful attainment.' (12) And they persuaded the general to change his station slightly.

The plain where the fighting was enacted was named Solachon, taking the same name as a nearby district. (13) From there Theodore, whom Byzantines call Zetonumius, and who had also served in the office of *magister* among the Romans, originally drew his descent;[10] and indeed that Solomon, the emperor's eunuch, who organized the Carthaginian war in Libya while Justinian controlled the imperial chariot. This has been recorded by the historian Procopius in the volume of his history.[11]

(4. 1) When the Persian lines came to grips with the Roman divisions, the brigadier Vitalius pushed forward more boldly than the other ranks and quickly routed the opposing force; then he wrought very great slaughter and took possession of the Persian baggage, which Romans in their native tongue are accustomed to call *touldon*.[12] (2) Then indeed the victors were occupied with the booty, but the general was dismayed and angered at the sight of these acts of disorder. (3) Therefore he improvised a clever plan: he took off from his own head his helmet, which was distinctive and conspicuous, and placed it on Theodore Ilibinus, who was the general's bodyguard; next he instructed him to beat with his sword the merchants of plunder. This in fact came about and was of particular benefit to the formation. (4) Since they supposed that the general was on the prowl and

---

[10] This Theodore was probably the son of Peter the Patrician; he held the position of *magister officiorum* and *comes sacrarum largitionum* under Justin II (cf. iii. 15. 6 and n.); Zetonumius, i.e. money-seeker, would be an appropriate nickname for a man in these financial and administrative positions (for which see Jones, *LRE* 575-84; 427-38). Peter the Patrician, however, is known to have come from Thrace, not Mesopotamia.

[11] Procopius, *Wars* iii and iv; at *Wars* iii. 11. 9 Solomon's place of origin is described as the eastern frontier near Dara.

[12] The standard 6th-c. military term, see Maurice, *Strategicon* v.

correcting the looters' error, they turned their attention to the battle, and took their share in the labours of war. The routed opposition escaped to the central section of the Persians, where the Kardarigan was in command. (5) So the central Persian division became deeper through the addition of the fugitive left wing, and the opposing Roman force would have had difficulty in standing their ground if they had not dismounted from their horses and engaged in hand-to-hand combat. (6) So the centremost lines were equal to the fight and their fighting was prolonged; as a result it came about that the battle-line stood on the remains of the dead, since the face of the earth was covered because of the continuity of corpses upon its surface. (7) But since the evil was unending, some divine purpose gave judgement against the foreign tribe, making the battle incline to the other side, and a voice sped through the Romans with great resonance, ordering them to strike at the enemy horse. Accordingly, the Romans obeyed this particular order and overcame the opposing force. (8) The Romans supposed that the shout had come from the captain Stephen, and after the fighting the Romans asked whether that Stephen had himself in fact been the originator of the tactic. (9) But he made denial and swore a great oath that he had never produced such an ingenious enterprise; for he was reluctant to seek glory thereby and to distort divine operations into his personal shrewdness. (10) The third Roman division, that is to say the left, confounded the opposing contingent and the survivors were hotly pursued as far as Daras, which was twelve miles distant from the site of the engagement.[13] (11) Then, as the Roman victory became so clear, the barbarians acknowledged their defeat and turned to flight. The central Persian section, together with its commander, fled and escaped the danger on a certain hillock. (12) When the Romans had heard that some of the enemy were on a hillock sheltering in a state of shock from the victors, they immediately encircled the strong point and ordered the enemy to surrender. But they scorned death and swaggered to the verge of madness. (13) Therefore the Romans ignored them, since they were unaware that the Kardarigan had crept on to the hillock and was paying close attention to the danger. (14) And so the Kardarigan, although he had no food and was hard-pressed by hunger, held out on the hillock for three or four days,

---

[13] Dara, the former Roman fortress, had been captured by the Persians in 573 (iii. 11. 2). The distance between the site of the battle and Dara indicates that the Romans had in fact advanced several miles to the east of the river Arzamon in order to confront the Persians (cf. n. 2 above).

since the unforeseen danger had thrown the Persian general into utter panic: for the convergence of unexpected changes is terrifying, since they alter opinions as well as actions.

(5. 1) When they returned to the general, Stephen was subjected to a harsh rebuke because he had not reduced the remnant; but he rebutted the general's criticism with a defence most appropriate for a leader, saying: (2) 'I know both how to respect the limits of victory and to fear the summit of Fortune. For she holds the scales which hate wrong, and she is not accustomed to tolerate success that flaunts itself more than necessary.' And so when the Persians thus found that the descent was free, they crept down the lower slopes. (3) After they had descended from the ridge, they encountered some Romans who were returning and congregating at the camp; therefore, many were slaughtered and more than a thousand captured, who were dispatched to Byzantium.

(4) Before the approach to battle, the Kardarigan ordered the Persians to burst open those skin flasks of theirs: thereby he stimulated the Medians to more reckless bravery, by making this fact clear to them, that they would die of thirst if they did not grapple with great dangers, since the Romans were stationed by the river Arzamon and were guarding its course with considerable industry. (5) Nor indeed did his boldness stand him in good stead: for it is foolish, by trusting in the dice of Fortune, to be confident at the heights of peril, and to glean favourable outcomes from previous errors. For if the opening is unwise, the conclusions too will take their course in accordance with the antecedents. (6) This in fact destroyed many of the Medes after the defeat: for when they came across wells, some of the Persians gulped down water too insatiably, and so sank into great trouble, since their stomachs, under the sudden incursion of water, could not endure to contain the excessive burden of water.

(7) The Kardarigan reached the vicinity of Daras and made an attempt to enter the town; for the townsmen, or rather the Persians guarding the city, refused to open the gates for the Medes, since indeed Persian custom permits that fugitives should not be admitted. (8) After they had abused the Kardarigan and added their insults to the disaster, they persuaded him to return home to the accompaniment of most shameful words.

(9) As day was waning, a sudden visitation of panic affected the Roman camp and a rumour spread around that the Persians had acquired a reinforcement and were on the very point of attacking the

rampart. (10) Therefore Heraclius, the father of the emperor Heraclius, and another of the leaders, on horseback and protected by steel, ranged about with irresistible impetus on the tracks of the barbarians; and they came to the hillock where those who had recently escaped with the Kardarigan had bivouacked. (11) Therefore they rushed to the heights and gazed round from an excellent vantage-point, and the enemy were not to be seen. Then, after they had made a clear search and there was no possibility of deception in their reconnaissance, they returned to the Romans. (6. 1) At a certain point on their route they observed a Roman soldier in the throes of death, his body adorned by four wounds; (2) a Median arrow had penetrated deeply through his helmet and planted itself in his upper lip; another had in turn entered his other lip from below and was extended in antithesis, as it were, so that by means of opposing shafts his tongue was marked with a cross by the counterposed conjunction of the barbs, and hence the hero was unable to shut his two lips. (3) On his left arm he also bore a spear's incursion, and a further wound in the side from a Median javelin; this indeed was the epitaph even for his bravery. (4) And so Heraclius' companions, seeing the hero bathed in his noble blood and marvelling at his courage, set him on horseback and carried him to the camp. (5) Next, they drew out and extracted the other missiles implanted in his body, but the one in his side they were unable to withdraw; for those who are instructed in these things, the skills of Chiron and Machaon,[14] whispered among themselves that with the departure of the weapon his soul would also pass away. (6) But that Macedonian, or Leonidas in spirit, a Callimachus or Cynegeirus,[15]–but it will suffice to call it Roman–when he heard the doctors' words, asked if the Romans had been victorious. When the bystanders assented and said that the Latins had raised the trophy, he tested their words on oath. (7) When he had learned that the Romans had in reality gained the lighter pan in the balance of war, whereas the Persians had the opposite turn of the scale and were being dragged down to calamity by the weight of defeat, he leapt up with a gasp, saying that the statement was a great consolation and relief for his pain, and that he now awaited death. (8) With a nod he fawned upon the onlookers, as it were, to

[14] The Centaur Chiron was renowned for his medical skill, while Machaon was son of Asclepius, god of healing.

[15] The Macedonian is a reference either to Alexander the Great or to his father Philip; Leonidas was the heroic Spartan commander at Thermopylae; Callimachus was the Athenian commander at Marathon, where he lost his life along with Cynegeirus, the brother of the poet Aeschylus, who was killed in the fight over the Persian ships.

withdraw from his side without mercy that far-famed Median dart; for he said that the man departing this world would never find any other such good provision to take with him from among things mortal. (9) They say that the hero was on the roll of the Quartoparthoi, which is the appellation borne by the men stationed at the city of Beroe in Syria.[16] When that fatal weapon was extracted from his side, that great and most noble spirit of the hero sprang forth with it, hastening to reach the Elysian land, I might say in poetic terms; but I am ashamed to besmirch with myth the dignity of the triumphs.

(10) On the next day the general held a review of the soldiery: he favoured the wounded with gifts, gold and silver decoration was a reward for courageous spirit, and he weighed out the recompense according to the extent of the perils. (11) For some people received promotion as a prize for fortitude, another man a Persian horse, fine in appearance yet good in battle, another a silver helmet and quiver, another a shield, breastplate, and spears. The Romans inherited possessions equal to the battle's inheritance of corpses. (12) But at midday the general dismissed the parade and dispatched the wounded to the cities and nearby forts, so as to heal and soothe the pangs of their wounds through the gentle sorcery of the works of Asclepius. (13) He himself took the rest of the force and invaded Median territory; and wherever the Persians lacked foresight they suffered severely. The Roman onslaught was irresistible and unapproachable for those who encountered it.

(7. 1) And so the Roman general quite suddenly, like a hurricane at sea or a violent thunderbolt, visited the district of Arzanene, and he wrought havoc in the Persian state. The inhabitants of Arzanene descended into the hollows of the earth, for the story is current among us that at a depth they have constructions in the manner of cave-like houses. (2) Accordingly their own safety was for a time treasured up in these same underground shelters. Now indeed the people of Arzanene had stored away bread and barley-cakes in the caves, which they thought to be good for defence. (3) But after briefly beguiling

[16] The Quartoparthoi (the Legio Quarta Parthica) had earlier been stationed at Circesium (*Not. Dig. Or.* 35. 24); it is not known when they were transferred to Beroe (Aleppo) in Syria. The account of this wounded hero has been narrated by Theophylact in deliberately elevated language. This good story of a very insignificant incident in the Solachon campaign is perhaps more likely to have been retailed by the elder Heraclius than by John of Epiphania, and the switch of source might help to explain why Theophylact decided to write up the story so grandly; cf. ii. 18. 15-25 for similar treatment of another attractive story.

perception, they were before long discovered by the Romans, when captives revealed the underground mysteries and displayed the secret in the open. (4) Therefore the Romans tested for those lurking underground through echoes, and the testing by means of resonances was an infallible guide that revealed the rites of the bowels of the earth. (5) The people of Arzanene, however, were led up as if from the very foundations of their fellow initiate earth to the day of slavery, to describe in more tragic terms their tragedy.[17]

(6) But when the Romans had finished the task of groping around in the nether regions, and the barbarians did not escape the most hateful fate, thereafter they camped near the fort of Chlomaron.[18] On the next day two men deserted who were brothers in blood as well as in purpose. (7) One was named Maruthas and the other Jovius, and the two were both leaders of Arzanene. After they had deserted and been accorded a friendly audience with the general, thereafter they most eagerly desired goodwill. (8) Then, since speech most commonly takes precedence over action, they first fawned upon the general, as it were, with well-chosen discourse, and these in fact were their words of goodwill: (9) 'General, if you wish the Romans to take possession of Arzanene, we will show you certain places which are particularly impregnable because they are supported by their strong position. The course of good counsel enjoins that forts be built.'[19] Such were the primary points of the barbarians' speech to the general. (10) Their words were not inconsistent with the general's intentions, for the director of the Roman camp was eager to acquire places of this very type, but had meantime out of uncertainty restrained the enterprise by delaying the investigation. (11) So when the general had received such tidings, as if he had chanced upon some godsend, with a ready enthusiasm he dispatched his second-in-command Heraclius, and sent along with him as well the guides to the strong point. (8. 1) And so he set out on his way; but the Kardarigan was marching against the Romans, having enrolled throngs, who were not soldiers but men inexperienced in martial clamour; he had in addition assembled

---

[17] 'The day of slavery' is derived from Homer, *Iliad* vi. 463.

[18] Chlomaron, the chief town of Arzanene and the seat of the Persian governor and of a Nestorian bishop, had been unsuccessfully besieged by Maurice in 578, after his capture of the nearby fortress of Aphumon (iii. 15. 14; Menander, fr. 57; John of Ephesus vi. 15, 34).

[19] These sites for prospective forts were probably intended to command the routes across the Taurus and Hakkari mountains, which connected Arzanene with Persarmenia and lower Mesopotamia.

a herd of baggage animals and camels, and was moving forwards. This was a show bereft of truth, a shadow of things that were otherwise, like a marvel contrived for stage deception. (2) Accordingly he encountered Heraclius' party, which was progressing on reconnaissance of the country; twenty men accompanied Heraclius. (3) They were unarmed because of their ignorance of what was to happen. No helmet protected their head, no breastplate their breast, steel to ward off steel, a bodily defence that escorts and accompanies the man it protects. For good fortune had enfeebled them, since victory does not know how to maintain the conqueror at the same fortitude. (4) And so when Heraclius observed the spectacle, he simulated boldness and pretended to continue his forward march. When his stratagem was revealed, as the enemy were approaching and were just about to come to grips with his men, he and his party made for a high ridge. (5) When the foe launched an onslaught against them, they moved again to another ridge, and from that one again to another, and by a succession of moves they evaded the enemies' schemes. By night he sent a messenger to Philippicus to inform him of the barbarian approach.

(6) When the general had brought this envoy into his own tent and learned that the barbarians were intending to attack on the following day, he reassembled his army, which was dispersed hither and thither ravaging Arzanene, by commanding the trumpet to sound the recall. (7) And so it rang out, while they returned to camp in eager haste. A certain man who bore the appellation Zabertas (this man was invested with the responsibility for the garrison of Chlomaron in fact) secretly slipped out of the fort and silently followed behind the Roman force, moving noiselessly and carefully; when he had outflanked the Roman soldiery, he hurried off to join the Kardarigan's men. (8) Therefore the Persian fugitive guided his fellow countrymen, leading them up to confront the Roman throng, showing them a safe place that was a defence against attacks because of the calm of its strong position. For, like some respected intermediary, a great ravine lay in the middle and separated the two forces. For the barbarian was well aware that the Persians would not withstand their conqueror if he attacked directly and suddenly, since they could not bear the sight of the enemy because of the freshness of their misfortunes. (9) It was for this reason that Zabertas spread the Persians in opposition along the lip of the ravine. The ravine was interposed like a ready-made ditch, a good custodian which had both sides in its trust; there indeed the Romans and barbarians remained for some time. (10) The Romans in their eagerness for

an engagement strove to leap across the ditch; but the Persians deflected the attack because the ravine was biased in their favour, and for a time the slaughter received deferment. (11) After this the Persians came to the rear of the Romans, cheating observation at night; for, circumventing the ravine secretly, they moved around and by a circular march came behind the Romans. Hence the Persians gained the confidence to camp on the upper slopes of the mountain where Chlomaron was sited. (12) Accordingly, it came about that the Romans departed from there and fortified a camp in the foothills of the mountain. The forces were such close next-door neighbours to each other that they could discern each other's voices and clearly hear the neighing of the horses. It was for this reason that the Romans abandoned the siege of Chlomaron; for thereafter it was not possible for them to reduce the fortress.

(9. 1) On the following day, about the first watch of the night at the time of the deepest sleep, an uncontrollable terror deranged the general and drove him in a frenzy to inexplicable flight. (2) Therefore he was so terrified and, since he could not endure the onset of fear, he departed on his way without communicating his retreat to any of his attendant army. (3) Such was the intensity that his consternation had reached; and yet the Mede did not have the power to balance the Romans, and furthermore hunger was pressing the barbarians severely. (4) So the general reached Aphumon, which was at that time under Roman control.[20] Therefore terror, panic, confusion and perplexity afflicted the Romans; the crisis was beyond control, for it was prolonged by the moonless night. (5) And so they fled, negotiating impassable tracks and effecting a perilous retreat, and the cause of the flight was not examined, while the barbarians were puzzled by the Roman manœuvre and comprehension was unattainable. (6) Then the troops converged on the intervening ravine, and were encompassed by extraordinary troubles, since in the pitch darkness the baggage animals were virtually annihilated in the ditch by slippages.

[20] Aphumon was situated on the opposite side of a valley, probably that of the Redwan river, from Chlomaron (John of Ephesus vi. 34). The motive for Philippicus' withdrawal to Aphumon was perhaps less discreditable than Theophylact's highly rhetorical account pretends: the Roman siege of Chlomaron had been thwarted (ii. 8. 12), since the Kardarigan had managed to bring up reinforcements, and so it was now essential for Philippicus to organize a new attack or to arrange a diversion so that the Roman army could retire in safety. It is possible that the elder Heraclius, who had been sent out on reconnaissance (ii. 7. 11-8. 5), was in fact partly to blame for the Kardarigan's success in relieving Chlomaron, and that the fierce criticism of Philippicus reflects the desire to avoid criticizing the Heraclius family (cf. n. 7 above).

(7) As the Romans were massed together and whirled apart, pushing and being pushed by turns, it was impossible for them to find an escape from the confinement: such trouble did the general's folly engender. (8) And indeed by heaven, if a mere ten Persian slave-boys, I mean those who transport the equipment from the camp and serve the barbarians, if they had cried out on that day to the effect that the Persian army was pursuing them and was on the point of allocating slaughter, the whole Roman contingent would have perished, so as to endanger, I think, the survival of anyone to report the disaster. So great was the trouble which the womb of folly brought forth for them.

(9) Therefore, as dawn's rays were dispersing the darkness, the Roman army was with difficulty extricating itself and crossing to Aphumon. Hence the forces abused the general and insulted him to his face. (10) The Persians followed unhurriedly and cautiously, for they did not have the courage to come to grips openly, since it had not become apparent to them that the enemy was panic-stricken. (11) Then they followed in the rear and struck the tail of the Roman force with arrows, and the Medes shot as if at a butt: such was the disorderly retreat of the Latins. (12) Accordingly, even one of the mules that carried the general's bedding was struck by a barbarian missile and confusion immediately arose: for the report was distorted to the effect that even the general's baggage had been taken by enemy hands. After this the missiles flew at random and transmitted to the Romans very grave wounds. (13) Nevertheless the barbarians did not harass the retreat overmuch, partly through fear, and partly because they suspected that the Romans were devising some plan and disguising under a cloak of retreat some cunning deceit against them. (14) At midday, when everyone had assembled by the general, the soldiers poured insults and abuse against Theodore: for this man had in fact undertaken the supervision of the watch but, surrendering himself to indolence, he had neglected his task, and the trouble had thereby gained ground.[21]

(15) The Roman baggage was also captured by the Persians, and the Persians encountered a very great benefit, since the famine, which had sorely afflicted them like an implacable tyrant, was banished. (16) The general effected his retreat with great peril and forded the

---

[21] Theophylact's elaborate rhetoric has probably exaggerated the extent of the Roman mishap: at any rate, the army extracted itself from a difficult position, and during the rest of the year the Romans were able to construct fortresses (ii. 9. 17) and ravage extensively (ii. 10. 4) without encountering Persian opposition.

river Nymphius; such was his utterly shameful escape from Persia. On
the following day he reached Amida, losing much of his force, since
the Persians were harrying the rear of the Roman force. (17) The
general, whose hopes had been dashed,[22] restored forts below Mount
Izala, and furthermore repaired the old forts which had been
neglected and were gaping through the passage of time and the war;
one of these forts was called Phathacon, the other Alaleisus, and he
stationed garrisons in them, organizing the control of Mount Izala
from there.[23] He gave part of the army to Heraclius, since he was himself overwhelmed by pain and unable to fight.

(10. 1) Heraclius marshalled his soldiery and camped opposite the
foothills of Izala, or rather the banks of the river Tigris. This begins its
course from the northern regions of Persia, winds through the Roman
territory, and circles, loops, and meanders, so that it virtually doubles
its length through its circuitous detour; (2) it also encircles part of
Mount Izala and, returning home, it enfolds the place called
Thamanon;[24] then with a gentle course it flows out through the
Melabason mountain, and wandering towards the south it comes to
rest. (3) The Melabason mountain was native to Media, and beyond it
one can see the Carduchian ranges jutting out, as the geographers
plausibly declare in setting out for us their perception.[25]

(4) Accordingly Heraclius left Thamanon,[26] advanced towards the
southern parts of Media, and ravaged the whole of that area. He even
traversed the Tigris and urged the army forward, burning everything
of importance in that part of Media. Then he re-entered the Roman
state, circled past Theodosiopolis, and once again rejoined the men

[22] We translate the vulgate text. De Boor accepted the reading of the Vatican MS,
which adds 'Persian' to specify which general is being mentioned; however, this forced
him to postulate a lacuna, since in the remainder of the sentence (as in the preceding
sentence) the subject is clearly the Roman general Philippicus.

[23] The location of these forts is problematical. Alaleisus was probably sited in the
Bitlis pass (the *cleisoura* Balaleison), which connected Arzanene and Persarmenia, while
Phathacon should probably be identified with Atachas, which guarded another of the
passes across the Taurus. Hence Philippicus was continuing the strategy of isolating
Arzanene which he had begun during the siege of Chlomaron (ii. 7. 9-10). Neither of
these locations is in, or close to, Mount Izala (the Tur Abdin), and it appears that there
is some confusion in Theophylact's geographical information.

[24] The Tigris 'returns home' because Thamanon was a district or settlement on the
east bank of the river in Persian territory, so that the river has now come back to its
native land.

[25] The reference to geographers may indicate that Theophylact lifted this brief
description of the Tigris from a geographical handbook.

[26] This is the first precise indication of Heraclius' position and suggests that his
camp (ii. 10. 1) had been located on the east bank of the river.

with Philippicus.[27] (5) After these particular things had been accomplished contrary to expectation, the general broke camp: for the season of winter was doubtless already present, and the annual monetary payment had been dispersed to the Roman army. (6) When spring-time seasons had engendered the terrestrial greenery,[28] the general gave two-thirds of the entire Roman force to Heraclius, the father of the emperor Heraclius, but the other portion to Theodore, the man from Tur Abdin, and to Andrew: this man was indeed the intermediary for the Saracen tribe which was aiding the Romans.[29] (7) He instructed them to use the tactics of sallies and raids and to swoop down again on the Persian state. For the general was sick and unable to apply himself to military conflict.

(8) In this particular year Comentiolus came to Anchialus, assembled the army, carefully reviewed the bravest of the throng, and separated them from the ineffectual force.[30] He arranged three divisions and dispersed these separately against the barbarians. (9) He appointed Martin brigadier of the right flank, while he made Castus captain of the other wing; the general took charge of the centre of the force. The number of the fighting force was six thousand; for four thousand were non-combatant because of feebleness of spirit, and these the general ordered to stand guard over the rampart, as it is called, along with the baggage. (10) And so Castus took his contingent, ranged across the country on the left hand, and came to Zaldapa and the Haemus range; but at dawn he swooped down unexpectedly on the barbarians, and finding them off guard, he distinguished himself with the spear and won a glorious victory; he killed a very great portion of the barbarian throng. (11) Therefore, he embellished his victory with many spoils, which he entrusted to one of the bodyguard to take back. Would that he had not; for on the following day the barbarians assembled and recovered this booty.

(12) But Martin came to the vicinity of the city of Tomi, and spied out the Chagan and the Avars encamped there. So the Romans laid an

---

[27] Since Heraclius' raid had begun at Thamanon to the east of the Tigris, he therefore crossed back to the west bank to ravage Beth Arabaye and continued westwards to Theodosiopolis (Ras el-Ain). It is improbable that Theophylact understood the geography of this raid.

[28] i.e. 587.

[29] i.e. the Ghassanids; Andrew was perhaps their patron, acting as the intermediary between the imperial administration and the tribes.

[30] Theophylact now returns to the Balkans and the narrative of i. 8. 11, where Comentiolus was appointed general to oppose the Avar invasion that had begun in autumn 586.

ambush and then suddenly launched a fierce attack; a sort of watery death came upon the barbarians, in that an ebb-tide suddenly swallowed up the enemy, as it were. (13) The Chagan had the good fortune to find an unexpected and providential salvation, and flight had an assistant, since it was not noticed that an island in the marsh preserved the barbarian: for in truth he would have been captured and have brought the Romans a glorious ransom. For this extreme and most spectacular peril befell the barbarians. On the fifth day it was indeed possible to extract the truth from the Avar deserters as well. (14) Next, in the morning, Martin withdrew to the place which the general had prescribed on the previous day, and Castus too linked up with him, coming to the same place as Martin. The divisions mutually gave and received the greatest strength from their conjuncture and obtained strongest security from their union. (11. 1) Comentiolus dismissed the compact and agreements of the previous day, accomplished absolutely nothing indicative of astuteness, and, on account of the multitude of barbarians, did not set out towards Castus and Martin to withdraw them towards the rear and to be implicated in their triumph.[31] (2) The accusation is also reported that Rusticius, the commander of one of the contingents, admonished the general that he was neglecting his arrival and disregarding his rendezvous with Castus and Martin because of the impenetrable uncertainty of fortune, and that it was not the wish of the emperor which was pressing him not to undertake such perils. (3) And in fact the general gave ear to Rusticius and eagerness replaced indolence. After Martin and Castus heard that the general had reached Marcianopolis, they withdrew to him. When the sun began its circular light-giving orbit, Comentiolus moved with the whole army to his own camp, where he had also left the rejects from the Roman army.

(4) After that indeed he moved camp to the defiles of the Haemus, ascending towards the peaks and the upland valleys. The place is named Sabulente Canalion in the native appellation. But come, let us sketch this in word and try to shape it with eloquent power.[32] (5) This

[31] The description of Comentiolus' movements is obscure. This point marks the beginning of the anti-Comentiolus bias in Theophylact's Balkan narrative. It is probable that Comentiolus had sent his two subordinates to harry the Avars in advance of the slower-moving main Roman contingent (cf. the tactics of Maurice, *Strategicon* xi. 4, 180-224), so that Castus and Martin gained credit while Comentiolus appeared to be less active (cf. book viii n. 9).

[32] Comentiolus had probably retreated south-west from Marcianopolis, across the higher parts of the Haemus (Stara Planina), and then descended into the fertile Valley of the Roses (Sabulente Canalion), which lies between the main range of the Haemus

place is exceedingly beautiful and elevated, a flat area in the very centre of the mountain, an extensive plain that is bedecked all over with flowery fields. The green of its meadows is a festival and banquet for the eyes. (6) It has shady haunts which conceal the rider by the leafiness of the wood and produce abundant shelter for wayfarers at the midday hour, when even the inner recesses of the earth are seared by the sun's rays. And it is a delight to behold, but not easy to describe. (7) Round the place flows an abundance of waters, which does not distress the drinker by its excessive coldness nor enervate the man taking refreshment by the mildness of its communion, so to speak. Birds, sitting on the young shoots of the trees, entertain the audience rather musically with their tunes, sing for them soothing songs that banish care and obscure the memory of all troubles, and with their airs pass on great tranquillity to wayfarers. (8) Ivy, myrtle, columbine and all the other flowers perfect in a most beautiful harmony a super-abundance of intangible luxuriance for the nose, and with their fragrances they enrich the inhabitant, as though they were proffering some heart-warming preparation to the passers-by in an excellent bond of hospitality.

(9) Here indeed the general ordered his army to encamp on the next day and on the following one. In the morning the general commanded Martin, in the role of ambuscader, to search out the Avars in the vicinity of the wooden bridge over the nearby river, and to observe whether the enemy crossed the stream, while he ordered Castus to investigate the enemy movements at the stone crossing, what their plans were, and whether they were encamped on the opposite side.[33] (10) But when Martin had observed that the enemy was just on the point of crossing the stream, he retreated as if in retrogression and joined the troops under Comentiolus. (11) But Castus stealthily approached, crossed the river, and on arriving at the far side encountered the opposing

and the parallel subsidiary range of the Sredna Gora. The description of the luxuriant valley is based on Aelian's account of the Vale of Tempe (*Var. Hist.* iii. 1).

[33] The identity of this river is uncertain. According to Theophylact's narrative, the Avars ought to be north and the Romans south of the Haemus, so that a confrontation would only have been possible if one of the armies crossed the mountains. The Romans are unlikely to have recrossed to the north of the Haemus after retreating away from the Avars, and it is probable that the Avars had by now crossed to the south (an action that Theophylact records subsequently, ii. 12. 5-6). If this suggestion is right, the river is probably the Tundža, a major tributary of the Marica, which would have been sufficiently important to have two bridges in close proximity. Comentiolus was trying to retreat south-east to the safety of Constantinople, but found that the Avars were blocking his escape.

advance party, all of whom he robustly put to the sword. (12) After such achievements, he was unable to preserve his current good fortune, through the decrees of some malevolent demon: for he did not return towards Comentiolus, but set out for the wooden bridge in an attempt to rendezvous with Martin. (13) When his plan failed, since the sun was setting, he camped for the night on the spot. On the next day the enemy remained vigilant and crossed to the further side by the wooden bridge; for it was impossible to cross the stream elsewhere, since the river shelved steeply and its surging flood prevented those who approached from crossing. (14) While Castus was converging on the base and was returning to the camp, he encountered the enemy throng head on, so that the danger was overwhelming, with no possibility for stratagem. (12. 1) Then Castus was bathed in sweat, his spirit cast down in despair; he shrank back in terror and the misfortune was the prelude for great disaster. (2) At once his contingent scattered and, such was the panic, fled in different directions. Like hares or deer escaping a hunter's snares, they hid themselves in the valleys and blanketed themselves in the woods. (3) But some Romans were caught by the Avars; they suffered unbearable torment, underwent a variety of methods of torture, and were also threatened with a most painful form of death if they did not reveal where Castus had chanced to turn. (4) Accordingly they confessed and pointed out Castus hidden away in the middle of the forest like, as it were, an unpicked bunch of grapes. Therefore the brigadier was taken prisoner and became a splendid prey for the enemy. But along with Castus a very great part of his army was also bound fast by the foe.

(5) The fighting received further augmentation rather and blazed forth more furiously. For the Chagan released a great army, as if from some starting-line of woes, to ravage the whole of Thrace. (6) Then the enemy leapt forward to pillage through the borders of Mesembria, and next slaughtered the guards, who were heroically arrayed (there were five hundred of these who were guarding the strong points).[34] (7) A certain brigadier Ansimuth (this man was in command of an infantry army stationed in Thrace) collected his host as soon as he learned of the Avar incursion, and retreated for refuge towards the Long Walls. (8) He himself was in fact at the rear of the force, pushing the army inwards; it was this that handed him over alive to the barbarians: for he was captured, and became a spoil ready to hand for the enemy

[34] The strong points would have been located in the low passes across the Haemus immediately north of Mesembria (the modern Nesebär on the Black Sea coast).

vanguard, since the fool did not have his rear under guard. (9) Shortly afterwards the Chagan also poured the remaining portion of his horde into Thrace, and they made their entry through innumerable points, while Comentiolus' men were marching from the left.[35] It was for this reason that the Romans hid in the forests of Haemus and the enemy bypassed them to scatter in several sections across Thrace. (10) On the third day Comentiolus summoned to his own tent the captains and tribunes and the most capable of the contingent, and communicated exactly what he intended to do. (11) On the following day he gathered the cavalry and infantry, summoned an assembly, and exhorted the meeting not to show their backs to the barbarians, but to place everything second to courage. (13. 1) But one of the tribunes stood up in the middle, grumbling, and brazenly dismissed the general's instructions. He said that it would be expedient both for the army itself and for the general to withdraw to the rear, using the following words:

(2) 'Men, experts in war, stalwarts in spirit, that is when opportunity is our ally and when fortune is weighted in our favour; men, for whom the common lot is danger, while the salvation of all is indivisible. (3) However much cowardice is reproached, recklessness in contrast is equally reprehensible. Hesitation is the most exalted mark of intellect, when it does not shame good counsel but puts prudence in good order. (4) But before any of my words have peeped forth from their own mother my heart, and been delivered to your ears by you as midwife, put aside the general's trustworthiness a little, lest perchance you block your ear to advisers, lest the speaker be forestalled by an obstacle like a closed door, and lest you cast out our words before you have welcomed them in. (5) For trustworthiness is an autocratic quality whose strength is innate, but it possesses the will like a rudder and steers its audience exactly where it wishes. (6) Men, the general exhorts you to resist the enemy and orders you to sail head on, the few against the many, and this even after Castus' destruction. (7) You are also my witnesses that not all are good in the battle-line, if, that is, I do not cause some offence by exposing the truth to you: for in my opinion false praise is more reprehensible than truthful censure, since events are not the slaves of panegyrics. (8) Did not the general recently order those unfit for battle to guard the rampart? These men numbered four thousand, so that the remnant was very nearly equal to those engaging, the non-combatants to the fighters, and the healthy were matched

---

[35] Comentiolus was still trying to retreat from the west (left) south-east towards Constantinople (cf. n. 33 above).

by the lame. (9) I will pass over in silence how many steadfast spirits were destroyed in the recent misfortunes, and how the enemy sheared off our chief supporting weight; and, if I am not mistaken, the recent disastrous failure was greater than our success which occurred a little earlier. (10) Castus killed many of the barbarians and took possession of their booty, but on the next day the barbarians recaptured it, and now I shall also tell a most ill-omened epilogue: they seized that man too, took prisoner his soldiers, and bound on a glorious triumphal crown. Castus could not escape detection when concealed in the wood. (11) And yet a marshy island hid the Chagan, and did not declare to Martin the man lurking within, but kept him concealed like some secret mystery from the uninitiated. (12) And now those relatively small successes delude the emperor, and he will not dispense additional allied assistance for us, since he has not yet learned of the more recent ill fortunes. (13) I am sure that those recent upsets, which spun them around, will also make the enemy more provident, and that in future they will take great care to guard their safety on account of that minor misfortune. (14) I have spoken enough, men, with regard to our future expediency. May fortune grant that I am disappointed in my expectation, by deploying her own personal assistance on your behalf.'

(15) Then, after the tribune had spewed forth these ignoble words, and had terrified the meeting with his speech, while the multitude was quiet and aghast at his fearful descriptions, a certain veteran sprang up from the assembly, shouted in reproach at the tribune, and asked the assembly to admit a speech in opposition. (16) When the multitude agreed and by their hands instructed him to speak out, he began his speech something like this, loudly imploring them in his aged voice and impelling respect for his words with a veteran's tear.

(14. 1) 'Men of Rome, unless you would belie the name by your actions; men, that is if your hearts are masculine like your body. Even though the tribune is expert at high-flown talk and at confusing the issue, nevertheless deeds are more vigorous than words and do not tolerate empty sounds. For he does not scare us like children with his sophistries. (2) First of all I should like to ask him a question: in all honesty, O tribune, to whom were you directing this harangue? Rustics you would have deceived with this talk, men who use the winnowing-fan rather than the sword, with a leather jerkin as breastplate, plough-oxen rather than a proud, high-prancing horse, unskilled labourers who obey the farmers' commands. (3) Why did

you assume you were addressing an assembly of women, insulting our nature as well as our race? With words you misrepresent deeds, bringing shame on the council. Did you not realize that you were pouring forth disgraceful words in the presence of men? Or do you not see an assembly of the Roman people, proud of their zeal, vigorous in arms, knowledgeable in their experience of danger and providence for future advantage? Why, in your opinion, did a minor reverse curtail an endowment of great successes? (4) Let the enemy, who was not dismayed by his misfortunes, put you to shame. That man who recently became a swamp-dweller, as it were, who was a fugitive on the island and who adopted reliance on the waters as an unreliable salvation, he now bravely marshals his line, encourages the wounded, and persuades them to welcome for their wounds greater blows from the enemy, like drugs which soothe the most intense pains. (5) For he is forgetful of his former troubles: for the man who did not expect his difficulties to change must despair of success. (6) How did the Romans advance to great power, and expand their tiny city-state to such great might? In my opinion, it was through their proud spirit, their seething desires, their innate daring and love of danger, their belief that it was death not to die for glory. (7) If their spirit was like the tribune's, they would not have conquered Europe, held Libya in subjection, dispatched tax-collectors to Asia, or possessed as their servant the Nile, which shipped the wealth of Egypt in the summer season to the Roman cities, and with merchantmen turned the sea into dry land, as it were. (8) And how fantastic was the tailpiece to your speech! "There will be no reinforcements", he says. Who entrusted you with the codes of this prophecy? Or did you take over the oracle of cowardice as if from some Pythian priestess? Along with everything else hesitation has this too–laudation: a self-taught prophet and diviner is always the quickest to invent a spontaneous delay for actions. (9) I am amazed if the barbarians are rushing around near the Long Walls and the emperor has not been aroused, when such great confusion is surging in the city. (10) One thing, men, is established as an invincible ally, the courage which surpasses everything, rendering possible what is impossible for others, while more bravely enduring what frightens the multitude. (11) Then let each man advance into battle today inspired, and let us affix a great seal of glory to our deeds: for I will not insult actions with names, and call recklessness courage or rashness bravery. (12) This much from me, a veteran who loves danger. But if it seems right to anyone else as well, let him judge likewise; but if not, still allow me at least my fervour: for excellence has not achieved equal favour among all men, nor are pledges taken seriously by all. For courage is a lofty quality that is hard to reach and inaccessible to the majority, either because of strength of cowardice or lack of ambition for the better.'

(15. 1) When the old man had made this speech ring around the assembly, he kindled the multitude, and urged them on to confrontation, in the best men inspiring uncontrollable eagerness, but for the more slothful goading, as it were, with lashing words and transforming their cowardice. (2) A great shout was stirred up from the council, and they made the meeting resound with their acclamations in admiration at the old soldier's noble spirit. At once, united as brothers in the same resolve, they disbanded the council and all turned to arm.

(3) Then, eager for war, they swooped down from the Haemus to Calvomuntis and Libidurgon. They saw the Chagan loitering not very far away, but with his tents pitched carelessly about four miles distant, because his horde was dispersed across the whole of Thrace.[36] (4) So Comentiolus marshalled the army, arranged it into a single formation, and permitted it to march. He instructed it to move towards the Astike, to spend the night on guard, and on the morrow to fall on the Chagan like a whirlwind and inflict very great slaughter on his company. (5) But some fate decided to pervert the general's prescriptions; for like a drone it wasted the hives of prudence, and ravaged. the general's bee-like labours. (6) For when the sun showed its back to grim-faced night, and the beautiful light-bearing torch had shrouded its radiance and given way to nocturnal power, one of the baggage animals shed the load it was carrying. (7) It happened that the animal's owner was marching in front; those following behind saw that the beast of burden was dragging in some disarray its intended load, and ordered its master to turn to the rear and to rectify the baggage-beast's miscarriage. (8) This in fact became the cause of disorder and produced a spontaneous backward rush to the rear. For the utterance was incorrectly repeated by the majority, the word was distorted, and it appeared to indicate flight, as if the enemy had suddenly appeared before them and cheated their expectation. (9) The army fell into tremendous uproar, a great outcry arose among them, with piercing

---

[36] These two places, which are otherwise unknown, should probably be located in the Sredna Gora range, which separates the Valley of the Roses from the Thracian plain. The Chagan was perhaps camped near Beroe (Stara Zagora), which was the first Thracian city that he attacked (ii. 16. 12).

shouts everyone cried out to return, and one man ordered another in native parlance to turn to the rear, amidst utmost confusion, shouting 'Turn, turn', as if a night battle had unexpectedly come upon them.[37] (10) So the whole contingent was rent asunder, as if it were the harmony of the strings of a lyre. Hence the Chagan escaped this second very grave danger, with all possible speed abandoned his usual haunts, moved to another location, and had a lucky salvation even more extraordinary than his earlier one. (11) The Romans also acted similarly, the flight was reciprocal, an ill-founded panic threw the Roman camp into turmoil, and a spurious danger confounded it. (12) Nevertheless the majority of the Avars were slaughtered when an unexpected engagement brought the two armies together: for some of the Roman division wheeled about and engaged the enemy most resolutely.

(13) When the Chagan had recovered his breath from these twin confusions, after banishing the squall caused by the attacks and gathering the barbarians, he attacked the Roman cities and captured the fort of Appiaria. It does not seem to me superfluous to relate the manner, and to bestow a brief account like an intercalation in the sequence.[38] (16. 1) There was a certain soldier, whose name was Busas, a good man in battle, whose courageous spirit had won him more renown than all the other heroes in combat, since he always anticipated them in danger, whenever he so much as heard a trumpet sound the battle-cry. (2) At that time this man was resident in the fort. Now Busas decided to ride in the meadows near the fort, and next to extend his ride rather further because his hunting would perhaps be more successful. (3) Therefore the barbarians captured Busas and the hunter fell into a snare. When they had him captive, they threatened to strike him with the spear; he begged them not to do this, but rather to trade his life for a ransom, since the death of Busas and scorn of splendid gifts would not benefit the barbarians. (4) Then the barbarians accepted the promise and did not reject the exchange. Therefore they

---

[37] Theophylact's account of this incident is obscured by grandiloquent rhetoric; for a clearer account, see Theophanes 258. 10-21. The Roman confusion was caused by the shouting of 'torna, torna', a standard military command for an about-turn (cf. Maurice, *Strategicon* iii. 5, 44). On this, see *Byzantion* 52 (1982), 426-7, and 53 (1983), 327-8.

[38] This sentence suggests that the following account of the capture of Appiaria did not originate in the source which Theophylact was following for the main part of this campaign-narrative (cf. *Byzantion* 53 (1983), 328-9). Appiaria was located by the Danube (at the modern Tutrakan), so that the insertion of the story causes Theophylact's narrative to jump, without warning, from the Thracian plain (ii. 15. 3-4) across the Haemus mountains, and then back again to the cities of Thrace (ii. 16. 12).

brought the captive to the fort and proclaimed to those within the stronghold that they would slaughter Busas before their eyes if they did not redeem him with gifts and friendship. (5) Busas too begged the Romans not to ignore him now that, as if at some critical point, he was being weighed in the balance of salvation and death; he implored them to measure out for him reciprocal services, with cries and tears he recited the brave deeds which, at immense risk, he had been allocated for the benefit of the Romans, (6) he ran off the list of his ordeals, displayed the contests that were recorded in the wounds on his body, demonstrating the manifestations, as it were, of his labours, clearly laid bare the scars of the enemy missiles and, to sum up, demanded from his beneficiaries that, as a result of his sufferings, he obtain immunity from suffering. (7) They refused, since they had been corrupted by a certain man whom report derides as having consorted in stolen pleasures with Busas' wife. But they dismissed the barbarians in dishonour. (8) Then Busas, being in greater danger, entreated the barbarians that his death be briefly delayed, and that as payment for the temporary reprieve he hand over the fort to the barbarians: for he thought that those who forgot a favour should suffer first, and that inhumanity should have the initial share of misfortune, so that the evil might first make its advance against itself. (9) When the enemy had obtained a greater offer, they were better disposed towards clemency; they guaranteed on oath to spare Busas and not in fact to slaughter him, but to grant the power to natural death, whenever it might wish to loose his vital bond; for if the agreement was brought to completion by him, they would not inflict on him this fabricated and unnatural death. (10) Next Busas taught the Avars to construct a sort of besieging machine, since they had as yet no knowledge of such implements, and he prepared the siege-engine for a long-range assault. (11) Shortly afterwards the fort was overthrown, and Busas exacted punishment for inhumanity by giving the barbarians skilled instruction in the technology of siegecraft. For, as a result, the enemy subsequently reduced without difficulty a great many other Roman cities by using the invention as prototype.

(12) Now indeed he attacked Beroe; but at the cost of a very great waste of time and after encountering many labours, he attained the end of his struggles without reward, because the local inhabitants arrayed themselves in opposition more spiritedly.[39] Nevertheless they

[39] The narrative has now returned from the Danube to the Thracian plain. The inappropriateness of the insertion of the Busas story, with its reference to Avar skill in siegecraft (ii. 16. 11), is highlighted by the fact that the Chagan did not actually manage

purchased an agreement for a small sum of money, for this provided him with a plausible cloak for the failure. (17. 1) He also vigorously besieged Diocletianopolis, but the city also marshalled itself in opposition strongly and prevented him from attacking with confidence; for they stationed catapults and other defences on the walls, and it was impossible for the barbarians to approach and engage at close quarters. (2) Then he departed disgruntled, after experiencing the proverbial fate of the wolf: for he had gaped at vain hopes.[40] At once he moved to Philippopolis, invested the city, and strove to take it. (3) The town's inhabitants fought back most skilfully and inflicted many injuries from their ramparts and battlements, so that the Chagan willingly abandoned the fight, respecting their inviolability on account of their courage. (4) In the morning he crossed the forests of the Astike, as it is called, came up against Adrianopolis, and attacked the town fiercely, but the townsmen bravely resisted.

(5) The news of the capture of Castus and Ansimuth was buzzing round Byzantium, and great uproar surged over the city. The emperor was publicly insulted by some ignorant gossips from among the multitude, whose fortunes were undesirable and intellects unenviable: they composed slanderous chants against him,[41] disparaging him, mocking the ill fortune in verse, and ascribing the failure to folly rather than to chance. (6) But the insult did not engender wrath in the emperor: for with regard to anger the emperor's soul was barren and held no communion with the flame of wrath. (7) The enemy handed Castus back after receiving exceptionally lavish payment, as can be gathered from the elders among us, and there is no harm in belief.[42] (8) The emperor marshalled his own thoughts against the enemy, and equipped himself for hostilities with greater preparation. He appointed as general John, the one whom the masses are accustomed to call Mystacon, (9) and also elected Drocton as outrider to him, as it were, a second-in-command to whom he entrusted some power. This man was a Lombard by race, a very brave fighter and a weighty force in war.[43]

to capture any of the cities which he besieged immediately afterwards (ii. 16. 12-17. 4), Beroe (Stara Zagora), Diocletianopolis (Hisar), Philippopolis (Plovdiv), or Adrianopolis (Edirne).

[40] A reference to the fable of the disappointed wolf, Babrius 16, esp. vv. 6 f.

[41] This probably refers to the circus factions, who were normally responsible for organizing popular chants.

[42] Although this comment might indicate that Theophylact has gathered some oral information about Castus' ransom, it is perhaps as likely to be an empty periphrasis to embellish the reference to lavish payment.

[43] Drocton (Droctulft) was in fact a Swabian who had been brought up by the

(10) When they came near Adrianopolis, they raised the barbarians' siege, and on the second day the fight was accomplished. Then in the engagement with the barbarians the Romans were victorious and turned the fighting in their favour, since the second-in-command Drocton outmanœuvred the enemy. (11) For by feigned flight his wing gave the enemy the impression of turning their backs, as though the Romans were afraid of the opposition; next he turned about in pursuit, came up behind the barbarians, and slaughtered those whom he encountered. (12) Accordingly, at the hour of midday the Avars retreated, scattering in different directions and being carried in headlong flight wherever chance took them. The general did not pursue the opposition: for he practised moderation in success and was cautious, as is reasonable, of the height of prosperity. (13) For fortune is prone to wheel about and is unreliable, and victory visits men in turns, so that I may intersperse in my narratives a touch of the Homeric poem.[44]

(18. 1) And so at this particular time Heraclius made another invasion into the Persian state, and trouble became endemic among the Medes.[45] (2) When he had arrived, he attacked a certain very strong fort; this was situated upon a lofty rock.[46] The under-general arranged his siege-engines and machines. (3) The Persians also devised various counter-stratagems against his schemes, and wove things like robes: after collecting hairs and intertwining the warp with the weft, they produced long tunics and packed these densely with chaff; after making them solid, they hung them upon the wall and on these they received the bombardments, mitigating the hardness of the discharges through the softness of the countering preparation. (4) Many of the missiles flew right over the fort, but others were also brought down on the stronghold itself. Heraclius admitted no respite in the bombardment, alternating those engaged in the work day and night. (5) For those who had recently participated in the labours received relief from the succeeding force, while fellow labourers in turn replaced those, and others again together took over the toil from those. (6) It was for this reason that those protecting the stronghold grew weak and their strength grew faint. In this very way the fort was captured and

Lombards and created a Lombard duke. He also fought for the Romans in Italy and was buried in San Vitale at Ravenna; his career and epitaph are recorded by Paul the Deacon, iii. 18-19.

[44] Homer, *Iliad* vi. 339.

[45] A return to the narrative of ii. 10. 6-7, the campaign of 587.

[46] The location of this fort is unknown, but it is likely that Heraclius was continuing the Roman assault on Arzanene (cf. ii. 9. 17 with n. 23).

came into Roman possession; after its capture the general installed a garrison in it.

(7) The men under Theodore and Andrew restored Matzaron (this was also a fort) which had become antiquated in the course of time; this was in fact not far distant from Beïudaes.[47] While Theodore was occupied in the construction, farmers came to him inciting him to invest Beïudaes and intimating that it was inadequately garrisoned. (8) At once the men with Theodore and Andrew decided to suit action to words, and they spent the night engaged in a forced march. (9) They had intended to attack Beïudaes by night. Being unable to accomplish their intention, they appeared before the fort with the dawn chorus of birdsong. The natives had prior knowledge of the Roman approach, and they remained unafraid because of the impregnability of the site; thereafter, confident in the rock, they showed their faces and opened proceedings with deterrent missiles. (10) There was in fact only one entry to the fort, and this was difficult to approach with hostile intent. For the entrance was entrusted to one tower placed in advance of the stronghold, as if it were founded on stones of adamant–or anything whose nature is more solid.

(11) So the Romans dismounted from their horses, bombarded the rock, and the overtures of the conflict were effected by discharges of arrows; those in the fort defended themselves now with stones, now with catapults, and created a deluge as if from some unseen lofty vantage-point, banishing as it were the alien enemy by means of the heights. (12) While the Roman force was occupied, some brave Romans defended themselves with linked shields and, gradually moving step by step and enhancing their boldness with supreme heroism, led the way for the following troops; they moved forwards without regard for the deluge from the rock, and dislodged the barbarians from the rock. (13) The besieged abandoned their allied rock, retired into the fortress, and surrendered the entrance to the enemy. The Romans took possession of the fortifications on the rock and besieged the fort exceedingly strongly. (14) Those standing on the parapet were unable to scare off the opposition, since they could not endure the innumerable missiles, but forthwith were suddenly to be seen showing their backs instead of their faces.

[47] Theodore and Andrew were operating in the Tur Abdin. Matzaron (modern Maserte) was located about 10 miles from Beïudaes (also known as Sina Judaeorum or Sinas; the modern Fafi), which was in fact a Roman fort that the Persians must have captured during the course of the war (perhaps in 573 during the siege of Dara).

(15) A certain man Sapeir, who in physique was like the Tydeus celebrated by Homer, but in resolve far exceeded Tydeus (for he was a Heracles in courage, or any man who has ever been stronger than he; for I do not hesitate to place Heracles in the second rank for magnitude of courage, even though we lack a parallel),[48] he rushed at the stronghold carrying sharp spikes, and walked on high. (16) He inserted one spike in the tower at the joints of the construction (for the fort was composed of dry stone), and mounted the spike with his foot. Next, ingrafting, as it were, the other spike in turn, he supported the remaining one of his two feet on it and, grasping the stones placed above, held fast with his hands, and thus devised his ascent. (17) While the besieged were unable to endure the sight of the missiles, that man Sapeir firmly gripped the parapet, and he would have captured the stronghold at that first assault, if one of the Persian division had not suddenly appeared at one of the battlements projecting out from the rampart, and pushed off that hero. (18) He slipped and was borne downwards together with the battlement, 'head foremost in the dust, on his forehead and shoulders' in a Homeric mishap.[49] Nevertheless he did not perish, since his comrades caught him on their shields and saved the injured man: for the iron of the javelins had pierced him very slightly. (19) He resolutely went back to that task and yet again leapt up, clasped the parapet with his hands like an octopus with clinging tentacles, and held on to the parapet in a firm grip. (20) But the Persian foe effected a stratagem kindred to the other: since the parapet had recently been weakened by the Roman bombardment, he pushed over the hero along with it and let them fall downwards. (21) And then the danger-loving soldier was carried down with the parapet in his embrace, but at the dreadful spectacle his allies stretched out their earlier rescue for the daredevil. (22) But when the wounded man recovered from his fall, he gladly undertook a third attempt as well, as though some irresistible divine power was urging him to the labour. (23) After he had crept up and finally mounted the garland of the rampart, he drew his sword and slew that same Persian, that drone of his own courage; therefore he separated the head from the neck and sent it off to the besiegers. The Romans

[48] At *Iliad* v. 801 Tydeus is described as 'small in body, but a fighter'. The story of Sapeir is presented by Theophylact in much more pompous terminology than is normal for a military narrative; cf. the account of the wounded hero of Solachon (ii. 6. 1-9 with n. 16). For the concept of a man better than Heracles, applied naturally to the emperor Heraclius, see George of Pisidia, *Exp. Pers.* i. 65 f.

[49] *Iliad* v. 586.

were encouraged by the sight of what had happened and were eager for dangers. (24) A certain brother of that Sapeir (this man was senior in age), after being a spectator of his courage, immediately also became an emulator of the undertaking and climbed up, himself devising a means akin to his kinsman's; next after him yet another followed and after this one many more. (25) For the first to seize the stronghold were now raised by ropes, they bombarded the gates, and the Roman army was finally able to enter. Having thus mastered the enemy, they reduced the fort; some they killed, others they spared and transferred to a captive fate. After pillaging the possessions, they put guards about the stronghold and withdrew from there.

(26) Since the winter season was approaching,[50] Philippicus retired to the Constantinian city, leaving Heraclius as general. And so Heraclius inflicted penalties for desertion on the vagrants from the Roman force; and those who had bidden farewell to labour, and who were aimlessly wandering hither and thither, were converted to good sense by punishments.

[50] Winter 587/8.

BOOK THREE

(I. I) AND so Philippicus had learned during his journey that Priscus had been accredited as general by the emperor; on reaching Tarsus he composed messages to Heraclius which indicated that, after leaving the army, he should return to his own city when he came to Armenia,[1] and surrender the army to Narses, the commander of the city of Constantina. (2) And through jealousy against Priscus he disclosed the emperor's decree which had recently reached him, and ordered that it also be revealed in public to the soldiers. The decree indeed diminished the soldiers' remuneration, and the reduction was in fact by one-quarter.[2] And it happened as the general had commanded. (3) With the arrival of spring, the one was demoted while the other began his command. And so Priscus, after reaching Antioch, ordered the soldiers to assemble at Monocarton; on coming to Edessa he encountered Germanus, and greeted and embraced him courteously when he arrived from his residence (for this man graced the throne of Damascus);[3] he brought him to dinner and entertained him on the next day.

(4) Then after four days the general left Edessa, took with him the luminary of the priestly seat, and went to the camp. For the day was at hand on which it is customary for Romans to celebrate that saving Passion, through which the only-begotten Son of God, he who is co-honoured equally with the Father in nature and dominion, took the world in his care.[4] (5) The general's feelings were as follows, namely that he ought not to celebrate the annual day of the Resurrection in

[1] Heraclius probably held the post of *magister militum per Armeniam*, with headquarters at Theodosiopolis (Erzurum), presumably the city to which Philippicus directed him to return from the army's camp at Monocarton.

[2] Cf. Evagrius vi. 4, p. 224. 25-8; the reduction in pay was probably offset by the provision of a standard issue of arms and by improvements in conditions of service. Maurice attempted similar reforms in 594 (vii. 1. 1-7).

[3] Germanus, the leader elected by the mutineers (iii. 2. 4-5), was *dux* of Phoenice Libanensis (Evagrius vi. 5, p. 225. 2-4). Theophylact has probably confused this Germanus with an unnamed bishop whom Priscus met at Edessa (probably the bishop of Edessa or Constantina), and wrongly assumed that Germanus was the religious, not the military, leader of Phoenice Libanensis. De Boor unnecessarily suspected a lacuna at this point.

[4] i.e. Easter was approaching.

a city, while the Roman army in the open might appear to keep a somewhat gloomier feast, being bereft, as it were, of a city's rejoicing. It was for this reason that he took the priest with him and moved to Monocarton. (6) Germanus went on ahead to make known to the soldiers the presence of the general. Then after two days the brigadiers and indeed the whole of the battle array met the general about three miles from the rampart. (7) An ancient custom was honoured in the camp, that the man who was about to assume the reins of generalship should, when the soldiers came to meet him, dismount from his horse, walk through the middle of the soldiery, and favour the camp with his salutations. (8) When Priscus did not in fact do this, but even utterly vilified this particular ancient custom, the army did not bear the insult with moderation. On the first day of the festival the general remained untroubled. (9) But when the third day had passed and the reduction in the soldiers' remuneration was no longer in concealment, but became clear to the whole throng,[5] extreme anarchy made its entry: the masses converged on the general's tent, some carrying stones, others swords, as the occasion served each man. (10) The general came to hear of the commotion and enquired the cause. When they gave no answer to his enquiry except 'The unity of the whole array has been overthrown, the camp is leaderless', the commander Priscus was bathed in sweat and cowered in great fear, his mind being completely at a loss as to what exactly he should do. (11) And so he uncovered the image of God Incarnate, which Romans call 'not made by human hand', gave it to Eilifreda, and ordered him to go round the army,[6] so that by respect for the holy object, the anger might be humbled, while the disorder take a change towards good sense. (12) When the multitude was not brought to its senses thereby, but even pelted the ineffable object with stones, the general, chancing upon a horse of one of the emperor's bodyguards, naturally abandoned himself to flight, and cheated the peril with an unexpected salvation. (13) Accordingly he encountered the grooms who were pasturing the soldiers' horses, and, escaping their clutches with the

[5] Philippicus had already had the imperial decree published (iii. 1. 2), so that its provisions would have been known long before Priscus' arrival at the camp. The inconsistency in Theophylact's narrative may have been caused by the fact that two versions of the mutiny were current, an 'anti-Priscus' version that highlighted his arrogance and made him appear responsible for the unpopular imperial decree (cf. Evagrius vi. 4, p. 224, 19-34), and a 'pro-Priscus' version which blamed Philippicus' jealousy for rousing the dissension (iii. 1. 2) and which praised Priscus' efforts to restore order (iii. 1. 11, 1. 14-2. 3, 3. 1-5). The third day of Easter was Easter Sunday, 18 Apr. 588.

[6] Cf. ii. 3. 4 with n.

utmost danger, he reached the gates of the city of Constantina shortly after leaving the encampments at Monocarton. (14) Accordingly, turmoil also arrived in the city along with the general. And so the inhabitants of Constantina remained with hearts dismayed at events, but by means of couriers the general inscribed letters to the leaders of the cities and the commanders of the forts, that they should not deprive the soldiers of anything customary, or be cast down at heart by the sudden turn of events. (15) He also requested that medical expertise should present itself to him and apply dressings to the wounds on his calves; for he was in great pain from the bruises which the discharge of stones had dispensed to him.

(2. 1) And so the revolt continued to rage in the camp; for the general's tent was torn apart, Priscus' possessions were also pillaged by the throng, the leaders of the contingents fled as well, and the anarchy increased to great evil. (2) Shortly afterwards the general sent the prelate of Constantina as ambassador to the camp, asseverating that he was assuaging the soldiers' grievance, that the emperor Maurice had changed his mind, and that he was bearing a royal letter which ordered that the soldiers' stipends be reinstated at the customary level. (3) The general Priscus blamed Philippicus, and rumoured that he had been the originator of the disorder, because he had advised Maurice to reduce the soldiers' stipends. These things Priscus compiled at random. (4) And so the priestly ambassador went on his way as he had been ordered; but the soldiers assembled and sanctioned the election of a general. It was for this reason that they summoned Germanus, introduced him into the council, and decided to entrust to him the reins of generalship. (5) But when he rejected the camp's demand, they insisted that he comply with the election, and added threats that the punishment for disobedience would even be death; the soldiers' resolution prevailed, and Germanus was proclaimed general after he had secured on oath matters of future expediency, that the Romans would refrain from pillaging the subjects, and that disorder would be banished; it was also agreed that they campaign against the foe. (6) The general, fortified by these agreements as if by impregnable breastplates, was content to lead the Romans. So the priestly ambassador came to the general and camp. (7) And so he urged the army to turn towards sense; but they were antagonized by the priest, and did not admit his words to their ears, but banished like a barbarian captive the proposals made to them by the ambassador; they even exhorted that Priscus be cast out of the city. (8) And so they

attempted to tear down the royal statues (this in fact happened), and they also obliterated the pictorial representations which had by the art of painting been composed on panels and boards for the honour of the emperor; for they said that they would not endure to be ruled by a shopkeeper.[7] (9) The prelate of Constantina made these things known to Priscus. Then Priscus also sent the leader of the clergy of Edessa as ambassador to the soldiers. But the priest, after coming to the army and expending many words, made his return without success. (10) The dreadful consequences of the disorder were surging over the east, and everywhere evil was underpinned by evil, so that I may also mention a poetic catastrophe;[8] some squandered resources, others engaged in violent highway robbery, others plundered in the fields, while the mutiny flourished and provided an amnesty for the crimes. (11) And so Priscus made these events known to the emperor Maurice in letters, but the emperor instructed Philippicus again to preside over the east.

(3. 1) Accordingly those in the army elected delegates, forty-five in number, and sent a message that Priscus should withdraw from Edessa. (2) So these came before Priscus in the city of Edessa and conveyed to him the camps' resolution. (3) And so Priscus defended himself at length and persuaded the emissaries that he had not participated in the injustice of the enterprise. And so they proclaimed to Priscus that they would quench the raging beacons of the soldiers' anger; but Priscus took up residence at Edessa, gaping at hopes.[9] (4) Next the ambassadors arrived at the camp, recounted Priscus' defence, and also attempted to tame the revolutionary caprices of the mutiny. (5) This lifted them to the peak of danger. For they were condemned to be stripped of office and only just averted death; for this was the pronouncement of wrath. They were then expelled from the camp, and the affair of the ambassadors was terminated with such outrages.

(6) Accordingly the leaders of the disorder marched against Priscus and, marshalling a fighting force of five thousand men, sent it to Edessa. So at that time Theodore came to Edessa, promising the arrival of Philippicus; it was for this reason that Priscus left Edessa and came to Byzantium. (7) The Romans in the camp were still

---

[7] For Maurice's reputation for parsimony and avarice in financial matters, cf. John of Nikiu xcv. 1, 21-2, and John of Ephesus v. 20, who charitably explains the reputation as the result of the severe financial shortages caused by Tiberius' excessive liberality.

[8] Homer, *Iliad* xvi. 111.　　　　　　　　　　　　　　[9] Cf. ii. 17. 2 with n.

enmeshed in the disorder when they learned that Philippicus was about to reach Monocarton, and they agreed on oath that they would not tolerate his command of the army. (8) The Persians, revelling in the Roman misfortunes, poured over the Roman state and attacked Constantina, and there came upon the cities a double war, which was nurtured and enriched both by their own men and by their enemies. (9) So the concourse of the Romans remained without fighting, completely unconcerned, as if it were disposing its attention on events connected with someone else's business. Germanus equipped a thousand men from the fighting force, suddenly appeared at Constantina, and liberated it from the anticipated evils. (10) With difficulty the general spurred on and incited the Roman contingents with speeches, assembled four thousand men, and ordered them to invade Persia. (11) Aristobulus (this man was in fact the head of the emperor's royal house called that of Antiochus)[10] visited the soldiers on a mission from the emperor. Partly by bribery and partly by persuasion he mitigated the savagery of the mutiny. (4. 1) So after the Romans were converted to peace, they moved camp to Martyropolis and a detachment from the camp again invaded Persia. And so Maruzas, the Persian general, appeared and provided a hindrance to the Roman attack. (2) Accordingly the Romans retreated homewards across Arzanene and the Nymphius river, while Maruzas also followed behind the Romans. Accordingly, the Romans converged with the opposing barbarian near Martyropolis, and a most famous battle took place between Romans and Persians; a magnificent and glorious victory was accorded to the Romans. (3) For the general of the Persians was killed, three thousand of the Persians were taken as captives, the leaders were made prisoners of war,[11] and only about one thousand of the barbarian contingent reached Nisibis. (4) Then, since the slaughter was great and glorious for the Romans and the booty glittering, the assembled camp dissolved its hostility against Maurice, honouring the emperor with great booty and sending to him in addition the Persian standards, which Romans call *banda* in their ancestral utterance. (5) Philippicus was camped at the city called Holy,[12] cowering in fear at the disorder and awaiting the reversal of the anarchy.

---

[10] On the *domus Antiochi*, a large property in imperial possession that was organized for charitable purposes, see Janin, *Constantinople* 310. Aristobulus, whom Pope Gregory (*Register* i. 28) addressed as *ex-praefectus* and *antigrafus*, served on an embassy to Persia during the latter stages of the war and visited St Golinduch in prison (*Passion of Golinduch*, ch. 21).

[11] These are probably the captives who were described by John of Ephesus vi. 43.

[12] i.e. Hierapolis (modern Membij) in Syria.

(6) Accordingly, the winter season inherited the war in the ever-moving, alternating change of the solstices, and the Roman camp was disbanded. When spring arrived and provided the earth with a gentle, happy aspect,[13] the customary distribution of gold was dispatched to the soldiery by the emperor. (7) The war between Romans and Persians was flourishing and restive. As for the Getae, that is to say the herds of Sclavenes, they were fiercely ravaging the regions of Thrace; the Medes encountered the Roman generals and were squandered in slaughter; (8) the elder Rome withstood the incursions of the Lombards; in Libya the forces of the Maurusii were continually attenuated and declined towards abasement and exhaustion as a result of the multitude of Roman successes. (9) And so thus they laid down their reins as well as their shields and, bowing their necks to the Romans, embraced repose, while the Phasis was not clouded by bloodshed: for its peaceful stream was for the meantime encompassed by translucent quiet as it irrigated the Colchians, since it had nowhere acquired a Median colonist. And this broadly was the disposition and arrangement of Roman affairs.[14]

(5. 1) Now at this time deeds not unworthy of mention were accomplished against Media. But come then, let us also insert these adornments into the body of the history like a gem-studded necklace, an intellectual feast for the eyes, a delight and festival, so to speak, for the ears.[15] (2) There is a fort (Giligerdon is its name) which is constructed in the interior of Media in the region known as Bizaë, not far from the city of Bendosabora. Adjacent to this fort there is also a prison; the barbarians call this Lethe.[16] (3) The place is dedicated to royal wrath, like a fertile tract to a god, and it would not be inapposite

---

[13] Spring 589.

[14] There is no parallel in Theophylact for this general survey of the empire's affairs, and there is only one other reference to events in the western part of the Mediterranean (vii. 6. 6-7). The Getae were a Thracian tribe who had settled on the Danube in the 4th c. BC; the name was frequently used as an appropriate classical synonym for the Goths; its application to the Slavs (cf. vi. 6. 14; vii. 2. 5) is less appropriate, but Marcellinus Comes (s. ann. 505, 517, 530) provides a parallel for Theophylact's usage. Theophanes 261. 27-9 records that the Lombard attacks on Rome began in autumn 587. Pope Gregory, writing in AD 591 to Gennadius the exarch of Africa, refers to his successes against the Moors (*Register* i. 59, 72-3). The mention of Phasis and Colchis is explained by the narrative of the following year's campaign (iii. 6. 7-7. 19).

[15] The sentence indicates that Theophylact is switching to a different source for the following story.

[16] The castle of Lethe, i.e. Oblivion, was a famous place of detention (cf. Procopius, *Wars* i. 5); it was situated in south-west Persia, in the region of Beth Huzaye (Bizaë), near the cities of Susan and Gundishapur (Bendosabora), where Roman prisoners had been settled in the 3rd c. AD.

if someone were to call the fort a precinct of hatred. Here, then, are enclosed all those caught in the nets of the king's displeasure, some of them his subjects, others prisoners of war. (4) So when Justin the younger was commanding the Roman state, the king of the Persians reduced the city which is called Daras;[17] so the king made his decision and the people of Daras became inhabitants of this fort. (5) In it there were also Kadasenes (the tribe is a barbarous one from Media),[18] and in truth others too whose fate had been to suffer misadventure, and the fort embraced a common congregation of men in distress. (6) So common misfortunes brought harmony to the different races and those divided by race, custom, and speech were trained in concord by their affinity in sufferings and were united with their brother in distress. (7) Then the men of Daras gave the lead in bravery and at the first shout, using the available tools of war, they slaughtered the guards; and after the killing flared up more fiercely (for there was a multitude of soldiery garrisoning the fort), the Romans were victorious and led out of the fort as well their fellow sufferers in adversities. They returned to the Roman land after many experiences and achievements.

(8) After the Romans had experienced those notable triumphs, preparations were still being made for the battle at Martyropolis, which we spoke of beforehand, when Maruzas even, the general of the Persians, chanced to fall in the engagement, the brigadiers of the two wings were captured, and the head of the general Maruzas came to Byzantium.[19] (9) Philippicus was still being rejected by the Roman force and was deprived of command: for the masses did not accept as guardian the man who had recently achieved success by the Arzamon. For the multitude is naturally easy to influence and hard to please, and it likes the ceaseless movement of change. (10) Then Philippicus, after being among the villages of the Cilicians,[20] returned again to Syria with imperial letters and was reluctantly received by the Romans after Gregory, who at that time controlled the high-priestly throne of Antioch, had reconciled the armies to the general.[21]

[17] In 573 (cf. iii. 11. 2).
[18] The Kadasenes, or Cadusians, inhabited the mountains along the southern shore of the Caspian Sea.
[19] The switch of source (cf. iii. 5. 1 and n.) for the story of the prisoners at Lethe has occasioned a minor dislocation of the narrative, so that Theophylact now refers for a second time to the Roman victory at Martyropolis in 588 (cf. iii. 4. 2-4).
[20] Cf. Evagrius vi. 13, p. 231. 20-1; Philippicus was in fact at Tarsus.
[21] For a more detailed account of the reconciliation, which occurred on Easter Eve, 9 Apr. 589, see Evagrius vi. 10-13, pp. 228. 27-231. 29. Gregory was Patriarch of Antioch from 570 to 592.

(11) Just at that time Martyropolis was captured by Persians, not by the laws of war, but through the wiles of treachery, which are wont to steal what cannot be gained from opponents in battles. (12) The author of the trick was in fact Sittas; this man, after deserting to the Persians, persuaded four hundred of the barbarians to arm themselves, pretend that they were about to come over to the Romans, and appear before the city. (13) When this had taken place, Sittas persuaded the townsmen to admit the barbarians as turncoats to the Romans. Then the evil swiftly took place and the barbarians appropriated the city. (14) When Philippicus had learned this, he moved camp and encircled the city with a rampart; for this reason the king of the Persians also launched an expedition and fitted out against him Mebodes, the son of Surenas; these titles are held in honour among Persians.[22] (15) Since Mebodes did not have a sufficient force, the Persian king also dispatched Aphraates, who was allotted the general's reins of war against Armenia. Then after battle was joined, the Romans faltered and were not equal to their objective, while the barbarian camp was victorious.[23] (16) And so an additional force reached the Persian garrison in Martyropolis, and the city was strongly defended by the Persians, while Philippicus was at once dismissed and the emperor elevated Comentiolus as general.

(6. 1) Accordingly, the general came to the forecourts of Persia itself and near Nisibis (this was of old called Antioch in Mygdonia), he engaged the Persians near the place known as Sisarbanon. (2) While the battle was in progress, Comentiolus turned his back on the engagement, and after his flight had become lengthy and his escape had culminated at Theodosiopolis, Heraclius the father of Heraclius the emperor, with exceptional courage won distinction for valorous deeds, and was conspicuous through his glorious achievements with the spear.[24] (3) So the general of the Persians was killed, whom the

---

[22] The title Mebodes (Māhbōdh) denoted a high priest (Justi, *Iranisches Namenbuch* 185); Suren was the name of one of the greatest families of the Parthian and Sassanian kingdoms (Justi, 316-17); Mebodes' father was the Persian satrap of Armenia who was murdered in 572 (iii. 9. 9).

[23] Evagrius vi. 14, p. 232. 23-8, who was reluctant to mention failures by Philippicus, describes this as a Roman victory with heavy Persian casualties, although he admits that some Persians achieved their objective of entering the city.

[24] The length of Comentiolus' supposed flight to Theodosiopolis (Resaina), several days' journey to the west, is incredible, and it appears that Comentiolus' cowardice has been invented, or exaggerated, so as to magnify the achievements of Heraclius. Contrast Evagrius vi. 15, p. 233. 5-10, who records that Comentiolus was wounded in fierce fighting after his horse had been slain.

account revealed as Aphraates, since Mebodes too had already, I think, been killed by a Roman missile in the fight against Philippicus. After the Romans had carried off the glory on account of the flight of the Persians, the corpses of the barbarians were of course plundered and became the possessions of the victor. (4) On the next day, after the Romans had attacked the Persian camp and gained control of this, they sent proof of their trophies to the emperor, golden swords, Persian diadems, gem-studded belts which the barbarians illumine with pearls, and the standards of the engagement, which Romans in their ancestral tongue are accustomed to call *banda*. (5) On receiving the general's missives announcing victory, the emperor was delighted and overjoyed; he decreed that chariot-races should be held and ordered the factions to dance in triumph as is the custom for Romans when they celebrate.[25]

(6) Since in our narratives we have terminated the story about Aphraates, come then, come and let us plant in the meadows of the history the Roman actions in Suania. For indeed artists who have depicted the larger and more conspicuous elements do not lay aside their masterpiece before they have depicted on their tablets the smallest elements of the whole as well. (7) In the eighth year of the reign of the emperor Maurice, Baram the general of the Persians was dispatched with the barbarian forces against Suania by Hormisdas the king of the Persians.[26] Since the Persian attack came as a surprise, industry replaced indolence. (8) For Suania was ravaged most severely, and the trouble could not be checked: for she lacked a general, since Colchis was leaderless and orphaned of a guardian, because the war was flourishing in the east. (9) Accordingly, after the Huns, who dwell towards the north-east and whom it is customary for Persians to call Turks, had been outfought exceedingly mightily, so to speak, by Hormisdas the king of the Parthians, Baram transferred the war to Colchis. (10) For the Persian kingdom raised its head so high that the Huns were subjected to tribute by the Babylonians, although formerly the Huns levied from the Medes forty thousand gold coins as

[25] On the connection between circus factions and dancing, see Cameron, *Circus Factions*, ch. 8, esp. 225-7, and on the participation of the factions in triumphs, ibid. 250-1. This passage foreshadows the evidence cited by Cameron for the factions' official participation as a standard constituent of triumphal entries.

[26] i.e. 589/90. Early in 589, Maurice had organized an invasion of north-west Persia by Caucasian tribesmen, but this was repulsed by Baram, who had just concluded a successful campaign against the Turks on the Persian north-east frontier (Higgins, *Persian War* 38).

cause for inactivity. (11) The Turkish realm, then, had been made very rich by the Persians, and this particular nation had turned to great extravagance; for they hammered out gold couches, tables, goblets, thrones, pedestals, horse-trappings, suits of armour, and everything which has been devised by the inebriation of wealth. (12) Subsequently when the Turks broke the treaty and demanded that they be given more than the customary money and that there be a very heavy supplement, the Persians, intolerant of the burden of the imposed tribute, elected to make war. (13) When the Persians won a splendid victory, affairs together with fortune reversed their flow, and the Turks were subjected to tribute by the Persians and were also deprived in addition of the wealth which they had previously accumulated. (14) Persian affairs flourished again and distinguished triumphs were established for Hormisdas: for they took as booty the couches, tables, and thrones of gold, horse-trappings, jars, and everything which is marshalled for the honour of tyrants.[27]

(15) When Turkish affairs had proceeded according to his intention, he stretched out his sword against Suania, since the Scythian array had been debilitated by the Persians. (16) Then Baram, who had distinguished himself in the Turkish campaign occupied himself with Suania, secured a conspicuous booty which he dispatched to Babylonia, and moved camp to the river Araxes, which the barbarians call Eras. (17) When the emperor had heard of these events, he appointed Romanus as guardian of the war. So when the general arrived in Colchis, which customary parlance has renamed Lazica, he took counsel with the chief priest there, set out thence, and moved camp into Albania itself. (7. 1) Baram, on learning of the presence of Romans, was overjoyed: for he longed for a confrontation with Romans, since he doubtless believed that fortune smiled on him always. (2) It was for this reason that he crossed the nearby river and made a withdrawal towards Canzacon, as if he were luring the Romans into the interior of Persia. (3) So when Romanus perceived this, he became eager to turn back, making expediency rather than zeal his business. Since the troops grumbled to themselves, and were indignant and eager to move forwards, with sensible arguments the general soothed the army's swollen boldness. (4) He had also sent out fifty soldiers to track the movements of the enemies; these encountered two Persian scouts who

---

[27] Sebeos, ch. 2, pp. 11-12, and *Chron. Seert* 43, record that there was a quarrel between Hormisdas and Baram about the division of booty from the victory over the Turks, since Hormisdas suspected that he had not been sent his proper share.

were wearing Roman dress. They deceived their captors and dismissed the idea of danger, since they were accredited as Romans. (5) They proffered as guarantee of their story that by means of an unfamiliar track they would reveal during the night the enemy lying unguarded on their pallets. (6) And so the Romans, welcoming destruction and misled by the promise, were captured by the Persians; after being taken prisoner, they gave response to interrogation under torture, and made everything clear to Baram, how Romanus had lacked the confidence to invade the Persian land and about the smallness of the fighting force with him.

(7) So when these had been captured, three of their number were saved and announced the disaster to Romanus. And so Baram forded the river and again ravaged the Roman land, while the Roman leader moved back towards the rear. (8) On realizing this, the barbarians harried the Roman contingents, but the general collected an army from Colchis, and scrutinized the attitude of the Roman contingents, whether their hearts were courageous for confrontation. (9) Then, after the Roman multitude had been encouraged for battle, the Roman general separated the bravest from the weaker, took the fighting men with him, and arranged the rejects to guard the camp. (10) Then, as the fighting force approached ten thousand men, the general disposed two thousand to advance in front of the soldiery; they encountered the advance unit of the Persian army, all of which they nobly slaughtered, since a precipice was there and rendered flight unobtainable for the barbarians. (11) After the pursuit had become manifest and progressed as far as the barbarian camp, so that even Baram was disconcerted by the chain of events, the advance force of the Roman multitude retreated. (12) When this was revealed to the Roman general, although the Roman formation was eager to come to grips with the Medes, Romanus welcomed the repose from battle, out of fear of the overwhelming gathering of the barbarians. But when he was unable to curb his subordinates, who were fired by the recent successes, he equipped his forces for engagement. The barbarians also assembled. (13) So the two forces were camped in the plain of Albania; a steep-sided ravine that extended from the river Araxes kept them apart from engagement. And so the troops camped on the banks of this interposed stream and exchanged words with each other. (14) On the third day a messenger came from the Persians to Romanus with a demand for battle, that either the Romans should give ground to the Persians at the crossing or the barbarians to the Roman armies.

(15) Therefore the man invested with the command of the Romans summoned an assembly of his whole army, and demanded to learn from the multitude what would be the best course for them with regard to battle. When they advised the general to permit the enemy to cross, on the next day the proposal was put into effect. (16) Shortly afterwards each force prepared to deploy and, when Baram tried to steal victory, Romanus marshalled artifices against cunning. (17) On the fifth day both Romans and Medes equipped themselves for engagement, arranging the battle in three contingents. And so the central division of the barbarian force was worsted by the opposing armament; accordingly Baram, fearing the impact of the Roman charge, brought round a force from the left wing. (18) As a result the left contingent was debilitated by the force fighting against it, great slaughter surged around the Persians, Baram's affairs came to a crisis, the whole Parthian army took to flight, a great and glorious pursuit by the Romans ensued, and Baram's luck was extinguished together with his vanity. (19) And so flight mastered the one, while valour extended the other, as it were. The Persian dead were despoiled and deprived of burial, so that there was a ready feast for the passing wild beasts. (8. 1) When Hormisdas learned of this, he did not tolerate the niceties of misfortunes and abused Baram with most shameful insults, by allotting him female attire as prize for the ignominy;[28] furthermore he dismissed him from command, enacting this in royal dispatches. (2) From this began the war between Mede and Mede, for in return the general humiliated Hormisdas even, the man whom events had recognized as king of the Persians. (3) The insult was symbolized in the dispatches, and in the counter-statement that very Hormisdas was abusively recorded as the daughter rather than the son of Chosroes.

(4) A short time before this, the Armenians, who are neighbours of Persia, were subverted by certain Romans and organized a conspiracy to revolt; they undertook to desert to the Medes after they had murdered the man whom the emperor had made commander in Armenia, whose name was John.[29] (5) Since affairs in Armenia had lapsed into turbulence, the emperor Maurice dispatched to Armenia Domentziolus, a distinguished and loyal man who held an illustrious position among the leaders of the senate.[30] (6) And so he provided an

---

[28] *Chron. Seert* 43 records that Hormisdas sent Baram a red robe and a distaff.

[29] Probably John Mystacon, who had been fighting in Thrace in 587 (ii. 17. 8), but who was the Roman commander in Armenia in 590 (iv. 15. 2).

[30] Probably the same man as the Domitziolus, *curator* of the *domus Hormisdae*, who, John of Ephesus vi. 28 records, had been sent by Tiberius to resolve discontent among

impediment to the onset of the revolt, and he presented the instigator of the rebellion (his name was Sumbatius) in chains to the emperor. When the emperor had correctly organized the investigation of the accusation in a court of law, lest through the failure to examine the charge the course of punishment might be administered with unjust licence, the culprits confessed their crimes. (7) Next the judges presented their sentence and declared that men who had committed such acts should be dispatched from human affairs by the punishment of being thrown to wild beasts; when the theatre was full and those who had committed the crimes were about to be consumed by beasts, upon the acclamations of the people the emperor displayed clemency. (8) He was separated from the beasts and reaped unforeseen salvation, while the spectators magnified the clemency of the emperor's unexpected pity.[31]

(9) Since time renews, restamps, and transforms all things, moulding them now this way now that, and bringing change with the revolution of its perpetually moving circuit, tyrannizing the solidity of affairs through the axis of its rotation, constantly dissatisfied and sickened with security, having nowhere to stay its wandering, possessing no fixed abode through the irregular movement of its ebbs and flows,[32] at the present time there befell the Persian kingdom quite incalculable sufferings, which possess a narrative exposition that is not unornamented. (10) For when Baram did not terminate the hostility with Hormisdas which had suddenly sprung up quite recently, the monarch of Media, whom the history has recorded as Hormisdas, ordered a certain leading Mede to go to Baram, dismiss him straightway from office, bind him in fetters, and present him at once in disgrace at the palace. (11) And so Sarames (for this was the name of the man sent by the king) was overpowered by Baram, was handed over as victim to one of the largest elephants, and terminated his life in a most bitter death. (12) After Hormisdas had been outfought by

the Roman troops in Armenia. Phocas had two relatives called Domentiolus, and it is possible that the tyrant's family was related to this distinguished and loyal senator.

[31] Sebeos, ch. 10, pp. 37-9, records at greater length the revolt of the Armenian noble Smbat Bagratuni, although he connects it with Armenian discontent against military service in Thrace in the 590s. According to Sebeos, Smbat was spared but exiled to Africa, after successes in the arena against a bear, a bull, and a lion had inspired the crowd and the empress to beg Maurice to show mercy.

[32] This section is markedly bombastic, as to a slightly lesser degree is the whole of iii. 8. This chapter marks the transition from the account of Baram's revolt to the flashback to the early history of the war in iii. 9-18, and was for this reason written up by Theophylact in a grand style.

Baram and deposed from kingship, and the younger Chosroes, Hormisdas' son, had been ousted at the time of his proclamation and had consequently approached the Romans, that age-old Persian war which had lasted for two decades of years was concluded.

(9. 1) But before we describe in greater detail the accomplishments of Baram and the events connected with the approach of the younger Chosroes, let us return the narrative to the reign of the younger Justin, turning the account aside towards the past just a little: (2) for hence we will recount the causes of this ancient Persian war; for thus the pages of the history will be adorned by the completeness of the narrative.[33]

(3) When the emperor Justinian had migrated to the inviolate sphere, after directing the Roman sceptres for thirty-nine years, the younger Justin succeeded to the control of events;[34] this man was in fact a nephew of the emperor Justinian. (4) Accordingly in the seventh year of the reign of the younger Justin,[35] the Romans broke the treaty through the levity of the king; the blessings of peace were shattered and rent asunder; there came upon Romans and Medes war, the receptacle of evils, the inn, so to speak, for all ill fortunes, the archetypal destroyer of life, which it would not be unfitting to call a putrefaction of human affairs. (5) The fifty-year agreement which had been concluded between Romans and Persians was destroyed and cut short by the great folly of the king,[36] and hence came the evil procession of Roman misfortunes. (6) The Romans blamed the Parthians and proclaimed that they were architects of the war, alleging that the Homerites (the race is Indian and is subject to the Romans) had been incited by them to revolt; and that next, when those people had not succumbed to these overtures, they had suffered irreparably from attacks by the Persians, since the peace between the Persians and the Roman state had been dissolved.[37] (7) As an additional cause of

---

[33] Contrast i. 3. 5, where Theophylact refuses to describe the capture of Sirmium on the grounds that it had been adequately recorded by Menander.

[34] In 565; for the following passage (as far as iii. 12. 9), the text of Theophylact's source, John of Epiphania, survives (FHG iv. 271-6).

[35] i.e. 571/2.

[36] For the details of this treaty, agreed in winter 561/2, see Menander, fr. 11.

[37] The Homerites, who lived in the south-west of the Arabian peninsula, had been the object of Roman diplomatic activity earlier in the 6th c. They had been subject to the Axumites, who lived in Ethiopia and were Roman allies, but subsequently (c. 565-75) a Persian-supported pretender to the Homerite throne was installed and thereafter a Persian governor imposed; see Tabari, pp. 220-37. The term 'Indian' is regularly used of the peoples bordering the Red Sea.

grievance they alleged that, on the occasion of the very first Turkish embassy to the Romans, the Persians had tried to corrupt the Alans by bribes, so that the ambassadors should be slaughtered as they passed through them and their passage be allotted impediment.[38] (8) The Romans, eager for a pretext, embraced warfare and from minor ephemeral beginnings they devised for themselves great processions of troubles: for bellicosity procured for them no profit. (9) The Medes, in proclaiming that the Romans were originators of the war, adduced the following causes, that the Romans had received the Armenians (who were in fact in the category of subjects to the Persians), after they had progressed to revolt, and slaughtered Surenas, whom the Persian king had made the regional commander of the Armenian state;[39] (10) furthermore, in addition to this, the Roman unwillingness to pay in accordance with custom the annual payment of 500 pounds of gold, which the emperor Justinian had conceded in the agreement, as if they thought it unworthy to be tributaries under the Persian king.[40] (11) But this was not the case, but the payments were made for the defence of the fortresses which were garrisoned for their joint preservation, so as to prevent the influx of the irresistible might of the innumerable neighbouring nations and the destruction of each kingdom.[41]

(10. 1) So when the peace had been dissipated and the treaties

---

[38] For a detailed account of the initial Roman diplomatic contacts with the central Asian Turks, see Menander, frr. 18-22. Fr. 22 records that Sarodius, the leader of the Caucasian tribe of the Alans, had warned the Roman ambassador Zemarchus, who was returning from an embassy to the Turks, that the Persians intended to ambush him on his journey through the land of the Mindimians. The Romans and Turks had probably already agreed to launch a concerted attack on Persia (frr. 20, 32), and the possibility of such joint action would have been enough to persuade the Persians to try to interfere with the embassy.

[39] The Armenians' revolt against Persia and their appeal to Justin II are described by John of Ephesus, ii. 18-20, vi. 11, Evagrius v. 7, and Menander, fr. 36. The Armenians had been negotiating with Justin since 569/70, but were driven into open rebellion when the Persian satrap, Cihor-Wsnasp, a member of the Suren family, attempted to introduce Zoroastrian practices; he was murdered in Feb. 572.

[40] Payment for the first seven years had been made in advance by Justinian in 561/2, and for the next three by Justin II in 569. Menander, fr. 36 records that Sebochthes was dispatched to Constantinople in 572 to request the next payment.

[41] The fortresses were intended to control movement across the Caucasus through the Caspian Gates. During the 5th c., and intermittently in the 6th, the Romans had contributed to the cost of the Persian defence of these forts in recognition of the fact that both empires benefited from the maintenance of this barrier: on this and other matters of common interest to the two empires, see N. Garsoïan, 'Byzantium and the Sasanians', Cambridge History of Iran iii (1). 574-9. This section explaining the Roman payments is Theophylact's own addition to the analysis in John of Epiphania.

between Romans and Persians overturned, Justin the emperor of the Romans dispatched to the east as general Marcian, a distinguished man who was on the register of the patricians, and who was in fact not unrelated to the royal family.[42] (2) Then Marcian crossed the Euphrates and came to Osrhoene when summer had already passed its youth and prime. Since the barbarians had no thought of conflict, Marcian equipped three thousand of the soldiery and dispatched them against the district whose name was Arzanene. (3) Then the force invaded and, since the attack came as a surprise to the Medes, the Persian empire suffered gravely during that time: for it was ravaged and plundered and a not inconsiderable booty was carried off. (4) In the following year of the reign of the emperor Justin,[43] Marcian collected his forces and made his advance from Daras, the barbarians encamped by Nisibis, the Romans and Persians came to grips near a place in Persia which is known as Sargathon, the Medes faltered, and the Romans won the fight. (5) For this reason they besieged and tried to capture Thebothon, which is a Persian fort; then, after they had warred against the fort for many days and affairs had not turned out according to their objective, they retired to the city of Daras.[44] Next they invaded enemy territory again and decided to invest Mygdonian Nisibis, since these were their orders from the emperor. (6) But the king of the Persians, Chosroes the elder, set out from Babylon with a Median army, crossed the Tigris, entered the desert region, and moved camp across it, so that his march would not be observed by the Romans; he came near Abbaron, a place in Persia which is five days' journey distant from the Roman city of Circesium. (7) The man named as Adormaanes he dispatched as general across the river Euphrates to ravage Roman territory, and dispatched with him six thousand of the soldiery, while the Persian king himself marched along the river Aboras and executed a surprise attack on the Romans besieging Nisibis.[45] (8) And so Adormaanes came near to

[42] He was Justin's nephew.

[43] i.e. 573.

[44] These initial manœuvres in the 573 campaign suggest that the Romans were trying to isolate Nisibis, first defeating the Persians at Sargathon, 8 miles west of the city, and then attacking Thebothon, 30 miles south-east of Nisibis on the route to Singara. Marcian abandoned the siege of Thebothon after ten days and returned to Dara to celebrate Easter.

[45] Chosroes would have crossed the Tigris at Ctesiphon, marched to Perozshapur (also known as Abbaron or Ambar) on the Euphrates, and then up the Euphrates as far as its confluence with the Aboras (Khabour), where Circesium was situated (about 200 miles from Abbaron). At this point Adormaanes set off across the Euphrates, while

Circesium, crossed the river Euphrates, and ravaged the Roman land; since the Persian presence was not opposed by any stratagem to curtail the progress of the barbarians' movements, Adormaanes came to the vicinity of Antioch without effort, destroyed the magnificent buildings outside the city, since the opportunity was favourable, and came to Koile Syria. (9) He pitched camp near Apamea; and after the men of the city had sent an embassy with splendid gifts and agreed a ransom, the barbarian was deflected only to the extent of making a promise, but they were cheated and beguiled by barbarian tricks. On the third day Adormaanes enslaved the city; subsequently he also consigned it to the flames and returned to his own country.[46]

(11. 1) Since the overtures of the war had been inauspicious for the Romans, the Roman monarch was thoroughly dismayed and disconcerted at the barbarian successes. Angered by the misfortunes which encompassed him because of bad counsel, he sent Acacius, the son of Archelaus, to Nisibis after dismissing Marcian from his command.[47] (2) And so Marcian gave way to the royal decree and departed from Nisibis; when the Romans had reached Mardes, the Persian king came to Daras like a hurricane and assailed the township for six months, circumscribing the city with mounds and ramparts. After diverting the town's water supply, constructing towers to oppose its towers, and bringing up siege engines, he subdued the city, although it was exceedingly strong.[48] (3) When the emperor Justin heard of this, he was stricken by the impact of the disaster; shortly afterwards he was also afflicted by a sickness of derangement and, fearing the additional generation of subsequent troubles, he arranged with the Persians an armistice for the present

Chosroes continued up the Aboras and across the desert regions of Beth Arabaye to reach Nisibis by surprise.

[46] Adormaanes' attack against the prosperous cities of the Orontes valley coincided with Chosroes' dispersal of the Roman army at Nisibis and his subsequent siege of Dara (iii. 11. 2), which inevitably prevented the Romans from halting Adormaanes' depredations; cf. John of Ephesus vi. 6.

[47] The order of Theophylact's narrative (which follows that in John of Epiphania) wrongly suggests that Marcian was replaced because of the failure to oppose Adormaanes, whereas it was in fact because of his failure to capture Thebothon and to besiege Nisibis with sufficient energy to satisfy the impatient Justin (cf. Evagrius v. 9, pp. 204. 25-205. 28). According to Theophanes Byzantinus § 4, Marcian was replaced by Theodore Tzirus; if this is true, Acacius may have been sent to Nisibis to announce the change of commander.

[48] The Romans in fact fled in panic from Nisibis, probably because they suddenly heard of Chosroes' surprise approach. The siege of Dara, which ended in Dec. 573, is narrated most fully by John of Ephesus vi. 5.

year.[49] (4) But when the sickness attacked him exceedingly spiritedly, so to speak, he decorated Tiberius with adoption, made him partner in the empire, and proclaimed him Caesar. This man was in fact the commander of the emperor's bodyguards and shield-bearers, whom it is customary for Romans in normal parlance to call *comes excubitorum*.[50]

(5) But I will also present the emperor's advice which he gave in a public speech to Tiberius Caesar, on the occasion of the proclamation, not beautifying the ugliness of the diction, nor making any change to the inelegance of the expression; (6) but I will spread out nakedly, as it were, in my narrative the exposition of his words, so that the veracity of what follows may appear from the simplicity and authenticity of the nature of the diction.[51] (7) Then, after the senate had come together and the priestly hierarchy assembled along with their leader, the man who steered the rudder of the church,[52] the emperor, as if he had been standing on a rostrum, presented the following speech to Tiberius:

(8) 'Behold, God magnifies you; God grants you this apparel, not I; honour him,[53] that you may also be honoured by him. Honour your mother, who was once your queen;[54] you know that you were first her slave, but are now her son. (9) Do not delight in bloodshed; do not be party to murders; do not repay evil with evil; do not resemble me in hatred, for I have collected payment as a mortal (for indeed I was fallible), and I have been paid in accordance with my sins. But I will plead my case at the tribunal of Christ against those who have done this to me. (10) Do not let this apparel incite you as it did me. Attend thus to all men as you do to yourself. Recognize what you were and

---

[49] Menander, frr. 37-8, records that the truce was arranged by the doctor Zacharias, a personal emissary of the empress Sophia. The truce began in spring 574.

[50] The *excubitores*, commanded by a *comes*, were the most important functional element of the imperial bodyguard in the 6th c.; see Jones, *LRE* 658.

[51] This speech was not recorded by John of Epiphania, and Theophylact's digression from his main source, which is marked by this elaborate introduction, continues until iii. 12. 6. Justin's speech, which was recorded by shorthand-writers, is also preserved by John of Ephesus iii. 5, and in brief form by Evagrius v. 13, pp. 208. 32-209. 6. For a discussion of these versions, see Averil Cameron, 'An Emperor's Abdication', *Byzantinoslavica* 37 (1976), 161-7. The speech is based on sentiments in the *Ecthesis* of Agapetus Diaconus; its contents are similar to Tiberius' speech to Maurice at i. 1. 5-20, although the style is different, being much closer to the language of Agapetus and the New Testament.

[52] The Patriarch of Constantinople, John Scholasticus (565-77).

[53] Reading αὐτόν ('him') for αὐτό ('it'), since the latter would have to refer to the royal apparel, an item certainly not worthy of honour (cf. i. 1. 18); the balance of the sentence is improved if God is referred to in each clause.

[54] i.e. the empress Sophia.

what you are now. Avoid arrogance and you will not go wrong. You know what I was, what I became, and what I am. All these are your children as well as your slaves. You know that I have honoured you above my own kin.[55] You behold these men here, and you behold all those in the state. (11) Pay attention to your army; do not entertain informers. Do not let men say to you that your predecessor behaved thus; for I say this from what I have suffered. Let those who have possessions enjoy them, but give to those who have not.'

(12) After the Patriarch had made the prayer, and everyone had uttered the Amen, and the Caesar had fallen at the emperor's feet, the emperor said to him: (13) 'If you are willing, I am; if you are unwilling, I am not; may God who made the heaven and the earth himself implant in your heart all that I have forgotten to say to you.' This was spoken on the seventh of December, on the sixth day, in the ninth indiction.[56] (12. 1) When the emperor had terminated his discourse, the applause welled up from the audience and he received acclamations like the violent effusion of a shower. For, in truth, the election provided for the Caesar was not undistinguished.

(2) And so the Caesar, fulfilling the procedure of an imperial proclamation, inscribed letters and dispatched these to the king of Persia.[57] (3) At the start of spring, he sent ambassadors and renounced the war, since he was eager for a glorious achievement: for his request was for a truce, since nothing is more precious than peace, at least to men of intelligence who remember their mortal lot and their very brief passage in life. (4) He also recruited multitudes of soldiers and rendered the recruits' hearts eager for danger through a flowing distribution of gold, purchasing from them enthusiasm for death by respect for payment.[58] (5) Then the Caesar's ambition for magnanimity quenched the outrage of the barbarians and the dangers were bridled, while the afflictions ceased to burn, the disasters which had flooded

---

[55] Relatives of Justin II, who might have been preferred to Tiberius, were Marcian his nephew (iii. 10. 1), Baduarius (vi. 10. 10 with n.), who was married to Justin's daughter Arabia, and Justinian the son of Germanus (iii. 12. 6 with n.), who was a distant cousin.

[56] i.e. Friday (the sixth day of the week), 7 Dec. 574 (which was in fact the eighth indiction). Theophylact must have copied this date, which is the only precise date in the whole *History*, from the source (probably a chronicle) which provided him with the text of Justin's speech. John of Ephesus' text of the speech also concludes with an exact dating formula.

[57] For the customary procedure, cf. iii. 17. 1; viii. 15. 2.

[58] According to Evagrius v. 14, pp. 209. 27-210. 2, the recruits were mainly drawn from the Balkans.

upon the cities were checked, and with a sudden providence it was recognized that evil was absent.

(6) In this particular year Justinian, who was the son of Germanus and was numbered among the highest officials, was appointed general.[59] (7) And so the general attentively corrected the former lack of military training in the armies, moulding the unformed and transforming the undisciplined into good order. (8) But the emperor was still gathering forces and collecting allies from the nations, importing with great outlay of money irresistible additions to the armament. For the influence of money when it is sensibly managed can effect a return to the better even for those who have previously failed. (9) But when the period of the truce had been spent and the limit of the armistice between Romans and Persians had been extinguished, the Persians came near to Daras,[60] since this was the objective of Tamchosro, a high dignitary among the Persians who was guiding the reins of generalship. The Romans also encamped close beside it. (10) Neither force initiated the engagement, and after both sides had spent a long time staring at each other, the soldiery sought a negotiated agreement. Then a treaty was made on the terms that on the eastern front the war should keep peace and practise inaction for three years, but that in Armenia the conflict should be free from restraint.[61]

(11) Therefore the Roman general marched past the city of Amida and camped in the districts of Armenia, while the Persian king also followed and crossed the Euphrates with a great multitude.[62] (12) When the Romans heard that the Persian king was conducting the campaign in person, the Romans' spirits failed them, and not without due cause: for the royal presence had granted the Persians considerable success in their earlier actions and had given the Romans the weaker weighting. It was for this reason that the Roman general

[59] Theophylact now returns to John of Epiphania for information. This switch of sources may explain the double reference to Tiberius' recruitment (iii. 12. 4-5, 8). Justinian the son of Germanus was a great-nephew of the emperor Justinian and a distant cousin of Justin II.

[60] i.e. spring 575. The extant fragment of John of Epiphania ends at this point.

[61] Menander, frr. 39-40, 50 records the negotiations which led up to this truce, which was in fact arranged by ambassadors dispatched by Tiberius. When the Romans refused to accept some of the Persian conditions, Tamchosro was sent to ravage Roman territory between Dara and Constantina until the agreement was finalized. The three-year treaty was probably concluded in early summer 575.

[62] These events in fact occurred in the following year, 576, as can be deduced from Menander, fr. 41 since, following the conclusion of this treaty, there was time for a further embassy from Tiberius to Chosroes before the start of the Persian invasion, which arrived in Armenia in the spring.

climbed onto a mound, gathered the army round about on the plain, and began with these words:

(13. 1) 'The day now present, Romans, will be the beginning of great benefits for you, if you are persuaded by my words. Arm your spirits, I say, before your body; let your hearts do battle before your hands. Let each brave danger for another, and you are saved. (2) Philosophers (for I call you philosophers or soldiers, since you alone have death as your profession), demonstrate to the barbarian that your zeal is immortal. (3) Let your spirits be undaunted. Resolve to strike or be struck, receiving the opponents' missiles on your body as if it were another's. Let the falling enemy stand as witnesses to your courage; let their dead also narrate your triumphs. (4) Comrades–you are my comrades both in toils and tumults because of the war–the engagement is established as the test of courage and cowardice, and is the arbiter of souls: for this day will either convict us of effeminate cowardice, or with garlands and glorious triumphs will proclaim our manly bravery. (5) Do not, by turning your backs on the barbarians, let your soul be at all affected by love of body. Death, this sweet thing which we daily assay, is a kind of sleep, a sleep that is longer than this normal sleep, but is very brief in comparison with the day that is to come. (6) Men, be ashamed of dishonour combined with salvation: this is an undying death, and a coward's tomb never conceals the man who has been allotted disgrace. (7) Let not the Persian king disconcert you heroes because of his ownership of impotent hordes, his boasting, his raised eyebrows, his stiff-necked arrogance, the conceit that he has acquired as far as words are concerned. Is not the nation haughty and pompous, procuring its power by bombastic grandiloquence? (8) Forget the former misfortunes by recalling the supplements of allied forces; forget the past failure which was brought forth by the general's folly, with the disorder of those under his command acting as an evil midwife. (9) Nothing is terrible for the brave; for these the steel is fodder, as it were, while the pains of blows are a stimulant that kindles them to grasp greater dangers. Therefore guard your backs undisclosed to the enemy; show that they are not initiated to your hinder parts. (10) I know that wounds are founts of triumphs. Flight leads to slavery, and not salvation: for a cowardly beginning cannot preserve a promise of safety. Cast off your bodies before your breastplates, life before shields. Fight with all your limbs, let there be no limb that does not share the perils. (11) Fortify your line with interlocked weapons, barricade your ranks by the integration of cavalry,

fence yourselves round in a harmonious stance, like a building of
close-fitting stones. Do not let spears leap from your grasp, strike
without being deprived of your weapons.

(12) 'The Persians do not have an immortal nature; Median luck is
not immovable; barbarian hands are not tireless; the Parthians do not
have an advantage in limbs or possess double souls; their bodies are
not adamantine. Even Persians are initiates into the mysteries of
death. In this respect war is just, for it does not marshal immortals
against mortals. (13) The Romans have hired Justice as an ally, since
they have once again sought peace; the Medes have marshalled Justice
in opposition to themselves, since they abhor peace virtually always
and honour belligerence like an auspicious god. (14) Ours is not a
false religion, nor have we set up spurious gods as leaders; we do not
have a god who is scourged, since we do not elect a horse for worship;
(15) we do not do obeisance to a god that turns to ashes, who is now
ablaze but is soon not even visible; smoke and fuel do not constitute
religion, but their fading proves their falsehood.[63] (16) The barbarian
exults in cheerful circumstances, but success is unaccustomed to
remain stable when it ascends unjust altars. Injustice is often successful, but is also turned towards destruction. Accordingly, advance to
war as befits your appellation, lest we damage our names as well as our
affairs. (17) Let us not betray our allied shields, but let us embrace
these like beloved girls in their prime, and fight on their behalf as if
these were fatherlands which accompany our travels. Be Spartans in
combat. Let each man be a Cynegeirus, even though he has not
boarded ship.[64] Nothing is more effeminate than flight, nothing is
more abominable than capture. Therefore it is fitting either to die or
to shape hopes of victory. (18) Contemplate the newly-sown
recruitments of the Caesar. No reject has been implanted among the
companies, and the array is undefiled: for thus was the emperor's
ambition contented.

(19) 'Then I, the orator, will be the first to take war in hand, and in
my disdain at avoiding suffering I will eagerly engage the hands of all
for suffering. The impulse of my words cuts a way forward, and the
accomplishment is precursor of contemplation: for an inspired spirit
can range itself even against the laws of nature. (20) Today angels are

[63] For a concise account of Zoroastrian religion, in which fire-rituals played a central
role, see J. Duchesne-Guillemin in the *Cambridge History of Iran* iii (2), ch. 23.
[64] Cynegeirus was killed during the fight over the Persian ships which concluded the
battle of Marathon (cf. ii. 6. 6).

recruiting you and are recording the souls of the dead, providing for them not a corresponding recompense, but one that infinitely exceeds in the weight of the gift. (21) Let no one with a pleasure-loving soul wield a spear, let no one who loves the rites of luxury take part in battle, let no one who takes great pride in possessions share the undertaking: the battleground demands lovers of dangers. Come then, let us put an end to words with deeds, and let us divert contemplation towards engagement.'

(14. 1) Then, after such words had re-echoed among the forces, the ranks were excited for engagement, glad to endure anything and eager to run risks for valour: for they had disposed their hearts in accordance with the general's exhortations. (2) When the Medes had heard of the valorous resolve of the Romans, they ordered themselves for battle; the horses were adorned with cheek-guards and breastplates, while the soldiery also armed themselves; they mounted their horses and with haughty march slowly advanced in close-packed formation against the Romans. (3) Then the Romans also formed up and raised their standards. Next the trumpets sounded forth, the dust was whirled aloft; the clamour poured forth and, inundating the place, surging with the din of whinnying, and eddying with the clashing of weapons, it naturally transformed every utterance to indistinctness. (4) And so the barbarians extended the length of their line, intending thereby to create an impression of a countless multitude on the forces contending in opposition. (5) But the Romans made a deep formation whose density gave it weight, so that the array appeared to be virtually solid and to stand steel-resistant, riveted and counterforged, like immovable statues which seemed only in posture to grasp at war. The barbarians were dismayed at the sight, so that thereafter the Median spirits were seduced by the spectacle towards the weaker moves of cowardice. (6) And so the Babylonians fired arrows against the Roman companies, so that the sun's rays were hidden by the discharge of missiles, and on account of the furious outpouring of shafts a winged roof, improvised by the flight of darts, appeared to be spread in the air above their heads. (7) The Romans engaged in hand-to-hand combat, resisting the barbarians with spears and swords, and cutting short the assault of the missiles' onslaught; hence they rendered the opponents devoid of stratagems and took the lead in warfare. (8) Accordingly, a most memorable battle between Romans and Parthians occurred, the Persian disposition was broken because their ranks were not organized in depth, the rearguard of the Babylonian

armament was at a loss, and there was no counter-resistance; next, when the opposing force pressed heavily, the barbarians faced destruction and veered away in flight. (9) And the Persians were initiated into disappointed expectations, while they learned by the example not to take pride in their misdeeds. (10) And so the Babylonians were defeated and fled as fast as they could, while the Romans held the initiative and gave the Parthians an experience of evils. Furthermore, in addition to this they also looted the Persian camp, pillaged the king's tent, and carried off as glorious booty all their equipment. They captured the elephants and dispatched them to the Caesar along with the Persian spoils. (11) When the king of the Persians had been defeated and made his retreat homewards in shame, on coming to Melitene he burnt the beauty of the city, since he found that it was undefended and luxuriating in complete quiet. After crossing the Euphrates and withdrawing through Arzanene, he inscribed the disgrace of the failure in a law: for he decreed that in future it did not befit the Persian king to engage in expeditions to war.[65]

(15. 1) And so when the king of the Persians had thus paraded his misfortune in the law, he was at a loss as to what exactly he should do. But the Romans exploited the Persian failures and marched towards the interior of Babylonia, ravaged and pillaged everything in their path, and what they encountered became a victim of destruction. (2) Then they became marines on the Hyrcanian sea and, after great achievements and the infliction of misfortunes on the Parthians, they did not return to their own territory: for the winter season intervened on their actions and disaster waxed fat in Persia. With the arrival of spring the Romans retired, carrying off success too as travelling-companion.[66]

[65] John of Ephesus, vi. 8-9, provides the best account of Chosroes' invasion of Armenia (there is also an account at Evagrius v. 14). John does not mention a Roman victory in pitched battle, an omission that would be surprising if there had really been such a triumph as Theophylact describes, and instead he records that the two armies faced each other *without* fighting, immediately *after* the Persians had sacked Melitene; thereafter the Persians attempted to flee across the Euphrates by night, but their retreat was disorganized by the Romans and many Persians were drowned; the royal Persian baggage had been captured much earlier in the campaign, when the Romans almost trapped Chosroes in the Armenian mountains. John's account of these events is more detailed and plausible than Theophylact's. It is probable that Theophylact's account of the battle (iii. 14. 1-8), which is highly rhetorical and is composed of stylized descriptions of trumpets blaring, dust whirling, and arrows flying, is sheer invention, based perhaps on a misunderstanding of a brief report of this campaign in John of Epiphania. Chosroes' law is recorded, with minor variants, by John of Ephesus vi. 9 and Evagrius v. 15.

[66] The Roman expedition, which had ravaged through Azerbaijan as far as the Caspian (Hyrcanian) Sea, only returned to Roman territory in 577; cf. John of Ephesus vi. 10.

(3) And so, since the Medes could not endure the events, in their vexation they brazenly insulted their own king, for the attrition of the war and the prospect of future hardship distressed them exceedingly. (4) For, unlike Romans going on campaign, Persians do not receive payment from the treasury, not even when they are assembled in their villages and fields; but the customary distributions from the king constitute a law of self-sufficiency for them, they administer these provisions to obtain a subsistence, and hence are forced to support themselves together with their animals until such time as they invade a foreign land. (5) Therefore the king of the Persians, fearing the mutinies in his army, resolved to participate in discussions about peace with Tiberius the Caesar; on learning this, the Caesar decided to enter into negotiations. (6) So he dispatched men empowered to settle the discussions concerning a concordat, having appointed as ambassadors John and Peter, who belonged to the highest rank of the senate (they were in fact patricians), and Theodore who was honoured and respected among Romans in his office as *magister*.[67] (7) And furthermore Chosroes dispatched Sarnachorganes, a man highly regarded in the Persian state on account of his rank, together with other most notable men, delivering through them respite to the war.

(8) At that time then, a fierce battle was joined between Romans and Parthians for Armenia, with Tamchosro commanding the Babylonian force and Justinian leading the Roman throng; the Romans fell short of their former glory.[68] (9) It was for this reason that the Medes rejected the peace-treaty and their love of war was rekindled again, since they were incapable of moderation because of their recent successes. (10) And so the ambassadors, after accomplishing their objective to the extent of discussions, went homewards, abandoning the embassy bereft of peace. When events had turned out thus, Tiberius the Caesar appointed as his general Maurice, who was at that very time leader of the emperor's bodyguards, and dis-

---

[67] The negotiations are described in detail by Menander, frr. 46-7 and John of Ephesus vi. 12; they began in winter 576/7 and lasted for more than a year. Menander, fr. 46 records that Theodore, the son of Peter the Patrician, was at this time *comes sacrarum largitionum* (for which see Jones, *LRE* 427-38), although he had earlier held the post of *magister officiorum* in succession to his father; the other ambassadors, John and Peter, were honorary ex-consuls, and the doctor Zacharias also participated in the negotiations.

[68] The battle is described by John of Ephesus vi. 10; during the remainder of 577 the Persians prolonged the peace negotiations in order to delay Roman preparations for the resumption of hostilities at the end of the three-year truce in spring 578.

patched him to the provinces of Armenia.[69] (11) While the treaty which had come into being between Romans and Medes in the east still had an abundance of time, the barbarian general Sarnachorganes contravened the treaty and rapidly sent men against Constantina and Theodosiopolis.[70] (12) And so the general of the Chaldaeans took his force and ravaged the districts of Constantina and Theodosiopolis, while Tamchosro, who was invested with the command of the Persian armies in Armenia, on realizing that the assembled Roman forces now perhaps greatly outnumbered his own men, left Armenia, marched past the Roman fort of Citharizon, and, on coming near Amida, attacked the countryside and villages; next he returned home by way of Arzanene.[71]

(13) The Roman general Maurice, seeing that the barbarians had left Armenia and were engaged in ravaging on the eastern front, set out with his whole army and arrived in the land of the Persians; although his body was stricken by a fierce fever, he persisted in his labours in spite of his illness. (14) So the Romans invaded Arzanene and, since there was no resistance, they reduced the very strong fort whose name was Aphumon, razed some other forts, and administered great slaughter to the Persian state. (15) They took prisoner a total of one hundred thousand of the Persians, and the men of the army, by granting a third portion to Maurice the Roman general, made the wages of war not incurable. And so the general signified the presence of the captives to the Caesar, but the Caesar distributed the booty on Cyprus.[72]

(16. 1) Accordingly, after Arzanene had thus suffered harm from the Roman spear, the general changed course and summarily invaded the lands of Arabia situated not far from Nisibis.[73] (2) Next, after laying waste as far as the river Tigris, he dispatched Curs and Romanus across to the other bank to ravage the entire enemy territory; but, after he himself had laid waste the fort of Singara, since the winter

[69] Maurice, who had succeeded Tiberius as *comes excubitorum*, was appointed supreme commander of the eastern armies during the winter of 577/8, after the death of the general Justinian had led to quarrelling between his subordinate commanders (John of Ephesus vi. 27).

[70] Menander, fr. 50 records that the raid began forty days before the end of the truce, i.e. in spring 578.

[71] For further details about Tamchosro's raid, see Menander, fr. 52 and John of Ephesus vi. 14.

[72] Compare John of Ephesus vi. 15 and Evagrius v. 19, p. 215. 16-26. Agathias iv. 29. 8-9 reports that the sight of Maurice's ravaging severely affected Chosroes and indirectly led to his death. In spite of Maurice's successes in Arzanene, he failed to capture by siege the chief city, Chlomaron (Menander, fr. 57).

[73] i.e. Beth Arabaye.

season was peeping in, he collected his forces and arrived among the Romans. (3) In this particular year Justin, the emperor of the Romans, withered away from disease, after encountering great punishments for his violent deeds.[74] (4) So when he was on the point of departing the present life, he co-opted as lord of the monarchy the emperor Tiberius, a man who was both kind and humane, superior to financial gain and without regard for money, whose sole idea of happiness was that his subjects should flourish and abound in great wealth, and who considered the common bliss of mankind as an excellent and inviolate treasury. (5) This man hated the pomp of tyranny and, in his eagerness for the affection of his fellow men, he preferred his subjects to rule jointly with him rather than that his charges should be tyrannically enslaved, wishing to be called father rather than master by his subjects. (6) Since he steered the ship of power like an honest trader, it was natural that along with events, the war also was granted a turn for the better.[75]

(7) At the start of spring, Chosroes, the king of the Persians, was ensnared by disease and terminated this present life, after appointing as successor his son Hormisdas,[76] a man who in wickedness had overshot the impious habits of his ancestors. (8) For he was a violent man, a most insatiate lover of gain, who gave no place to justice; he rejoiced in deceit and wallowed in falsehood, clinging to hostilities rather than peace. (9) He was most hostile towards his subjects, the most powerful of whom he subjected to eternal fetters and chains; others he cut apart with the sword, while some he consigned to the bowels of the Tigris, and the river constituted an unclothed tomb for those consigned to death by the king (for it was not in fact kept hidden). (10) For it is said that Hormisdas had received from the magi a prophecy that he would discard power after being overthrown by his subjects, and that he would shamefully lay down the rudders of authority and kingship alike. (11) Those who believe these things are foolish in their impiety: for demons frequently make marvellous predictions which are probably not destined to come to pass in events, so that through terror at the prophecy of these things the wishes of the impious powers who provide the oracles may in fact somehow reach fulfilment by a most villainous stratagem of wickedness. (12) For hence Hormisdas inflicted the sword even on the common people themselves and, by

---

[74] Justin died on 4 Oct. 578; his madness was the punishment for his misdeeds.
[75] For Tiberius' good reputation, cf. Evagrius v. 13 and John of Ephesus v. 20.
[76] Chosroes I died in Feb. or Mar. 579.

destroying many thousands of the commons in his fear of the future, he stored up for himself among his subjects implacable enmity. (13) He also reduced military pay by a tenth, and compelled the army to face great dangers, so that through the destruction of the Babylonian force his royal throne might remain established free from revolt.[77]

(17. 1) So Hormisdas donned the tyrants' diadem; in his bragging and arrogance he cut short normal procedure, as though he did not deign to send the ratification of his proclamation to the emperor Tiberius.[78] (2) And so the emperor proclaimed to Hormisdas an end to the war, asking for peace to be made on equal terms for both sides. But he insulted the embassy and demanded that the Romans should openly pay tribute, that the Armenians and Iberians should be among his subjects, the Romans making this provision for him, and that the Caesar should make no further requests for Daras, even though his father Chosroes had been willing to respond to discussions with the Caesar on equal terms, and had not rejected the restoration of Daras to the realm of the Romans.[79] (3) When Hormisdas' arrogance was made plain to the emperor Tiberius and summer had again arrived, Maurice collected his forces and reached Persia, after sending Romanus, Theodoric, and furthermore Martin to the far side of the Tigris to lay waste the interior of Media. (4) And so they invaded with the mass of the army, and pillaged the fertile and most fruitful areas of the Persians; after spending the whole of the summer season in the slaughter of Persians, they ravaged Media, and wrought extensive destruction.[80]

(5) With the arrival of winter, the Roman leader came to Caesarea in Cappadocia, but as the summer came round again,[81] he arrived in the east with the whole Roman army at the city of Circesium. (6) Next, he subsequently hastened through the desert of Arabia to reach the land of Babylonia and then to steal a victory by the shrewdness of the enterprise. (7) In this he was accompanied by the leader of the

---

[77] For Hormisdas' bad reputation, cf. the criticisms in Bindoes' speech (iv. 5), as well as Tabari, pp. 267 ff. and *Anon. Guidi* 1; he was, however, regarded as a friend of the Christians (*Chron. Seert* 42) and was known for his justice towards the poor (A. Christensen, *L'Iran sous les sassanides* (Copenhagen, 1944), 436-7). The reduction in military pay presumably refers to a cut in the 'customary distributions' mentioned at iii. 15. 4.
[78] For normal procedure, cf. iii. 12. 2; viii. 15. 2.
[79] Menander, frr. 54-5 and John of Ephesus vi. 22 describe these lengthy negotiations, which probably dragged on throughout 579. Theophylact's account of the campaigns of Tiberius' reign omits one year, and he probably failed to realize the slowness of this diplomacy.
[80] This campaign lasted throughout the summer of 580.   [81] i.e. 581.

nomadic barbarians (his name was Alamundarus) who, they say, revealed the Roman attack to the Persian king: for the Saracen tribe is known to be most unreliable and fickle, their mind is not steadfast, and their judgement is not firmly grounded in prudence.[82] (8) Therefore, as a result of this, the king of the Persians transplanted the war to the city of Callinicum, after electing Adormaanes as a not untalented custodian of the expedition.[83] (9) Then, after Alamundarus had like a drone destroyed the beehives, or in other words had ruined Maurice's enterprise, the manœuvres of the expedition against the Medes became unprofitable for the Romans: for they returned to quench the disasters at home. (10) Next the general consigned to burning flames the grain ships which had accompanied him down the river Euphrates; he himself, with the pick of the army, came with all speed to the city of Callinicum. (11) When the Parthian contingents came to grips, the Roman spear won supremacy; then flight came upon the Persians and their insolence received a check.[84]

(18. 1) In the following year Tamchosro, the general of the Medes, assembled large Persian forces and came near Constantina. There was indeed knit in this year a great and most famous battle between Romans and Parthians.[85] (2) And so the general of the Medians, who was in the forefront of the contest, lost his life by the spear, the barbarians faltered, and the Romans were victorious. The barbarians were persuaded to turn away to their own territory, appropriating ignominy as well as suffering. (3) Therefore the general, after fortifying the key strongholds, returned to Byzantium. When the common end befell the emperor Tiberius, the general assumed the royal and lawful power of the Roman realm, like a noble and glorious reward for success, and divested himself of the secondary lot.[86]

(4) Now I have recorded in the earlier passages the subsequent actions of Romans and Persians. Therefore I must return to the continuity of the narrative, wheeling round the history, which is perhaps running a little off course, towards its subsequent and easily perceptible goal, from which in fact we briefly digressed after presenting

[82] John of Ephesus iii. 40, vi. 16-18, and Evagrius v. 20 also record this campaign. Maurice's intention was to sack Ctesiphon by a surprise march down the Euphrates.

[83] The Persians advanced to Callinicum on the Euphrates in order to cut the line of Maurice's retreat. John of Ephesus' account preserves Alamundarus' version of events.

[84] According to John of Ephesus, there was no battle and the Persians retreated with impunity.

[85] In June 582; John of Ephesus vi. 26 describes the battle (his date is wrong by one year).

[86] In Aug. 582, cf. i. 1.

in public the attendant events connected with Baram at that time. (5) But first let Baram's fatherland and lineage, the stages of his fortune, and his progressive achievements be described in a few words, so that the historical recital may be in all respects harmonious and comprehensive.

(6) I heard a certain Babylonian, a sacred official who had gained very great experience in the composition of royal epistles,[87] say that Baram originated from the region whose name is Rhazakene, but that this Persian tyrant, who had initiated the overthrow of the tyrant Hormisdas, belonged to the house of Mirrames.[88] (7) For seven peoples among the Medes, allocated by ancient law, perform the sagacious and most honoured of their actions; and he stated that procedures could not be otherwise; (8) and they say that the people entitled Arsacid hold the kingship and these place the diadem on the king, another is in charge of the military disposition, another is invested with the cares of state, (9) another resolves the differences of those who have some dispute and need an arbitrator, the fifth commands the cavalry, the next levies taxes on the subjects and is overseer of the royal treasuries, the seventh is appointed custodian of arms and military uniform; Darius the son of Hydaspes inscribed this very law in the royal precincts.[89]

(10) They say that Baram, who came from the house of Mirrames and the Arsacid people, was formerly enrolled among the bodyguards of the king, that shortly afterwards, as commander of a unit of soldiers, he joined in campaign with Chosroes the son of Kabades, when the Babylonians reduced Daras while Justin the younger possessed charge of the Roman sceptre. (11) And so Baram, together with the

[87] This rare mention by Theophylact of an oral source may refer to a Persian ambassador to Constantinople during Heraclius' reign.

[88] Baram's family came from Rai (i.e. Rhazakene), near modern Tehran.

[89] For a discussion of Persian administration, see V. G. Lukonin, *Cambridge History of Iran* iii (2), ch. 19, particularly pp. 698-708 on the king's council and the categories of nobility. Although a limited number of noble clans dominated the administration of Sassanian Iran, and certain offices passed by inheritance within certain families (Procopius, *Wars* i. 6. 13), there is no evidence to corroborate Theophylact's description of a rigid sevenfold division of high office. Such an arrangement could hardly have survived from the reign of Darius son of Hydaspes, Achaemenid king of Persia from 522 to 486 BC; it might, however, have been invented by the earliest Sassanians as part of their attempt to portray themselves as legitimate successors to the Achaemenids. Under the Achaemenids, the descendants of the seven Persian nobles who had conspired to overthrow the false Smerdis (the conspirators included the future king Darius) perhaps used their lineage to claim special status, and Darius certainly granted his six fellow-conspirators particular honours (Herodotus iii. 84).

Persian king Chosroes the elder, invaded as far as Armenia itself, distinguished himself in the campaign, and soon after was even
appointed general of the Persian company. (12) When fortune had
thus gradually raised him up, so that he was even proclaimed *darig-
bedum* of the royal hearth (whom Romans indeed name *curopalates*),[90]
he continued into extreme folly: he was inflated greatly and uncontrol-
lably as a result of his victories against the Turks, and felt the pangs of
the embryo of tyranny. (13) And so like a spark in the ashes he concealed the motive for his grievance from Hormisdas the king, but
whipped up the multitude by deceitfully contriving to make it appear
indeed that the Persian king was angry against his army and had in
addition even threatened death on the Babylonian soldiers because of
their misfortunes in the engagement in Suania. (14) He also produced
forged edicts of Hormisdas which curtailed the customary distributions to the contingents from the royal treasuries.[91] And hence the
whole multitude was infuriated and proceeded to mutinous insubordination.

[90] On these titles, see M. L. Chaumont, 'Chiliarque et curopalate à la cour des
Sassanides', *Iranica Antiqua* 10 (1973), 157-65.
[91] Hormisdas had already reduced military payments by one-tenth (iii. 16. 13).

BOOK FOUR

(1. 1) WHEN the mutiny had been secured by oaths and the revolt founded upon agreements, Baram collected allies and the civil war among the Persians gained strength. The hatred for Hormisdas recruited for Baram an additional force of supporters; (2) for the Persians encamped at Nisibis, who had quite recently been defeated by the Romans in pitched battle,[1] were diverted towards revolt on hearing the unexpected news concerning Baram, and eagerly pursued enterprises akin to his. (3) When this was announced to Baram, he sent ambassadors to Nisibis from his own number, and through his seductive promises intestine strife was concocted more fiercely among the Medes. (4) And so they received the ambassadors and went towards the city of Nisibis, but when they were near the city gate they encountered Chubriadanes, who was a respected holder of office among the Persians and who had been appointed by Hormisdas as overseer of the conduct of the war. (5) They hurled this wretch from his horse, lopped off his extremities, cut his head from the neck vertebrae, and sent to Hormisdas these tokens of an irreconcilable revolt; after putting the man to a cruel death, they entered the city and turned to pillaging his property.

(6) At Nisibis as well then, strict oaths were exchanged that Hormisdas should be deposed and be created a commoner instead of king. So, when they had proceeded thus far in their actions, Persians went on embassies to Persians and leaders were sent to Baram, who was waiting at the crossing of the Zab.[2] (7) This river, whose course is small as it gushes forth from the towering mountains where it rises in the north, subsequently, as it is borne southwards and is watered by many torrents, becomes navigable and joins the Tigris. (8) Baram received the messengers and made a great show for them with a splendid welcome; he ordered that there should be patrols by armed troops and that all paths be secured so that Hormisdas should not

---

[1] Comentiolus' victory at Sisarbanon (iii. 6. 1).

[2] i.e. the Greater Zab; the river is normally difficult to cross, hence the strategic importance in the subsequent narrative of the crossing point, which was probably that on the road from Mosul to Arbela/Erbil.

even receive news of the misfortunes. (9) The king raged and glared furiously, bellowing and gnashing his teeth; since he could not find a passage for his reconnaissance, he was distraught with despair like those possessed.

(2. 1) During this time the Roman general Comentiolus captured the fortress of Akbas and broke camp for winter,[3] while Baram gradually advanced against the territory of Media.[4] (2) But Hormisdas collected forces from the nearby districts and appointed the Persian Pherochanes as commander of the campaign; in the Roman tongue his name signifies the title of *magister*.[5] (3) And so Pherochanes asked the king that Zadespras, whom Hormisdas had bound and put away in prison, should be released from his chains to join him on the campaign. (4) This man had in fact been condemned to prison by the Persian king because he had been caught appropriating a considerable sum of money from Martyropolis. Hormisdas was annoyed by the request, but Pherochanes persisted in his demand until the king's will was overcome and Zadespras was released from his fetters.

(5) So Zadespras set out on campaign with Pherochanes, but as soon as he came close to the mutineers, in the vicinity of the river Zab, he at once deserted and went to Baram, measuring out for Hormisdas repayment for his injury in prison. (6) Then, after this had happened, Baram was greatly elated and expected that all the opposing army would also come over to him. Pherochanes sent ambassadors to Baram, asking him to change his mind and put a stop to the mutiny, and earnestly entreated him with royal gifts as well; for such were his instructions from the Persian king. (7) Pherochanes failed to buy off hostility and Baram instead financed the mutiny thereby. Then provisions ran short, since Pherochanes the Persian had previously

---

[3] Winter 589/90. Comentiolus had reorganized the siege of Martyropolis (cf. Evagrius vi. 15, p. 233. 16-26), which had been disrupted by Philippicus' defeat outside the city (iii. 5. 14-16). The capture of Akbas would have enabled him to hamper communications between the Persians inside the city and those in Arzanene across the Nymphius river.

[4] Theophylact normally uses Media as an imprecise synonym for Persian territory, not as a precise technical term to denote the region of Media on the Iranian plateau. However, neither sense would be appropriate here: Baram's troops remained north of the Zab (cf. iv. 2. 7), so that he was not advancing towards the royal capitals in lower Mesopotamia, but equally he would not have moved towards the Iranian plateau, since this would have taken him back along the route he had traversed when marching from Albania to Mesopotamia. The clause was probably Theophylact's own comment on Baram's moves, and its inaccuracy reflects his geographical ignorance.

[5] Justi, *Iranisches Namenbuch* 95-6, s.v. Farruχān and Farruχhormiz gives 'lucky' or 'lucky Hormisdas' as the meaning of the general's title.

occupied the crossing,[6] and the usurper had spent a considerable time in that region. (8) And so Baram schemed to augment his outrage and suborned the troops arrayed against him with a memorable stratagem. (9) For he sent to the opposing force messengers who declared that the opposition was acting misguidedly in taking up arms against injured parties and reminded the Persians of Hormisdas' harshness, his cruel actions and unjust impiety; he laid bare Hormisdas' infidelity and, in short, marshalled an extensive and most compelling list of Hormisdas' crimes. (10) For enmity is ever fond of accusation and from small beginnings can fabricate great mountainous charges. (11) When Pherochanes' troops heard these claims, their minds were changed and they longed for revolution, despising the honourable and honouring the wicked. And thereafter they no longer made accusations of mutiny, but they regarded the enterprise as lawful, with justice as the source of the deeds. (3. 1) Then Zoarab (this man was leader of the Dilimnite tribe),[7] together with the younger Sarames, who at that time was enrolled in the general's guard but who subsequently became commander of the bodyguard of Chosroes the king, strove for different fortune, and conceived an extraordinary longing for a change of affairs; they formed a conspiracy and in a surprise attack murdered Pherochanes by night with absolutely no opposition. (2) After this had happened, everyone turned to pillaging the general's possessions. Then on the fifth day news reached the Persian king of the fate which had recently befallen the general. (3) Accordingly, Hormisdas, who was dismayed by the increase in his troubles, set out from Media, where he had been lingering, and approached Ctesiphon,[8] collecting his remaining forces and applying his attention as best he could to his own defence.

(4) When the inhabitants of the royal cities came to know of these events, they were panic-stricken and in their utter amazement at the revolution in affairs were at a loss as to exactly what to do: for unexpected news is accustomed to create confusion in the soul and to import a complete overthrow of rational thought when it is thrust on

[6] i.e. the crossing of the Zab.

[7] This tribe inhabited the area north-west of Tehran, the region from which Baram originated (iii. 18. 6).

[8] Hormisdas was probably travelling between the royal summer palaces on the Iranian plateau and the winter residences in lower Mesopotamia; hence Theophylact might here be using Media in a technical sense (cf. n. 4 above), but it would probably be wrong to assume that Theophylact understood the geography of Hormisdas' movements.

the ears with sudden advent. (5) On the third day[9] the prisoner Bindoes, the son of Aspabedes and a relation by birth to Chosroes the king of the Persians, who had resided in prison in chains being punished without reason by Hormisdas, was led away from detention by Bestam, who was in fact his brother, with no one present to prevent it.[10] (6) When Bindoes had found respite from his misfortunes, this mob from Pherochanes' army burst into the palace at about the third hour and encountered Hormisdas.[11] (7) He was sitting on the royal throne, his attire that of a tyrant and very costly, the gold gem-studded tiara gleaming brightly with its inset of rubies around which ran an abundance of pearl. Glistening in his helmet and emerald green he amplified his splendour,[12] so that the eye of the beholder was all but petrified by insatiable amazement. (8) His trousers were gold-decorated, costly products of the weaver's hand, and his apparel was as luxurious as his arrogant appetite desired. And so the king asked Bindoes how his removal from detention had occurred, about his bold manœuvres, and what the improvisation of the attendant force meant. (9) But he, in full hearing of the king, railed and blasphemed against Hormisdas, since his tongue was no longer curbed because security for free speech ensued from the disorder. (10) Then, since no one hissed Bindoes down nor was present to censure him and spare the royal dignity, Hormisdas asked the officials whether the state of affairs pleased them. (11) When everyone jeered at Hormisdas, Bindoes grasped Hormisdas by the hand, lifted him from the throne, stripped the diadem from his head, and handed him over to the bodyguard for detention.[13] (12) And thus Bindoes' fortune was reversed and Hormisdas suffered for his deeds, learning that one should not injure those who have done no wrong.

[9] The chronological indications in this passage are not helpful (cf. 'the fifth day', iv. 3. 2); it would, for example, have been useful to know how long Baram and Pherochanes manœuvred near the Zab. Theophylact's information was probably derived ultimately (via John of Epiphania) from a member of the Persian court, whose main concern would have been the sequence of events that involved the king.

[10] Bindoes and Bestam were maternal uncles of Chosroes II.

[11] The movements of Pherochanes' army after the general's death have not been recorded; it appears that part had not joined Baram, but had retreated in disorder to Ctesiphon, where it was joined by Bindoes (cf. iv. 9. 1 with n.).

[12] The text is suspect at this point and the reference of 'emerald green' is uncertain. The sense is, however, fairly clear, and the whole passage is phrased in deliberately grandiloquent and contorted terminology.

[13] Using eastern sources, it is possible to calculate the date of Hormisdas' deposition as 6 Feb. 590; for this date, and other calculations of Sassanian chronology, see Higgins, *Persian War*, esp. 26 ff.

(13) When his son Chosroes heard that Hormisdas had been deposed from the kingship, he departed from his customary haunts and made his escape to Adrabiganon,[14] in fear of the perils that had befallen Hormisdas, since he suspected that the misfortunes would perhaps transfer to him as well. (14) And so Bindoes tracked Chosroes' movements, but when in his quest events went according to his will and he had Chosroes in his grasp, he asked the boy to return to assume the royal throne. (15) And so Chosroes returned to the palace after receiving a binding guarantee of good faith. On the next day Hormisdas sent a message from prison which indicated that he wished to make a speech to the advantage of the Persian state; he requested the attendance of the satraps, officials, dignitaries, and all of the royal bodyguard, since his subject was not concerned with trivial talk. (16) Accordingly, when this had been announced to the leading barbarians, an assembly took place at the palace and Hormisdas too was led from prison, so that his proclamation might be brought to fulfilment. Then after the gathering had been organized in the palace, Hormisdas stood up in the middle and began as follows:

(4. 1) 'Spectators, would that you had not been the engineers of my royal misfortunes, for then you would not have acquired a king who was both orator and prisoner; men, you are now haughty enemies but were once subjects who obeyed in fear. (2) Spectators, would that you had not come forward this day as attendants and witnesses of such troubles. If weeping should recede, I shall utter words which will again invite weeping. (3) For I see you revelling in these misdeeds, clapping your two hands, gnashing your teeth, with lying sneers on your faces, immoderate in laughter, unbounded in insults and, if I am not mistaken, treating the venerable institution of kingship as an occasion for amusement. (4) For present among you, on display in your midst as a prisoner flogged by the masses, is the man who was recently revered as a god, the man who was swathed in purple now clad in rotten rags, the man who was daintily adorned with gold and pearl now afflicted and abused by an iron chain, (5) the man whose hair was well groomed and who was perfumed with myrrh now

---

[14] i.e. towards the north-east. Tabari, pp. 272-3, records that Chosroes had earlier fled to Azerbaijan (Adrabiganon) because he feared that Hormisdas would suspect him of complicity in Baram's revolt; Chosroes only returned to Ctesiphon on learning that the Persian nobles had overthrown and killed his father. Tabari's account is more credible than Theophylact's, for there was insufficient time for Chosroes' flight between Hormisdas' deposition on 6 Feb. and his own proclamation at Ctesiphon on 15 Feb. (iv.7. 1, with n.).

subjected to shameful discomfort, bestial in appearance from filth and dust, from running eyes and matted hair, the man who was enticed by countless varieties of foods now starving and almost deprived even of chance crusts, (6) the man who resided in gold-roofed chambers, lounged on golden couches, revelled in resplendent cloaks and wallowed in magnificent robes, now cooped up in prison and cast down on the earth with no scraps of cheap garments to wrap round him.

(7) 'But I see that the fame of my ancestors too is besmirched this day by your impious actions against me, theirs who should be cherished with divine honours because of the godlike protection that is daily exercised over their descendants. (8) But although you have overthrown the law of nature, set at naught the institutions of power, trampled down the order of monarchy, obliterated the regulations of justice, and banished retribution for violence, I will not forget my royal excellence, but out of goodwill for the community of my race will describe what is advantageous for the Persian state. (9) Satraps and all you who are assembled at this royal place, mobilize a united policy against the mutiny; do not allow this lofty and most powerful monarchy, venerable and most fearful to the men who inhabit the world, to be further abused. (10) Otherwise you will destroy a great dominion, overturn the origin of many triumphs, cast down the summit of greatest glory, rend asunder an impregnable monarchy, and hence you Persians will be deprived of prosperity, when power has been removed from you and the institutions of kingship have been set at naught because of the tyranny. (11) For discord is the precursor to disorder, disorder is anarchy, anarchy which takes its origin from tyranny is the start of dissolution. This gives birth to multiple rule and disarrays previous advantages; through unstable authority and divisive discord it destroys the unity and harmony of the dominion, and compels the friends of tyranny to suffer rather than to do in all things. (12) A slight gust of wind has sunk the ship of monarchy when it is steered by many rudders, since its helm is divided between the contradictory designs of the many, as each one severally tries to steer the bark to his particular goal. (13) Assuredly, unless you winnow out the tyrants, you will lead the kingdom into servitude and be a plaything for the nations when you have acquired vulnerability through the discordant conduct of life. (14) Baram is still at hand, he is still armed and dissembling, he still persists in his insolence as he wields his sword against Persia. Let him perish and become a prey for wild beasts, do

not let this man's corpse be honoured with burial lest you implant the putrefaction of a vile spirit in the bowels of the earth. Let Chosroes too strip the diadem from his head; he does not possess a royal spirit, he is not adorned with a leader's intellect, his mind is not authoritative. (15) His impulses are uncontrolled, his temper is naturally furious, he is suffused with a look of inhumanity, he is unable to respect the practices of forethought, his manner is arrogant, his appetite naturally hedonistic, everything is subordinated to his wish, he does not wait for what is expedient, he does not cherish good advice, he dismisses generosity, he is enmeshed in avarice, a belligerent warmonger, who has no appetite for peace.[15]

(16) 'Today I will by my words appoint for you as king the youth, a son of mine who is innately good, a brother to Chosroes by birth but not a brother by inclination. (17) Did I not bring round Persian affairs to excellent good order while I guided the Babylonian state with the rudder of magnanimity? Proof of my words is that the Turks are paying tribute, the Dilimnites have surrendered their necks and weapons to us, the Romans have lost famous cities and bewail their new fortunes with the loss of the old. (18) I who accomplished all this have also suffered because of the mutability and instability of fate. It is in your power to maintain expediency as your objective or, spurning what is good, to reject second thoughts and, after repentance of your errors, to weep in despair over what exactly you should do about matters at hand.'

(5. 1) Then, after Hormisdas had poured out this discourse of admonition, Bindoes the Persian contrived a spluttering laugh and cursed Hormisdas' exhibition of oratory; he stood up in the middle and addressed the assembly roughly as follows:

(2) 'Fellow kinsmen, comrades, tyrant-haters—provided, that is, you do not tolerate tyrants continuing to make laws. Even now that he is a commoner the tyrant does wrong. (3) He still assumes the language of authority, undertakes to give orders, acts the king in oratory, ordains laws on the rostrum, denounces generals, rejects monarchy, and appoints the next ruler; (4) he has everything at his disposal, more even than the munificence of dreams could bestow on the deluded, and yet he is incapable of realizing this much, that those who in their actions have failed to arrange their own affairs skilfully

---

[15] This tirade against Chosroes was clearly composed by Theophylact to reflect the Roman opinion of Chosroes after his invasions of the empire during Phocas' and Heraclius' reigns (cf. viii. 15. 7).

are not naturally reckoned in the category of advisers. (5) How then will he deposit for us a truly sound and trustworthy guarantee for his proposal? Or did he not trick us by pledging his own fate as security, since he wished to see us as fellow prisoners and as participants in the same sufferings although we are innocent? For as subjects of tyranny we did not share his crimes. (6) How is it that he has stirred his voice against tyranny, that man who left no Persian custom free from tyranny, who ruled like a bandit, who adulterated his power with violence, who poured down a deluge of murders throughout the whole period of his rule, who with corpses almost made the Tigris dry land, the man who created an abundance in tombs, fattened the sword on blood, and procured a dearth of men, so that by fortifying wickedness through depopulation he might obtain immortality for tyranny?[16] (7) The man who has not judged advantageously in his own affairs is an arbiter for children's intellect. Abandon this absurdity, Hormisdas! Tyrants do not lecture after their overthrow, men who have become subjects do not make laws, men condemned to death do not act as advisers. (8) Since, then, it is not open for you to tyrannize your subjects in the future, like a coward you have practised an outrage against your children by choosing to wrong the elder through the younger, so that there may never be any respite for your wickedness.

(9) ' "The Turks are made our tributaries."[17] But this was not the product of your intelligence: Persian deaths and the courage of generals have gloriously constructed these achievements of forethought. (10) "The Romans have been stripped of cities and towns."[18] But the Persians will not be persuaded, for the deeds do not correspond to the words: or are they not waiting at our threshold, toying at warfare and with a sudden swoop showering an endemic slaughter on the Persian army? And because of your bellicosity there is no hindrance. (11) Your treasuries are full of gold, but the cities, mansions, fields, valleys, and farmsteads are also full of lamentation: it has been the common fate to share the same misfortune so that you yourself, showered by wealth, may take your fill of a most ill-fated prosperity.

(12) 'Depart from here, then, having paid the penalty for your crimes. Let the destruction of one man be a lesson in prudence and let this be a most equitable law, a salvation for those to come: for the proclamation of kingship does not herald a feast of pretension but an irreproachable superabundance of good management.'

[16] For Hormisdas' reputation, cf. iii. 16. 7-13 with book iii n. 77.
[17] Picking up Hormisdas' claims at iv. 4. 17. [18] See n. 17 above.

(6. 1) And so the assembly jeered at Hormisdas, insulted him, disparaged his forthright speech, and were moved to extreme rage; infuriated, they glowered and revelled in the gusts of bravado. (2) In a great outburst of indignation, they brought to the middle Hormisdas' son, that unfortunate youth, then slaughtered him in full view of Hormisdas as gratification for their wrath. (3) But this was not the limit to the occasion they provided for malevolence, but they also placed Hormisdas' wife in the middle and sliced her in pieces from the bladder, the sword exacting a wicked judgement on her limbs. (4) And so such destruction of his wife's life in open audience, together with his wretched son's, constituted the material of tragedy. When Hormisdas had been an indubitable witness of that ill-fated story, he was allotted blindness, and this was for him the moral, as it were, of his misfortunes. (5) For after they had heated iron needles to glowing-point by placing them in closest contact with fire, they thrust them into the pupils of his eyes. Thus with a torture of molten eye-shadow they adorned Hormisdas[19] and decreed on him permanent darkness for the future, since they suspected that he might perhaps escape and provide trouble for the Persian state: for they clearly remembered what Kabades had accomplished after laying down the Persian sceptre.

(6) For this Kabades had been the father of Chosroes the former king of Persia; but since he was a murderous man who exercised power violently and converted monarchy into tyranny, the Persians deprived him of office, shut him away in prison, and committed him to be nursed at the bosom of hardship.[20] (7) His wife made frequent and regular visits to him each day, tended him with her ministrations, and by her advice persuaded him to endure with equanimity the acts of unfavourable fortune. (8) Now the commander of the prison, who was an officer and held authority over a company of soldiers, fell in love with the wife; so Kabades, when he heard this, urged his wife to share the governor's bed and endure every squall of fortune that befell her. (9) When this had happened the watch relaxed, the strict guard was slackened, and vigilance became slave to indolence. Hence Kabades procured a transformation of his troubles, dressed himself in his wife's clothing, and escaped from the prison, leaving behind his wife dressed

---

[19] Translating σπβίζοντες, Dindorf's conjecture for the unattested τιβίζοντες.

[20] These events are narrated by Procopius, *Wars* i. 5-6; Kabades was imprisoned in the famous Castle of Oblivion mentioned by Theophylact as the gaol of the Dara captives (iii. 5. 2).

in his clothes. (10) Then in the company of Seoses, a most trusted friend, he approached the Hun tribes whom history has almost universally recognized as Turks.[21] He was then entertained most hospitably by the king of the Hephthalites and he acquired very considerable forces; he defeated his opponents in battle, returned to the palace, and regained power. (11) And so Kabades measured out for Seoses the recompense for the bond of friendship and decorated him with the most pre-eminent offices, while he savagely exacted punishment from those who had injured him. It was with these particular events in mind that the Persian satraps pecked out Hormisdas' eyes.

(7. 1) So, when the assembly had fully vented its rage, Chosroes was led up to the royal throne and, standing in the golden apse, as is the custom at Persian proclamations, he received royal homage while acclamations washed around his ears.[22] (2) And so for a time he treated his father with kindness as consolation for his captivity, and gave him a share of the royal table, sending him on golden dishes savouries, joints from royal hunting, choice cuts of antelope, gazelle, and wild ass, fragrant wines and preparations of elaborate aperitifs, carefully baked bread, milk, cakes, and anything else that is preserved for the festive board of gluttonous tyrants. (3) But Hormisdas spurned the king's generosity and most boorishly insulted those who ministered to him, for he naturally condemned despicable pity and rejected insolence which feigned piety. It was this which finalized Hormisdas' death, for his flanks were beaten by cudgels, the vertebrae of his neck were crushed by clubs, and he ended his life most bitterly.[23]

(4) Chosroes, after defiling the prelude of his rule with such pollution, held a festival to celebrate the advent of his power, lavishing much gold on the most distinguished men in the Persian kingdom and leading the masses from prison, thereby pretending that he would not succeed to his father's inhumanity. (5) On the sixth day he summoned

[21] These Huns were not Turks, but Hephthalites (cf. Procopius, *Wars* i. 6. 10, and the very next sentence in Theophylact). For Theophylact's equation of Huns and Turks, cf. i. 8. 5, iii. 6. 9.

[22] Chosroes was crowned on 15 Feb. 590, see Higgins, *Persian War* 26-8.

[23] Both Sebeos, ch. 2, pp. 13 f., and Tabari, pp. 272-3, record that Hormisdas was killed by Persian nobles before Chosroes' proclamation as king; according to Michael the Syrian (x. 21) as well, Chosroes was not implicated in his father's death. Theophylact had an interest in denigrating Chosroes (cf. n. 15 above), and his account is suspect, since the description of the delicacies from the royal table is clearly a piece of rhetorical invention; there were only two weeks between Chosroes' coronation (iv. 7. 1) and his flight from Baram (iv. 9. 9), a much shorter period than Theophylact's narrative might suggest.

Baram to his presence by courier,[24] pacified him with costly royal gifts to terminate the mutiny, and even promised to assign to him the position of second in power, to remit his previous offences, and to provide as guarantee of the agreement a mediating oath. (6) On receipt of the royal letter, Baram answered to Chosroes in the following words: for I will now set down Baram's actual composition, word for word.[25]

(7) 'Baram, beloved of the gods, conqueror, pre-eminent, enemy of tyrants, satrap of grandees, leader of the Persian force, prudent, commanding, god-fearing, irreproachable, noble, fortunate, shrewd, venerable, politic, provident, gentle, humane, to Chosroes the son of Hormisdas. (8) I have received what was written by your defective and minimal intelligence and I have not accepted what was dispatched by your brazen enterprise: for you should not have used either royal letters or gifts in dealing with us, especially since your election has come upon the Persian state in such an irregular way and the noble and distinguished did not take part in the voting along with the unranked and lower-born. (9) So, lest you encounter your father's dangers, lay down the crown in the holy places and withdraw from the royal places, while those caught in the transgression, whose daring has been like your own, must again be put away in prison. (10) For it is not a prerogative of your power to release without investigation malefactors from the punishment appropriate to them under the laws. (11) When you have done this, come to us and you will at once become a regional commander of the Persian state. Farewell and think wisely of what is advantageous. Otherwise perish like your ancestor.'

(8. 1) At full speed the letter-bearer soon reached the palace and conveyed to the king the tablet containing Baram's composition. On the following day,[26] the Persian king summoned everyone and revealed to the ears of the assembly Baram's haughty message. (2) The satraps and the others who were resplendent with positions of rank were enraged by Baram's extraordinary boldness; they roused the king to a frenzy of anger and publicly proscribed that same Baram as the tyrant of all Persia. (3) The Babylonian king, however, feared that by menacing words he would exasperate the tyrant to further disobedience. He kept his thoughts to himself and, as if with a false curtain of flattery, he evaded Baram's demand with a further demand that

[24] i.e. 20 Feb., counting from Chosroes' proclamation (Higgins, *Persian War* 30).
[25] This letter, and the following ones, may well be translations of the originals, which Theophylact's source John of Epiphania would have been well placed to see. The extravagant salutations give an air of authenticity, cf. iv. 8. 5, 11. 1.
[26] 21 Feb. 590.

his opponent desist from pride,[27] inscribing to him in a letter the following words in effect. (4) I consider it not unimportant that the actual arrangement of wording should be set out, so that, by a precise exposition of the facts, those who are eager for strange and engaging narratives can draw off the truth unsullied.

(5) 'Chosroes, king of kings, master of dynasts, lord of nations, prince of peace, saviour for mankind, among the gods a righteous immortal man, a god most manifest among men, exceedingly glorious, victorious, who rises with the sun and bestows eyes on the night, distinguished in his ancestry, a king who hates war, bounteous, who employs the Asones[28] and preserves the monarchy for Persians, to Baram general of Persians and our friend. (6) We have received a reminder of your far-famed courage and were gladdened to know that you are in health. In your letter were set out certain words which did not spring from your heart. It was perhaps the drafter of the letter who, drunk on much wine and enfolded by unmeasured sleep, composed vain absurd dreams. (7) But since at the present time the trees have shed their raiment and dreams are powerless, therefore we were not perturbed. We received the royal throne rightfully, we did not overturn Persian customs, and we do not attempt to imprison again those saved from prison;[29] for it is not fitting for a king's gift to be deprived of force. (8) Now, we are so firmly confident of not relinquishing the diadem that, even if there are other worlds, we expect to rule over those as well. We approach you as befits a king, either persuading with words or subjugating with arms. If you wish to prosper, take thought for what is needful. Good health to you who will be our best ally.'

(9. 1) So after the king of the Medes had dispatched this to the usurper Baram, forces were gathered from every quarter. He assembled the army and collected as quickly as possible the men from the region of Adrabiganon, those stationed in the area of the river Zab, in addition to those encamped at Nisibis.[30] (2) Next, after he had marshalled in one place the forces which had been amassed for him and gratified them with money, he then appointed commanders: ordering Sarames to command the companies on the right, and

---

[27] The text is defective but the sense is clear.
[28] The significance of this allusion is unknown.
[29] The text is again defective but the sense is clear.
[30] Chosroes had no time for lengthy military preparations at Ctesiphon before Baram's arrival; he could merely have assembled the supporters whom he had collected during his flight to Azerbaijan (Adrabiganon), loyal remnants of Pherochanes' army that had been encamped by the Zab, and any fugitives from the rebellious Nisibis army.

directing Zamerdes to lead the left side, he ordered Bindoes to take the central division and to hold the rearguard. (3) Then the Persian king set out from the royal capital and came to a certain plain where there ran a river flowing in the middle between the two forces.[31] (4) Then the two armies took up their position on the banks of the river, and many messages from Chosroes and Baram were ferried across from first light until the rising of the evening star, but their discourse was scattered on the air; when peaceful fortune had completely failed to grant a resolution, battle was knit and fighting gave birth to a visitation of great troubles.

(5) Then sallies now occurred and skirmishes and those very actions which are the bellicose preludes of the engagement. So Baram surrounded himself with a ditch and made other dispositions for the safety of his fighting force, (6) but Chosroes lacked the courage to circumvallate himself on the plain: throughout the day his appearance suggested eagerness for battle, but when night fell he protected his forces by containing them within the city. Consequently a serious loss of morale befell Chosroes' contingents. (7) But when the cowardice of the opposing force had become clear, thereafter Baram was encouraged not to steal the victory: for he thought it wrong that those whom it was possible to coerce openly should make accusations of deceit and sully his triumph because of trickery. (8) But Chosroes put to death certain people whom he suspected of associating in the tyrant's undertakings. On the second day he observed that the spirits of his forces were downcast, and he therefore looked to flight and made advance preparations for the escape of his harem. (9) With matters standing thus, since Chosroes refused to meet him in an engagement, on the seventh day Baram organized a night attack when there was no moon and assaulted Chosroes' contingents.[32] (10) Accordingly, there was fearful consternation, and great confusion immediately arose; at first the enemy directed the slaughter against the baggage animals, but then the massacre switched to Chosroes' allies as well and, after many had been slain, the army changed its opinion, deserted to Baram, and united with his forces. (11) Now Chosroes was unable to endure the climax of his misfortunes, and with a handful of bodyguards he escaped from this great and most unexpected peril as fast as his feet would carry him.[33] (10. 1) And having thus been ousted

---

[31] The river was probably the Nahrawan canal, which ran a few miles east of Ctesiphon.

[32] On 28 Feb. 590 (Higgins, *Persian War* 29-30).   [33] On 1 Mar. 590.

from his kingdom, he left Ctesiphon and crossed the river Tigris; he was in despair about exactly what to do; some advised him to approach the eastern Scythians, whom we are accustomed to call Turks, others to save himself in the mountains of Caucasia or Atrapaïca.[34] (2) Thus Chosroes was at a loss how to evaluate the advice. Accordingly he very properly entrusted the reins of his flight to the supreme God; after looking up to heaven, and turning his thoughts to the Creator, disregarding the false gods and placing none of his hope in Mithras, he naturally decreased the swift slide of his perils, and by changing faith he also changed fortune towards the better. (3) And so bidding farewell to the bridle and casting aside the guiding reins, he determined that he would be directed by his mare, and that by entrusting to God and the horse the determination of his escape, the rider should be steered towards an advantageous course by the mount: for thus the occasion consented to improvise for the world a mighty occasion for actions.[35] (4) And so that royal mare carried its fugitive rider into the desert; after crossing this and going along the river Euphrates, he drew near to the forts of Abbaron and Anathon, which were subject to tribute under the Persian state.[36] Setting out from there, Chosroes came to the vicinity of the city of Circesium. (5) He camped ten miles away and sent messengers to Circesium to make known his arrival, his changed fortune, and his flight to the Caesar; he asked to be returned to his own country and sought to win support from the Romans. So it was in the third watch of the night that his messengers approached the gates. (6) When the ambassadors had indicated to the gatekeepers the reason for their passage through the wall, those responsible for the gate-watch quickly came before the city's commander and with all

---

[34] After Chosroes had crossed from Ctesiphon to the west bank of the Tigris, the direction of his flight was in fact virtually determined, since it would have been difficult to flee north-east, back across the Tigris and past Baram's army, to the Turks or to the Caucasus or Azerbaijan (Atrapaïca). Chosroes may already have made initial preparations for seeking Roman help against Baram, perhaps asking the Nestorian Catholicus Mar Isho-Yahb to accompany him on his journey (*Anon. Guidi* 2), or using the Arab leader Naman, who was a Christian, to act as an intermediary to test the possibility of Roman support (*Chron. ad an. 1234* 80).

[35] Although it is also preserved by Evagrius (vi. 17, p. 234. 2-4), this story of Chosroes' reliance on divine providence to determine the course of his flight is most implausible, since Chosroes was in fact hotly pursued by Baram's soldiers (see iv. 12. 1-2), and some preparations for a flight to the west may already have been made (see n. 34 above). Chosroes probably invented the story as part of the Christianizing propaganda that was designed to help him gain assistance from Maurice.

[36] Chosroes follows the route of his grandfather's invasion of the Roman empire in 573. The route is confirmed by *Anon. Guidi* 2.

haste reported the turn of affairs to the commander. The commandant of the fort was called Probus. (7) So at dawn Probus brought Chosroes into the city and entertained him with courtesy and hospitality; he accorded the utmost humanity to Chosroes' wives, who were carrying infants at their breasts, and with strict propriety he looked after the bodyguard and attendants, of whom in fact Chosroes had thirty. (8) On the second day Chosroes king of the Persians asked Probus to send a written embassy to the Caesar, and after composing a royal message he dispatched it to the emperor via Probus. (9) On the following day Probus made Chosroes' presence known to the general Comentiolus, who was residing at Hierapolis, and also sent to him Chosroes' written request to the Caesar. Comentiolus gave the couriers a report to carry to the emperor of the events which Probus had revealed[37] to him at Hierapolis. (10) On hearing the news, the emperor Maurice was delighted and revelled in the improved prospects; removing the Persian seals, he sought to comprehend and discern precisely what was written on the tablets.[38] (11) The substance of the Persian king's request was in effect arranged as follows: for I will set out the petition word for word without adorning its phraseology, so that through its uncultivated diction we may see an undistorted reflection of the motivation for the request.[39]

(11. 1) 'Chosroes king of Persians greets the most prudent king of the Romans, the beneficent, peaceful, masterful, lover of nobility and hater of tyranny, equitable, righteous, saviour of the injured, bountiful, forgiving. (2) God effected that the whole world should be illumined from the very beginning by two eyes, namely by the most powerful kingdom of the Romans and by the most prudent sceptre of the Persian state.[40] (3) For by these greatest powers the disobedient and bellicose tribes are winnowed and man's course is continually regulated and guided.[41] And one can see that the sequence of events is consonant with our words. (4) Since, then, there are certain malignant and evil demons abounding in the world, who are eager to confound all God's excellent dispositions, even though their enterprise does not

[37] Translating Bekker's emendation διαγνωρισθέντων for the MSS διαγνωσθέντων.

[38] Maurice is likely to have received Chosroes' letter towards the end of Mar. 590.

[39] Cf. iv. 7. 6 with n.

[40] Cf. Peter the Patrician, fr. 13 for the use, possibly anachronistically, of the image of the twin eyes or lights of the world in the context of Roman-Persian negotiations in 297. Cf. Malalas 449. 19-20 for the salutation of a letter from the Persian king, the eastern sun, to the Roman emperor, the western moon.

[41] Cf. iii. 9. 11 with n.

achieve its result, it is right for God-loving men of piety to take the field against these, having received from God a treasury of wisdom and the strong arm and weapons of justice.

(5) 'Now in these days the most malicious demons have attacked the Persian state and accomplished terrible things, mobilizing slaves against masters, subjects against kingdom, disorder against order, and disadvantage against expediency, and supplying weapons to every opponent of goodness. (6) For Baram, that abominable slave who was exalted and glorified by our ancestors, failed to contain his great glory but has shied away towards destruction; wooing kingship for himself, he has confounded the whole Persian state; everything which he accomplishes and endeavours is in order that he may quench a great eye of power, (7) and that thereby the fierce, malevolent tribes may gain authority and power over the most meek kingdom of the Persians, and then subsequently thereby in the course of time gain irresistible might, which will not be without great injury to your tributary nations as well. (8) It is then fitting for your peaceful providence to give a saving hand to a kingdom that is being ravaged and coerced by tyrants, to support a power that is on the point of dissolution, to establish in the Roman state the cause of salvation, as if it were a universal trophy, and to proclaim yourselves the founders, saviours, and physicians of the Persian state. (9) For the most powerful rulers ought continually to accomplish all that is in the interests of justice; thereby, even when they have departed the present world, they will have eternally incorruptible praise for their magnanimity, and will establish an example that servants ought not to take arms against their masters. (10) It is, then, right that you should guide the current irregularity of affairs in the Persian state; for thereby the Romans will receive through you a more glorious reputation. (11) These words which I write, do I, Chosroes, address to you as if I were in your presence, I, Chosroes your son and suppliant. For the chance course of events will not make you disregard what is proper to my rank and title.[42] May the angels of God who grant blessings preserve the kingdom for you free from disgrace and tyranny.'

(12. 1) While the Caesar was reviewing this embassy, Baram bestowed favours on the satraps and Babylonian nobles and demanded their allegiance. He assumed all the royal accoutrements which Chosroes the Persian king had in his train and came to the palace.

---

[42] Evagrius vi. 17, p. 234. 8-13, records that Maurice was deeply affected by the reversal of fortune which was demonstrated by Chosroes' appeal.

He selected from the army picked men for an expedition, and ordered them to track down Chosroes and bring him to his presence in chains.[43] (2) Now these failed to accomplish their orders from Baram, but encountered Bindoes, who was a staunch supporter of Chosroes the Persian king. They disgraced him with chains and brought him to Baram on the seventh day.[44] (3) Baram, although he was appropriating the Persian kingdom and was consumed by lust for it, did not openly exhibit the machinations of his heart, since he feared that he might meantime be discovered to have organized the whole course of his actions for this precise reason. (4) He desired his rule to be affixed by senatorial decree, and the proclamation of his power to be clothed in a certain legal force, thereby contriving for himself that his kingdom be beyond reproach and furthermore that his undertaking be unopposed. (5) But when, in spite of all this dissembling and manœuvring, the plotter of the scheme did not gain credence, he was angered at the magi whose opinions were contrary. Since, then, his ambition had totally failed to achieve its goal and objective, he came into the open. (6) Accordingly, during the course of the great and famous festival which the Persians are ordained by an ancient and venerable practice to hold in honour of the sky,[45] he seized the royal diadem, proclaimed himself king, and appeared resplendent on the golden couch; he ordered the barbarians resident in Martyropolis to maintain a strong guard and not to pay the least attention to Chosroes. (7) Then Baram's proclamation was revealed to the Romans who were besieging the city,[46] for they captured the man bearing the tyrant's orders.

(8) So now Chosroes came to the city called Hierapolis, and indeed Comentiolus the general did not leave dishonoured the man who was temporarily deprived of his kingdom: for such was the emperor

[43] The statement that these events occurred while Maurice was considering Chosroes' appeal is incorrect, since Baram acted very quickly to organize a party to pursue Chosroes (cf. nn. 44, 45 below). It is possible that Theophylact was misled by the order of John of Epiphania's narrative, which perhaps reported in full Chosroes' appeal to Maurice before returning to describe Baram's contemporaneous actions.

[44] Tabari, pp. 280-2, records (probably correctly) that Bindoes accompanied Chosroes on his flight, but then donned the royal robes and allowed himself to be captured in order to ensure that Chosroes escaped from the close pursuit by Baram's soldiers. The seventh day is calculated from the day of Chosroes' flight on 1 Mar. (iv. 9. 11), so that Bindoes returned in chains on 7 Mar.

[45] The Nauruz festival; Higgins, *Persian War* 8-11, calculated the date of the festival as 9 Mar.

[46] The blockade of Martyropolis was probably maintained throughout the winter of 589/90, although the main Roman army had retired to winter quarters (iv. 2. 1).

Maurice's decision, and his decree was translated into action. Therefore Comentiolus came to the place known as Bedamas to meet Chosroes, organized royal provision for him, and gave him a magnificent guard. (9) On the ninth day Chosroes dispatched a satrap known as Miragdun as messenger to the Persian garrison in Martyropolis to notify them of the change in fortune, and that it was wrong for them to be in possession of the city, since the magnanimity of the emperor had remoulded the Persians into non-combatants and friends. (10) From among the Persian notables he dispatched Bestam to Armenia,[47] ordering him to go to Adrabiganon and establish for him the allegiance of the Persians living there. (13. 1) These were the actions which he thus performed in public, but, with his innately knavish disposition which placed all things second to deceit, he scorned the law of hospitality and cast underfoot the guarantees of friendship by sending on the fifth day a messenger to the Chaldaeans encamped at Martyropolis, ordering them to maintain their guard most strictly and to pay no attention to his public instructions: for the Persian nation is worthless and from the outset their life is one of treachery, humbug, and boasting.

(2) Then, since he had encountered a temporary delay in returning to his kingdom,[48] Chosroes tried to approach the Roman emperor. Now Maurice, when he realized Chosroes' objective, prevented him by a royal letter from coming to his presence, without regard for reputation but effecting for Chosroes the advancement of his interests: for he considered that Chosroes must not travel far from the Persian state, lest Baram might thereby establish his tyrannical enterprise more firmly. (3) At the start of spring Chosroes sent ambassadors to the emperor;[49] and so on the third day the emperor convened a royal assembly and received the open homage of the ambassadors. Then, when silence pervaded the meeting and the emperor had granted the Persians permission to deliver a speech, the most distinguished of the ambassadors, giving his speech a preliminary enrichment of tears and

[47] It later emerges (see iv. 15. 3, 5 with nn.) that Bestam did not reach Armenia until about mid-July, which suggests that he had not been dispatched by Chosroes before late June. Theophylact has not made clear, and probably did not realize, how long the initial negotiations between Chosroes and Maurice had lasted.

[48] There has been no suggestion of any delay in Theophylact's narrative, but see n. 47.

[49] Spring 590. Since Bestam was sent to Armenia in June (see n. 47) and Chosroes had experienced some delay (iv. 13. 2), these ambassadors can hardly have been dispatched at the start of spring. Spring (ἦρος) may be an error by Theophylact for summer (θέρους).

thereby trying to capture the emperor's pity, began with these words:[50]

(4) 'Thrice-greatest king, if the request were from your closest friends, the occasion would possess propriety, the manner eloquence, the argument persuasion, the suffering mercy, the theme its justification, the necessity swift arrival of assistance, the embassy respect and, in a word, the sufferings would possess pity to match even the disasters with which they were identified. (5) But since all these things, along with everything else, have escaped Persia's grasp, it remains either for Chosroes to be bathed in benevolence through your virtue or for the Medes to destroy a great kingdom by tyranny. (6) I am well aware that one of those not initiated into the rites of good sense might say that it would benefit the Roman state for our Babylonian nation to lament long in perdition after casting aside its kingdom, power, and great strength, and for Roman power to wax fat in unmolested peace; he would be ill informed about what is disadvantageous to Roman might. (7) For it is impossible for a single monarchy to embrace the innumerable cares of the organization of the universe, and with one mind's rudder to direct a creation as great as that over which the sun watches. (8) For it is never possible for the earth to resemble the unity of the divine and primary rule, and to obtain a disposition corresponding to that of the upper order, since it is steered hither and thither towards the breakers by mankind, whose nature is unstable and whose judgement most worthless because of its tendency towards evil.

(9) 'Therefore, even though the Persians were to be deprived of power, their power would immediately transfer to other men. For events will not tolerate lack of leadership, nor such great fortune lack of direction. For as thought will not be separated from reasoning, so the greatest powers in the world will never be, as it were, bereft of a helmsman. (10) Or did not the Medes possess prosperous Chaldaea after the Babylonians, the Persians after the Medes, and after these the Parthians, as if by some succession of inheritance? It is obvious to shepherds and goatherds alike that the whole flock does not act at a single pipe blowing a pastoral tune. Something similar is accustomed to happen in human affairs as well. (11) Sufficient proof is the insane, unreasonable ambition of a Macedonian stripling: for Alexander became an immature sport of fortune and, when she smiled on him a little in mockery, he swaggered in his mastery of Europe, undertook to

[50] The speech is a rhetorical expansion of the themes of Chosroes' letter (iv. 11).

master the sea, desired to hold the sceptre of Babylon, yearned for
Indian power, threatened to subjugate Libya, and constrained his
kingdom to expand as far as the sky is spread and the sun's eye shines
with sparkling rays. (12) He attempted to subjugate the temporal universe to a single unitary power. But, sooner than this, ambition was
quenched along with power, and affairs proceeded once more divided
up into a leadership of multiple tyranny, so to speak. For concord has
never come to unite the inharmonious.

(13) 'Accordingly, what prosperity would events devolve upon the
Romans if the Persians are deprived of power and transmit mastery to
another nation? What mark of honour would the Roman race acquire
if it rejects as suppliant a king who is the most famous and brave of all
on earth? (14) Or what citadel of piety will you have if you have
despised the unfortunate? When, O king, will you ever take up the
contest on behalf of justice and mobilize for war if you forgo this opening? When will the beauty of worship ever blossom for you if not at the
present opportunity? Now you may either confirm your title by your
actions, or by your misdeeds acquire falsehood for your appellation.
(15) What more kingly display than this will you make during the
whole period of your rule? What other such occasion for exultation
could be available for the Romans? What guarantee of your fairness, O
king, will be more respected among the nations than this? (16) Now
through a brief alliance you will derive eternal peace, and what the
Romans have utterly failed to accomplish by innumerable conflicts,
unbounded cares, and a flood of financial outlay, this you will now
carry off effortlessly through a virtuous spirit, which the occasion
demands but the king disposes, and you will pluck a trouble-free
peace without toil. What could be more advantageous to the Romans
than this? (17) Let not any of Hormisdas' wickedness dwell in your
heart. He has learned from his sufferings not to abominate peace. Chosroes has not inherited his father's misdeeds: sons do not inherit their
father's inclinations in their entirety along with his possessions.
(18) Hormisdas was ill disposed, Chosroes is now well disposed; he
carries round your benefaction incarnate in his person, which he will be
ashamed to forget since he has numerous witnesses to your piety.

(19) 'Do not let usurpers prevail, lest you should share the pre-
cedent. Or is not evil the masses' great ambition, is not human nature
disposed to desire the worse, its impulse hard to redirect towards the
better? (20) We have heard that the usurper has also dispatched ambassadors to you, demanding to have as accomplice in crime the man who

has done no wrong, and all but contriving that a ruler join in revolution with a fugitive. What could be more inglorious and abominable to the Romans than this? (21) What foundation of loyalty to you will he use to underpin his promises, that man whose premise is one of utmost ingratitude, who has organized a contingent against his benefactors, and embraced every form of evil in order to depose from his kingdom a ruler who has done nothing wrong? A premise of evil does not usually protect a promise of friendship. (22) An imprudent beginning will also have a totally inexpedient conclusion: for the sprout does not progress in contradiction to the seed. Baram may perhaps attempt to angle for injustice with gifts; but I have heard it said by one of your nation, who is wise in subtleties, that from wicked men "gifts are no gifts and are not beneficial".[51] (23) The wages of debauchery are unable to bring a harvest of enjoyment, and the profits of crime to possess an unrepented crop growing in the furrows: for before pleasure there is pain, and before gratification a diversion to grief, since fine objectives have been surrendered and even righteous acquisitions are removed in addition.

(24) 'In exchange we give back Martyropolis, we will offer Daras as a gift, without payment we will lay war in the tomb and build a house of peace by bidding farewell to Armenia, on whose account war ill-fatedly gained free rein among men. (25) Even if the gifts do not befit the necessity, still this is our highest principle, to exercise moderation in promises rather than to grease the ears with great offers and incur undying enmity when we fail to accomplish their realization, wickedly storing up against the future health of peace great occasions for evil. (26) I have made sufficient defence of the profitable course for Romans and Persians. But if I have disregarded any element of a more complete treatment, then, O king, supply the omission: for it often happens that reason abandons the contest, since necessity is incapable of tolerating discipline or obeying the dictates of reflection when concomitant circumstances are constantly ferrying the mind back and forth in confusion.'

(14. 1) When the ambassadors had thus completed this discourse and their request won persuasion and favour from the fluency of the speech, the senate and emperor decreed that the Romans would help Chosroes and prepare most energetically for war against Baram,[52]

---

[51] Sophocles, *Ajax* 665, a quotation that is reused at vii. 15. 11.

[52] John of Nikiu xcvi. 10-13 and Sebeos, ch. 2, p. 15, record that Maurice, with the support of Domitianus of Melitene, overruled the opposition of his council and in particular of the Patriarch John Nesteutes, who preferred to allow the Persians to weaken themselves in civil war.

(2) since the emperor thought it unworthy for the Latin realm to provide arms for criminals and brave danger for injustice because of a substantial promise,[53] or for the Romans to be eternally branded with undying reproaches because they had undertaken a most shameful policy. (3) So on that day the decree was proclaimed and publicized throughout the royal city, while on the fifth day the ambassadors were admitted to the Caesar's presence, were honoured with royal gifts, and obtained the emperor's decree in writing. (4) Furthermore the emperor dispatched to Chosroes, together with the ambassadors, Samen, Chosroperozes, and the others whom the Romans had already captured earlier in the course of the war.

(5) And so when Chosroes had perused the contents of the Caesar's missive and rejoiced at the Romans' virtue, he left Hierapolis together with Comentiolus and came to the city of Constantina. Shortly afterwards the bishop of Melitene, who was in fact Domitianus, also came to Chosroes on the emperor's instructions; this man, who was connected by birth to the emperor Maurice,[54] was a priest by office but more than priestly in the ordering of his life, pleasant in speech, quick in action, most shrewd in counsel. (6) He was accompanied by Gregory, the leader of the priesthood of Antioch, for this too was the emperor's decision and his word was translated into deed. So, when the priests had reached Constantina itself, they consoled Chosroes with words and gifts, arranging for him in his despondency the attainment of his hopes.

(7) And so Chosroes dispatched ambassadors to Nisibis, reminded the Persians of their goodwill for the royal family, and urged them with gentle exhortation that they should not tolerate the rule of tyrants and scorn the ancient and ancestral law, which had grown venerable in the Persian kingdom and which had never been invalidated by the recent coup. (8) But when Baram was informed that Chosroes was safe, that he had been hospitably received by the Romans, and that this had also been sanctioned by the emperor through the ambassadors, he sent ambassadors to ask the emperor not to provide any assistance to the fortunes of Chosroes, and promised to surrender to the Romans the city of Nisibis and the territory as far as the river Tigris. (9) Now Baram's deceit was to no avail, for he could not corrupt the emperor's sanctity. A few days later, he was revealed in his swollen pride to be cheating his allies, a burden on Persia, and insatiate in his enterprises

[53] Baram's offers are recorded at iv. 14. 8.
[54] Domitianus was either a cousin or a nephew of Maurice.

as he exacerbated the savagery of his tyranny. (10) And so the most eminent satraps in his force secretly united in a plot[55] to assassinate Baram and to restore the affairs of the Medes to tranquillity. (11) Now the leaders of the plot against Baram were Zamerdes and Zoanambes the Persian: these same men also selected as many other associates as possible from the Babylonian army, and fomented their conspiracy. (12) They surmised that it would be to their advantage to have as a collaborator Bindoes as well, who was confined in custody by Baram, and they accomplished their desire in action: they suddenly burst into the prison, released Bindoes from his bonds, chose him as leader of the plot and, during the night, attacked Baram in the palace.[56] (13) Now in the second watch of the night Baram became aware of the conspiracy, arrayed his guards and ordered them to arm, prepared the troops which had recently reached him from foreign nations, and stoutly resisted his assailants. (14) A fierce night battle took place, Baram gained the upper hand and captured the originators of the enterprise; once day had grown bright, he chopped off the functional parts of their limbs and then, after spreading out the remainder of their bodies, he allowed them to be trampled by the elephants and to obtain this all-consuming death.

(15. 1) Now Bindoes together with his companions unexpectedly escaped the disastrous peril and came as quickly as possible to Adrabiganon. So he encamped there, collected a large number of Persians and, as it were, tamed the rebels to espouse Chosroes' cause. (2) On the tenth day he sent a messenger to John, whom the Romans were accustomed to call Mystacon, informing him of the recent actions and seeking to learn how Chosroes' attempted rapprochement with the Romans had fared. (3) And so John conveyed the news by letter to the emperor and detained Bindoes' ambassadors while he awaited the outcome of his report to the emperor.[57] (4) The emperor Maurice commanded John to ally himself whole-heartedly with the supporters of Chosroes' cause, and to give them complete assurance of proper behaviour so that Baram's tyranny might tend to lose strength. (5) On

[55] The text may be defective but the sense is clear.

[56] According to eastern sources (see Higgins, *Persian War* 45), Bindoes remained in prison for seventy days, or for three to four months, which would place this revolt against Baram in June 590.

[57] Since John, the Roman commander in Armenia, was uncertain about how to receive Bindoes, it is clear that he did not yet know of Maurice's decision to give Chosroes full support. Bindoes could not have approached John before late June or early July (cf. n. 56), which suggests that it took longer for Maurice to decide to support Chosroes than Theophylact's narrative (iv. 13. 2-14. 6) implies (see Higgins, *Persian War* 42-5).

the previous day Bestam, whom Chosroes had sent to Armenia, reached John;[58] and so John revealed Bindoes' presence to Bestam and with the greatest joy imparted the significance of what had befallen Baram. (6) And so Bestam was overjoyed at the news and sent a messenger to Chosroes to inform him of these facts. Bindoes acquired great courage when he saw that circumstances were again smiling on Chosroes, and on receiving the emperor's money he distributed it to his company, according to the strength of their individual support. (7) When those stationed at Nisibis learned that the emperor was friendly to Chosroes and was deluging him with great forces of allies, they revised their opinion and came to Constantina. The city-protector was lubricated with promises by Chosroes, and virtually transferred to Chosroes the whole of Arabia and the lands as far as the river Tigris in full gratification of his hopes.[59]

(8) But those in possession of Martyropolis, although they were beset by the Roman siege, complying in effect with Chosroes' secret injunctions did not surrender the city to the Romans, but even put up a very stout resistance. (9) Accordingly, when Chosroes' villainy became apparent, with shrewd calculation Domitianus counter-marshalled irresistible counsel and dispersed the festering sore of the Persian deceit like an excrescence of blisters. (10) For he summoned to his presence the most prominent members of the city garrison and won over some with words, while others he bribed with gifts; he reminded them of the Roman siege which confronted the city, of Chosroes' request for the emperor's assistance, and of the uncertain fortune which beset Baram. (11) So great was the power of his speech that those holding Martyropolis were divided in their opinions, . . . 'willing but with reluctant heart'; for let me now use the Homeric tongue to portray his thoughts.[60] (12) Next he dispatched to Martyropolis the chief eunuch, whom Romans are accustomed to call *praepositus* and who had been seconded for his royal bodyguard,[61] with

---

[58] It must now be mid-July at the earliest, since John has had time to communicate with Maurice about Bindoes. This indicates that Bestam had probably been dispatched by Chosroes from Hierapolis (iv. 12. 10 and n.) in late June.

[59] Nisibis probably defected to Chosroes towards the end of 590, since Baram apparently did not yet know of the change of allegiance when he sent Zadesprates to take control there (probably in Dec., see v. 1. 2 with 13. 5).

[60] *Iliad* iv. 43. The Homeric tag applies to Chosroes, since it illustrates *his* thoughts, and the following sentence continues with Chosroes as subject. Accordingly, de Boor postulated a short lacuna.

[61] The *praepositus sacri cubiculi*, the head of the imperial household, who had been dispatched to Chosroes in a military capacity.

a recommendation to the Persians to leave the city and encamp near Nisibis. (13) And so, since Chosroes the king had changed his mind, the Persians arranged a truce with the besiegers and withdrew from the city. Then, after the leaders had arrived at Constantina, Sittas too was discovered in their midst, the man who had by trickery handed over Martyropolis to Hormisdas the Persian king.[62] (14) And so Domitianus indicated to Chosroes that he was engaged in impiety towards his Roman benefactors in trusting a traitor who had wrought great injury on the Romans; he reminded him that Sittas had also been a friend of Baram, (15) and that it was most inexpedient for him to esteem a faithless murderer, lest the massed Roman troops might perhaps do away with Chosroes himself as well as Sittas, and Baram gain respite from his struggle. (16) Chosroes concurred with this, bought off the immediate crisis with flattery, and delivered Sittas to Comentiolus. On the second day the general tortured him in full view of the army, handed him over to the fire, burnt him to ashes in the flames, and exacted punishment from Sittas for his misdeeds.[63]

(17) And so Domitianus, in a manner befitting a priest, busied himself to the greatest possible extent with matters connected with the recovery of the city, and he handed over to the general Comentiolus the Romans who had conspired with the barbarians for the capture of the city. (18) Then, after these had undergone punishment worthy of their crimes against their country, the priest inaugurated the festival for the city's salvation and arranged a feast for its gloriously victorious martyrs.[64] Standing on the lofty pulpit in the church, he chanted a new victory-hymn to Christ, and addressed words such as these to the ears of the assembled people:

(16. 1) 'Not only in wars and engagements and battle-array does David sound the war-cry on his trumpets, but also on the famous day of feasting does he trumpet to the supreme God. For it is fitting for God to be hymned even on the instruments of war, since he is supreme commander of the battle-array and a strong and powerful champion in wars. And from where glory is born, it is no doubt essential that praise also should surely proceed.[65] (2) Come, let us also sound the war-cry

---

[62] Cf. iii. 5. 11-13.

[63] According to Evagrius vi. 19, p. 234. 34-5, Sittas was stoned to death at Martyropolis.

[64] Higgins, *Persian War* 47, suggested that the festival might have been held on 16 Feb., the day of commemoration for the Persian martyrs whose relics were enshrined in the city.

[65] Many of the phrases of this sermon are borrowed from the Scriptures; for details of parallels, see S. Leanza, 'Motivi cristiani nelle storie di Teofilatto Simocatta', in

on spiritual trumpets, I mean on the trumpets of intellect, not of horn as was the Jewish custom: for we are not caused by density of intellect to be ordered to honour God with the limbs of unreasoning creatures. (3) So let us arrange a festival, not extending merely as far as the altar-rails,[66] but unto the upper hierarchy of God himself, whose high priest for ever after the order of Melchizedek exists and is honoured, being seated on the right hand of the Majesty. (4) For in truth he has acted mightily with his arm, humbling peaks of arrogance, casting down the mighty from their seats, and once more inscribing against Babylon the greatness of the spirit. (5) For lions are enslaved, serpents choked, Bel and Mithras sold into slavery, and the fire mitigated, the fire which could not even conquer the clothing of the martyrs although it was liberally sprinkled with tar and pitch.

(6) 'Once again the right hand of the Lord has acted powerfully by condemning the pride of the Chaldaeans, writing his proclamation not on a wall, but in heaven. The sceptres of Babylon are rent asunder, the throne of insolence is cast down, the wine-sodden kingdom abased, the humbled are once more honoured, and the conquered hold sway. (7) Once again the city made barren by war can be seen rejoicing like a mother in the blessing of children. Let no one don raiment unworthy of this royal festival. (8) Let us all wear white attire in purity of life, lest by dressing our souls in an apparel unworthy of the feast we may appear unworthy of transformation and receive the judgement consequent on failure. (9) Celebrate, celebrate, O city of exultation, for your light has come and the glory of the Lord has risen upon you. This the Holy Spirit declares to me, and I rejoice at the proclamation; and the present glory has surpassed its former brightness. (10) For in ancient, bygone times you had acquired companies of martyrs overflowing every path and highway of your vitals.[67] (11) Your return is more glorious than your capture: for what trickery stole, fear has now

---

Umanità e storia, scritti in onore di Adelchi Attisani (Messina, 1971), ii. 553-74. Most allusions are to the Psalms, the most widely known book of the Septuagint, and to Daniel, which was particularly appropriate for the celebration of success against Persia. For the exultant tone, compare *Chron. Pasch.* 727. 15 ff., the emperor Heraclius' victory-message to the inhabitants of Constantinople, proclaiming his triumph against the Persians; also George of Pisidia, *Heraclias* ii.

[66] Literally 'the horns of the altar', which would recall the trumpets of horn used by the Jews in the previous section. De Boor proposed to delete διήκουσαν, 'extending', but such a word has to be understood to provide sense.

[67] Marutha, founder and first bishop of the city, had collected relics of Persian martyrs and enshrined them in his new city (see V. Minorsky, *Encyclopaedia of Islam* iii (1936), 159, s.v. Maiyāfāriḳīn).

surrendered, what the villainy of a barbarian monarch wickedly despoiled, a most public slavery now excellently repays. (12) The slave has dispatched this as an offering to you, O martyrs, in his search to gain as allies those whom he had earlier godlessly disregarded, being taught piety by failure just as the Pharaoh of old was brought to honour God by beatings and admonitions. (13) This, martyrs, is your offering from the Babylonian tyrant and foreigner, the fugitive from his own kingdom who is now obedient to the Romans rather than hostile: for such great deeds have you executed against your enemies. (14) The tyrant was confounded at these things, and fear and trembling came upon the earth. For he who was from the beginning has punished the heathens, and this is the transformation of his right hand. From the very peak of heaven is its going forth and its end is as far as the bounds of the earth, and we have beheld its glory full of grace and power.

(15) 'As the prophet says, let the neighbouring "rivers clap their hands",[68] now let the Euphrates in accordance with its name rejoice at the splendours of its Creator and let the Tigris transform its ferocity into benevolence, for it has been liberated from the debauchery of slaughter.[69] (16) Let us sing a song of salvation to the Lord, let us sing to him together with his martyrs a victory hymn. Let us proclaim his glory by the rivers of Babylon as we exult in the spirit, for we have not been condemned to Jewish lamentation, nor been reproached by the shame of captivity at the hands of these brigands. (17) Let us appoint the Lord as leader of the festivity, lest we forget the upper Jerusalem and lest our tongue stick in our throat because it wickedly fails to magnify the wonders of God. Now is the daughter of Babylon wretched indeed in accordance with the Scripture,[70] she who is mounted on arrogant sceptres, and blessed is the piety of the emperor, which has not imposed on her the corresponding destruction nor returned the recompense that she has rendered to us. (18) For there is fulfilled this second covenant which enjoined on the spiritual Israel not to measure out the repayment for evil; this day the king is not rejected for pitying his enemy, nor has Samuel for this reason jealously skirmished with the all-powerful Lord.[71] (19) For Jesus the Christ, the ancient of

---

[68] Ps. 97 (98): 8.

[69] A pun on the rivers' names, the Euphrates suggesting the verb εὐφραίνομαι, 'rejoice at', and the Tigris the ferocity of a wild beast.

[70] Ps. 136 (137): 8.

[71] King Saul was rejected by God for disobeying his orders and sparing Agag, king of the Amalekites; God's judgement against Saul was pronounced by Samuel, who grieved at Saul's rejection but did not in fact oppose God's will (1 Sam. 15).

days and venerable, knows that mercy is more pious than sacrifice; he assigns his Father's kingdom to those who pity; motivated by love of humanity, he assumed the form even of a slave, went about among mankind, knew the manger, submitted to swaddling clothes, fled the tyrannical sword, went to Egypt, (20) then dwelt in Nazareth, and was proclaimed a Galilean; he excelled in wisdom, was abused by envy, was tested by Sadducees, associated with sinners, was handed over to suffering, received a cross, was reckoned among the unrighteous, welcomed a tomb, passed over to resurrection, and was glad to suffer all things, enjoying only one benefit from us, namely that we too are saved.

(21) 'Let us sing to the Lord, but not a song of departure since this is a festival of advent: both city and church are restored, ancestral law is renewed, true faith is strengthened, and I behold Christ celebrating in the centre of the church and bearing round on his shoulders the symbols of victory: the triumph is the cross through which the barbarian is expelled and the Roman admitted. (22) Let us sing to the Lord a hymn of departure as well: for like a boar from a thicket, from the city is banished the Babylonian tribe which had attempted to trample underfoot the holy things and raged to tear apart the pearls of faith with their nails. (23) Let us imitate those who are renowned in Babylon and become fellow revellers in their dance, for even now the fire of the Chaldaeans has been made inefficacious to consume the city of the martyrs; let the heavens be glad, let the earth exult, and let the plains rejoice for the war-loving nations have been cast down. (24) In the words of the prophet, they have recognized that they are men,[72] and now they have not failed to comprehend the nature of their construction; what they could not learn in their prosperity, it can be seen that they have learned in their distress. (25) Improvising these words for you in our joy, we have delivered to you an unrehearsed hymn, a banquet for angels, a simple and unadorned feast: for God likes to be honoured even with disordered words and to accept the modest offerings of his retinue, assessing the manifestation of thanksgiving according to the repentance of the heart not the weight of the gift. (26) Now let us not cease from praising the Father, nor rest from adoring the Son as God by nature, nor refrain from honouring the Spirit as being by nature one of the three persons: for God is the Trinity, to whom be glory without end from countless ages unto ages.'[73]

[72] Ps. 9: 20.

[73] This statement of Christian orthodoxy, which concludes the aggressively Christian speech, illustrates the difference between Theophylact's attitude to the composi-

(27) After the priest had propounded his discourse of highest praise in such a manner, the congregation applauded the noble sentiments of the speech, and many tears mingled with joy flowed over the church because of the compunction of his words; the festival was prone to tears although it had no cause of suffering, for thus did the occasion, which was free from sorrows and grief, summon up tears. (28) And so the priest, after offering the bread and consecrating the wine in the incarnate mysteries, blessed the congregation through their partaking. And in such a way the city celebrated with festivities for seven days.

tion of classicizing historiography and those of his predecessors, Procopius and Agathias, who tended to avoid explicit discussions of Christian matters.

BOOK FIVE

(1. 1) BUT Baram, after failing to win the goodwill of the Romans, gathered an assembly and held a discussion concerning matters at hand; from the more eminent, he appointed as generals those who possessed superiority in courage, so that with countering forethought he might, so to speak, set inviolability in the balance against Chosroes' affairs. (2) And so he positioned Miradurin with a large force at the fort of Anathon, which is built beside the Euphrates in the vicinity of Circesium,[1] and to Nisibis and neighbouring Arabia he also dispatched Zadesprates, who had quite recently been Pherochanes' fellow-campaigner.[2] (3) And so Zadesprates left Babylon and dispatched messengers to Solchanes to give notice of his arrival at Nisibis.[3] (4) Now when Solchanes had learned from the messengers about Zadesprates' overweening arrogance, on the following day he convened a meeting and ordered the messengers to expound in the assembly's hearing what their demand was, without curtailing it at all through fear. (5) And so they fully complied with the command, and detailed the message from the man who had sent them. Confusion then ensued in the assembly, everyone reviled Baram, Solchanes abused and dishonoured the messengers, and dispatched them to Chosroes afflicted with inescapable chains. (6) Chosroes solicited Solchanes with promises, urging him to make proper disposition of the visitations of fortune, but Chosroes himself was dispirited by despair and intimidated at the tyrant's attacks. (7) Then reverence for holy religion came upon him, and he again transported his mind to the supreme God; he supplicated Sergius, glorious among martyrs (whom the nomad tribes are also accustomed to revere), to assist him in his troubles.[4] (8) He solemnly promised to offer as first-fruits of victory

---

[1] The fort of Anathon was in fact about 100 miles to the south-east of Circesium on the Euphrates.   [2] See iv. 2. 3-5.

[3] Although there are no indications of dates in this section, it can be calculated that Zadesprates must have left Ctesiphon (Babylon) in Dec. 590, since the date of Chosroes' prayer to Sergius is known (see n. 4 below).

[4] Sergius, whose major shrine was located at Sergiopolis/Resafa, was the favourite saint of the Monophysite Arab tribes of upper Mesopotamia. Chosroes probably hoped that an appeal to Sergius would encourage the Arabs to support his cause. Chosroes' vow was made on 7 Jan. 591 (v. 13. 5).

the famous symbol of the Lord's Passion (this is designated a cross), to fashion it from beaten gold, and to cover it with pearls and radiant Indian stones:[5] for in his necessity the occasion had made him implore more piously. (9) But Solchanes accomplished an extraordinary enterprise most worthy of narration, and killed the enemy commander through a courageous plan. For he equipped Rhosas, who was also called Hormisdas by the Persians, with a cavalry troop and dispatched him against the multitude arrayed in opposition; but he strictly ordered Rhosas to entrust the accomplishment of his enterprise to trickery. (10) And so Rhosas diligently followed Solchanes' orders and approached the enemy. On the second day[6] Zadesprates arrived in the district of Charcha, a village which is alike most productive and well-populated, and when night fell he camped near it. (11) He felt suspicion of an enemy sighting, in case they might perhaps come upon him suddenly, and he exercised forethought for the protection of his body. Therefore, divorced from fear he apparently passed the night revelling in the tower located in the place, whose structure consisted of unhewn stone.

(12) Then Rhosas came up close to the general and, when he had discovered the place where in fact this man was resting for the night, he took a guide and advanced. After approaching the fortification, he ordered one of his force to run ahead to tell the general that there was a messenger from Baram bringing him reinforcements. (13) And so in the middle of the night he came to the makeshift fort and, deceiving the guards in their native tongue, he demanded that they proclaim the news to the general. Then those wretches received the message with joy and transmitted the word to Zadesprates, as if they were hurrying over some favourable matter that merited urgency. (14) And so Zadesprates, who was still wine-soaked and half-drunk, had his sleep interrupted; carelessly accepting the report, he told the Persians to take courage and ordered them to open the gate of the fort. This indeed became an extemporary and self-chosen death for him, which had folly as the origin of peril. (15) And so Rhosas' troops streamed into the fort and made free with their swords. On seeing the unexpected calamity, the general went to the roof of the turret and sought to elicit security from his captors; but when they threatened to destroy the

---

[5] 'Indian stones' are probably just a general reference to precious stones, and do not denote any particular gem (cf. vii. 6. 4). For the conjunction of pearls and Indian stones, cf. Nonnus, *Dionysiaca* xlii. 239.

[6] This should probably be the second day counting from Rhosas' departure from Nisibis.

building by fire, he came to the enemy. (16) Then his opponents executed him, pillaged everything in the fort, and returned to Solchanes carrying Zadesprates' head and all that chance had allowed them to appropriate by trickery.

(2. 1) And so Solchanes, taking pride in these preliminary duties, dispatched to Chosroes at Constantina the head of the opposing general and the riches which his good counsel had effortlessly looted.[7] (2) And so Chosroes abandoned his ill-omened expectations, divorced despair, and converted his prospects to a more favourable outcome. (3) At about this time the soldiers dispatched by Baram to Anathon also rebelled, killed their commander, and sent his head to Chosroes. (4) So Chosroes, on seeing that he was being crowned by the concurrence of these particular successes, derived a guarantee for the future from what had already occurred, and, confessing that the Christ who is reverenced and honoured among the Romans is the greatest God of all, repudiated his former religion with unrestrained tongue.[8] (5) On the tenth day he sent some of his leading followers to the emperor Maurice, and indicated the transformation in his attendant circumstances; he asked him to put a stop to delay among the allied forces and to assist with all speed, and that he be provided by the emperor with a financial endowment, guaranteeing to return the loan to the Romans once he had recovered his own kingdom. (6) The Roman emperor bestowed on him the massive sum of money in addition to the military alliance. Then Chosroes wrote a receipt for the loan, dispatched it to Maurice, and received the abundant financial wealth; this he divided up and distributed among the attendant Persian forces.

(7) Now Gregory, the leader of the eastern priesthood, left Constantina and moved to Antioch. Shortly afterwards, Chosroes ordered Sarames to go to the emperor with an appeal that the Caesar remove Comentiolus from his command as general, alleging that Comentiolus had insulted him and had vitiated the recruitment of allies by delays. (8) Then Sarames came to Byzantium in accordance with his instructions, and recounted his mission to the emperor. And

[7] Chosroes received Zadesprates' head on 9 Feb. 591 (v. 13. 6).

[8] Chosroes suggested that he might accept Christianity as an inducement for the Romans to support him. Although exaggerated reports of the Persian king's conversion circulated in the west (see e.g. Fredegarius iv. 9), and Chosroes did maintain good relations with Persian Christians for most of his reign, he never repudiated the Zoroastrian religion (see e.g. the letter which Pope Gregory sent to Bishop Domitianus, commiserating on his failure to convert Chosroes, *Register* iii. 62).

so the Roman emperor demoted Comentiolus from the leadership of the return to Persia, and gave the command to Narses, who was in fact the general's bodyguard.

(3. 1) Then at the beginning of spring[9] the new general, taking with him Chosroes and accompanied by the man who was at that time bishop in Melitene, whom report has revealed as Domitianus, moved to Mardes, a fort three parasangs distant from the city of Daras.[10] (2) And so the men of Nisibis in Arabia, all the other potentates, and the commanders of the contingents proclaimed Chosroes king;[11] they handed over kinsmen to guarantee their oath, and made advance preparations for Chosroes' return to his kingdom. (3) And so the Persian king arranged for these to be guarded by Romans; then the general set out from there for Daras and encamped. When Chosroes beheld his allied Roman forces glorying in might and equipped with arms in wondrous array, he gave no place at all in his calculations to his former suffering, and migrated to new hopes. (4) Accordingly the barbarian king entered the city, and installed himself in the walled precinct[12] at the notable shrine of the city, where the Romans performed the mysteries of religion; this was an excessively boorish and insolent action, since he was still labouring under necessity, and his affairs lay on the sea of chance. (5) Now the inhabitants of Daras were enraged by his move, since the elder Chosroes had made no move to insult their religion after he had captured the city. (6) Therefore Domitianus, unable to endure the insolence of the barbarian, threatened to take the forces and return to Constantina. Then Chosroes, being dishonoured thereby and regretting his rashness, dispatched some of his most distinguished followers to Domitianus, and begged him to show mercy on repentance. (7) And so the priest, after inflicting a suitable insult on the barbarian, returned to Daras, having expelled Chosroes from the precinct. On the sixth day the emperor sent to Chosroes at Daras a gemstudded belt, a royal crown, and golden couches and tables; he organized a royal escort for him from his own guardsmen, and generously handed it over, lest he should appear contemptible to the Romans and Persians through lack of a kingly retinue.

[9] Spring 591.
[10] The standard parasang is about 3¼ miles; the actual distance between Dara and Mardin is about 15 miles, or 4 parasangs.
[11] This ceremony was used by some Syriac writers in their chronological computations as the beginning of Chosroes' reign; see Higgins, *Persian War* 47-9.
[12] The precise sense of the Greek is unclear; Chosroes had probably appropriated part of the complex of ecclesiastical buildings attached to the Great Church at Dara.

(8) So Chosroes was encircled on every side by a royal bodyguard equal to that with which Romans are accustomed to honour imperial sceptres. So when the Medes saw the great strength lavished on Chosroes by the emperor, they changed their views, bade farewell to the tyranny, and came over to Chosroes. (9) Baram's support weakened day by day, while for Chosroes events proceeded according to his wishes as his forces were swelled. So Chosroes at once proposed to exhibit an act of great goodwill to the emperor Maurice. (10) Therefore he voluntarily inscribed in a royal epistle that the city of Daras was subject to the emperor Maurice, and sent to Byzantium the satrap Dolabzas, a man of distinction,[13] to convey the keys of the city and the record of the gift. (11) And so the ambassador came to the royal town, surrendered the city to the Romans, and had an audience with the emperor. The Roman emperor exalted Dolabzas with royal gifts and, calling Chosroes his son,[14] once more confirmed the promise of his earlier proclamations.

(4. 1) Chosroes safeguarded his wives and children in the Median city of Singara, since the city was very strongly fortified because of the conflict and was most difficult for the enemy to capture, as it was rendered naturally unapproachable by siege because of the dearth of water supply.[15] (2) After this he issued orders to Mebodes and, giving him a guard of two thousand men from the army, decreed that he march via Singara on the royal cities and destroy the palace guards created by Baram. (3) But the tyrant, on learning that Chosroes was advancing with the Roman contingents, gathered his army and brought it out on campaign. And so Mebodes, afraid of the king's command, went on his mission. At the beginning of summer[16] when the corn was swelling in ripeness, Chosroes left Daras with his allied army and moved forwards. (4) When they reached Ammodius, fourteen measures distant from Daras,[17] Domitianus assembled the Roman army and its commanders, went up on to a mound, and instructed the forces with the following words:

(5) 'Men, the moment devises for you an occasion for great deeds

<hr>

[13] Dolabzas may well be the same man as the Persian ambassador Dalauzas who arrived at Constantinople in Oct. 590 (v. 16. 6).

[14] Cf. Evagrius vi. 17, p. 234. 11.

[15] Singara had in fact been captured by Maurice in 578 (iii. 16. 2).

[16] Summer 591.

[17] There is no word for 'measures' in the Greek, and it is difficult to see what unit of length has been omitted, since Ammodius is about 5 miles, 1⅓ parasangs, or 40 stades, to the south of Dara. A possible solution to the problem is that Theophylact, or his source John of Epiphania, carelessly substituted '14' for '40' and omitted 'stades'.

and the circumstances a just purpose. The location requires daring; the cause proclaims piety and rejects tyrant-loving outrage. So, be allies worthy of the fight, for you are returning to enemy territory where victory is exceedingly glorious and the weight of the other fortune is also told. (6) Further, the engagement is the occasion for great glory and is the beginning of famous action, since all the nations of the world are inscribing your story in their minds. The enterprise is renowned, the campaign memorable, the contests immortal: trophies are not escorted to tombs of oblivion. (7) Therefore it is advantageous to contend in suffering everything or to throw away your bodies with glory. If you are victorious, this will be the limit of your labours, this will be the entry of peace. Do not be robbed of wounds, lest as punishment you lose salvation. Draw blows to your breasts, so that you may also embrace triumphs. (8) Let no one receive a scar on his back: the back is incapable of seeing victory. In the contest be united in spirit more than in body, comrades in toils but not in cowardice. Let him who has not taken up the inheritance of danger be disowned. In death reach out for victory. Trophies are bought with wounds and blows. Sloth provides no glory. (9) There is nothing sweeter than death in war, for if there is no advantage in growing old and being struck down by wasting disease, assuredly it is more appropriate for you heroes to die in the battle-line while you are young, reaping glory for your tombs. For nature is unable to make fugitives immortal. (10) Let the body not fear to be stripped of life.[18] Life has not found a place free from destruction. Nothing in the present world is a stranger to sorrow. Everything is mingled with grief. A most tyrannical necessity governs human life. (11) Do not be amazed that a brief allotted time enriches life's boundary, and that great scope is provided by it, which gives authority to ease while men stray after pleasures.[19]

(12) 'Be brave in spirit, rejoicing at the change of events. For the king of Babylon has come among us, led in slavery together with Persia's fortune, and along with his body he has all but handed over to us his power as well, making religious piety the summit of his hopes. (13) The Persians do not welcome the tyranny. Baram is seated on faithless altars, for he is not endowed with royal birth. Therefore, since he has encompassed the foundation of his power with laws of insolence, he will soon be overthrown. For violence is incapable of

[18] A negative has to be added to de Boor's text.
[19] De Boor suspected corruption in the last phrase, whose grammar is deficient and sense unclear.

existence without contention. (14) Lay up these things, recorded in
unformed letters, in the storehouses of your heart, and let not the purport of my speech be poured away and scattered to the winds, lest you
may be assigned shame which is more grievous than failure. (15) May
you have as guide of your campaign the Chief General of the Host of
the Lord, the only-begotten Son of God, the God before the ages who
grants you conclusions more auspicious than your hopes.'

(5. 1) So, when he had cast these words upon the ears of the forces,
the Roman throng was filled with a divine inspiration; fortifying their
eagerness with irresistible strength, they were in a frenzy to proceed
thereafter to the decisive action itself, being whipped up for combat by
a prudent madness. For even the power of words can scorn death.
(2) Then they departed from there and moved forward. Chosroes'
bodyguard was drawn from the Romans, since the protection of his
fellow countrymen did not gain his confidence. (3) And so Domitianus returned to the Roman empire, after confirming Narses as commander of the campaign; the army pitched camp near the river
Mygdon. (4) Sarames preceded the army, gathered stores of provisions, and prepared sufficient food for the requirements of the allies.
On the third day the Romans reached the Tigris itself and for the time
being delayed any further advance, while they awaited the Roman
forces in Armenia.[20] (5) But Chosroes, after marshalling in good order
one thousand of his personal guards, commanded them to cross the
river and seek out what was the strength of the opposing force. (6) And
so these forded the river and came to the river Zab; on hearing that
Bryzakios, who had been sent by Baram with a considerable force to
spy on the Roman approach, was camped in the vicinity, they marched
on him, attacked suddenly in the first watch of the night, won the
battle, and captured Bryzakios, whose ears and nose they chopped off
with a cleaver and sent to Chosroes the king.

(7) Chosroes was greatly elated at the good fortune of his attack;
after discovering the intentions of the enemy, he incited the commander of the Roman force not to squander the opportunity which was
offering them invincible success. (8) For this reason, the forces
crossed the stream[21] and entrenched their camp at the place known as

[20] The army would have reached the Tigris in the vicinity of the modern
Fechkhabour, 60 miles east of Nisibis. The contingent from Armenia (cf. v. 8. 6-7) was
probably meant to march through Azerbaijan, where more support could be collected,
and then across the Zagros mountains, so that Baram would have to turn his attention to
two different threats.

[21] i.e. to the east bank of the Tigris.

Dinabadon, where Chosroes feasted the Roman and Median leaders. When the dinner was already in progress, Bryzakios was led in chains into the middle, with his nose and ears mutilated. (9) After he had been the victim of the diners' jests, the king, as though favouring the banqueters with a memorable dinner-time spectacle, in an unspoken injunction commanded his attendant bodyguards with a gesture of the hand, and put this man to death: for it is not the custom for Persians to speak while feasting. (10) And so they stabbed Bryzakios and killed him as they had been ordered. Then, after bloodshed too had been blended with the meal, Chosroes gave a concluding pleasure to those at table: for after drenching them with perfume, he wreathed them with flowery crowns, and ordered them to drink to victory. (11) And so those who had been entertained at the banquet departed to their own tents, describing everything which had befallen them during the feast; and Bryzakios was the centrepiece of the articulation of their story.

(6. 1) On the morrow Chosroes the king and the allies crossed the river Zab. But Mebodes the Persian, who had been sent to Singara, advanced on Babylonia; on approaching the royal cities, he sent to the overseer of the royal treasury a message that he should prepare a great supply of food and set aside a suitable grant of money, since the allied forces were converging on him in large numbers; and that death would be the punishment for sloth. (2) And so the man invested with care of the treasury showed Mebodes' letter to the comptroller of the royal treasures, who had been left by Baram at the capital. (3) But the latter's spirits were dismayed, and in the middle of the night he collected his soldiers, left Seleucia, and went to Ctesiphon. (4) It is said that the Seleucus called Nicator constructed Seleucia between the two rivers,[22] one of which, the Tigris, discharges its full flow into the Persian sea, while the Euphrates is divided into three on reaching this region and, losing its own name, is called by different appellations. (5) One of its offshoots disappears after being dissected, as it were, into great channels and ditches: this is also what makes that particular region very fruitful. The second branch flows on into Babylonia and spreads over the Assyrian marshes to form a lake. (6) The third flows through the vicinity of Seleucia and empties into the Tigris, providing impregnable security

---

[22] For the foundation of Seleucia, cf. Strabo xvi. 1. 5 and Pliny *NH* vi. 30. 122. Seleucia itself was abandoned during the third century AD, being superseded by the adjacent new foundation on the west bank of the Tigris, Veh Ardashir (see J. M. Fiey, *Sumer* 23 (1967), 7-8); Theophylact's Seleucia is probably Veh Ardashir.

for the town, since it fortifies the city with its pools of water, as if with a rampart's garland.[23]

(7) On the second day, after Mebodes had heard that Seleucia was unguarded, he approached it by night, ordering the Romans to give the battle-cry and talk in their native tongue, and to strike with the sword indiscriminately and at random anyone they encountered. (8) And so the inhabitants of Seleucia were stricken by irresistible fear and willingly surrendered the city to Mebodes. As a result, extraordinary confusion prevailed, so that even Ctesiphon was affected by the panic, and a rumour reached the barbarians living in the adjoining city that Seleucia had been captured by a Roman army. (9) Then, in their terror they held a mass assembly, and without argument determined to surrender to the Romans. And so he left his refuge in that place and came to nearby Antioch,[24] which Chosroes son of Kabades had constructed after capturing Syrian Antioch, and to which he apparently transplanted the latter's population.[25] (10) After occupying Ctesiphon, Mebodes took charge of the royal treasures, and proclaimed and heralded Chosroes as king, as if he were present. Ctesiphon is the greatest royal capital in Persia. It is said that the emperor Justinian provided Chosroes son of Kabades with Greek marble, building experts, and craftsmen skilled in ceilings, and that a palace situated close to Ctesiphon was constructed for Chosroes with Roman expertise.[26] (11) And so the barbarians who inhabited Babylonia, eager for change, preferred Chosroes' cause. But Mebodes sent a message to Persian Antioch written in Roman script. The letter ran as follows,

[23] For a map which marks the major canals in this area, see J. Newman, *The Agricultural Life of the Jews of Babylonia* (London, 1932), frontispiece. The third of Theophylact's offshoots of the Euphrates is the Nahr Malka canal, which emptied into the Tigris a few miles below Veh Ardashir. In this part of Theophylact's narrative, there are several short digressions on points of antiquarian interest, geography, and ethnography (cf. v. 6. 10-11, 7. 7-9). These were no doubt intended to suggest that Theophylact had conducted special research to enhance his narrative, but it is perhaps more likely that the information was merely lifted from John of Epiphania, whose participation in an embassy to Ctesiphon would have given him some experience of conditions in lower Mesopotamia.

[24] This must refer to Baram's treasurer, who had crossed to the east of the Tigris on hearing of Mebodes' approach (v. 6. 2-3).

[25] For Chosroes I's capture of Antioch in 540, see Procopius, *Wars* ii. 8-9. On the New, or Better, Antioch, located on the east bank of the Tigris to the south of Ctesiphon, see Fiey, *Sumer* 23 (1967), 25-8.

[26] There is no evidence to corroborate Theophylact's account of Justinian's gift to Chosroes, and it is possible that both materials and craftsmen had actually been captured by Chosroes at Antioch, where marble was included amongst the booty plundered from a church (Procopius, *Wars* ii. 9. 15-16).

word for word: for I consider it right that the exposition of the actual arrangement of the words should be set forth exactly as it was.

(7. 1) 'Romans, believers in Christ Jesus our Lord, send greetings to the inhabitants of Persian Antioch. We have not accepted this labour either in obedience to the emperor's commands or swayed by Chosroes' promises, but we have come to this land in order to rescue from the entrails of Persia you who have grown old in misery. (2) Therefore, so that our objective may achieve fulfilment and your yearning, brothers, may result in joy, surrender to us those who have fled to your city of Antioch and those who support Baram's cause. For we wish you to know that if you disregard this point you will not have occasion to bless the outcome.'

(3) So, when this letter had been delivered to the inhabitants of Antioch and had become public knowledge, the people of the city came together, arrested the man,[27] and handed him over to the man sent by Mebodes, along with those who had gladly accepted Baram's cause. (4) But Mebodes, after learning in detail about his opponents' affairs from the prisoners, tortured their commander and mutilated him by cutting off his nose and ears; he sent him to Chosroes, while he consigned the others to the jaws of the sword. (5) On the sixth day he condemned to death and killed with the sword many Jews who had been closely involved in Baram's revolution. (6) For the support which Baram had received from the Jews for his usurpation had not been inconsiderable. For at that time there was living in Persia a large number of the said race, who had abundant wealth.[28] (7) For after the capture of Jerusalem by the emperor Vespasian and the burning of the temple, many of the Jews, shrinking from Roman might, migrated from Palestine to the Medes and returned to their primal nurse,[29] whence their forefather Abraham had in fact come. (8) Then these people, by trading in valuables and journeying across the Red Sea, had

---

[27] This again (cf. v. 6. 9) must refer to Baram's treasurer.

[28] On the Jewish communities of Persia, see Newman, op. cit., and G. Widengren, 'The Status of the Jews in the Sassanian Empire', *Iranica Antiqua* 1 (1961), 117-62. Widengren (p. 147) suggested that the Jews might have supported Baram because Hormisdas had closed the Jewish teaching institutions at Sura and Pumbaditha.

[29] In the MSS μεταναστεύουσι(ν), 'migrated', is used for both verbs; we have adopted de Boor's suggestion of παλιννοστοῦσι, 'returned', for the second. There were substantial communities of Jews in lower Mesopotamia long before Jerusalem was sacked by Vespasian and Titus in AD 70, indeed from the sack of Jerusalem by Nebuchadnezzar in 586 BC. Josephus *AJ* xviii. 371-9 records the troubles of the Jewish community in Seleucia, where more than 50,000 Jews were massacred in about AD 39. Theophylact says that the Jews 'returned to their primal nurse' because Abram had come from Ur of the Chaldees (Gen. 11: 26-31).

through financial transactions invested themselves with great wealth. Hence they were most ready to slide towards the revolts and conflagrations of the people of Babylonia. (9) For they are a wicked and most untrustworthy race, trouble-loving and tyrannical, utterly forgetful of friendship, jealous and envious, most immutable and implacable in enmity.[30] (10) So Mebodes subdued these and handed them over to a variety of deaths. So, when he had gained control of the capitals, he made a selection of the more valuable adornments and dispatched the choicest to Chosroes.

And so the Romans and Persians with Chosroes arrived at the place called Alexandriana in four days. (11) The place had obtained its name from the actions of Alexander of Macedon, for the son of Philip had gone there with his Macedonian force and Greek allies, razed a very strong fortress, and slaughtered the barbarians in it.[31] (8. 1) Then, moving from there, the Romans and Persians on the second day invaded the region called Chnaithas.[32] At first light on the next day Narses, the commander of the eastern contingents, dispatched Comentiolus, brigadier of the right wing of the army, with one thousand horse to secure in advance the crossing of the second river Zab.[33] (2) When this had happened, those sent out on reconnaissance by Baram learned of the deed, returned to Baram, and reported these facts to him. But Baram tried to secure prior control of the next bridge.[34] (3) He fostered his hopes with the encouragement that the Roman contingent in Armenia would not be able to join up with the Roman eastern forces on account of the difficulty of the terrain.[35] (4) On the fourth day Narses captured men dispatched on reconnaissance by Baram and, after interrogating them to the utmost under the lash, discovered the nature of his enemy's intentions. Next, he gave an adequate force to Rufinus, son of Timostratus, and then ordered him to appropriate the other crossings. (5) On the following day, in the

[30] This brief tirade reflects the anti-Jewish feeling prevalent in the Roman empire during Heraclius' reign, after the Jews had collaborated with invading Persian armies; cf. A. Sharf, 'Byzantine Jewry in the Seventh Century', *BZ* 48 (1955), 103-15.

[31] Alexandriana should most probably be identified with Arbela, where Alexander captured the royal Persian treasures after the battle of Gaugamela in 331 BC (Arrian, *Anabasis* iii. 15. 5).

[32] The army was continuing to move in a south-easterly direction.

[33] i.e. the Lesser Zab; Narses was probably now advancing east towards the modern Koi Sanjaq, which is situated on the Lesser Zab.

[34] This bridge probably crossed one of the tributaries of the Lesser Zab in the vicinity of Koi Sanjaq.

[35] The two Roman armies were separated by the Zagros mountains.

first watch after nightfall, the general set out, took possession of the crossings,[36] and suddenly invaded the territory of the Nanisenes.[37] At midday Baram's men, who had seen these events, reported them to the tyrant. (6) But he, now that he had failed in his objective, separated his forces towards the north and east in order to cut off the amalgamation with the Roman force expected from Armenia.[38] Baram was already accomplishing the journey with some alacrity and had arrived at a certain lake on his route,[39] when it happened that the contingent from Armenia appeared in close proximity. (7) When the Roman scouts espied Baram's army, they sent a message to the general John that Persian cavalry squadrons were apparently moving against them. And so John arranged his forces in battle-array, while Bindoes took charge of the Persian phalanx; the Roman disposition was commanded by the general John. (8) A river separated Baram from the Roman and Persian forces with John, and prevented them from engagement. On the second day the Roman troops along with Bindoes turned away towards the south.[40]

(9) And so Narses and Chosroes set out from the territory of the Nanisenes and, moving forwards, reached the vicinity of a certain village called Siraganon by its inhabitants.[41] On the fifth day Narses discovered that the Roman reinforcements from Armenia were nearby. (10) For this reason he dispatched couriers to John, and instructed the general that he must not engage the Persians until the two forces had joined up together and made their strength invincible. (9. 1) While Chosroes was encamped at this very place, the messengers sent by Mebodes came before the king with their announcement of glad

[36] The various 'crossings' referred to in this passage are rather confusing, and Theophylact himself is most unlikely to have known exactly what was happening. It appears that Baram had been trying to encircle Narses' army somewhere in the area drained by the Lesser Zab and its tributaries; this decisive action by Rufinus enabled Narses to extricate himself from the trap.

[37] If the territory of the Nanisenes is to be located in the vicinity of Rowanduz, as is probable, this would indicate that Narses had abandoned his southward march and returned north to cross the Zagros range by the route that ran from Rowanduz across the Keli Shin pass.

[38] Although the Greek would suggest that Baram disengaged his troops separately towards both north and east, it emerges from the subsequent narrative that he moved his whole army north-east from the Lesser Zab to Azerbaijan.

[39] Lake Urmiah in Azerbaijan.

[40] The two armies probably faced each other across the river Tatavi, which flows into the southern end of Lake Urmiah, with John's army on the east bank and Baram's on the west. Thereafter John would have moved south to outflank Baram in an attempt to advance towards Narses and Chosroes.

[41] This march brought Narses and Chosroes to the vicinity of Lake Urmiah.

tidings. (2) And so, after he had learned of Mebodes' actions in Babylonia and had received the royal trappings sent to him from Ctesiphon, he joyfully exulted in the restoration of his affairs and publicized his success to Narses and the Roman forces. (3) On the fifth day, and after three encampments, the Roman army united with John's divisions.[42] And so the forces, by coming together in one body, mutually gave themselves and received in return great strength. (4) It is said that Chosroes brought with him more than sixty thousand soldiers, including the allies, whereas the battle was knit by Baram with forty thousand men.

(5) Now indeed Baram planned to steal the victory and to burst upon the Roman force by night, but the difficulty of the terrain provided an impediment to his attack, at sunrise he became visible to the Romans, and his trick was brought into the open. (6) At the third hour Baram's troops, eager for battle, advanced with shouting and clamour, while the Romans were directed to the engagement in disciplined silence and without noise. Narses was angry with the generals Bindoes and Sarames, who were unable to calm their barbarian forces into untroubled quiet. (7) Then the Romans also shared their own discipline with the barbarian allied forces, and persuaded them to arrange their formation in order and refrain from foolish clamour. (8) Accordingly the Roman army was arranged in three divisions; the central section was controlled by Chosroes and Narses, the right by the Persians Mebodes and Sarames,[43] who led the Median phalanx, and the other by the general John, the commander of the troops from Armenia. Their opponents too were in fact drawn up in the same way, and were likewise arranged in three divisions. (9) Now the Roman army was restless in its resolve and unrestrained in aggression, whereas their opponents were dismayed by the strength, number, and order of the Romans, and withdrew to the mountain slopes. For this reason five hundred of Baram's company laid down their arms and went over to the Romans. (10) And so Chosroes, who was by nature fiery in action,[44] urged the Romans to advance towards the hillsides. But in their prudence the Romans consigned this very idea to the bosom of folly, they did not disperse at all from their ordered cohesion, and by other means they deferred the advance towards the

[42] The armies probably united a short distance to the south of Lake Urmiah.
[43] Mebodes was still in lower Mesopotamia, and the name must be a mistake for Bindoes.
[44] We have translated Bernhardy's conjecture αἴθων, 'fiery', for the MSS ἄκων, 'involuntary', which gives no sense.

mountain heights. (11) But the barbarians were compelled by their
own king to grapple with the foolish risks, and were soundly routed
by their opponents when they dared to climb the mountain. The
enterprise would have been punished with severe losses if the
Romans had not checked the barbarian pursuit by deploying themselves to confront them.[45] (12) The sun had already declined towards
its setting when Baram retired to his camp with his allied force,
gratified by these achievements, while the Romans, on coming to
their camp, denounced Chosroes' folly.

(10. 1) When Baram realized that the Romans were extremely
aggrieved at Chosroes' recent interfering orders to them while they
were at a peak of eagerness for confrontation, he broke camp at daybreak and retired towards difficult country, which was steep and
unsuitable for cavalry. (2) So, after this, he came to the plain which
extended nearby, where the city of Canzacon is situated;[46] Baram
moved camp and from there led his forces elsewhere, planning
thereby to shake off Roman aggression. (3) But on discovering
Baram's move, the Romans moved camp very close to the enemy by
forced marching; then they approached the river Blarathos,[47] where
they encamped for the night, and when day came they reached a
broad plain. (4) And so the Roman generals marshalled their troops,
instilled in the soldiers many good instructions, and prepared for
battle in triple formation. The Romans provided a password for their
barbarian allies as well, teaching them the name of the Virgin
Mother of God, lest they might kill their allies as enemies because of
the difference in race, since in the confusion of battle those on their
own side would present an indistinguishable aspect. (5) And a
strange event occurred, for the saving name of Mary came to the
Chaldaeans as well.[48] Baram arranged his own strength in three contingents, the tyrant controlling the centre of the line, while the commanders of the allies held the force on either side. (6) Then indeed
he arranged for elephants, the Indian beasts, to be led forward as a
sort of bulwark for the cavalry, and he mounted the bravest of his
fighting force on the beasts and prepared to fight. Neither side was

---

[45] In this section Theophylact uses 'barbarian' first to denote the Romans' Persian
allies and then their Persian opponents, which causes some confusion.

[46] Baram has now retreated about 60 miles south-east of Lake Urmiah.

[47] Baram has continued south from the plain of Canzacon to the valley of the river
Saruk (Blarathos).

[48] The Roman battle-cry was probably 'Ave Maria'.

without its share of these beasts as allies.[49] (7) Now Chosroes reviewed the ranks, protected by a guard of five hundred men. But when the two forces had gazed at one another and been gazed at in turn, the standards were raised and were gently upheld by the breeze, the trumpets whirled and whipped up the engagement as they boomed abroad these mysteries of war; finally, the middle ground was cut anew and bereft of its proper bounds. (8) Then when the engagement came to close quarters, Baram forsook the centre of his force and moved to the left. Then he contributed great strength to those who received him, and, as one might expect, devastated the opposing division in a sudden thrust with a massed array. (9) And so the Romans on this side were scattered and turned to flight, since they could not endure the weight of the opposing force. Therefore, when Narses saw this, he ordered troops to commingle quietly with the weakened men and stopped the flight of the enfeebled force. (10) And so Baram attacked the centre of the Roman might and tried to turn Narses to flight. Then Narses, without being in the least concerned about the elephants, stoutly resisted Baram, charged the middle of the opposing force, and completely disrupted the cohesion of the Median formation. (11) After this action, the rest of Baram's forces faltered, while with victorious strength Narses cast the cavalry from their mounts and felled the infantry with the spear. (12) Then, as the pursuit became fierce and slaughter blossomed on the field, six thousand Babylonian fugitives came to a certain hillock in a bid for salvation; but the Romans encompassed the hillock and overpowered the fleeing force. Then they took many prisoners and led them in chains to Chosroes. (13) And so the Persian king handed over some to the jaws of the sword, while others he presented as toys for the feet of the beasts.[50] When he had learned that some of the captives were of the Turkish race, he sent them to the emperor Maurice to publicize Roman strength and offer the emperor first-fruits of victory. (14) On their foreheads was inscribed the sign of the Lord's passion, which is called a cross by the ministers of the Christian religion. So the emperor enquired what was the meaning of this mark on the barbarians. (15) And so they declared that they had been assigned this by their mothers: for when a fierce plague was endemic among the eastern Scythians, it was fated

---

[49] This sentence probably means that both flanks of Baram's army were protected by elephants, rather than that both armies had elephants, since the Romans are unlikely to have been able to provide Chosroes with fighting elephants.

[50] i.e. of elephants, probably those captured from Baram (v. 11. 2).

that some Christians[51] advised that the foreheads of the young be
tattooed with this very sign. The barbarians in no way rejected the
advice, and they obtained salvation from the counsel.

(11. 1) But the Romans (for I would redirect my account towards its
goal), took as booty the tyrant's tent, wives, children, gold ornaments,
and royal trappings. And so they gave the more valuable items to Chosroes, but he gloried in the spoils and proceeded to greater arrogance.
(2) When the sun declined, the Romans observed that the barbarians
seated on the elephants were hurling missiles and using their bows.
Therefore they encircled these, won a second battle, captured the
beasts, and handed them over to Chosroes. (3) Then, after the battle
had been brought to such a conclusion, the Romans returned to their
own camp, as night was apparently already rising over them. On the
next day, the Roman army assembled at dawn and despoiled the
corpses of the slain. (4) Then, after acquiring great riches, they went to
Chosroes' royal tent. The commanders of the Roman army marshalled
ten thousand men to track down Baram, appointing as their brigadier
the commander of the divisions from Chalcis;[52] they gave the barbarian
allies to Bestam. (5) Then, after camping on the battlefield for three
days, Chosroes and the Romans withdrew on the fourth, because they
could smell the corpses and were unable to endure the choking stench.
So they came to the vicinity of the city of Canzacon. (6) Chosroes the
king, priding himself on these felicitous events, held a victory-feast for
the Romans; he remained on his couch, enjoying the music of strings
and flutes, as is the custom in Persian victory celebrations. (7) He
lingered in the place until the tenth day; when he learned that Marinus
and Bestam had returned to him from the pursuit of Baram, and he
realized that the rout of his enemies was unmistakable, he directed the
Romans back to their country, while he gathered the Persian contingent and entered Babylonia, having shown utter disrespect to his
Roman allies. (8) And so the Roman generals expounded[53] a spoken
moral to the barbarian, that he should not forget the kindness and
salvation which he had received from the Romans. Then, after depositing such words with him, the Romans returned homewards. (9) But

---

[51] These Christians were probably Nestorian missionaries, whose activities in this
period extended from Persia along the trade routes to China.

[52] The sentence may be defective, since ταξιάρχας, 'brigadiers', is in fact in the
plural; the commander of the Chalcis troops is probably the Marinus who is mentioned
below (v. 11. 7), and his name should perhaps be inserted at this point.

[53] We have translated de Boor's suggestion διεξῇεσαν for the nonsensical ἐξῇεσαν of
the MSS.

Chosroes, in fear that an assassination might perhaps be organized against him by his countrymen, asked the emperor Maurice to send a thousand of the army for the protection of his person.

(12. 1) A story has reached us that Golinduch came to Hierapolis at that time, during the return of Chosroes to his kingdom.[54] But let it be declared of the woman, in the poet's words, 'who and whence';[55] for indeed let us not exclude the story about her which is adorned with the greatest glories. (2) Now this woman was born in Babylonia of the race of the magi; her father was a distinguished satrap who levied Persian taxes. When she reached her prime, of the age which is bright for marriage, he gave her away to a prominent man. (3) Once, when she was dining with her husband, it seemed that she suddenly became paralysed, next her body remained motionless, and sensation somehow returned to her much later. When the witnesses of the suffering, if indeed this divine ecstasy should be represented as suffering, enquired what it was that had befallen the young woman, she replied as follows: (4) 'Great indeed are the punishments I have seen stored up on our threshold, and a luxuriance of great blessings ministered to those who adore the greatest God, whose worship by the Christians is established as a subject for mockery among the Persians.' (5) Now her husband derided his wife's words, but when indeed he realized that her resolve to change her religion was unshakeable, he decided to thrash her to her senses; he even threatened that she would be punished with death, as it is customary for the Persians to do to those who reject the doctrines of the magi.[56] (6) And so divine love gave wings to her mind, she sealed her ears as it were, and let his words be scattered on the winds. Then, there also came to the woman an illumination of another and greater divine manifestation; (7) for an angel, brighter than radiance in form and raiment, stood before her, once again revealed to her the vision of the future, and predicted her husband's imminent death. (8) And so the woman's husband laid down his life in accordance with the angel's prophecy, while the woman departed from Babylonia and came to

---

[54] A *Life* of Golinduch, composed (probably in Syriac) by Stephen, bishop of Hierapolis, survives in a Georgian version, which is translated and discussed by G. Garitte, *AB* 74 (1956), 405-40; a highly rhetorical Greek adaptation of this *Life* by the presbyter Eustratius also survives, see P. Peeters, *AB* 62 (1944), 74-125. Theophylact's version is considerably closer to the tradition of the *Life* by Stephen than to Eustratius' adaptation. Theophylact's information about Golinduch may have been lifted from John of Epiphania, who could have consulted Stephen's *Life* directly; T. Olajos, *Acta Antiqua et Archaeologica* 1 (1978), 7-38, suggested instead that Theophylact used a Greek translation of Stephen's *Life*.   [55] Homer, *Odyssey* xv. 423, etc.

[56] Although Christianity was generally tolerated in Persia, proselytism was forbidden.

Nisibis, where she encountered the Christian priests and confessed the greatness of the Spirit.[57] (9) So they initiated her into these truly divine and ineffable doctrines of the Christians; when this was revealed to the magi, they went in search of the woman. (10) So they came to Nisibis and in flattery made preparations more elevated than her rank, attempting thereby to lead the female astray; but when they were defeated and their speech was ineffectual, they locked up the woman for a long time in a harsh prison.[58] (11) Then, since God oversees all things and at no time leaves himself without a witness, with the assistance of the guardian angel she departed from the prison and came to the land of the Romans.[59] (12) And so, journeying as far as Jerusalem, she proclaimed the manifest and indescribable greatness of God; after offering up prayers at the most holy tomb of the great God, even our Saviour Jesus Christ, and venerating with adoration the cross of the passion, she returned to Hierapolis. (13) She made many predictions about what would befall Chosroes, and revealed his approach to the Romans before the commencement of the events.[60] After conducting her life like an angel and arranging the considerations of soul and body as befits the saints,[61] she departed from this world,[62] binding on with undefiled triumphs the crown of endurance.

(13. 1) The Roman emperor dispatched bodyguards to Chosroes. Then the Persian king called to mind the decisive assistance which he had received from above,[63] and he dispatched as a gift to Sergius,[64]

[57] The presence of the Nestorian theological school made Nisibis one of the most important centres for Christianity in Persia. On Nisibis, and the numerous monasteries in its vicinity, see J. M. Fiey, *Nisibe, métropole syriaque orientale et ses suffragants des origines à nos jours* (*CSCO* subsidia 54, Louvain, 1977). Georgius of Izala was another noble Persian who moved to Nisibis after conversion to Christianity (J. Labourt, *Le christianisme dans l'empire perse* (Paris, 1904), 224-9).

[58] In the castle of Oblivion, according to the *Lives*.

[59] According to the *Lives*, Golinduch was led out from prison to execution, but an angel saved her from death. She, however, insisted that her head be chopped off, so that she should not be deprived of martyrdom; it was then reattached to her body, and thereafter she was known as the living martyr.

[60] At Hierapolis, Golinduch met Domitianus, when he was preparing for an embassy to Persia before Hormisdas' death (this embassy is not mentioned by Theophylact), and predicted the imminent overthrow of Hormisdas and the flight to the Romans of Chosroes; subsequently she met both Domitianus and Chosroes, during the latter's flight, and made various predictions. See the Georgian *Life* 17 (*AB* 74 (1956), 438-9).

[61] The word 'arranging' has been supplied, in accordance with de Boor's suggestion that διαθεῖσα, or a similar word, has fallen out of the text.

[62] On 13 July 591, see Peeters, *AB* 62 (1944), 74.   [63] Cf. v. 1. 7-2. 1.

[64] Evagrius vi. 21, pp. 235. 11, 236. 14-16, states that the offerings were first sent to Gregory of Antioch, who dedicated them to Sergius only after Maurice had been consulted.

most glorious among martyrs, a gem-studded cross made of gold,
(2) the one which Chosroes the son of Kabades, when he reduced the
city, had taken as booty and deposited in the palace of the Persians,
while the emperor Justinian was still in control of the Roman
sceptres.[65] So on this cross, Chosroes fashioned at its head another
cross of pure gold and inscribed on it the reason for the offering.
(3) He sent a letter written in Greek characters to the Barbaricon, as it
is called,[66] along with the treasure, and the letter was also signed with
the royal seal. The contents of the letter were in fact in the following
terms, for I will not alter the original wording:[67]

(4) 'This cross I, Chosroes, king of kings, son of Chosroes, when we
departed to Romania on account of the devilish operations and
wickedness of the most ill-starred Baram son of Bargusnas[68] and of his
associate cavaliers, and on account of the coming of the ill-starred
Zadesprates from the army towards Nisibis for the seduction of the
cavaliers of the district of Nisibis to rebellion and complicity in revolution, we also sent cavaliers with an officer to Charcha, (5) and
through the fortune of the most holy and renowned St Sergius, when
we heard that he was the granter of petitions, in the first year of our
reign, on the seventh of January, we petitioned that if our cavaliers
should kill or defeat Zadesprates, we would send a gold-bejewelled
cross to his shrine because of his most holy name. (6) And on the
ninth of February they brought before us the head of Zadesprates. So,
since we were successful in our petition, because each part was unambiguous, to his most holy name the cross which came from us, together
with the cross sent to his shrine by Justinian, emperor of the Romans,
which was brought here in time of estrangement between the two

---

[65] This cross must have been among the treasures which the inhabitants of Sergiopolis had given Chosroes in 542 in their attempt to buy off his attack (Procopius, *Wars* ii.
20. 7); Chosroes had still attacked the city but, *contra* Theophylact, failed to capture it
(Procopius, *Wars* ii. 20. 12-16).

[66] This must be part of the shrine of Sergius.

[67] Chosroes' votive offerings to Sergius are also recorded verbatim by Evagrius vi. 21,
pp. 235. 18-238. 12. There are only very minor differences between the versions in
Evagrius and Theophylact, and these were explained by M. J. Higgins, 'Chosroes II's
Votive Offerings at Sergiopolis', *BZ* 48 (1955), 89-102 (cf. also Allen, *Evagrius* 259-61) by
the fact that Evagrius was transcribing the actual inscriptions from the dedications (cf.
Evagrius vi. 21, pp. 235. 16-17, 236. 18-19), whereas Theophylact's account ultimately
derived from the letters sent by Chosroes to accompany the gifts. The language of the
letters is formal and unusual, the grammar is loose, and Theophylact's claim to have
presented an accurate report is not unjustified.

[68] Baram was son of Bahrām-Gušnasp (see Justi, *Iranisches Namenbuch* 363 s.v.
Wereþraghna no. 23). Evagrius' version of the name is less accurate.

states by Chosroes our father, king of kings, son of Koades,[69] and which was discovered in our treasuries, we have sent to the shrine of the most holy Sergius.'

(7) And so the satrap delivered the cross and the king's letter according to his instructions. In the following year the Persian king proclaimed as queen Seirem, who was of Roman birth and Christian religion,[70] and of an age blossoming for marriage, slept with her, and thereby debased the customs of the Babylonians. (14. 1) In the third year he entreated Sergius,[71] the most efficacious in Persia, that a child by Seirem be granted to him. Shortly afterwards this came to pass for him,[72] and once again he naturally honoured his benefactor with gifts. Using Greek expression he dispatched a letter; the letter was as follows, word for word:

(2) 'To the great martyr Sergius, Chosroes, king of kings. I, Chosroes, king of kings, son of Chosroes, have dispatched the gifts accompanying the patten not for the sight of men, nor so that the greatness of your most holy name may be known from my words, but because the truth about events has been recognized as well as the many favours and benefactions which I had from you: for it is my good fortune that my name should be carried on your holy vessels. (3) During the time when I was in Berthamaïs,[73] I petitioned of you, holy one, to come to my aid and that Seirem conceive in her womb. And since Seirem is a Christian and I a pagan, our law does not grant us freedom to have a Christian wife. (4) So on account of my gratitude to you, for this reason I disregarded the law, and I held and hold from day to day this one among my wives as legitimate, and thus I resolved now to beseech your goodness that she conceive in her womb. (5) And I petitioned and ordained that if Seirem should conceive in her womb, I would

---

[69] i.e. Kabades, the form of the name which Evagrius vi. 21, p. 236. 11, uses. Although Chosroes' message states that Justinian had dedicated the cross, Evagrius observed that it had in fact been dedicated by Justinian's wife Theodora (vi. 21, p. 235. 13-14).

[70] Seirem (or Sirin, in the vulgate MSS and Evagrius) was in fact Aramaic by race, a Christian from Huzistan, who was one of the most influential supporters of the Monophysites in Persia. *Anon. Guidi* 5 records that Chosroes had a second Christian wife called Maria the Roman (a story which was subsequently embroidered, so that Maria became Maurice's daughter, see Tabari, p. 283).

[71] In the third year after Chosroes' return, i.e. in 593/4; see Higgins, *BZ* 47 (1955), 90-2.

[72] *Anon. Guidi* 8 records that Shirin (Seirem) conceived and gave birth to a son, Merdanshah, after Gabriel of Sinjar, a Christian doctor at the royal court, had let blood from her arm.

[73] The area of Beth Aramaye in lower Mesopotamia; the vulgate MSS and Evagrius give the reading Βερααμαῖς, which was wrongly introduced into the revised edition of de Boor's text.

send to your most holy shrine the cross that she wears. And with regard to this both I and Seirem have this purpose, that we should have possession of this cross in remembrance of your name, holy one. (6) And we have resolved that for its value, although this does not extend beyond four thousand three hundred standard *miliaresia*, five thousand standard coins should be dispatched in its place.[74] (7) And from the time when I had the said petition in my mind and made these calculations until the time we came to Rhesonchosron, ten more days did not elapse and you, holy one, not because I am worthy but because of your goodness, you appeared to me in a dream at night and thrice declared to me that Seirem had conceived in her womb. (8) And in the dream itself, I thrice answered you in return and said, "Thank you, thank you". And because of your holiness and charity, and because of your most holy name, and because you are the granter of petitions, from that day Seirem did not know what is customary for women. (9) I was in no doubt of this, but trusted in your words, even because you are holy and a true granter of petitions. After she did not experience womanly ways, from this I recognized the power of the vision and the truth of what you had spoken. (10) So straightway I sent the same cross and its value to your most holy shrine, giving orders that from its value one patten and one cup should be made for the sake of the divine mysteries, but indeed also that a cross, which is owed, be fixed on the honoured altar, and a solid gold censer and a Hunnic curtain adorned with gold;[75] (11) and that the remaining *miliaresia* are for your holy shrine, so that through your fortune, holy one, in all things, but especially in this petition, you may come to the assistance of myself and Seirem. And what has come to us through your intercession by the mercy of your goodness, may it also advance to completion at the wish of myself and Seirem, so that both I and Seirem and everyone in the world may have hope in your power and still trust in you.'

(12) Accordingly, the emissary quickly came to the shrine and placed the king's gift along with his message on the holy altar.

(15. 1) But Baram, who had not been subdued by Chosroes,

---

[74] The *miliarensis* was a Roman silver coin that had fallen out of use in the fifth century AD. It is used as a convenient synonym for the standard Persian silver coin, the dirham.

[75] Chosroes' letter now suggests that Seirem's cross was after all dispatched (contrary to § 5 above). On Sassanian silk textiles, which were famous for their richness of design and decoration, see D. Shepherd, *Cambridge History of Iran* iii (2). 1107-12. The description 'Hunnic' probably refers to the design on the curtain.

shook off[76] extreme peril. Therefore the Persian king committed to death all who had associated in the usurpation, and Bindoes himself he buried in the bowels of the Tigris, on the grounds that he had stretched forth his hands against the king.[77] (2) The treaty between Romans and Persians was made on equal terms,[78] and thus indeed that great Persian war was brought to a glorious conclusion for the Romans.

(3) But I will not overlook what Chosroes, who was well versed in the burdensome folly of the Chaldaeans concerning the stars, is said to have prophesied at the height of the war. (4) For when the renowned John, the general of the Armenian force, jeered at him on account of his lack of order,[79] and said that it was wrong for a king to be perverse in his ways and outlandish in the impulses of his heart, they say that the barbarian said to the general: (5) 'If we were not subject to the tyranny of the occasion, you would not have dared, general, to strike with insults the king who is great among mortals. But since you are proud in present circumstances, you shall hear what indeed the gods have provided for the future. (6) Be assured that troubles will flow back in turn against you Romans. The Babylonian race will hold the Roman state in its power for a threefold cyclic hebdomad of years. Thereafter you Romans will enslave Persians for a fifth hebdomad of years.[80] (7) When these very things have been accomplished, the day without evening will dwell among mortals and the expected fate will achieve power, when the forces of destruction will be handed over to dissolution and those of the better life hold sway.'[81]

[76] We have translated de Boor's suggestion ἀπεκρούσατο, 'shook off', rather than the MSS ὑπεκρούσατο, 'interrupted'.

[77] Baram was soon murdered in eastern Iran while trying to collect fresh forces. Bestam, who had been sent to oppose him, subsequently assumed the leadership of his troops on learning of Bindoes' death, and maintained a serious rebellion for ten years (see Sebeos, ch. 12, pp. 40-4 and Goubert, *Byzance avant l'Islam* i. 283-6). *Anon. Guidi* 4 records that Bindoes was crucified at Beth Lapat, after having his right arm and leg amputated.

[78] This is not strictly true, since the Romans, apart from regaining their lost cities of Dara and Martyropolis, also received a large part of Persian Armenia. The treaty was equal in the sense that there were no financial payments by either side.

[79] This probably refers to the occasion described at v. 9. 10-10. 1.

[80] This prediction refers to the events of the early 7th c., when the Persians defeated the Romans for approximately twenty-one years (a threefold cyclic hebdomad) and were then defeated by Heraclius in a campaign which lasted six years (until 628). The Roman victory is placed in the fifth hebdomad, presumably because the prophecy was reckoned to include one hebdomad of peace, which is not mentioned, but which preceded the three hebdomads of Persian conquests.

[81] This prophecy of a messianic Golden Age is similar to the apocalyptic promise in

(8) Not long afterwards Probus was invested with the high-priestly care of the city of the Chalcedonians, and apparently heard extraordinary things from Chosroes.[82] (9) For when the emperor Maurice dispatched this man to Chosroes at Ctesiphon, at high noon one day Chosroes had him summoned to the palace where, bathed in sweat, he demanded of the priest to see an image of the Mother of God. (10) So the priest, who carried with him her likeness on a tablet, granted a view of it to the Persian king. He worshipped the panel, and declared that its archetype had stood beside him and told him that the victories of Alexander of Macedon would be bestowed on him; and yet already Chosroes had received the return to his kingdom and overpowered the tyrants through the strength and power of the emperor.[83] (11) Probus also recounted with respect to Nineveh that there existed certain remnants of the tower whose construction men had undertaken in Babylon, and that its brickwork, in accordance with the account of the high priest Moses, was baked exceedingly carefully by fire.[84]

(12) But since in the construction of our narrative we have terminated as far as possible the theme of the Persian war, let the pen which navigates the books with ink again proceed to events in Europe, so that, anchoring in the harbour of its goal and carrying as cargo spectacular actions, it may complete the reports which are worthy of record.

(16. 1) When day had indeed but recently smiled on affairs in the east, not making her appearance mythically in the words of Homer from a barbarian bed, and rejecting the appellation rosy-fingered,

the Syriac *Christian Romance of Alexander* (ed. and tr. E. A. W. Budge in *The History of Alexander the Great* (Cambridge, 1889), 155, 158), a work that was revised in 629/30, soon after Heraclius' victory. Compare also the prediction for world rule by the Romans after the defeat of Persia in George of Pisidia, *Hexaemeron* 1845 ff. (*PG* 92. 1575). Golinduch also made apocalyptic prophecies in 590/91 (see the Georgian *Life*, *AB* 74 (1956), 439).

[82] The *Chron. Seert* 67 describes an embassy from Maurice to the Persians conducted by a bishop of Chalcedon named Marutha, who witnessed a miraculous cure effected by the Nestorian Catholicus Sabrisho (596-604). This embassy should probably be identified with Theophylact's. For further information about Probus, who had formerly been a Monophysite and had participated in doctrinal controversies, see A. Van Roey, 'Het Dossier van Proba en Juhannan Barboer', in E. Van Cauwenbergh (ed.), *Scrinium Lovaniense* (Louvain, 1961), 181-90, and Olajos, 'La carrière de Théophylacte', 44-5.
[83] Theophylact interprets the prophecy as foreshadowing the conquest of the east from the west (the exact replica of Alexander's victories), a success which Chosroes had already achieved with Maurice's help. Chosroes, however, perhaps intended the prophecy to convey a more general promise of extensive conquests, possibly in particular conquests of Egypt, Palestine, and Asia Minor (areas conquered by Alexander): hence, he may have publicized the prophecy to justify and corroborate his Near Eastern conquests in the early 7th c.
[84] i.e. the Tower of Babel (see Gen. 11, particularly v. 3).

since the sword was not actually reddened by bloodshed,[85] the emperor transferred his forces with all speed to Europe and prepared an expedition to Anchialus: for he had learned that the Avars were again wishing to roam abroad.[86] (2) Accordingly, since the barbarians were in fact expected, he marshalled himself in preparation. And so the more distinguished of the senators entreated that the Caesar appoint a general for the war, and that the imperial offensive gain deferment.[87] (3) When they did not persuade him, the leader of the high-priestly ranks[88] asked the emperor to stand down from command and to invest another with the conduct of the contest. When even this man's pleading was not respected, the empress, together with her children, implored and supplicated her husband the Caesar to have second thoughts. (4) But when even her request did not have a respected aspect or persuasive strain, the emperor Maurice went out a distance of one and a half parasangs from the capital; this place was called the Hebdomon in fact by the Byzantines.[89] (5) Now on that day

[85] In Homer (e.g. *Odyssey* ii. 1), 'rosy-fingered' is a standard epithet of dawn, who is said to rise from the bed of Egyptian Tithonus (*Odyssey* v. 1).

[86] The chronology of the following campaign (v. 16. 1-vi. 3. 8) is extremely obscure, and there are various contradictory indicators. This opening section suggests that the campaign began after the reinstatement of Chosroes (i.e. in autumn 591 at the earliest), but events are then dated to Maurice's ninth regnal year (14 Aug. 590-13 Aug. 591), and specifically to Oct. 590 by the solar eclipse (v. 16. 5 with n.); the campaign concludes with the arrival of an embassy from the Frankish king Theodoric, who did not ascend the throne until after Christmas 595 (vi. 3. 6-7 with n.); the campaign is immediately followed by Priscus' first Balkan campaign (vi. 3. 9-6. 1), which appears to have begun in early summer and to have ended in autumn (see book vi n. 17 for the chronological problems of Priscus' campaign). Many of the events of Maurice's campaign are very strange, quite unlike any other military narrative in Theophylact, and they are clearly intended to presage disaster for Maurice.

The solution to these problems probably lies in the sources which Theophylact was using (see Introduction, pp. xxiii-xxv). He has mistakenly amalgamated separate reports of two different campaigns—a brief and factual report of an expedition by Maurice in Oct. 590 to inspect the damage caused by the Avars at Anchialus (cf. Theophanes 268. 3-4), and a much longer, but imprecise, account of an imperial expedition in the vicinity of the Long Walls (see vi. 3. 2-5 with nn.) that occurred in 596 or later (cf. vii. 15. 7 with n.); the latter account was characterized by a love of miracles and marvels. On this, see also Whitby, *Byzantion* 53 (1983), 312-45, esp. 331-2.

[87] In the 6th c. it was not customary for emperors to lead military expeditions in person, hence the senate's reaction to Maurice's preparations. Maurice had, however, already led an expedition to defend the Long Walls in 584 (i. 7. 2).

[88] i.e. the Patriarch John Nesteutes.

[89] The Hebdomon was a fashionable suburb at the seventh milestone from the centre of Constantinople, and was the site of an imperial palace; see Janin, *Constantinople* 446-9. The use of the Persian parasang as a unit of measurement is an obfuscatory affectation that Theophylact maintains in books vi-vii (vi. 1. 4, 2. 1, 4. 4, 9. 1; vii. 5. 6, 13. 9); he had already used it once in his eastern narrative, v. 3. 1.

a very great eclipse of the sun took place; this was in fact the ninth year of the emperor Maurice.[90] There followed also violent gusts of wind, a fierce southerly, so that even the pebbles of the deep were virtually churned up by the turbulence of the swell. (6) And so, on hearing that the Persian Dalauzas had come to him,[91] the emperor hastened back to the royal city, settled the embassy's petition as skilfully as possible, and once more set out on the object of his expedition. (7) Since he was also eager to obtain some divine guardianship to accompany him on campaign, he spent the night in the great religious precinct which had been constructed by the emperor Justinian: the shrine is dedicated to the name of the Wisdom of God.[92] (8) Accordingly, since no dream vision appeared to him, he prayed with the army at the house of the Mother of God outside the city, spent the day in religious celebration and partook of the God-incarnate banquet;[93] the church is known as that at Pege.[94] (9) On the next day the emperor set out from there and came to the Hebdomon as it is called; on the sixth day he reached Rhegium,[95] where a countless throng of beggars gathered and asked for a gift from the emperor. (10) And so the emperor enclosed the massed throngs in the palace there, judged them worthy of charity, and, by dividing up a quantity of silver, beguiled the affliction of poverty for the assembled multitude. When dawn came he sounded the trumpets and began the journey.

(11) Then, on coming to Rhamphus,[96] he was escorted by his body-guards and the formation stretched out at length. The emperor was delighted by the bearing of the formation of his escorting force; the soldiery walked behind, while the wood of Christ's cross was raised aloft on a golden pole and preceded the emperor and the attendant force. (12) At the second hour an enormous beast, which was in fact a boar, came at the Caesar; then the royal horse was thrown into confusion at the beast's sudden approach and rebelliously struggled to

---

[90] Maurice's ninth regnal year began on 14 Aug. 590. The eclipse can be dated to 4 Oct. 590; see F. K. Ginzell, *Spezieller Kanon der Sonnen- und Mondfinsternisse* (Berlin, 1899), 227.

[91] Dalauzas is probably the same man as the Persian Dolabzas who came to Constantinople to surrender the keys of Dara in spring 591 (v. 3. 10).

[92] i.e. the church of St Sophia in Constantinople.

[93] i.e. Holy Communion.

[94] The Church of the Source, or Spring, which Justinian had constructed a short distance outside the walls of Constantinople (Procopius, *Buildings* i. 3. 6-8). For further information, see R. Janin, *La Géographie ecclésiastique de l'empire byzantin* i (3) (2nd edn., Paris, 1969), 223-8.

[95] Maurice was proceeding by the Via Egnatia along the coast of the Sea of Marmara.

[96] The precise location is unknown.

throw its imperial rider from his seat. (13) But the emperor sat most firmly, holding the bridle, and in spite of itself the horse became obedient; casting off its terror at the sight, it changed its mind and was governed by the reins once more. (14) And so the beast was not attacked by anyone, and in its irresistible might had an unpunished passage, while after the disappearance of the beast, the emperor traced on his forehead the sign of the cross, as it is customary for Christians to do at miracles; he continued on his march, wondering at these truly extraordinary events which attended him.

BOOK SIX

(I. I) ACCORDINGLY, when the emperor came to Selymbria, he set out by sea for Perinthus, which more recently men have been accustomed to call Heracleia.[1] Then swift-sailing ships were at hand, which had nothing lacking for royal embarkation in the completeness of their equipment. (2) Accordingly, at the start of the emperor's voyage, violent rain fell and uncontrollable blasts of wind ensued, so that the oarsmen and rowers bade farewell to their oars, stopped rowing, and entrusted the boats to fortune; the emperor, together with his fifty-oared ship, avoided wreck and escaped to an unexpected salvation in Daonion.[2] (3) In this very place the emperor spent the night and, when the sky cleared in the morning, he mounted the royal horse and came to Heracleia. Then he entered the precinct of the church of the martyr Glyceria, bestowed the greatest honours on the precinct, and provided funds for the transformation to new beauty of those parts of the church burnt down by the Avars;[3] he marshalled his forces and left the city. (4) Then, after moving four parasangs,[4] he encamped at sunset in a certain place whose site was flat, which was well populated and abounded in a wealth of provisions. In this very place the emperor sited his camp. (5) While the emperor's attendants were surrounding the royal tent with screens as protections for the sake of propriety,[5] a woman screamed out, her cry re-echoed and was emitted more frequently, for birth-pangs were afflicting the woman. (6) And so one of the emperor's bodyguards went out to stop the female's cacophony, but when he reached the cottage and learned the cause of the cry, the woman gave birth. The offspring happened to be a deformity of nature: (7) for the child had no eyes, eyelids, or eyebrows, and its

---

[1] The distance between Selymbria and Heracleia is only about 22 miles, and it is not clear why the emperor boarded ship for this short journey.

[2] Daonion was situated about half-way between Selymbria and Heracleia.

[3] Theophylact has not, so far, recorded an Avar attack on Heracleia. However, if the suggestion is correct that Priscus' first Balkan campaign (vi. 3. 9-6. 1) belongs to 588 (see n. 17 below), then it is probable that the destruction occurred during that campaign, since the Avars penetrated as far as Heracleia (vi. 5. 8).

[4] i.e. about 15 miles.

[5] We have accepted de Boor's suggestion (Index verborum, p. 367 s.v. αὐλαῖος) that τὰς αὐλαίας be taken as a noun meaning 'screens'.

hands and arms were abnormal and misshapen: at its hip it had a tail appropriate to a fish. Now the bodyguard recounted the nature of this particular spectacle to the emperor and dragged in the father, the mother, and the child. (8) And so when the emperor had viewed the monster, he questioned the monster's parents about how this had ensued; after learning nothing at all from the parents, he terminated the inspection and commanded that the monster be killed. And so the monster's mother was sent away but the child greeted the sword.

(2. 1) On the second day the emperor moved on, marched to the place called Enaton, and built a camp after a journey of two parasangs.[6] At this particular place the most distinguished of the royal horses, which gleamed with golden trappings, suddenly fell, ruptured itself, and perished. (2) But since in all these signs he saw omens of ill-fated and exceedingly terrible affairs in prospect for him, the emperor was sorely distressed, and in fear of the future was prematurely disturbed by the present.[7] On the next day a herd of deer encountered the emperor himself in the course of his march. (3) Now the emperor's attendants shot at the animals with bows and spears. So the largest of the herd of deer was struck, and a fierce pursuit from the hunters naturally occurred. (4) As the sun was sinking and the hind was bounding away and escaping the hunt by the speed of her feet, the rest gave up, but one of the emperor's bodyguard and a man of Gepid race persisted in the chase. (5) Then, while that same hind reached a certain thicket in her swift flight and concealed herself in the foliage of the copse, the men proceeded, all the more eager for success because of the rivalry of the hunt. (6) And so, when the Gepid saw the youth dressed in bright clothing, fastened with an elaborate gold belt, and his horse with its golden bridle, he killed the poor unfortunate, treacherously murdering him in a ravine. (7) And so, in place of the hind, the bodyguard became a sinful quarry for a most sinful desire, having occasioned the plot from his own circumstances and person:

---

[6] The location of Enaton is unknown; the name ought to denote a settlement nine miles from a more important locality, presumably Heracleia in this case. Maurice, however, had now marched a total of 6 parasangs (vi. 1. 4 and 2. 1) from Heracleia, i.e. about 23 miles; this would have taken him far beyond the ninth milestone, unless his progress had, unknown to Theophylact, involved considerable marching and countermarching, so that the expedition was still in the vicinity of Heracleia (cf. nn. 13, 14 below).

[7] Cf. v. 16. 14; vi. 11. 1; vii. 12. 10 for other portents. All these omens are naturally to be interpreted as portents of Maurice's overthrow. Their significance is less clear in Theophylact's account, where most of the portents are inserted too early in the narrative, than in the chroniclers (e.g. Georgius Monachus 656. 17-658. 17), where the portents directly precede the narrative of Maurice's overthrow.

for the gold decoration, a decorated[8] travelling companion and fellow-journeying plotter, became for him nets and snares and toils. (8) In the first watch of the night the perpetrator of the murder returned to the camp while the emperor and his companions were despondent in their uncertainty, since they did not see the bodyguard anywhere at all. (9) Then a farmer encountered the horse as it was wandering aimlessly, and brought it back to the camp; so the emperor suspected that this man was responsible for the murder, and handed him over for examination under torture.[9]

(10) On the following day three men, Sclavenes by race, who were not wearing any iron or military equipment, were captured by the emperor's bodyguards. Lyres were their baggage, and they were not carrying anything else at all. (11) And so the emperor enquired what was their nation, where was their allotted abode, and the cause of their presence in the Roman lands. (12) They replied that they were Sclavenes by nation and that they lived at the boundary of the western ocean;[10] the Chagan had dispatched ambassadors to their parts to levy a military force and had lavished many gifts on their nation's rulers;[11] (13) and so they accepted the gifts but refused him the alliance, asserting that the length of the journey daunted them, while they sent back to the Chagan for the purpose of making a defence these same men who had been captured; they had completed the journey in fifteen months; but the Chagan had forgotten the law of ambassadors and had decreed a ban on their return; (14) since they had heard that the Roman nation was much the most famous, as far as can be told, for wealth and clemency, they had exploited the opportunity and retired to Thrace; (15) they carried lyres since it was not their practice to gird weapons on their bodies, because their country was ignorant of iron and thereby provided them with a peaceful and troublefree life; they made music on lyres because they did not know how to sound forth on trumpets. For they would quite reasonably say that for those who had no knowledge of warfare, musical pursuits were uncultivated,[12] as it

[8] The word κατάκοσμος, 'decorated', may be corrupt.

[9] This story is concluded at vi. 10. 4-18 (see n. 56), a passage that is followed (vi. 11. 1-2, with n. 62) by a record of prodigies similar to those noted above (vi. 1. 6-7).

[10] i.e. the Atlantic; there is no evidence to corroborate this statement that Slavs were living so far to the west.

[11] In 601 the Avars concluded an alliance with the Franks and Lombards, and obtained Lombard help for the siege of an island in Thrace (Paul the Deacon iv. 20, 24). It is likely that they had made earlier attempts to gain assistance from the peoples on their northern borders, over whom they had some influence (John of Ephesus vi. 24).

[12] The word ἀγρότερα (Vatican MS), 'uncultivated', may be corrupt; the vulgate

were. (16) And so, as a result of their words, the emperor marvelled at their tribe and judged that those same barbarians who had encountered him were worthy of hospitality; in amazement at the size of their bodies and the nobility of their limbs, he sent these men under escort to Heracleia.

(3. 1) On the third day ambassadors were dispatched from the royal city and the request from the senate came to the emperor; its purpose was an endeavour to secure the return of the imperial expedition. And so the emperor utterly rejected the embassy and ordered the ambassadors to go back. (2) On the fourth day the emperor redirected himself forwards. A number of soldiers came upon a narrow bridge and encountered difficult, marshy terrain, so that the crossing was hard to traverse. Nearby were the sources of the river which the local inhabitants call Xerogypsus.[13] (3) The force was in disarray near the crossing, clamour sprang up by the bridge, surprised shouting came upon the multitude, and some were pushed over the edge by the crush in the throng; the emperor dismounted from his horse, took up a staff, and became the architect of order; by commanding the masses to refrain from pressing, he provided fluency for the march, and by the removal of the confusion he gradually showed safety to the soldiers. (4) And so the emperor thus passed the whole day at the bridge without food, and provided a way through in the difficult terrain. When the sun sank towards its setting, he encamped two miles from the bridge. (5) On the next day he sited camp at Anchialus,[14] and, after making a stay here for a total of fifteen days, he returned to the imperial city on the news that ambassadors had reached Byzantium from the Persian king. (6) On the third day the ambassadors from Celtic Iberia arrived at the imperial city; these are in fact called Franks in more modern

MSS read αἱρετώτερα, 'preferable'. If ἀγρότερα is retained, Theophylact's sense is not totally clear: perhaps, peaceful people have not been stimulated by the practice of war to develop the full range of 'civilized' musical pursuits (i.e. trumpets as well as lyres), so that their musical skills could be described as 'uncultivated'. The vulgate reading gives much simpler sense (peaceful people naturally prefer music to war), but it is probably a scribal conjecture to resolve the obscurity of the text.

[13] The Xerogypsus was one of the tributaries of the river Ergene; its sources were near Tzurullon (modern Çorlu in European Turkey, 17 miles from Heracleia). This indicates that Maurice's expedition had not advanced far from Heracleia (perhaps only 20 miles), and was still in the vicinity of the Long Walls.

[14] It would have been physically impossible for the imperial expedition to move in one day from the Xerogypsus to Anchialus on the Black Sea coast, a distance of about 100 miles. Theophylact clearly did not realize the implausibility of this part of his account, an implausibility that resulted from his amalgamation of separate reports of two distinct expeditions by Maurice (cf. book v n. 86).

parlance; the names of the ambassadors were Bosus and Bettus. (7) These had been sent to the emperor by the monarch of their nation, whose name was Theodoric;[15] he requested to join in alliance with the Romans on agreement to levy tribute, and to undertake the war against the Chagan for gifts. (8) And so the emperor honoured the ambassadors with gifts and instructed that the alliance should be offered to the Franks without payment, since he would not tolerate the Roman nation to be subjected to tribute by the barbarians.[16]

(9) The Chagan demanded from the Caesar that the agreement receive a supplement; but, when the emperor did not grant to the barbarian's words their objective of a hearing, he at once received war in return.[17] Therefore the Chagan ordered the Sclavenes to construct

---

[15] On Frankish-Byzantine diplomatic contacts during this period, see Goubert, *Byzance avant l'Islam* ii (1), esp. ch. 3. This embassy cannot be identified with any of the missions recorded by other sources (Goubert 90); Guntram Boso, an important Frankish noble, visited Constantinople at the start of Maurice's reign, but he cannot be identified with Theophylact's Bosus, since he was killed in 587. Theodoric II came to the throne of Burgundy at about Christmas 595, although, since he was still a minor, effective power was wielded by his grandmother Brunhilda.

[16] The main objective of Maurice's diplomatic dealings with the Franks was to encourage them, by means of gifts, bribes, and the manipulation of members of the Merovingian royal family who had fallen into Roman hands, to co-operate with the Roman authorities in Ravenna for the defeat of the Lombards in northern Italy (Paul the Deacon iii. 17, 22). Although there is no evidence to corroborate this proposed alliance against the Avars, it would have been sensible for the Franks to offer to co-operate with the Romans, particularly after 596, when Queen Brunhilda was forced to buy off the Avars, who were attacking the Franks in Thuringia (Paul the Deacon iv. 10-11).

[17] The date of this campaign (Priscus' first Balkan campaign) is a serious problem. In Theophylact's narrative it appears to follow directly after Maurice's expedition to Anchialus, but this connection is suspect, since Theophylact muddled the chronology of that expedition (see book v n. 86), and his information on Priscus' exploits originated in a different source from those on which he relied for the account of Maurice's march (see Introduction, pp. xxiii-xxv). Priscus' second Balkan campaign is firmly dated to 593 (see n. 35 below), and it is probable that, unknown to Theophylact, there had been a gap of some years since the end of this first campaign. The weakness of the Roman army during the first campaign also suggests that it should be dated before the reinforcements arrived in the Balkans from the eastern frontier (autumn 591 at the earliest); in the subsequent campaigns of Priscus and Peter, the Roman army appears quite strong and the Avars strangely quiet (cf. n. 37 below). J. Marquart, *Osteuropäische und ostasiatische Streifzüge* (Leipzig, 1903), 486, noted that there were striking similarities between this narrative in Theophylact and the account in Michael the Syrian (x. 21) of the Balkan events of 588, an account that was based on a lost passage of John of Ephesus' contemporary history. It is an attractive proposition to date Priscus' first campaign to 588. The agreement which the Chagan was demanding to have revised was that made in 584, under which the Romans paid 100,000 solidi annually to the Avars (i. 3. 13, 6. 4). Although the Avar invasion in 587 had ended with a minor Roman success near Adrianopolis (ii. 17. 8-13), after which the Avars withdrew, overall the Avar successes had been sufficiently sweeping to encourage them to demand an increase in payments before they invaded the empire again.

large numbers of boats so that he could control the crossing of the Ister.[18] (4. 1) The inhabitants of Singidunum ravaged the Sclavenes' labours by sudden attacks,[19] and consigned to flames their nautical enterprises. (2) It was for this reason that the barbarians besieged Singidunum; the city reached the extremity of disaster and had feeble hopes of salvation. (3) But on the seventh day the Chagan ordered the barbarians to abandon the siege and to come to him. When the barbarians became cognizant of this, they left the city carrying off two thousand gold darics,[20] a gold-inlaid table, and clothing. (4) Therefore the Chagan moved five parasangs, camped at Sirmium, and organized hordes of Sclavenes in timber operations, so that he could cross the river Saos, as it is called, by boat.[21] (5) And so he pressed on with the campaign, while they provided shipping in accordance with his order: for such are the things which fear of appointed officers can accomplish. So, shortly after the barbarian had acquired skiffs ready for use, the barbarians crossed the adjacent river. (6) And so the Chagan marshalled a detachment of his force, and ordered it to hasten ahead and give the Romans a frightening encounter with authority. On the fifth day he came to Bononia. (7) The emperor appointed Priscus as commander in Europe,[22] and equipped him with an improvised

---

[18] The Avars were not skilled in nautical matters and relied on other races to provide this expertise; cf. Paul the Deacon iv. 20 for Lombard shipbuilders in Avar service, and *Chron. Pasch.* 724 for Slav *monoxyla* at the siege of Constantinople in 626. The Slavs, on the other hand, were renowned for their ability to adapt to life near rivers and swamps and for their skill at boating; see Maurice, *Strategicon* xi. 4, 23 ff., and *Miracula S. Demetrii* ii. 1, §§ 179 ff.

[19] Singidunum, which the Avars captured in 583 (i. 4. 1-3), had clearly been reoccupied by the Romans after the peace of 584. It was the Roman fortress furthest upstream on the Danube, and hence was an important base for observing Avar actions along the upper Danube. Although Theophylact suggests that it was civilian inhabitants who disrupted the Slavs' preparations, such daring action is only likely to have been undertaken by a military detachment stationed at Singidunum.

[20] i.e. solidi; this is another example of Theophylact's affectation of Persian terminology (cf. book v n. 89).

[21] Sirmium was situated about 50 miles west of Singidunum; the Chagan had probably earlier been encamped between the two cities (since he had to move 5 parasangs, about 19 miles, to reach Sirmium) to supervise both siege and boat-building operations. When the Avars captured Sirmium in 581/2, the river Sava was crossed by two bridges that had been built for the Avars under compulsion by Roman engineers; one bridge was already rotten then (John of Ephesus vi. 24, 30; Menander, fr. 66), and by now both bridges had clearly collapsed, a factor that made it harder for the Avars to cross to the south bank of the Danube to ravage.

[22] If this campaign is to be dated to 588 (see n. 17 above), Priscus' appointment would have immediately followed his return to Constantinople from the east. In 588, Priscus had been appointed commander of the eastern army which mutinied at Easter, 18 Apr. 588, when Priscus tried to fulfil Maurice's instructions to introduce changes in military

force. And so Priscus made Salvianus second-in-command, furnished him with one thousand cavalry, and ordered him to occupy in advance the secure strong points. (8) And so he enclosed the passes of Procliane, pitched camp, and bivouacked;[23] on the fifth day, when he was beyond the strong points, he encountered the advance party of the barbarians; accordingly, recognizing that he did not possess a force sufficiently strong for an engagement, he made his escape once more to the safety of the strong points. (9) When the barbarians attacked the passes, their advance received a check, since the opposing Roman expeditionary force provided an impediment to the barbarians' moves. And so in consequence, there came about a fierce engagement between Romans and barbarians. (10) Then the battle lasted all day, and, although many were slain by the barbarians, the Roman second-in-command gained the upper hand. In the first watch of the night the barbarians came to the Chagan and described the outcome of events. (11) Accordingly, in the morning the Chagan equipped Samur with eight thousand men and dispatched him, but the Romans were not astonished by the massive reinforcement, and steadfastly endured the engagement. After the barbarians had been defeated, the Chagan took his forces and advanced to battle. (12) But Salvianus was dismayed by the innumerable horde of forces, and in the second watch of the night he abandoned the passes and returned to Priscus. (5. 1) The Chagan, after spending three days in the region in front of the strong points, on the fourth discovered that the Romans had fled; at the first hour on the fifth day he began his journey and traversed the difficult terrain of the passes. So, on the third day he came to the place called Sabulente Canalin.[24] (2) Next he reached Anchialus, and setting out from there he came to the church of the martyr Alexander,[25] which he gave as

pay (iii. 1-2); Priscus was quickly replaced in the east (iii. 2. 11) and returned to Constantinople (iii. 3. 6), probably during May 588, so that he would have been available for reappointment in the early summer of 588.

[23] Priscus' strategy was to try to secure the passes across the Haemus mountain-range and so protect the Thracian plains from ravaging. There were probably four or five major routes across the Haemus that were in use during the 6th c.; for details, see C. J. Jireček, *Die Heerstraße von Belgrad nach Constantinopel und die Balkanpässe* (Prague, 1877). Salvianus was probably defending the Šipka pass.

[24] Sabulente Canali(o)n should probably be identified with the Valley of the Roses (cf. book ii n. 32), which extends westwards from the southern end of the Šipka pass.

[25] This description of the Chagan's movements is incomplete: there is no reference to the length of the march from Sabulente Canalin to Anchialus, and the church of Alexander is very probably the shrine near Drizipera which the Avars also sacked in 598 (vii. 14. 11). The Avars may well have captured Anchialus (cf. Michael the Syrian x. 21), a major disaster for the Romans, which would have been tactfully overlooked by Theophylact's source, because of its bias in favour of Priscus (see Introduction, pp. xxiii-xxiv).

prey to the all-consuming fire; after moving three miles he encountered those sent on reconnaissance by the Roman general. (3) And so the barbarian investigated under torture what the captives' objective might be. He groped around for the cause of their journey, and became aggrieved at his inability to learn the unadulterated truth: for they frustrated him with fictitious stories.

(4) After the fifth day had passed, he transported his camp to Drizipera,[26] and made an attempt to reduce the city; but, since the citizens arrayed themselves bravely, on the seventh day the barbarian constructed siege-engines. (5) So, violent uproar afflicted the city and, as their hopes of safety were tossed at sea, they resorted to a pretence of boldness: for, opening the city gates, they threatened to spurn the rampart and do battle with the barbarians on equal terms. (6) And so, after effecting their deployment to the extent of orders and formation, they were stricken by cowardice and did not go out of the city. But the barbarians were prevented from attacking by some divine solicitude. (7) For at midday they imagined they saw countless Roman divisions in close formation, moving out of the city and hurrying to the plain in eagerness to do battle and die in combat.[27] Then the Chagan was glad to flee precipitately; the opposition was an illusion, a bogyman of vision and a bewilderment of perception.

(8) On the fifth day the Chagan reached Perinthus, which Romans call Heracleia.[28] When Priscus suddenly saw the barbarians, he provided no delay to the assault. (9) Accordingly, after engaging the Chagan's troops for battle, he turned his back on the enemy forthwith, since he could not endure the impact of the fight because of the abundance of the opposing force. But the Roman general retired to Didymoteichon with the infantry.[29] (10) After this he came to Tzurullon

---

[26] If the church of Alexander was that near Drizipera (cf. n. 25 above), the Chagan did not have to move camp but merely to turn his attention from the extramural church to the city walls.

[27] Such miraculous explanations for the unexpected withdrawal of besieging armies are not uncommon; cf. Evagrius iv. 28, pp. 176. 24-177. 2, for the Persians at Sergiopolis (the truth is recorded by Procopius, *Wars* ii. 20. 10-15), or *Miracula S. Demetrii* ii. 3, § 222, for the Slavs at Thessalonica. The real reason for the Chagan's retreat from Drizipera may have been the need to confront Priscus' army.

[28] Although Theophylact has just recorded a precipitate Avar flight from Drizipera, it now emerges that the Avar advance has continued unchecked to Heracleia, 33 miles to the south-west on the Sea of Marmara. The Chagan probably intended to prevent Priscus' army from retreating to the safety of the Long Walls of Constantinople.

[29] Priscus has now been forced to retreat west, away from Constantinople, to the security of the fortress of Didymoteichon on the Hebrus (Marica) river. Theophylact does not record what had happened to the Roman cavalry, but it is possible that they had managed to escape the Avars to reach the Long Walls.

and took over the city as a refuge for his forces.[30] But the barbarians invested the city and vigorously besieged Priscus. (11) So, when the emperor heard of this, he was greatly dismayed, feared the outcome, and derived extreme confusion from the news of the occurrence. But on the fourth day he proposed a plan which was inspired by sagacity. (12) For, issuing a summons to one of his bodyguard, he ordered him to allow himself to be captured by the barbarians and to declare that he was carrying imperial letters to Priscus, so that the barbarians, after reading these as if they were some sort of godsend, would become personally cognizant of the purport of the contents; and that as a result they would be terrified and deceived into retreating homewards. The wording of the message was in fact like this:

(13) 'To Priscus, the most eminent commander of the combined forces in Thrace.[31] The enterprise of the sinful barbarians has inflicted no disturbance whatsoever on our piety: on the contrary indeed, it has made us even more concerned for their destruction. (14) And let your Eminence know this, namely that the Chagan is obliged to make an ill-fated and ignominious retreat with numerous losses to the country which he was assigned by the Romans.[32] For this reason your Eminence shall stand firm in the city of Tzurullon together with the most fortunate army, and shall resolve that the accursed Avars wander around. (15) For we have sent by sea ships and an army, to go to their households and take everyone captive; and consequently the accursed Avar leader may be forced ignominiously and with a heavy punishment to return to his own land from our state.'

(16) And so the fictitious messenger delivered the command to completion. On the seventh day he was captured by the barbarians and voluntarily delivered the royal missives. But when the Chagan had learned its contents in his native tongue through an interpreter, he was foxed by the message; in extreme terror, he arranged terms with Priscus for a minimal sum, and returned to his own country as quickly as possible: for the force of the deceit misled the barbarian most masterfully.[33]

[30] Tzurullon was located midway between Drizipera and Heracleia, so that Priscus was marching east in an attempt to slip behind the Avars at Heracleia, who were blocking his direct retreat towards Constantinople.

[31] i.e. *magister utriusque militiae per Thraciam*, the commander of Roman cavalry and infantry forces in Thrace.

[32] i.e. to Pannonia, an area that the Romans could pretend to have assigned to the Avars, since it had once been a Roman province; cf. i. 5. 14.

[33] Michael the Syrian x. 21 records that the Avar retreat was occasioned by the payment of 800 lb. of gold, and the rumour of an offensive by the Turks, a nation whom the Avars dreaded, against their homeland. The payment of 800 lb. of gold, or just under

(6. 1) And so, at the beginning of autumn,[34] the general broke camp and came to Byzantium, while the disbanded Romans streamed into Thrace and found subsistence in the villages. (2) At the start of spring, the general was sent by the emperor to the Ister so that the Sclavene races, by being prevented from crossing the river, might unwillingly provide security for Thrace:[35] for the emperor told Priscus that the barbarians would not remain quiet unless the Romans kept a very strict guard on the Ister. (3) And so Priscus took charge of the cavalry force, while Gentzon was ordered by the emperor to command the infantry troops. Thus, in the middle of spring, the Romans assembled near Heracleia. (4) On the seventh day, the general gave orders to move camp; he held a review of the allies, counted his forces, and made their annual distribution of money. (5) So he set out from there and after four camps came to Drizipera; after waiting there for a total of fifteen days, he reached Dorostolon in twenty camps.[36] (6) And so the Chagan learned by report of the Roman offensive, and hence dispatched ambassadors to Priscus. So, when the ambassadors came to Priscus, Koch, who was the barbarian, began the embassy as follows:[37] (7) 'What is this, O gods? Among those for whom devoutness is appropriate, impiety has newly been established close at hand. The Romans have broken peace, the law of treaties is debased, guarantees of agreement are scorned, respect for trust is squandered, the

60,000 solidi, was hardly minimal, but was less than the previous annual payment of 100,000 solidi.

[34] This is the first indication provided by Theophylact of the time of year during this campaign. It is only possible to guess at the total length of the campaign, since Theophylact has not supplied comprehensive chronological indications (cf. n. 25 above), but there would have been sufficient time for the various actions if Priscus was appointed commander in early summer (cf. n. 22 above).

[35] There was most probably a gap of several years between the events of vi. 6. 1 and 2. Priscus' second Balkan campaign can be dated to 593 by counting back the campaign-years in Theophylact's narrative from the final campaign of Maurice's reign in 602. In July 593, Pope Gregory sent a letter (*Register* iii. 51) to Priscus, *patricius orientis*, to congratulate him on regaining the emperor's favour: the nature of Priscus' disgrace is unknown, but it is tempting to suggest that it was the consequence of the disastrous conduct of his first Balkan campaign (588), and that his reinstatement to favour was marked by his appointment as general in Thrace in spring 593.

[36] Priscus' advance to Dorostolon on the lower Danube confirms that he was concerned to combat the Slavs (cf. vi. 6. 2, 14), not the Avars, whose homeland was in Pannonia on the upper Danube.

[37] The following speech is similar in sentiment to that delivered by Comentiolus to the Avars in 583 (i. 5), and to the Chagan's brief remonstrance to Priscus in 595 (vii. 10. 5–7). It is noticeable that the Avars cannot back up their complaints with action, an indication that the balance of forces in the Balkans has changed from the situation during Priscus' first campaign.

mediating oath has perished. (8) The Ister sees a spectacle of war, a camp, and Priscus arrayed in armour, him who recently escorted the peaceful marriage between Avars and Romans.[38] You do wrong, Caesar, in impiously stealing the battle. The enterprise is not royal nor the design authoritative,[39] but it is a robber's plan, an act accursed by the people. (9) Either lay down the adornment of your crown, or do not corrupt the decorum of authority. You have administered baseness to the barbarians: we should not have known about treaty-breaking, if we had not found you as teachers of deceit. Those whom war has not discovered at rest, neither has the eye of peace beheld demobilized. (10) In making war you do wrong; in making peace you are aggrieved. And when is your assurance of love for unwarlike quiet preserved? Have respect for the recent clemency, general. We preserved you to be friends, not enemies. Alas for that clemency which has brought forth grief and danger! (11) Those who derived salvation from us are now measuring out the contrary return. We make war with the gods on our side, since the citadel of oaths is besieged, the better is tyrannized by the worse, treachery has free rein, deceit is entrusted with leadership, and insults have openly taken the field. (12) And so, general, if you feel shame and admit your error, you will obtain only disgrace in punishment; otherwise you will have the requital as teacher to inflict repentance together with misfortunes.'

(13) Then, after the termination of this speech, although the force was distressed by the address, Priscus granted pardon to boldness and forgiveness to barbarian words. (14) Therefore, he offered no rebuttal to rashness, but declared that he was undertaking war against the Sclavenes, for the agreement and truce with the Avars had not in fact concluded the Getic war as well.[40] (7. 1) On the twelfth day the general constructed ships and crossed the river.[41] On hearing that Ardagastus[42] was sending the Sclavene hordes abroad to obtain booty, he delivered his attack in the middle of the night. (2) And so Ardagastus, bidding farewell to the visions of dreams and brought round from sleep by the increasing clamour, mounted an unsaddled mare

[38] i.e. the agreement of vi. 5. 16, to which the 'recent clemency' of vi. 6. 10 also refers.

[39] We have preferred de Boor's conjecture ἐξουσιαστικόν to the MSS ἐξουσίας ἔτι (adopted into the text by Wirth), since the latter damages the antithesis.

[40] i.e. the Slav war. The Slav tribes of the lower Danube were, at best, only loosely under Avar control, and the Avar-Roman treaty of 598 specifically allowed the Romans to cross the Danube to fight the Slavs (vii. 15. 14).

[41] The Danube.

[42] The Slav leader defeated in Thrace in 585 (i. 7. 5).

and made his flight. Now the barbarian fell in with Romans and, dismounting from the mare, engaged in hand-to-hand fighting. (3) But when he could not withstand the might of opposition, he took to flight across some rough country; so, as a result, Ardagastus had the advantage in moving since he had a physique that was accustomed to this. (4) Less favourable fortune came upon him, and the barbarian fell over the stump of a huge tree; hence he would have been for his pursuers an earnestly desired prey, if a river had not been his salvation, for he swam across and escaped from danger. (5) And so the Romans made the Sclavene hordes a feast for the sword, and ravaged Ardagastus' territory; they put their captives in wooden fetters and sent them to Byzantium.

(6) But Priscus became a cause of disorder among the troops, for he undertook that the emperor should obtain the first portion of the booty, the emperor's eldest son the second, then that the rest of the emperor's offspring should also be allocated shares, exporting the greater part because of the abundance of the royal progeny.[43] (7) So, since the Romans were insulted by their attenuated spoils, mutiny visited them and confusion reigned. So the general shuddered at his deed, condemned the proposal in repentance of his previous ideas, and gave the victor's prize to second thoughts. (8) Then, at daybreak, he summoned the commanders of the forces and persuaded them with a web of words that he had done nothing improper on the preceding day. (9) Then, after the leaders of the contingents had unanimously sanctioned what the persuasive speech had established, the masses congregated around the general; and so the general began to address the Romans as follows in their ancestral tongue:

(10) 'Men, friends, soldiers, allies, who are heroes in battle but civilians in disorder; if you will reconcile your ear and set straight your heart, I will begin with admonition. (11) But my words may perhaps even cause some affront as I repair the error of your ways: for indeed in this it is right for the commander not to fear speech in any way for the reason that friendship is endangered. (12) Why is it that you have just recently combined against us with wanton and, as it were, exceeding insolence? I have caused offence by taking your spoils for the emperor. You are aggrieved at having your triumphs displayed; everyone is indignant against the general because he is bequeathing your heroism and trophies to the city, emperors, and people. (13) What witnesses

[43] In 602 Maurice had six sons and three daughters. It is not known how many of these children were alive in 593.

will you have to proclaim your heroic deeds? Who will be a spectator of your labours? Where are we to dedicate the tablets of glory? How, whither, when, and to whom are we to proclaim your bravery? (14) For if you shall be witnesses to what is recorded, your toil will be discredited, your success rejected, your trophies a fable, the elaborate guarantees of your accounts insecure, since your story will be isolated and persuasiveness be in short supply. (15) You who treat death like philosophers, who have chosen both to suffer and to do all things, would you not despise booty for the sake of goodwill? Will you not concede the spoils as tribute, so that you may extend your applause? Why are you enslaving your souls to avarice, you who are eager to subjugate the enemy and to purchase victory at the risk of life? (16) Love of possessions cannot form a foundation for glory, nor yet can ambition for money preserve the appetite for praise. So either abandon the one or do not debase the laws of soldiery.'

(8. 1) So, while the general was still in full flood of words, a Roman speaking the Attic of Themistocles,[44] applause sprang up among the troops, hostility turned to goodwill, blame to praise, jeering to approbation, and all was transformed and altered. (2) For the might of the tongue can rule nature, impose laws on necessity, rechannel processes of thought, change fortune, and transform, mould, and fashion everyone to obedience. (3) Then, after his speech had prevailed, Priscus sent off the fruits of their labours to the emperor, placing a guard of three hundred men on the booty and appointing Tatimer as their commandant.

(4) And so Tatimer began the journey to Byzantium, but on the sixth day he encountered Sclavenes and came into unexpected danger.[45] For at midday, while he was encamped carelessly and at ease, and the horses were grazing the grass, the barbarians attacked. (5) Whereupon a cry was raised, the Romans made a stand without their horses, and Tatimer rushed forward with a few men; on his coming close to the barbarians, great disaster befell him; for, being unable to endure a fight at close quarters, he had turned to flight when he was struck by untimely missiles, and with difficulty escaped the

---

[44] The 5th-c. BC Athenian statesman Themistocles, and the Attic style and dialect, symbolize the ideal of Greek eloquence to which Priscus has aspired in his speech to the army, delivered in Latin ('their ancestral tongue', vi. 7. 9).

[45] These Slavs probably ambushed Tatimer while he was crossing the Haemus mountains. This incident indicates that Roman control of the land south of the Danube was by no means complete, and that some groups of Slavs may already have established themselves in the Balkan uplands.

peril. (6) So, when the Roman infantry had come up and saved Tatimer, thereafter they undertook battle against the Sclavenes. (7) Then, after a fierce fight, the Romans overcame the Sclavenes, wrought great slaughter, captured fifty barbarians, and returned to their camp having preserved Roman booty from the Sclavenes. (8) And so Tatimer, his body more or less healed, reached Byzantium and brought with him a most distinguished booty; accordingly, the emperor was delighted at these occurrences, and kept vigil at the city's greatest shrine of God;[46] then with the populace he made prayers of supplication, and asked the Divinity to grant more glorious trophies.

(9) The commander Priscus ordered men to move ahead on reconnaissance. On the second day he did not detect enemy in the area; therefore he commanded Alexander to march at dawn into the region beyond the river Helibacia.[47] (10) And so Alexander crossed the adjacent river and encountered Sclavenes. But the barbarians, on beholding enemies in sight, made their escape to the nearby marshes and the savage woodland,[48] while the Romans tried to catch them. (11) But when they reached the mire, they fell into overwhelming difficulty, and the whole contingent would have perished if Alexander had not quickly extricated the Romans from the swamp.[49] (12) And so the brigadier Alexander encircled the place and tried to consign the barbarians to fire, but the flame languished and grew feeble because of the damp conditions, and Alexander's attack was inglorious.

(13) Now there was with the barbarians a Gepid, who had once long before been of the Christian religion. This man deserted to the Romans and also pointed out the means of entry. And so the Romans gained control of the entrances and overcame the barbarians. Alexander enquired by interrogation what was the captives' race; (14) but the barbarians, since they had fallen into mortal desperation, declared that they welcomed tortures, disposing the agonies of the lash about the body as if it were another's. (9. 1) But the Gepid described everything and revealed events in detail, saying that the prisoners were

---

[46] i.e. the church of St Sophia.

[47] This river is also the scene of action during Peter's campaign in 594 (vii. 5. 6). Its precise location is unknown, but it is probable that Priscus was still operating fairly close to Dorostolon, so that the Helibacia would be one of the tributaries on the north bank of the Danube in this area.

[48] 'Savage' (βάρβαρον, literally 'barbarian') may well be corrupt; de Boor suggested βορβορῶδη, 'swampy', as a possible emendation.

[49] This illustrates the problems of attacking the Slavs on marshy and wooded terrain; the advice at Maurice, *Strategicon* xi. 4, 82 ff., that the Romans should campaign in winter, was intended to resolve precisely these problems.

subjects of Musocius, who was called *rex* in the barbarian tongue,[50] that this Musocius was encamped thirty parasangs away,[51] that he had sent out the captives to reconnoitre the Roman force, and that he had also heard about the misfortunes which had recently befallen Ardagastus. (2) He advised the Romans to make a sudden attack and to catch the barbarian by the surprise of their onslaught. And so Alexander came to Priscus and brought the barbarians, but the commander consigned these to slaughter. (3) So that barbarian Gepid came before the general, described to Priscus the barbarians' intentions, and advised Priscus to attack the barbarian; as a pledge of success the Gepid agreed to trick the barbarian. (4) Then Priscus joyfully accepted the proposal and, lubricating the deserter with splendid gifts and securing him with glorious promises, he sent him to beguile the barbarian. (5) Therefore the Gepid came to Musocius, and asked to be provided by him with a number of canoes, so that he could ferry across those involved in Ardagastus' misfortunes. (6) And so Musocius, regarding as a godsend the plan woven against him by deceit, provided canoes so that the Gepid could save Ardagastus' followers. Then, taking a total of one hundred and fifty skiffs and thirty oarsmen, he came to the other side of the river which the natives call Paspirius.[52] (7) Priscus, in accordance with the agreement, began his march at dawn. But the Gepid man eluded the notice of his companions, and in the middle of the night came to the Roman commander; he asked to be given one hundred soldiers, so that he could destroy the barbarian sentries in the jaws of the sword. (8) Then the general marshalled two hundred men and gave them to the brigadier Alexander. When the Romans had come near the river Paspirius, the Gepid placed Alexander in hiding. (9) Accordingly, when night had fallen, the barbarians happened to be heavy with sleep and, since they had been drinking, they held fast to their dreams, whereas the Gepid dissimulated so as to destroy the barbarians. (10) In the third watch he moved away a short distance, came to the hiding-place, and led Alexander out of the ambush. And so he directed the Romans to the river Paspirius, exchanged signals, and came to the barbarians. Then, since the barbarians were still consorting with sleep, the Gepid gave Alexander the

---

[50] Cf. Maurice, *Strategicon* xi. 4, 128, for the use of the Latin word *rex* of Slav leaders; on the significance of Theophylact's phrase, see L. M. Whitby, *Byzantion* 52 (1982), 425-8.

[51] About 112 miles.

[52] The Paspirius must be another tributary on the north bank of the Danube; it cannot be located, since Theophylact has not recorded the direction in which Musocius' camp lay.

signal by means of Avar songs. (11) Alexander attacked the barbarians and provided the mortal penalty for sleep. When he had gained control of the skiffs, he dispatched messengers to the general to increase the impetus of the attack. (12) Priscus took three thousand men, divided them between the skiffs, and crossed the river Paspirius. Next, in the middle of the night, they provided the introduction to their attack. Now the barbarian was drunk and debilitated by liquor, since on that day there had been a funeral celebration for his departed brother in accordance with their custom. (13) And so great panic ensued; then the barbarian was taken captive, while the Romans revelled in a night of bloodshed. As day grew bright, the general put a stop to the slaughter; at the third hour the general ferried across his equipment and forces. (14) Then the Romans grew over-confident at events and inclined towards high living: subsequently they were sewed up in liquor and, adulterating their success with drunkenness, they disregarded sentry-duty, which Romans are accustomed to call *sculca* in their ancestral tongue.[53] (15) And so the vanquished assembled and measured out a return attack for the Romans, and the repayment would have been harsher than the success, if Gentzon had not deployed the infantry forces and been victorious in the battle. At dawn Priscus impaled the officers of the watch, and in addition severely flogged some of the soldiery.

(10. 1) The emperor sent Tatimer back to the commander carrying royal missives; the missives required the Romans to pass the winter season where they were.[54] Then, after Tatimer had arrived and the royal utterances became known, the army was kindled by commotion. (2) Then the Roman troops rejected the emperor's words and mutinied in an attempt to pass the cold season at home: for they refused to encamp in barbarian territory, since they claimed that the cold weather was insupportable and the hordes of barbarians irresistible. (3) But the general mitigated the army's insubordination with regulating persuasion; when the forces became obedient, the Roman commander broke camp in barbarian territory.[55]

[53] For *sculca*, a regular term in late Roman military usage, see Maurice, *Strategicon* ix. 3, etc.

[54] This accords with the recommendations of Maurice, *Strategicon* xi. 4, 82 ff.; the intention was to attack the Slavs when the bare forests offered less protection for ambushes, the snows would reveal the tracks of fleeing men, and the frozen rivers could be crossed more easily by the Romans. For the use of similar tactics in Lithuania, see E. Christiansen, *Northern Crusades* (London, 1980), 164-6.

[55] Although Priscus had apparently persuaded the army to return to obedience, the fact that he broke camp indicates that his invasion beyond the Danube was being

(4) Now at about this time, through some divine solicitude the man who had committed the murder at Anchialus during the pursuit of the hind by many of the emperor's attendants[56] (it is not beside the point to describe as well the causation of the active Providence which daily traverses the whole world, watches over mortal affairs with its untiring eye, and always administers to mankind retribution for acts of violence), the author of the murder was caught in the net of justice. (5) For after a time he came to the royal city and gave the embellished gold belt to a certain craftsman who worked in gold to melt down. And so the craftsman, after observing the highly-distinguished components of the belt, the violent manner of its removal, and the barbarian quality of his features, suspected that some theft had been committed by the man. (6) Then, he sent for seven men from the praetor of the people,[57] as he is called, and handed the barbarian over to the court. And so they brought the barbarian to the court-house, swaggering and vehemently resisting, brought forward an interpreter, and enquired where he had come by the remnants of the remarkable and exceedingly magnificent belt. (7) And so the murderer, who was in fact a Gepid, produced a very clever defence. What he said is as follows: Albuis had obtained the leadership of the Lombard nation;[58] (8) this man fell in love with a certain girl; the girl was in fact the daughter of Conimundus, the leader of the Gepids. When he was unable to persuade by speech, he proceeded to action by force. Accordingly, the lover organized an ambush and in a surprise attack snatched the maiden. From this, the war took its origins. (9) And so the Lombards had the upper hand in the war; it was for this reason that Conimundus dispatched ambassadors to the emperor Justin the younger, begging him for assistance. The victim sent magnificent gifts to the Caesar to

terminated in contravention of the emperor's command (cf. vi. 11. 3). Theophylact's account of the aftermath of this campaign is confused (cf. vi. 11. 2, 20 with nn.).

[56] This digression from the military narrative continues the story of vi. 2. 2-9. Theophylact probably separated the two parts of the story, which would in his source have formed a single narrative, in order to emphasize that the discovery of the murderer occurred some time after the event (vi. 10. 5). The murder in fact took place in the vicinity of Heracleia.

[57] i.e. the *praetor plebis*, who was responsible for order in the city (see Jones, *LRE* 692).

[58] For the background to Lombard-Gepid rivalry during Justinian's reign, see Bury, *HLRE* (2) ii. 299-304, and F. E. Wozniak, 'Byzantine Diplomacy and the Lombard-Gepidic Wars', *Balkan Studies* 20 (1979), 139-58. Albuis, or Albuin, was the king who led the Lombard migration to Italy in 568, after the Lombards had allied with the Avars to defeat Conimundus. Paul the Deacon i. 27 records that Albuin took Conimundus' daughter Rosimunda as wife after he had killed Conimundus in battle (and used his head as a drinking-cup).

ensure that the embassy's business would meet with the emperor's respect. (10) The emperor marvelled at the generosity of his suppliant and inclined to pity; he composed a letter which ordered the general Baduarius to collect the forces in Scythia and Mysia and to aid Conimundus.[59] (11) Then, when this was announced to Albuis, he trembled at the Roman forces; he requested with covenants and splendid gifts to be reconciled with the injured party, as it were, and pleaded that the marriage-link might be made according to marital customs. (12) But Conimundus would not tolerate the stinging insult and demanded that the insults find resolution in hostilities. Then the engagement ensued, the Romans were victorious, and the victors took possession of the spoils. 'Hence', he said, 'the acquisition of this splendid belt.' (13) Then he was examined by the attendant officialdom of the court, 'And who was this man who was wearing this conspicuous belt?' And so he joined one fabrication to another and said, 'It was in fact a bastard son of the Lombard *rex*,[60] as he is called, who was wearing this conspicuous belt; after slaying him and looting the corpse I received the belt as reward for my perils.' (14) And so the barbarian thus devised an exceedingly clever story, his account gained credence, and for a brief space he concealed the murder. Accordingly he was released from the charge but, after he had been dismissed, a certain man among the praetor's attendants intelligently examined his story and attempted to ascertain the time of the events narrated by the Gepid. (15) For this reason those in the court ran to catch up with the barbarian, and forced him to return once more to the court. So, when the barbarian had entered, the leader asked the time of the events recounted by him. (16) Then, since it was an exposition of quite ancient events, it was recognized that the story had occurred thirty years previously,[61] and that this man was not as old as the events he had described; the president of the court put the barbarian to torture. (17) Then his tongue created contradictory statements and, as the torments pressed the barbarian towards verisimilitude, the murderer became self-confessed and laid bare the misdeeds of his acknowledged undertaking. (18) And so that barbarian murderer had to pay the

---

[59] This expedition under Baduarius, who was son-in-law of Justin II, was probably dispatched in 566; the Gepids undertook to surrender Sirmium to the Romans, but repudiated the promise after defeating the Lombards.

[60] For *rex*, cf. vi. 9. 1 with n.

[61] The Gepid victory was achieved in 566, so that the thirty-year gap is roughly correct, since the Gepid murderer was probably discovered towards the end of Maurice's reign.

penalty for his savagery: it was voted that he be consigned to the teeth of beasts, and next he was offered as victim to all-consuming fire.

(11. 1) In this very year strange prodigies were born in the vicinity of the city, a four-footed child and another with two heads. Those who have diligently composed histories say that the appearance to cities of portents does not signify good. (2) And so the prodigies were exhibited to the emperor Maurice and consigned to slaughter.[62]

But the emperor dismissed the commander and made his brother, whose name was Peter, leader of the Roman forces.[63] (3) Now Priscus had not yet learned of this. Therefore he took his forces and crossed the river because the troops angrily refused to delay in barbarian territory, since they feared that the barbarians might perhaps attack suddenly and carry off the booty.[64] (4) But the Chagan was greatly amazed when he heard of the Romans' departure, and he next dispatched messengers to Priscus in his eagerness to discover the cause of the retreat. And so Priscus deceived the Chagan with the most plausible arguments possible.[65] (5) But after three days it was reported to Priscus that the Chagan was about to undertake an attack on the Roman forces, and that he had ordered the Sclavene hordes to cross the Ister: for he was in fact indignant and annoyed by the extensive successes of the Roman forces. (6) Now Targitius and the barbarian elite urged the Chagan to put an end to the war, for they said that his indignation against the Romans was unjustified. (7) Then Priscus magnanimously dispatched to the Chagan an ambassador, whose name was Theodore, a man clever and shrewd by nature, a doctor by profession and a free man in speech. This powerful man came to the Chagan.[66] (8) And so the barbarian became over-confident at what

---

[62] These prodigies resemble the miraculous events of Maurice's expedition (cf. vi. 1. 5-2. 2). In Leo Grammaticus, 139. 5-17, these portents and the moral about the opinions of historians are directly attached to the account of Maurice's Thracian expedition; cf. *Byzantion* 53 (1983), 318-19, 337-44.

[63] This abrupt transition back to the military narrative of vi. 10. 3 is another indication that the intervening material has been inserted, rather clumsily, from a different source (cf. n. 56 above).

[64] Priscus had already broken camp (vi. 10. 3) and now crossed to the south of the Danube. The booty for which the troops were afraid would be that gained in the defeat of Musocius.

[65] This section is confusing: it would be more natural for the Chagan to complain about the aggressive Roman crossing to the north bank of the Danube (cf. vii. 7. 3), and for Priscus to use plausible arguments to excuse this (cf. vii. 4. 7 for a comparable description of an apology for an act of aggression). There is further obscurity in Theophylact's account of this crossing of the river at vi. 11. 20.

[66] Theodore's influence at Maurice's court is shown by the letters addressed to him by Pope Gregory (e.g. *Register* iii. 64; v. 46).

had befallen him and swaggered exceedingly, declaring that he was master of every nation and that there existed no one, even as far as the sun extended its gaze, who would be able to confront him. (9) For this reason the ambassador, whose grasp of history was great, humbled the barbarian bombast with precedents. (It is not inconsequent to tell the history as well.) For he said, 'Listen, Chagan, to an ancient and very wise tale.' And when the opening had made the barbarian attentive to instruction, the narration of the history received no hindrance.

(10) 'They say that there once lived a man Sesostris, who was exceedingly fortunate and most eminent in the kingdom of Egypt. Ancient legend tells that this man prided himself on his wealth, and that his forces were completely invincible.[67] (11) But he became so besotted, so to speak, that the barbarian constructed a gold-inlaid carriage, wreathed it with precious stones, and sat in this; he bade farewell to mares and mules but encircled the necks of conquered kings with its yoke, and the unfortunate kings drew the chariot of Sesostris to the forum. (12) Then the Egyptian king did not behave moderately in success, but frequently and conspicuously reproached the defeated with their misfortune. They say that at a great and famous festival, when crowds of Egyptians had congregated, one of the kings subjected to the chariot-yoke would not draw the chariot, and repeatedly twisted backwards, and observed the motion of the wheels. (13) Then the haulage became inharmonious, since those appointed for this purpose were not acting with one accord, and the Egyptian king said to the one who was repeatedly twisting around: "Man, why are you shifting your gaze backwards? Why are you examining the wheels? What do you expect to achieve by gaping?" (14) But he said to Sesostris with great wisdom, "I have been marvelling at the movement of the wheels. It has an inconstant motion: now the parts of them in the air come back again to earth, while again the parts on the ground are subsequently exalted." (15) Wherefore Sesostris, they say, on hearing this, was taught not to be arrogant, and he decreed that the royal necks be released from the yokes and that thereafter the haulage be entrusted to mules. Let this be your lesson, Chagan. Nothing is less reliable than success.'

(16) And so the Chagan, in amazement at the man's good sense,

---

[67] The following story had been used for a similar purpose by Peter the Patrician during negotiations with the Persians in 561 (Menander, fr. 11). Sesostris' conquests were described by Herodotus ii. 102-11, and Diodorus Siculus i. 53-8. Diodorus i. 58. 2 records that four conquered kings drew Sesostris' chariot on visits to temples and cities, but does not report the moral about the revolving wheel.

reproved his arrogance, checked his boldness, and rearranged matters into a peaceful state. Accordingly, after being silent for many hours, he said to Theodore: (17) 'I know how to master even a swollen spirit, I know how to keep even wrath in line, although there is occasion for grievance. Theodore, I have made peace with Priscus, but let him too be a just friend to me. Let not the Chagan remain without due share of the booty. He has attacked my land and wrought injury on my subjects.[68] Let the results of success be shared.' (18) On these terms he bestowed favours and sent Theodore to Priscus. And so Theodore reached Priscus and recounted to him the barbarian's words, but Priscus convened an assembly on the next day and recommended the Romans to make the barbarian too a partner in the spoils. (19) But the Romans for a time did not accommodate themselves to expediency, and rebelled against the general. But with the aid of many subtle and unexceptionable arguments, the general persuaded the forces to give the barbarian some of the booty. (20) Then the Romans handed over the barbarian captives to the Chagan, and settled the dispute, although they left him without a share of the other spoils. Then the Chagan was pleased by the return of the barbarians and gave ground at the crossings.[69] (21) And so the Romans, after thus voluntarily ceding five thousand barbarians to the Chagan, came to Drizipera; the general reached Byzantium. Accordingly Maurice reproached Priscus and imputed errors of simplicity to him, since he had foolishly surrendered the booty to the barbarians.

[68] This is strictly untrue, since the Slavs on the lower Danube were not Avar subjects (cf. vi. 6. 14 with n.).

[69] Theophylact's description of the Chagan's actions is not entirely clear. The Romans had already retreated to the south of the river (vi. 11. 3), so that the Chagan could not have been blocking their retreat at the river crossings until he was persuaded by the return of the captives to give ground. It is possible that the Chagan, who had encouraged the Slavs to cross the Danube (vi. 11. 5), now withdrew them from the crossing points. The sense would be simpler if the Chagan 'gave pardon for the crossings', since the return of the prisoners had been intended to soothe his anger, so that he would excuse Roman aggression against the Slavs. But Theophylact himself was probably unclear about exactly what was happening, and so we have retained the text without emendation.

BOOK SEVEN

(1. 1) AND so Priscus was thus demoted while Peter, who was in fact Maurice's own brother, was proclaimed as commander by the emperor. Then Maurice inscribed royal letters, delivered these to the general, prepared for him to depart from the city, and ordered him to go to the camp.[1] (2) Now, one clause of the royal letters dealt with military pay; the clause proposed that payment would be organized in three parts, by clothing, equipment, and gold coin.[2] (3) Then the general departed from Perinthus and came to Drizipera, and leaving Drizipera he reached Odessus. And so the camp gave the commander a most distinguished welcome on his arrival at Odessus, but on the fourth day the commander attempted to publicize to the troops the royal dispatches. (4) And so the troops contemplated agitation, for they had previously heard the royal command. Then, after the general had hurriedly arranged a united assembly of the forces and had made the congregation listen to the emperor's utterances, the army shied away and, abandoning the general in disgrace, they pitched camp in uproar four miles away. (5) But Peter, being faced by revolt, concealed the more irksome parts of the royal commands; he also had to hand one of the royal ordinances which would be beneficial to the warring masses, and demanded that this be publicly proclaimed to the Roman troops. (6) And so the Romans assembled and reviled Maurice, but the commander intelligently and persuasively soothed the wrath of the camp and publicized to the men-at-arms the more pleasing of the emperor's letters. (7) They contained the following generous provisions: that Romans who had acted heroically and encountered some misfortune as a result of courage in danger should thereafter receive a respite, that these demobilized soldiers in the cities should be fed at imperial expense, and that servicemen's children who had lost their fathers in war

---

[1] The campaign of 594.
[2] On military pay, see Jones, *LRE* 670-4, and M. J. Higgins, 'Note on the Emperor Maurice's Military Administration', *AB* 67 (1949), 444-6. Maurice planned to reduce cash payments by offsetting against salaries the cost of state provision of clothing and equipment. Cf. iii. 1. 2 for an earlier attempt to reduce military pay.

should be enrolled for war in place of their parents.[3] (8) Accordingly, when he had put these proposals to the army from a lofty rostrum, he converted them, and persuasively reduced them to submission; hence their folly was also altered, and each reverted to goodwill towards the emperor Maurice. (9) Accordingly the Caesar was praised, being released from their recent slanders: for the masses are unstable and have never adopted a fixed position, but are transformed randomly and fortuitously by incidental pronouncements.

(2. 1) And so the general was thus reconciled with the camp regarding their grievances. On the fourth day, after he had acquainted the emperor with the mutiny of the forces, he set out from Odessus and moved towards the regions on his left;[4] on reaching Marcianopolis he ordered one thousand men to advance beyond the camp. (2) These, therefore, encountered six hundred Sclavenes who were escorting a great haul of Romans, for they had ravaged Zaldapa, Aquis, and Scopi, and were herding back these unfortunates as plunder; a large number of wagons held the possessions they had looted.[5] (3) When the barbarians observed the Romans approaching, and were then likewise observed, they turned to the slaughter of the captives. Then the adult male captives from youth upwards were killed. (4) Since the barbarians could not avoid an encounter, they collected the wagons and placed them round as a barricade, depositing the women and youth in the middle of the defence. (5) The Romans drew near to the Getae (for this is the older name for the barbarians),[6] but did not dare to come to grips, since they were afraid of the javelins which the barbarians were sending from the barricade against their horses. (6) Then their

---

[3] On provisions for veterans, see Jones, *LRE* 675; the children of deceased soldiers were probably enrolled at the rank held by their fathers.

[4] i.e. Peter marched westwards, or inland, from Odessus (modern Varna) on the Black Sea coast.

[5] This incident reveals how insecure Roman control of the Balkans was (cf. vi. 8. 4 with n.), because the Slavs were proceeding along a main road (since they had wagons) not far from the Roman cities on the Black Sea coast, and the main imperial army in the Balkans had been unable to prevent their ravaging. The extent of this Slav ravaging is a problem: Zaldapa was located to the north of Marcianopolis, but there are no places called Aquis or Scopi in the vicinity, and these should probably be identified with the more important cities of these names in the central Balkans. Thus these three places were quite widely separated, and it is unlikely that the same band of 600 Slavs had ravaged all three. It is possible that Theophylact, or his source, incorrectly combined a report of widespread Slav ravaging that devastated certain important places with the more detailed story of the encounter between the Roman army and one specific group of Slav raiders.

[6] Cf. iii. 4. 7 with n.

captain, whose name was Alexander, commanded the Romans in the ancestral Roman language[7] to dismount from their horses and grasp the enemy danger at close quarters. (7) Now the Romans dismounted from their horses, approached the barricade, and gave and received in turn discharges of missiles. (8) Accordingly, while the battle persisted on either side, a certain Roman burst in, went up and climbed on to one of the wagons that formed part of the barricade protecting the barbarians; then, standing on it he struck those nearby with his sword. (9) Then an indivertible peril came upon the barbarians, for thereafter the Romans broke the barbarians' barricade. The barbarians renounced salvation and slaughtered the remaining portion of the captives, but the Romans resolutely attacked and with difficulty, at long last, slaughtered the barbarians by the barricade. (10) On the second day the victors recounted these occurrences to the general. On the fifth day the general came to this place; when indeed he had seen the accomplishments of the advance guard, he rewarded the heroes with gifts.

(11) On the following day Peter came to a thick grove in search of hunting; now there was an enormous boar lurking deep in this vale and, as the barking of the dogs grew loud, the beast raised himself from his lair and made for Peter. (12) The general wheeled his horse in flight, but crushed his left foot by dashing it against a lofty tree. Accordingly, Peter was convulsed by unendurable pains and remained in the place, most grievously stricken by his accident. (13) But the Caesar was angered by the general's delay, and in astonishment at his military inactivity he addressed written insults to the general.[8] (14) Then Peter did not tolerate the emperor's epistolary denigration, and moved camp although he was still sorely oppressed by his affliction; after four changes of camp, he reached the habitations of the Sclavenes.[9] (15) On the tenth day the emperor Maurice dispatched to

[7] Latin was still the language of army commands (cf. vi. 7. 9, 8. 1), although its use in the east had otherwise declined very significantly by the end of the 6th c.

[8] Theophylact's account disparages most of Peter's actions. Hunting was recognized as an important part of military training (see Maurice, *Strategicon* xiiD, a chapter which is devoted to hunting because of its usefulness in war); its methods were analogous to those employed in securing captives (*Strategicon* ix. 5, 89), and would have been particularly appropriate for campaigning against the woodland Slavs. Cf. vii. 14. 5 for another instance when hunting activity may have been misrepresented by Theophylact, and vii. 7. 5 for hunting as an excuse to conceal Roman aggression.

[9] This indicates that Peter had crossed to the north of the Danube, although Theophylact has not specifically credited him with such energetic action. Because of the bias of his source, Theophylact has, unwittingly, seriously underrated Peter's achievements during this campaign, and the narrative should be interpreted in this light.

his brother a royal letter to remain in Thrace, for Maurice had heard
that the Sclavene hordes were directing their thrusts towards Byzantium. (16) Consequently the general came to the fort of Pistus, and
subsequently arrived at Zaldapa. On the second day he reached the
city of Iatrus, and next, after marching past the fort of Latarkium,
encamped at Novae.[10] (17) Then, when the inhabitants heard of the
general's imminent arrival, they came out of the city, provided him
with a most distinguished reception, and begged Peter to join the celebration for the festival of the martyr Lupus: for that day was the festal-
eve feast for the martyr Lupus.[11] (18) And so the general said that he
was unable to spend the day in the place because of the urgency of his
march, but the citizens amplified their request with superabundant
pleas, and compelled the general to take part in the festival. (19) And
so Peter, after being two days in the city, set out from there and
pitched camp at Theodoropolis; at the first hour he reached the place
called Curisca.

(3. 1) On the third day he established his quarters at the city of
Asemus.[12] But when the inhabitants of the city had learned that the
general was expected, they came out of the city to meet Peter, and made
his arrival at the city splendid. (2) From bygone times a garrison had
been organized in this city for the protection of the citizens, since the
barbarians swooped down like lightning around this city quite frequently. (3) Accordingly, when the garrison stationed in this city
learned that the general was about to arrive, they took up the standards,
which Romans call *banda*, and went out of the city; then, arrayed in
armour, they welcomed the general most gloriously. (4) And so Peter,
on seeing the magnificence of the city's soldiers, attempted to remove
them from the city and include them amongst his own forces. And so
the citizens and the city's garrison produced a decree of the emperor
Justin which granted the city this successive armed protection.[13] (5) On

---

[10] The movements described so briefly in this section indicate that Peter was actually
campaigning with considerable energy to deter the Slavs from crossing the Danube.
From Pistus (modern Ruse), Peter marched east to Zaldapa (modern Abrit), about 65
miles away; he then returned west to Iatrus (on the east bank of the Yantra river), a distance of about 90 miles, and then on to Novae (modern Svištov), a further 10 miles west.
Peter could not have reached Iatrus on the day after he came to Zaldapa. Theophylact
would not have known that his narrative was geographically impossible.

[11] Nothing else is known about this Lupus, whose feast day was 23 Aug.

[12] Peter's march has now continued 25 miles further west from Novae to Securisca,
and then a short distance south to Asemus.

[13] Both Justin I (518-27) and Justin II (565-78) had to take measures to protect the
Danube frontier, and either might have been responsible for this decree. In 447, Asemus
had defended itself against the Huns with exceptional vigour (Priscus, fr. 9. 3, 39-53).

the morrow the commander made objection and hastened to remove from the township those posted for its protection. For this reason the soldiers in the city took refuge in the city's church. (6) On hearing this, the general ordered the bishop to bring them out of the sanctuary;[14] when the priest angrily refused, the general dispatched the brigadier Gentzon with a body of soldiers to expel by force those who had taken refuge in the church. (7) On hearing this, those who had fled to the holy seats arrayed themselves in arms and blockaded the church doors from all sides. And so Gentzon, observing the opposition inside the sacred precinct, recognizing the outrageousness of his task, and at the same time respecting the sanctity of the church, departed without success. (8) But the general was infuriated at this, and demoted Gentzon from his command (Gentzon was leader of the infantry force). On the following day he summoned to his own tent one of the emperor's bodyguards, whom Romans call *scribo*,[15] and prescribed for him a shameful undertaking: his demand was for the city's bishop to be dragged in dishonour to the camp. (9) When the citizens had witnessed this, they all assembled together and forcibly thrust out of the city the man dispatched by the general against the priest; after closing the gates in the wall, they hymned the emperor with acclamations and covered the general with insults. (10) Peter was encamped in a fortified enclosure about a mile from the city. But since his enterprise was disgraceful, he left the city and proceeded to march forwards, escorted by great curses from the city.

(4. 1) On the sixth day, he marshalled one thousand men to reconnoitre the enemy, and these encountered ten hundred Bulgars. (2) Now the barbarians were marching off guard, since there was peace between the Romans and the Chagan.[16] But the Romans, on the general's decision, used their javelins against the barbarians. The Bulgars dispatched ambassadors to negotiate an end to the fight and to advise the Romans not to destroy the peace. (3) The officer of the contingent dispatched the ambassadors to the general, who was eight

---

[14] There is no evidence to confirm that Asemus was ever a bishopric. It is possible that the bishop of one of the many cities sacked by the Avars had taken up residence in this stronghold.

[15] For the *scribones*, cf. i. 4. 7 with n.

[16] The Bulgars, who were subject-members of the Avar federation, would have been protected by the treaty if they had been marching to the north of the Danube. Although Theophylact has not recorded that Peter had crossed the Danube, this is probably one of the omissions in his account of Peter's actions, since the Chagan's subsequent complaint and Peter's excuse (vii. 4. 6-7) also imply that the Romans were now operating north of the river.

miles from the spot. Peter, therefore, spurned their peaceful words and instructed the advance guard to put the barbarians to death by the sword forthwith. (4) And so the Bulgars formed up for battle as best they could, came to grips, and after joining combat most heroically, compelled the Romans to turn away in flight. (5) After these events, the barbarians also retreated a short distance, oft turning back as one small step replaced another, to blend a touch of the Homeric poem with our account,[17] since they feared that a supplementary force might perhaps join the vanquished and rally for battle again. (6) And so Peter, since his plan had failed, stripped the clothing from the brigadier of the advance guard and scourged him like a slave. Then the barbarians came to the Chagan and disclosed to him the sequence of events; and so the barbarian dispatched ambassadors to Peter, and reproached him for the apparent breach of the truce. (7) But Peter beguiled the ambassadors with plausible arguments, and alleged ignorance of the misdeed; then, with splendid gifts and a forfeit of booty, he converted the barbarian to good humour.

(8) On the fourth day he came near to the neighbouring river,[18] assembled twenty men, and sent them to cross the river and observe the enemies' movements. (9) And so these crossed the river and were all captured. The manner of their capture was this: it is customary that those detailed for reconnaissance always make their way by night but consort with sleep during the light of day. (10) These men had completed a long journey on the previous day; then at daybreak, being physically exhausted, they turned to rest in a certain nearby copse. (11) At about the third hour, when they were all asleep with no one keeping watch, the barbarians approached the copse. Then the Sclavenes dismounted from their horses, and proceeded to refresh themselves and give their horses some respite.(12) Accordingly, the Romans were detected by accident. The poor wretches were taken captive and interrogated to reveal what the Romans had planned; and so, despairing of safety, they recounted everything. (13) But Peiragastus, who was the tribal leader of that barbarian horde, took his forces, encamped at the river-crossings, and concealed himself in the woods like an overlooked bunch of grapes on the vine. (5. 1) But the general, the emperor's brother, consequently rejected the idea that enemy were

---

[17] An adaptation of *Iliad* xi. 547.

[18] If Peter's recent confrontation with the Bulgars had occurred to the north of the Danube (cf. n. 16 above), this unnamed river must be a tributary on the north bank of the Danube.

present and ordered the army to cross the river. Then, after one thousand men had traversed the river, the barbarians slaughtered all of them. (2) When the general realized this, he pressed the troops not to make the crossing piecemeal, lest by crossing the river gradually they should fall victim to the foe. Then, after the Roman formation had been organized in this way, the barbarians drew up on the river bank. (3) And so the Romans let fly at the barbarians from the rafts, while the barbarians, unable to endure the mass of discharged missiles, left the banks deserted.[19] (4) Then their brigadier, whom the story has already declared to be Peiragastus, was killed; for he was struck in the flank by a missile and death took him in hand, since the blow had reached a vital part. Therefore, after Peiragastus had fallen, the enemy turned to flight. (5) Then the Romans became masters of the river bank; next, encircling the barbarian hordes, they forced them into flight with great slaughter, but they were unable to press their pursuit very far because of their lack of horse, and they returned to camp.

(6) Then on the following day, the army's guides made a great error, with the result that a water shortage beset the camp and the misfortunes increased. Then the soldiers, intolerant of the dearth of water, assuaged their thirst with wine. On the third day the trouble intensified, and the whole army would have perished if a certain barbarian prisoner had not pointed out to them the Helibacia river, which was four parasangs distant.[20] (7) And so, thus, in the morning the Romans encountered water: then some inclined their knees forwards, as it were, and gulped down the water with their lips, others stooped down and drew up water in their hands, while others decanted the stream in pitchers. (8) On the opposite side of the river there was a leafy vale; barbarians were lurking therein, and greatest outrage came upon the Romans: for with javelins the barbarians struck the men drawing water. Therefore great slaughter ensued from concealment. (9) Then a choice between two alternatives was necessary, either to refuse the water and relinquish life through thirst, or to draw up death too along with the water. But the Romans assembled rafts

---

[19] Cf. Maurice, *Strategicon* xiiB. 21 for the tactics to be used when crossing rivers in the face of the enemy.

[20] The Helibacia river was probably located to the north of the Danube opposite Dorostolon (see vi. 8. 9 with n.). This would indicate that Peter had accomplished a remarkably aggressive campaign along the north bank of the lower Danube, for which he receives no credit in the biased account transmitted by Theophylact. Four parasangs are equivalent to 11 miles.

and traversed the river so that the enemy might be detected.
(10) When the soldiers reached the other side, the barbarians suddenly attacked and overcame the Romans; and so the defeated
Romans turned away in flight. Then, since Peter had been outfought
by the barbarians, Priscus became general; and so, after being
demoted from command, Peter came to Byzantium.

(6. 1) Now four years earlier (for we come back to the older events
of history) John, the helmsman of the church at Byzantium, departed
this life;[21] because he had completely out-thought the pleasures,
mastered the passions, and become emperor of the stomach, he was
called Nesteutes by the Byzantines. (2) It is also reported that a contract was drawn up for the loan of a large sum of money from the
emperor Maurice, and that his personal property was pledged as
surety in the terms of the loan. (3) After the priest had departed this
world, the emperor Maurice discovered, on investigating the chief
priest's possessions, that the man had practised indigence; he was
overjoyed at the priest's supreme righteousness, and he willingly tore
up the contract which had been arranged shortly before. (4) For they
say that the emperor discovered that the priest possessed nothing
other than a wooden pallet, the cheapest of woollen blankets, and an
unsightly cloak; for the man was ill clad but resplendent in frugality
of life. These things then, these the emperor Maurice valued more
than he would have great wealth and Indian stones, and he conveyed
them to the palace. (5) Accordingly, while exulting in the vernal fasts
of the Christians,[22] the emperor dismissed golden gem-studded
couches and Seric threads,[23] and passed the night on the priest's
wooden bedstead, as if he thought that he would partake of divine
grace thereby.

(6) During this period the Maurusii in Libya conspired together
against the Romans; when the hordes had congregated, the Carthaginians became greatly afraid. And so Gennadius, who was in fact at
that particular time the general of Libya, on seeing that an attack was
being organized against him by an innumerable mob, outfought the

---

[21] The Patriarch John Nesteutes (the Faster) died on 2 Sept. 595. Theophylact's campaign narrative has reached winter 594/5, so that he is not in fact returning to earlier
events. Theophylact probably derived the information in this chapter about John, the
Moors, and the comet, from a chronicle (cf. *Byzantion* 53 (1983), 317-18), and his chronological error in inserting this information illustrates the difficulties that might arise
when he attempted to combine material from different sources.

[22] i.e. Lent.

[23] i.e. silk clothing.

barbarians by guile.[24] (7) For he pretended that everything which the barbarians desired had been accomplished and, after diverting the barbarians to relaxation, he attacked them while they were feasting. Accordingly, there was much slaughter and a glorious booty, and the Carthaginian war was concluded. And so affairs in Libya were thus fairly and favourably settled for the Romans.

(8) In these days, a comet appeared in the firmament. Now, concerning these stars which appear to come into existence, the philosophers have had recourse to meteorological causation, which Stagirites and Platonists have inscribed on Helicon in the volumes of memory,[25] (9) while astrologers and certain historiographers declare that they presage future troubles. But, after bestowing upon our delayed narrative a discussion of these matters, let us constrain our history to strike for its goal.

(7. 1) At the beginning of spring,[26] Priscus left Byzantium; then he assembled his forces in the Astike and, on reviewing the number of the force, the general discovered that a great multitude of the Romans had perished. (2) Accordingly, he attempted to make Peter's failures clear to the emperor Maurice; nevertheless he was persuaded by certain advisers to conceal the errors.[27] (3) Then, after making a total of fifteen camps and crossing the river Ister, on the fourth day the general reached Upper Novae. On learning of this, the Chagan dispatched ambassadors to Priscus and sought to discover the reason for the Roman arrival.[28] (4) The general said that the regions were naturally suited for hunting, being good for riding and extremely well watered.[29] But the Chagan made plain that the Romans were entering foreign

[24] Gennadius was exarch, or governor, of Africa from at least 591 to 598 (Gregory, *Register* i. 72; ix. 9). John of Nikiu xcv. 13 records victories won by Aristomachus, governor of Egypt during Maurice's reign, against the Mauretanians and other barbarians named Marikos. Goubert, *Byzance avant l'Islam* ii (2). 207, suggested that troops from Egypt under Aristomachus' command might have assisted Gennadius in defeating the Moors.

[25] Cf. i. 12. 9 for a similarly pompous comment about natural phenomena. The 'Stagirites' denote Aristotle and his followers; Helicon is the seat of the Muses and the source of poetic inspiration. The comet appeared in Jan. 595, shortly before the death of John, Bishop of Ravenna, on 11 Jan. (Paul the Deacon iv. 10; Agnellus 98).

[26] i.e. 595.

[27] There is a clear contrast between the hostile treatment of Peter's actions and the laudatory attitude towards Priscus.

[28] Cf. vi. 11. 4 and vii. 4. 6 for similar complaints; on each occasion the Chagan is likely to have complained about Roman expeditions to the north of the Danube, although Theophylact's account of the two earlier instances is unclear or defective (see nn. ad loc.).

[29] On hunting, cf. n. 8 above.

territory, that Priscus had broken the treaty, and that the peace was being covertly disrupted by him. (5) Then Priscus said that the soil was Roman, but the barbarian that the Romans had lost possession of this by arms and laws of war. Then, while the Chagan was quarrelling and disputing about these regions, they say that Priscus reproached the Chagan with his flight from the east.[30]

(6) But since we have made reference to the Scythians, both those in the Caucasus and those who face northwards, come then, come, let us interrupt our history and present, like an intercalated narrative, the events which attended these very great nations during these times.[31] (7) When summer had arrived in this particular year, he who is celebrated by the Turks as Chagan in the east, dispatched ambassadors to the emperor Maurice;[32] he composed a letter and inscribed in it victory-praises. (8) The letter's salutation was as follows, word for word: 'To the king of the Romans, the Chagan, the great lord of seven races and master of seven zones of the world.' For this very Chagan had in fact outfought the leader of the nation of the Abdeli (I mean indeed, of the Hephthalites, as they are called), conquered him, and assumed the rule of the nation.[33] (9) Then he was greatly elated at the victory and, making an alliance with Stembischagan,[34] he enslaved the Avar nation. But let no one think that we are distorting the history of these times because he supposes that the Avars are those barbarians neighbouring on Europe and Pannonia, and that their arrival was prior to the times of the emperor Maurice.[35] (10) For it is by

[30] Cf. i. 5. 11 for a similar reproach in Comentiolus' speech to the Chagan in 583.

[31] The following digression, which is of some importance for the history of Central Asia in the mid-6th c., has been discussed at length by Haussig, 'Exkurs', *Byzantion* 23 (1953), 275-462, from which much of the information in the following nn. is derived. The digression combines reliable information about Central Asia, which must ultimately have been drawn from an official account of a Turkish embassy to Constantinople, with Theophylact's own misguided speculations about the so-called Pseudo-Avars.

[32] The military narrative has reached summer 595; however, from the contents of the Chagan's letter, it can be calculated that the embassy must have been dispatched at the very start of Maurice's reign (cf. n. 43 below).

[33] The Hephthalites were defeated in 558, after the Turkish Chagan and Chosroes I had joined forces against them.

[34] We have retained the reading of the Vatican MS, which was preferred by de Boor and Haussig 332, to the vulgate reading 'Stembischadan', which Wirth adopted into the text.

[35] Theophylact was unaware of the real chronology of this account of Turkish victories, and this ignorance gave rise to his misguided speculations about the Pseudo-Avars. Menander, fr. 10 indicates that some Avars at least had fled from the expanding power of the Turks before the Turkish conquest of the Hephthalites in 558; the first Avar contacts with the Romans were in 558/9 (Menander, fr. 4). The conquests recorded in the Turkish letter may not be placed in chronological order, but in

a misnomer that the barbarians on the Ister have assumed the appellation of Avars; the origin of their race will shortly be revealed. So, when the Avars had been defeated (for we are returning to the account),[36] some of them made their escape to those who inhabit Taugast.[37] (11) Taugast is a famous city, which is a total of one thousand five hundred miles distant from those who are called Turks, and which borders on the Indians. The barbarians whose abode is near Taugast are a very brave and numerous nation, and without rival in size among the nations of the world. (12) Others of the Avars, who declined to humbler fortune because of their defeat, came to those who are called Mucri; this nation is the closest neighbour to the men of Taugast; it has great might in battle both because of its daily practice of drill and because of endurance of spirit in danger.

(13) Then the Chagan embarked on yet another enterprise, and subdued all the Ogur, which is one of the strongest tribes on account of its large population and its armed training for war. These make their habitations in the east, by the course of the river Til, which Turks are accustomed to call Melas.[38] (14) The earliest leaders of this nation were named Var and Chunni; from them some parts of those nations were also accorded their nomenclature, being called Var and Chunni. (8. 1) Then, while the emperor Justinian was in possession of the royal power, a small section of these Var and Chunni fled from that ancestral tribe and settled in Europe.[39] (2) These named themselves Avars and glorified their leader with the appellation of Chagan. Let us declare, without departing in the least from the truth, how the means

a geographical sequence which symbolizes the conquest of the four regions of the world, and which progresses from the Hephthalites (vii. 7. 8) in the south, to the Avars (vii. 7. 9) in the west, the Ogur (vii. 7. 13) in the north, and the Kolch (vii. 8. 6) in the east.

[36] Theophylact is returning to the main theme of the digression, not to the main historical account.

[37] Apart from the Avars who fled to the west, and whom Theophylact ignored because (as a result of his chronological error) he believed that these could only be Pseudo-Avars, others apparently fled east to China (Taugast) and the Korean peninsula (inhabited by the nation of the Mucri).

[38] i.e. the Black river. The Ogur are probably the Oğuz, and the Til the river Tarim (Haussig 344).

[39] In Menander's account (fr. 43) of Valentinus' embassy to the Turkish Chagan during Justin II's reign, the Chagan disparagingly refers to the Avars as Varchunnitae, a name which could be rendered as Var-Huns, i.e. Avar Huns. It is quite possible that Theophylact's garbled information about the Var and Chunni has little independent value, but was merely adapted from Menander, to whom Theophylact turned in an attempt to resolve the muddle caused by his chronological error over the date of the Turkish embassy: Menander supplied Theophylact with the name Varchunnitae, and Theophylact then invented the story about how they came to acquire the name of Avar.

of changing their name came to them. (3) When the Barselt, Onogurs, Sabir, and other Hun nations in addition to these, saw that a section of those who were still Var and Chunni had fled to their regions, they plunged into extreme panic, since they suspected that the settlers were Avars.[40] (4) For this reason they honoured the fugitives with splendid gifts and supposed that they received from them security in exchange. Then, after the Var and Chunni saw the well-omened beginning to their flight, they appropriated the ambassadors' error and named themselves Avars: for among the Scythian nations that of the Avars is said to be the most adept tribe. (5) In point of fact even up to our present times the Pseudo-Avars (for it is more correct to refer to them thus) are divided in their ancestry, some bearing the time-honoured name of Var while others are called Chunni.

(6) But since we have, as it were, summarily detailed this information about the Pseudo-Avars, let us move our exposition towards the continuity of the narrative.[41] Then, after the Ogur had been quite soundly defeated, the Chagan handed over to the jaws of the sword the ruler of the nation of Kolch.[42] (7) Then three hundred thousand of this particular tribe were slain in the battle, so that the continuous line of fallen corpses extended for a four days' journey. (8) While indeed victory was thus gloriously smiling on the Chagan, the Turks clashed in civil war. A certain man named Turum, who was connected to the Chagan by birth, revolted and collected great forces. (9) When the usurper's party had gained the upper hand in battle, the Chagan sent an embassy to three other great Chagans. These were their names: Sparzeugun, Kunaxolan, and Tuldich. (10) Then, after their whole array had assembled at the Ikar (this is a place enfolded in great plains), and their opponents had valiantly arrayed themselves in opposition at that particular place, the usurper fell and his allied forces veered away in flight; after much slaughter the Chagan again became the master of his own territory. (11) The Chagan had made a declaration of these triumphs to the emperor Maurice via the ambassadors.[43]

[40] The Avars had already encountered the Onogurs and Sabir in the mid-5th c., when they displaced these tribes and forced them to move westwards; see Priscus, fr. 40 with Blockley's notes. These earlier dealings may help to explain the direction of the Avar flight after their defeat by the Turks, since the Avars knew that they were stronger than the tribes to the west.

[41] i.e. to the main theme of the digression again (cf. vii. 7. 10).

[42] Probably the Khalkh nation. Haussig 372 suggested that the enormous slaughter might indicate that the Khalkh should be identified with the Juan-Juan, the dominant tribe in Central Asia before the rise of the Turks.

[43] The suppression of Turum's revolt provides the climax of the Chagan's

The Ikar is four hundred miles distant from the mountain called Golden. (12) This particular mountain is located to the east, and is called Golden by the inhabitants partly because of the abundance of the fruits growing on it, partly because it is rich in flocks and baggage animals. It is customary for Turks to cede the Golden Mountain to the most powerful Chagan.[44] (13) The Turkish nations take pride in two things above all: for they claim that from the very beginning of time they have never witnessed an epidemic of plague,[45] and that there is a dearth of earthquakes in that land. But Bakath, a city founded once long ago by the Onogurs, was razed by earthquakes, and Sogdoane has experienced both plagues and earthquakes.[46] (14) Now the Turks honour fire to a quite extraordinary degree, they revere air and water, and they praise the earth; but they only worship and call god him who made the heaven and the earth.[47] (15) To him they sacrifice horses, cattle, and sheep, and they have priests who, in their opinion, even expound the prophecy of the future.

(16) At that time the Tarniach and Kotzager, who are also from the Var and Chunni, fled from the Turks and, on reaching Europe, united with the followers of the Avar Chagan. (17) It is said that the Zabender also originated from the race of the Var and Chunni. The additional force which accrued to the Avars was accurately assessed at ten thousand.[48]

(9. 1) And so, after concluding the civil war, the Chagan of the Turks managed affairs prosperously, while he made an agreement with the men of Taugast so that he might bring in secure peace from all sides and make his rule unchallenged. (2) The regional commander of Taugast is called Taisan,[49] which signifies 'son of god' in

letter. References in Chinese sources to the history of the Turks indicate that the revolt was defeated in *c.*582, which provides the *terminus post quem* for the dispatch of the embassy.

[44] Menander, fr. 43 records that Mount Ectel, which meant the Golden, was the seat of one of the Turkish Chagans.

[45] This is at variance with the story of the Turks who had been protected from a visitation of plague by the inscription of a cross on their foreheads (v. 10. 13-15); Haussig 386-7 noted that Chinese sources record that a serious famine and epidemic afflicted the Turks in 585.

[46] i.e. Bactria and Sogdiana, the regions beyond the north-east Persian frontier.

[47] i.e. Tengri, the great sky-god of the steppe peoples.

[48] These reinforcements for the Avars fled west at the same time as the suppression of Turum's revolt, i.e. in 582. In a conversation with a Turkish ambassador, Justin II was informed that the original group of Avar fugitives numbered 20,000 (Menander, fr. 18).

[49] For a detailed discussion of Theophylact's information about Taugast/China, see P. A. Boodberg, 'Marginalia to the Histories of the Northern Dynasties I; Theophylactus

the Greek tongue. The realm of Taugast is not troubled by discord, for lineage provides them with the selection of their leader. Statues are the cult of this nation, the laws are just, and their life is full of discretion. (3) They have a custom, which resembles law, that males should never embellish themselves with gold adornment, even though they have become owners of a great abundance of silver and gold as a result of their large and advantageous trading. (4) A river divides this Taugast; now once long ago the river was interposed between two great nations who were mutually hostile; the dress of one was black, and of the other scarlet-hued. (5) Then in our times, while Maurice was in possession of the Roman sceptres, the black-robed nation crossed the river and joined battle with those wearing the red clothing; next, having gained victory, it became master of the whole dominion.[50] (6) This Taugast in fact, the barbarians say, was founded by the Macedonian Alexander when he enslaved the Bactrians and Sogdoane and burnt twelve myriads of barbarians.[51] (7) In this city the ruler's wives have carriages made of gold, each of which is drawn by one bullock lavishly decorated with gold and precious stones; and even the oxen's reins are gold-inlaid. (8) And so the man who has assumed the dominion of Taugast used to pass the night with seven hundred women. The wives of the nobility of Taugast used silver carriages. There is a report that Alexander also founded another city a few miles away, which the barbarians name Chubdan; (9) and that when the leader dies, he is mourned for ever by his wives, who have their heads shaved and who wear black clothing; and that it is the custom for these women never to leave the tomb. Chubdan is divided by two great rivers, whose banks nod, so to speak, with cypresses. (10) The nation has many elephants. They associate in trade with the Indians, and they say that these Indians who face the northern regions are actually born white. (11) The worms, from which come the Seric threads, are possessed by the said nation in very great numbers and are in turn possessed of varied colour; the barbarians eagerly practise the husbandry of the said creatures. (12) But, so as not to misdirect

Simocatta on China', *Harvard Journal of Asiatic Studies* 3 (1938), 223-43. This information about China is most likely to have been transmitted to the Romans by the Turkish embassy which had brought the Chagan's victory dispatch.

[50] Boodberg 227 dated this conflict between two northern Chinese dynasties to 577.

[51] Haussig 389 f. suggested that there has been some confusion between the Chinese Taugast, to which most of the information in this passage relates, and a Taugast in Western Turkestan, the region of Bactria and Sogdiana, where Alexander the Great did found cities.

our narrative away from its goal, this is enough about the Scythians around Baktriane, Sogdoane, and the Melas river.

(10. 1) On the tenth day (for we will return to the affairs of Priscus) messengers came to the general's tent. Then Priscus heard that the barbarian was razing the walls of Singidunum, and was forcing the population to abandon their home and to make settlements in enemy land. (2) Therefore, with no concession to delay, Priscus sailed along the river and berthed at the island of Singan, which is situated in the Ister's stream thirty miles distant from the city of Singidunum. (3) And so Priscus disposed his forces about the island, brought up swift-sailing vessels, which the multitude is accustomed to call *dromon*s, and came to Constantiola. It was in this area that he encountered the Chagan, and the general held a discussion with the barbarian about Singidunum. (4) Now the barbarian sat on the river bank and gave his answers, while Priscus conducted the conversation from his station on the vessel. Accordingly, the Chagan is said to have begun the discourse and to have spoken to Priscus: (5) 'What are you doing, Romans, in the land which is mine? Why have you extended your steps beyond what is proper? The Ister is foreign to you, its swell hostile. This we have won with arms, this we have enslaved by the spear. Away with folly, Priscus. Do not destroy a peace which was transacted for you with numerous gifts. Respect the treaties, feel shame for the surety of the oaths. (6) Let good counsel lead the undertaking, and expediency the design of actions, lest we be brought to counsel after suffering. Let there be counsel before the design. You are injuring actions by rashness. The undertaking first harmed the one who took ill counsel. (7) You are stealing the war, general. You have adulterated peace with confrontation, by making agreements like a friend and grappling like an enemy. Now either abandon the one, or do not disrupt the repose.'[52] (8) The barbarian also said this, word for word: 'May God judge between Chagan and between Maurice the emperor. May the recompense that is from God at some time demand an account.'[53]

[52] Compare the speech by the Avar ambassador Koch at vi. 6. 7-12. Since Singidunum was located to the south of the Danube, the Avar complaints are not entirely honest. Priscus had been campaigning north of the Danube (vii. 7. 3), but this is likely to have been against the Slavs, since Upper Novae was a considerable distance from Avar territory. The presence of a powerful Roman fleet clearly irked the Chagan because of the impotence of the Avars in naval affairs.

[53] Compare the Chagan's pronouncement at vii. 15. 12 and, for a similar sentiment, the conclusion of an inscription erected at Philippi by a Bulgar Khan, *Die protobulgarischen Inschriften*, ed. V. N. Beševliev (Berlin, 1963), no. 14.

(11. 1) The story is that Priscus addressed these words to the Chagan by way of reply: 'You are wronging the city of Singidunum, my man. Why are you pulling down the walls and directing it into a miserable exile? You are a tyrant, and make accusations that you are being wronged. You use force, and spread rumours that you are being abused by Romans. (2) Leave an unfortunate people in peace. Keep away from a city where the billows of misfortune surge around. Pity the city which has frequently been ravaged by you. On your greed place boundaries; create for it a no man's land; teach it to pursue the mean; command it to halt at some limit. I believe that many worlds would not suffice for its appetite. (3) Boundless ambition does not obtain unshaken power; nothing insatiable is steadfast; that which is not measured in moderation does not have a capacity for ownership; the infinite is unattainable; the irreconcilable breeds strife. (4) Place a terminus on passion, manage the ungovernable with satiety; the greedy eye always has some new ailment. Actions are measured out in return for men, fate sounds a response to changes; there is nothing more fluid than good fortune. Victory prides herself on her wing, and the feet of triumphs slip. The nature of trophies is not immortal. (5) Today you behold the day smiling down, rosy and saffron-hued, all-gleaming and resplendent, so to speak; tomorrow you will behold this same day at once glowering and ill clad, besprinkled with thick mist and, to sum up, darkened to ugliness by compounded clouds.'

(6) Accordingly, in a rage the Chagan interrupted the discussion, and threatened in addition to destroy many cities. And so the barbarian left his seat and returned to his own tent, while Priscus had Godwin summoned, equipped him with a force of Romans, and ordered him to assist Singidunum. (7) Now Godwin sailed to Singidunum, for Singidunum is embraced by two rivers, the Saos and the Draos. When the barbarians at Singidunum saw that the Roman forces had constructed ships, they fortified the city by assembling the wagons in front of the town. (8) Then the barbarians did not wait for the Roman onset but, since they were also terrified of the city's population, they turned away in flight. And so in this way Priscus rescued an unfortunate people.[54] On the second day the Romans encircled the city with walls. (9) The Chagan was infuriated by these events and, mortified to the heart, he dispatched messengers to Priscus and

---

[54] The ability of the Romans to thwart this Avar attack on Singidunum, which was sited at the junction of the Sava and Danube rivers, illustrates the importance of naval power in ensuring the security of the Danube frontier.

publicly dissolved the treaties. On the tenth day the barbarian collected his own forces and mobilized the trumpet against the Ionian Gulf. (12. 1) Near these regions the country of Dalmatia is situated. Then, after several camps, the barbarian came to the place called Bonkeis and, when indeed he had reduced the city with his siege engines, he sacked forty forts.[55] (2) When the general heard of these terrible events, he equipped Godwin with two thousand soldiers and dispatched him to reconnoitre these actions. And so Godwin took the men picked from the army and began his march. (3) Accordingly, Godwin veered aside from the highways and made his way through rough country and unknown tracks, so that he should not come into extreme danger if an enemy sighting should appear and draw on him hordes of barbarians. Therefore, when he was near the barbarians, from a hidden vantage point he observed hordes of troops marching past. (4) Then he sent out thirty foot-soldiers with orders to track down the enemy; and so the Romans made their way by circuitous routes. Accordingly, at the second watch of the night, they lay in wait, as if in a corner, and kept track of the barbarians. (5) Accordingly they hid in the woods and, when the night passed as far as its middle signs, the Romans advanced with courageous spirit on the barbarians while they slept. (6) Two miles away they encountered three drunkards who were thoroughly intoxicated, took these captive, and by thorough interrogation they discovered all the enemies' intentions. And so the Romans put them in, chains and dispatched them alive to Godwin. (7) When the brigadier Godwin learned from them that the Chagan had marshalled two thousand troops to guard the booty, he was delighted at the news. Therefore he concealed himself in a ravine. (8) And so, in the light of day, the barbarians were escorting the plunder, but Godwin came upon their rear, and in a sudden attack destroyed them all with the spear; he recovered the booty and conveyed it to Priscus with magnanimous intent. (9) But the Chagan was cast down in great despair when he learned of this particular reverse; accordingly, for eighteen months and more nothing worthy of record was accomplished by the Romans and barbarians encamped on the Ister.[56]

[55] This Avar campaign towards the Adriatic (the Ionian Gulf) is the only occasion on which Theophylact mentions military action in the western part of the Balkans, even though it is probable that the Avars and Slavs made regular raids into this area throughout Maurice's reign. By 600, the Roman cities along the Adriatic were being pressed by Slav raids (Gregory, *Register* x. 15). The precise location of Bonkeis is unknown, and the name may indeed be corrupt (see de Boor's apparatus criticus).
[56] This cessation of hostilities lasted from autumn 595 until summer 597. During this

(10) In the course of the nineteenth year of the emperor's rule, a prediction of the future occurred and acknowledged the universal sufferings of the world;[57] for a certain man, who had severed himself from the present world, participated in the mysteries through the practice of contemplation, and retired to the solitary life,[58] unsheathed a blade and, after running with sword in hand from the Forum as it is called (this place is one of the city's landmarks) as far as the palace vestibule, he prophesied that the emperor together with his children would die slain by the knife. (11) There is a story that in the season of summer Herodian publicly predicted to the emperor Maurice his misfortunes; the man asseverated that the prophetic message had been manifested to him not without divine utterance.

(13. 1) And so at this time,[59] the man honoured among the Avars as Chagan collected his own troops, moved into Thracian Mysia, and then appeared before the city of Tomi. On learning this, Priscus approached the outraged city. (2) Accordingly the Romans and barbarians encamped in the vicinity of the city of Tomi and, when the winter season arrived, made no move to break camp. As spring appeared, famine beset the Romans. (3) With the imminent arrival of the great feast of the Christians, which celebrates alike the passion and resurrection of God the Saviour,[60] when famine was pressing hard on the Romans, the Chagan with strange providence sent the Romans an embassy whose mission was to put an end to the famine. (4) And so Priscus was doubtful and distrustful at the novelty of the mission; but when Romans and barbarians had given and received in turn guarantees, by arranging a five-day truce they effected immunity from fear. Accordingly the Chagan supplied the starving Romans with wagons of provisions. (5) For this reason, the instance of this barbarian charity has remained established right up to the miraculous tales of the present day. On the fourth day, when the Roman force was thriving

period, the Avars found it more profitable to turn their attention to the west, where they defeated the Bavarians and attacked the Franks in Thuringia (Paul the Deacon iv. 10-11).

[57] Maurice's nineteenth regnal year began on 14 Aug. 600; this prophecy has been badly misplaced by Theophylact, an error which he might have noticed, since he subsequently refers to Maurice's nineteenth year in the course of the military narrative (viii. 4. 9).

[58] i.e. he had become a monk.

[59] This indication of time does not pick up the regnal year (vii. 12. 10), but continues the chronology of the military narrative, which has reached summer 597 (see n. 56 above).

[60] i.e. Easter, which in 598 fell on 30 Mar.

with life from the vital necessities, the Chagan dispatched ambassadors with a request that he receive Indian spices from Priscus. (6) And so the general attended to the barbarian's request and dispatched pepper, the Indian leaf, cassia, and the thing called Saussurea.[61] The barbarian accepted the Roman gifts, and was most joyfully delighted to be made scented with spices. Then there was an armistice until the Romans had completed that great public festival. (7) Accordingly the opposing armies camped together, and there was no fear in either force. Therefore, after the conclusion of the festival, the Chagan dispatched messengers to request that the forces be separated from each other; and so in this way the barbarian was parted from the Romans.

(8) On the sixth day, when the Chagan had heard that Comentiolus was moving his forces and was about to arrive at Nicopolis,[62] he collected his army and took the field against Comentiolus. When Comentiolus heard that the Chagan had arrived in Mysia, he went to Zikidiba and constructed a camp. (9) On the seventh day he arrived at the city of Iatrus;[63] the barbarian was twenty parasangs distant from the Romans. In the middle of the night the Roman general secretly dispatched a messenger to the Chagan; next he ordered the Romans to arm themselves, giving the command as if incidentally: for he did not tell the Romans that there would be an engagement in the morning.[64]

[61] The 'Indian leaf' is probably cloves, cassia a form of cinnamon, and Saussurea another spice.

[62] Comentiolus appears to have been ordered to relieve the beleaguered Priscus by marching across the central part of the Haemus (probably by the Šipka pass), so as to attack the Avars from the west and threaten their retreat towards their homeland. It is possible that the Chagan's surprising generosity towards Priscus (vii. 13. 3-7) was prompted in part by the news that this second Roman army was advancing against him.

[63] Comentiolus' movements have not been clearly described. From Nicopolis, Comentiolus must have advanced a considerable distance to the north-east if he then moved to Zikidiba (presumably in retreat) on hearing that the Chagan was marching towards him. Comentiolus next rapidly retreated to Iatrus, about 140 miles to the west of Zikidiba.

[64] The following narrative of Comentiolus' confrontation with the Avars is extremely confused, and it is unlikely that Theophylact understood what happened. Comentiolus had probably not expected to have to oppose the whole Avar army with his own troops, since he was advancing to help Priscus, but Priscus had surprisingly come to an agreement (possibly a personal and unauthorized pact) with the Avars at Tomi. Comentiolus then retreated rapidly to avoid a confrontation, and his night-time message to the Chagan might have been to offer the Avars safe passage past his army if they would return peacefully to their homeland. The Avars were still 20 parasangs, about 75 miles, from the Roman army, so that a battle was not yet imminent. Subsequently the Avars moved swiftly to take advantage of Comentiolus' isolation, and this led to the disorderly retreat of the Roman army. Another version of these events, which represents the rout

(10) And so the Romans did not suspect that the general had ordered them to arm for the sake of battle, and they protected their chests with coats of mail, since they thought that the general wished to conduct a review of the army. (11) Then, as the sun cast its rays over the earth, the Romans saw the barbarian drawn up in good order and assiduously making his deployment against them. And so Comentiolus' forces cursed their commander, and accused him of responsibility for this unprepared disorder. Accordingly, utmost commotion arose, while the barbarians waited two miles from the Roman troops. (14. 1) Accordingly, when the Romans observed that the barbarians were putting into postponement their attack, they all armed themselves in proper military fashion, and there was an opportunity for them to correct their harmful oversight.[65] (2) Now[66] Comentiolus disordered the formations, at one moment transferring the forces from the central division to the left wing, at another moving men from the left-hand forces to the right flank.[67] Then through the indecisive rearrangement of the formations, he became responsible for great disorder. (3) Hence confusion befell the formations. Therefore the general secretly signified to the right wing of the battle-line that they should safeguard the baggage and take to flight at once. Then, before long,[68] the recipients of this order took it to heart and turned away in flight. (4) Hence, on observing this, the remaining Roman forces fell into confusion. Accordingly, as the sun set, the Romans made camp two miles away and bivouacked in this particular place, but the Avars did not move from the places where they had taken up position on the previous day. (5) In the middle of the night, the general formed up

as an attempt by Maurice to betray the Roman army to the Avars because of its disobedience, is preserved in a fragment of the 8th-c. chronicle known as the Great Chronographer; on this, see L. M. Whitby, *BMGS* 8 (1982/3), 1–9. The accounts in both Theophylact and the Great Chronographer are extremely biased against Comentiolus, and this contributes to the obscurity of events.

[65] If the Avars had just advanced 75 miles to confront Comentiolus, then this delay was perhaps occasioned by their need to refresh and regroup their forces. It is not clear why the coats of mail which the troops had donned (vii. 13. 10) were not regarded as proper military armament.

[66] We have accepted de Boor's suggestion that γάρ, 'for', be emended to γοῦν, 'now'.

[67] We have accepted de Boor's suggestion that λοφίαν, 'flank', should replace the nonsensical σοφία, 'wisdom', of the MSS. The reorganization of the Romans by Comentiolus may have resembled the manœuvre which Priscus carried out before a battle against the Avars (viii. 3. 9, where the manœuvre is described without criticism).

[68] The words ἀντὶ πολλοῦ, which we have rendered 'before long', are obscure and may be corrupt.

picked men on the pretext of being scouts, and ordered them to flee secretly. Next, in the morning, Comentiolus armed himself with the steel, so to speak, and pretended to be going hunting about four miles away.[69] It was on this account that he made his escape as fast as he could. (6) Then, at midday, the camp became aware of Comentiolus' folly and, when they had perceived that the general had turned his thoughts towards flight, they traversed the nearby river and fled forty miles from the camp in utmost disarray.[70] (7) Since their retreat was leaderless, they fell into extreme panic. The barbarians marched behind and crossed the river called Iatrus. Then, when the enemy attacked the Romans, helplessness and fear overtook the army. (8) Then the headlong flight of the Roman troops ensued; hence the barbarians blockaded the strong points of the passes,[71] which Romans are accustomed to call *cleisourae* in their ancestral tongue. (9) But many Romans were killed; since the slaughter of the Romans continued, the army formed a phalanx and dislodged the barbarian by force. Then the Avars withdrew from the passes under the weight of the attack. (10) And so the Romans thus regained the defiles at great peril. But Comentiolus reached Drizipera in ignominious flight, approached the gates of the town, and asked to be granted entry and to cleanse himself in warm water. But the townsmen sent off the non-combatant general with insults and stones, and Comentiolus came to the Long Walls. (11) But the barbarians gradually approached Drizi-. pera since the Romans were turned to the rear, sacked the city, and destroyed with all-consuming fire the church of Alexander, glorious among martyrs.[72] (12) On discovering the martyr's grave, which abounded in silver, they impiously pillaged it, by eviction outraged even the body lying in the tomb, and in their excessive pride at their victories they revelled in an orgy of festivities.

[69] For hunting in a military context, cf. vii. 2. 11-13 with n., and vii. 7. 4. There may have been a serious purpose underlying Comentiolus' 'hunting', that of removing ambushes from the planned route of the Roman retreat.

[70] The Romans were probably fleeing south past Nicopolis towards Veliko Tărnovo (the site of a Roman fort in the 6th c.), which is located about 40 miles from Iatrus, where the Romans had confronted the Avars. The river crossed by the Romans would have been the Iatrus (Yantra).

[71] Most probably the Šipka pass. A confused account of a Roman disaster is given by Sebeos, ch. 8, p. 35, who records that the Romans invaded enemy territory and crossed certain defiles, but were defeated and forced to flight; the barbarians cut their retreat by occupying the defiles, and the Romans only escaped to the fortresses in Thrace with great difficulty. This might be the same incident as the disaster described by Theophylact in this passage.

[72] The Avars had already burnt this shrine in 588 (vi. 5. 2 with n.).

(15. 1) Accordingly, in these days, our Jesus, in whom we trust, whose power extends over all the nations, who received from the Father as his inheritance the inhabited world and the ends of the earth as his possession, by no means allowed his kingdom to be unwitnessed by the Chagan. (2) For the barbarian hordes were stricken by a sudden visitation of plague, and their trouble was inexorable and would not admit any artifice. Accordingly, memorable penalties were exacted from the Chagan for his dishonour of the martyr Alexander: for seven of his sons were afflicted by swellings and a raging fiery fever, and departed this life on a single day. (3) And so in this way the Chagan had ill-fated good fortune in victory celebrations: for in the place of paeans, songs, hymns, clapping of hands, harmonious choirs, and waves of laughter, he had dirges, tears, inconsolable griefs, and intolerable punishment. For he was assailed by angelic hosts, whose blows were manifest but whose array was invisible.

(4) Then, while Comentiolus resided in the royal city, tumult also resided in his company; the city surged with clamour, perils were embellished by expectations, and every man while awake dreamt in imagination of ominous fortunes. (5) Then the affairs of the Byzantines reached such a degree of misfortune that they even resolved to abandon Europe, cross to Asia, and migrate to Chalcedon; (6) the city of Chalcedon is situated on the opposite shore from the royal city: for Chalcedon was regarded as a conveniently situated station for the Byzantines. (7) But the emperor took with him the bodyguards, whom Romans designate *excubitores*, assembled the army, and garrisoned the Long Walls; he also had with him a very large portion of the factions at Byzantium.[73] (8) On the eighth day the senate advised the Caesar to dispatch an embassy to the Chagan, and the emperor summoned Harmaton, appointed him ambassador, and dispatched him to the Chagan. (9) And so Harmaton came to Drizipera, bringing

---

[73] This imperial expedition in 598, which only proceeded as far as the vicinity of the Long Walls, should perhaps be connected with the expedition by Maurice and its attendant portents, which Theophylact narrated at v. 16-vi. 3. This 'earlier' expedition reached the Xerogypsus river (vi. 3. 2), which would have been an appropriate terminus for a defensive march against the Avars if the latter were encamped at Drizipera. The chronological problems of the 'earlier' expedition (see book v n. 86) would largely be resolved if it were redated to 598. This later date would also be more appropriate for the numerous portents of Maurice's overthrow that occurred during the expedition. In the Great Chronographer (cf. *BMGS* 8 (1982/3), 1-9), and the chronicles derived from it, Comentiolus' rout by the Avars was the occasion when Maurice's sins caused the withdrawal from him of God's favour; thereafter, Maurice's punishment was inevitable, and was clearly predicted by a succession of portents, including some of those associated by Theophylact with Maurice's expedition. On the *excubitores*, cf. iii. 11. 4 with n.

a mass of gifts, while the Chagan bewailed his current fortune, and mourned without restraint the loss of his sons and the injury to his forces. (10) The ambassador remained ten days and did not receive an audience with the Chagan, since his grief was bitter and his disaster indivertible. On the twelfth day the ambassador was admitted to the barbarian's tent. (11) And so the ambassador flattered the barbarian with soothing words, but the Chagan would not endure to receive the royal gifts, all but uttering the phrase of the tragedy: 'Enemies' gifts are no gifts and bring no benefit'.[74] And so by means of a long speech the ambassador persuaded the barbarian to accept the honour of the gifts. (12) On the following day the barbarian arranged the peace and contemplated retreat. The Chagan spoke as follows, word for word: 'May God judge between Maurice and between Chagan, between Avars and between Romans.'[75] (13) For he accused the emperor of rocking the peace, and his words were not wide of the mark: for in fact the Romans, as counterfeiters of peace and artificers of war, fell into the previously recounted misfortunes.[76] (14) For the conclusions of evil beginnings produce grievous manifestations. The Ister was agreed as intermedium between Romans and Avars, but there was provision for crossing the river against Sclavenes; the peace payments were also increased by an additional twenty thousand gold solidi.[77] On these precise terms the war between Romans and Avars reached a conclusion.

(16. 1) In this very year, while Menas was serving as the Egyptian prefect,[78] there was a manifestation of certain marvels at the streams of the Nile. For the controller of the Egyptian dominion had to visit the Delta, as it is called, a place which derives its appellation from the shape of the land. (2) Then, at about the first hour, while the commander was proceeding by the river banks, a man of astounding size rose up from the bowels of the river; his visage resembled that of giants, his stare was piercing, his hair golden mixed with some grey,

[74] Sophocles, *Ajax* 665, a tag already quoted by Chosroes' ambassadors at iv. 13. 22.

[75] Cf. vii. 10. 8, where the Chagan also makes this appeal on an occasion when the Avars appear to be the aggressors.

[76] Theophylact's judgement that the Romans were to blame for the war has no foundation in his narrative, since there had been a cessation of hostilities for eighteen months (vii. 12. 9), and previous Roman campaigns to the north of the Danube had largely been directed against the Slavs. Theophylact perhaps concluded that the Romans must have been guilty because God had favoured the Avars with victory.

[77] This should have raised the annual payment to 120,000 solidi from the 100,000 agreed in 584 (i. 6. 4-6).

[78] Menas probably held the post of *praefectus Augustalis*, governor of Egypt.

his cheek like that of men of good physique who frequent wrestling-schools; his loins resembled those of sailors, his chest was broad, his back that of a hero, his arms strong. (3) But only as far as his bladder did he present the history, while the watery element concealed the remaining limbs of his body: for he was like a man ashamed to display his genital organs to the spectators. (4) On seeing him the commander of Alexandria shrewdly assailed him with oaths. What he said was this: if this was a visitation of certain demons, let the apparition conclude the spectacle harmlessly and welcome quiet, but that if some solicitude of the Creator had displayed this particular vision, let him not terminate the contemplation until everyone had taken his fill of this marvellous sight. (5) According to report, that very being was the Nile, whom poets' utterances are accustomed to represent. And so that Nile creature (for I have not yet dared to call it man) continued in public view, conjured by the oaths, and provided for all the manifestation of his body. (6) At the third hour, there also rose straight up from the belly of the waters a creature of female form: for her nature was revealed by her appearance, her breasts, the smoothness of her face, her hair, the whole disposition of her visible body, her embracing and unwinding. (7) The woman shone with youthful bloom; her hair was much blacker than womankind's; the creature had the whitest face, a fine nose, a hand with lovely fingers, graceful lips; her breasts were plump, and on the phantom her nipple seemed to have newly peeped out a little in maturity. (8) But the watery element protected the woman's genitals from investigation, concealing the mysteries of the bed from the spectators, as if from those uninitiated into the secrets. And so the attendant officials and the commander enchanted their eyes until sunset. (9) At sunset, the visions sank into the primal depths of the waters, having arranged their display without speech: for in voiceless silence they displayed their story to their admirers.[79]

(10) But we should not overlook these particular marvellous descriptions which our predecessors as well have excellently devised about this very river: for since we derive our birth from there, it is natural and not unsuitable that we should have an affinity for the descriptions of the Nile.[80] (11) Concerning Apis one must concede to

[79] This apparition is also recorded at some length by Georgius Monachus 657-8, who says that many of the spectators were eaten by crocodiles after the Nile creatures had disappeared; compare also John of Nikiu xcvii. 34-7, who notes that the governor Menas was the son of Main, and that there was disagreement over whether the apparition was a good or bad omen.

[80] This is the only evidence that Theophylact was of Egyptian origin.

the inquisitive Herodotus,[81] while there are records by the ancients as well concerning the anthropomorphic Nile creatures. (12) What is signified by the presence of these, the Lydian dared to declare, he who is much more recent than the others and who was well known during the times of the emperor Justinian.[82] But we will disregard the continuity a little and describe the summer risings of the Nile, setting before our audience in a noteworthy record the more distinguished descriptions of the historians.[83]

(17. 1) This Nile is the greatest of all the rivers in the inhabited world; it flows past the territory of many men, Libya, Ethiopia, and India itself, surpasses the Ganges and Indus in size, and conceals its sources from men's vision. (2) Now, in the height of summer it receives augmentation, which is contrary to the nature of the other rivers in the inhabited world. But we are introducing in the present history, word for word, the reasons which have been expressed by the many and set forth by the ancients. (3) Now Hellanicus and Cadmus, and even Hecataeus, had recourse to mythical assertions, while the inquisitive Herodotus, who had much experience of history, if ever a man did, tried to provide the explanation for this, but is discovered to have pursued contradictory suppositions. (4) But Xenophon and Thucydides, who are praised for truthfulness, preferred to avoid these investigations. Ephorus and Theopompus, who above all men devoted themselves to these matters, completely failed to understand the truth: they did not realize the explanation, not because of negligence but because of the peculiarity of the country. (5) For from remote times until Ptolemy, who was called Philadelphus, these regions were completely and utterly foreign, and dangerous for those who entered. But

[81] Apis was the sacred bull worshipped at Memphis (Herodotus ii. 153; iii. 27-9).

[82] This reference is probably to John Lydus, de Mensibus iv. 57, which records that a festival held on 19 Mar. celebrated the apparition of a good demon in the Nile who, when the flood seemed to have failed and the Egyptians were starving, foretold that the river would still flood.

[83] The following discussion of the Nile flooding is not Theophylact's original research, but merely an unacknowledged paraphrase of the account in Diodorus Siculus i. 37-41 (translation by C. H. Oldfather in the Loeb edn., with limited nn.); Diodorus' account was, ironically, also an unacknowledged paraphrase of an earlier analysis, probably that by Hecataeus of Abdera. Theophylact, although abbreviating his source, keeps close to Diodorus' account and writes more stylish Greek under his influence; the most noticeable difference is that Theophylact is rather more polite than Diodorus had been to many of the earlier authorities who are refuted (e.g. vii. 17. 15-16, Herodotus). The causes of the Nile flooding had also been discussed by John Lydus, de Mensibus iv. 107, and Theophylact probably intended his own discussion to surpass John's: he succeeded in terms of length, but certainly not in originality or even in variety of authorities cited (John could include the Roman Seneca among his authorities).

after the aforementioned king had campaigned against Ethiopia with a Greek force, the facts about this region have become known exceedingly, so to speak, more accurately.

(6) Now the priests of Egypt assert that the Nile takes its formation from the ocean which flows around the inhabited world: there is no truth in what they say, but they resolve the problem with another, advancing as proof an explanation which stands in need of much proof, and leaving their description bereft of confirmation. (7) But those Troglodytes who migrated from the interior regions, who are also known as Bolgii, say that there are certain phenomena connected with those regions from which one might deduce that the stream of the Nile is constituted from many sources which combine at a single spot; (8) and in point of fact they say that it is naturally most fertile, beyond all the rivers throughout the inhabited world. But those who dwell on the island called Meroë (this is situated in the stream of the Nile) have called the river Astapous, which signifies when translated into the Greek language 'water out of darkness': for these assign the nature of this river to incomprehensibility. (9) Now Thales, who is called one of the seven sages, says that the Etesian winds, blowing against the mouths of the river, prevent the stream from flowing out into the sea, and that for this reason it becomes full and inundates Egypt, which is low-lying and flat. (10) It is easy to demonstrate the falsehood of this explanation, even though it appears to be plausible: for if the statement were true, then all the rivers which have mouths facing the Etesian winds would experience a similar rising. (11) Anaxagoras, who is called the physicist, held the opinion that the melting snow in Ethiopia was the cause of the river's fullness; even the tragic poet Euripides believed him and incorporated this in his poetry. (12) Now this assertion, we say, does not require much opposition, since its falsehood is obvious: for it is impossible for snow to accumulate in Ethiopia on account of the excessive heat; (13) for, in general, in those regions there is no frost, nor cold, nor, in short, any sign of winter, and in particular at the summer solstice. And even if someone were to say, by way of concession, that there were quantities of snow in Ethiopia, then again the inadequacy of the aforesaid explanation is proved most surely. (14) For it is agreed that every river which receives superfluity from snow gives off cold breezes, and also naturally thickens the air; but in the vicinity of the river Nile it is impossible to find formation of cloud, or cold breezes, or the nature of the air being thickened.

(15) Herodotus says that the Nile is of the size it appears during

its fullness, but that in the winter season the sun, as it travels over Libya, draws up to itself accumulations of moist essence from the Nile waters, and hence in the winter season the river becomes less; (16) but that when summer is present, and the sun makes its way towards the north, it dries up and reduces the rivers native to Greece; and that for this reason, the fullness of the Egyptian river at the summer solstice is not extraordinary. But out of respect for the man's love of learning, we will not denounce his mistake in detail. (17) For if this were consonant with the truth, then assuredly the sun would also draw up from the other rivers of Libya, and the rivers of Libya would also endure experiences akin to those of the Nile: but in truth it is impossible to see anything of this sort in the rivers of Libya. Therefore the historian has extemporized his explanation.

(18) Democritus, the brother of physics, maintains that in the winter season a mass of snow descends on the north but that, when summer comes, this is dissolved by the hot vapour; hence, he says, a great thaw occurs, and for this reason many very thick clouds are produced in the higher regions, since an abundant exhalation is being raised aloft; (19) these clouds are driven by the Etesians until they strike the highest mountains in the inhabited world, which are those in Ethiopia. Then somehow, being violently shattered on such heights, they produce enormous downpours, from which, he asseverates, the river grows full at the blowing of the Etesian winds. (20) However, one should not believe him: for the Nile begins to grow full practically at the summer solstice, when the Etesians are not yet blowing, but it ceases after the autumnal equinox, when the aforesaid winds have long since stopped. And so one must acknowledge Democritus' inventiveness, but one should not believe his words at all. (21) Ephorus adduces a strange explanation. He says in fact that the whole of Egypt is alluvial soil and indeed cold as well, furthermore that its nature is like pumice-stone, and that it has large and continuous fissures; through these it takes up into itself a mass of moisture, and during the winter season confines this within itself, but at the start of the summer solstice a sort of sweat subsists from it on every side, and for this reason it fills the river. (22) Now it is clear that Ephorus has not only not seen Egypt, but that he has not even learned attentively from those who have seen the state of this land. (23) For, first of all, if the Nile derived its increase from Egypt itself, it would not grow full in the interior regions where it is borne through a rocky and solid country; but in fact, it has its increase before it touches Egypt, while it flows

through Ethiopia for more than six thousand stades. (24) Second, if the stream of the Nile were lower than the crevices in the alluvial earth, it would have come about that the fissures were on the surface, over which it would be impossible for such a great mass of waters to cross; but if the river occupied a position higher than the crevices, it would be impossible for the conflux of waters from the lower hollows to the higher surface to occur. (25) In general, who would consider it possible for the sweat from the crevices in the earth to introduce such great increase in the river that practically the whole of Egypt is inundated by it? For I disregard the lie about the alluvial earth and the waters which melt away in the crevices, since the refutation is manifest from the following. (26) For the river Maeander in Asia has created much alluvial land, and yet you do not observe any occurrence whatsoever of the events associated with the overflowing of the Nile. (27) But also in Acarnania the river called Achelous, and in Boeotia the Cephisus, have deposited a considerable quantity of earth from the Phocaeans: from both these cases the lie of Ephorus is clearly refuted.

(28) So much for Ephorus; but some of the sages in Memphis have attempted to adduce the following explanation for the filling-up. They say that the earth is divided into three parts: one part is that of our inhabited universe (for such one must call it), another is antipathetic to these regions in its seasons, while the third lies between these and is completely uninhabitable on account of heat. (29) Now, if the Nile made its ascent during the time of winter, it would be clear that it received the conflux from our zone, because it is during these times in particular that heavy rains occur among us. (30) But since on the contrary it grows full during the summer, it is plausible that winter storms are being generated in the opposite regions, and that the excess of the waters in those regions comes to our inhabited world. Hence too, no one can reach the sources of the Nile, as the river would be carried from the opposite zone through the uninhabitable one. (31) A further testimony of this is the exceptional sweetness of the water in the Nile: for they say that it is considerably boiled down during its passage through the hot zone, and for this reason is sweetest of all the rivers, since indeed it is natural that the fiery sweetens all moisture. (32) But we will also answer this: for we say that it is impossible for a river to be carried up from the opposite inhabited world into our own earth, and particularly if one were to suppose that the earth is of spherical form. (33) For how could the Nile alone be carried from that

inhabited world to our regions? For it is probable that there are also other rivers, just as there are with us as well. (34) Furthermore, the reason for the sweetness of this river is totally absurd and completely unproven. For if the river were sweetened by being boiled down by the heat, it would never have been fertile nor have possessed diverse varieties of fish and beasts: for all water that has been transformed by the fiery element is incapable of generating life. (35) Therefore, since the nature of the Nile is completely reversed by the postulated boiling, one must consider false the suggested causes of the filling-up.

Oenopides says the following, that during the summer season the subterranean waters are cold, but that contrariwise in winter they are hot, (36) and that this is clear from the observation of deep wells: for at the height of winter the waters in the deepest wells are found to be warm, but the opposite when summer is present. (37) Wherefore it is also reasonable that the Nile is small and contracted during winter, because the heat under the earth consumes much of the watery essence while rains do not occur in Egypt, whereas in summer, when there is no longer subterranean consumption in the regions deep down, its natural vigour reaches fullness without hindrance. (38) But one must also reply to this: many of the rivers in Libya have mouths similarly located and take analogous courses, but do not rise up in a comparable manner to the Nile. For, on the contrary, since they are full in winter while they cease in summer, they refute Oenopides'. falsehood.

(39) Agatharcides of Cnidus has alone mastered the borders of the truth: for he said that each year in the regions of Ethiopia there are constant heavy rainstorms from the summer solstice until the equinox which occurs every autumn; (40) so it is reasonable that in winter the Nile contracts, when it has its natural course derived from its own sources alone, but that in summer it receives its increase because of the rains which are poured forth. As testimony for his statements, the occurrences in certain regions of Asia are also advanced. (41) For in the regions of Scythia which are towards the Caucasus, when time has made way, each year there occur exceptional snowstorms,[84] and this happens continuously for very many days; while in the parts of India turned towards the north there are also at certain fixed seasons falls of hail, great both in size and quantity; (42) but also near the river

---

[84] Diodorus specified that these snowstorms occurred after the passage of winter; Theophylact's phrase 'when time has made way' is obscure, and either the text is corrupt or he copied from a corrupt text of Diodorus.

Hydaspes continuous rains occur at the start of summer, and in Ethiopia the same happens some days later; this cyclical condition always causes severe storms in the contiguous regions. (43) So it is not at all surprising that in the inhabited area of Ethiopia above Egypt as well, constant rains beating down on the mountains make the river full in summer, particularly since its very self-evidence bears witness[85] by means of the barbarians who inhabit the regions. (44) But if the statement is of a nature contrary to what happens among us, one should not disbelieve for this reason: for indeed the south wind among us is stormy, but in Ethiopia it produces a clear sky, and the northern blasts, which are vigorous in Europe, are in that land gentle, vigourless, and altogether feeble. (45) And as the sun inclines towards the north pole, it happens that rains come upon Ethiopia during our summer and thence the Nile receives its increase, and on the other hand, when it withdraws towards the south pole, the Nile looks to contraction.[86]

(46) And so this is enough concerning the filling-up of the river, lest we adulterate the goal of the history; now we must goad our account to submit to the subsequent parts of the narration. Then, on his return from Alexandria, Menas wrote to the emperor Maurice about the manifestation of the anthropomorphic Nile creatures; on hearing this, the emperor was exceedingly downcast in spirit.

[85] In Diodorus the verb is passive, 'is attested by the barbarians', which provides better sense.

[86] This section is Theophylact's own addition to Diodorus.

BOOK EIGHT

(1. 1) IN these very times Chosroes, the king of the Persians, tried to defile the peace.[1] The barbarian's reason was in fact roughly this: many different nations are native to Arabia, whom the masses are accustomed to call Saracens; (2) some of these particular nations were Roman allies; a subdivision of these went into Persia during the time of the peace, and in their sally ravaged certain parts of Babylonia. Hence Chosroes decided to be aggrieved. (3) For this reason the emperor Maurice dispatched to Persia as ambassador George, who held the responsibility for the tax-collection of the eastern cities; Romans call this man praetorian prefect.[2] (4) And so Chosroes, in indignation at what had happened, affronted the ambassador and engineered for him a long delay in the barbarian country; so George spent many uncomfortable days in Persia without gaining any access to the king. (5) Then, since Chosroes' affairs were still subject to strife,[3] the barbarian sensibly took the view that he should not in the meantime initiate war against the Romans; then the Babylonian king admitted George into the palace. (6) And so George, having the moment as his ally, persuaded the barbarian not to dissolve the peace treaty. And so, in this way, Chosroes 'willingly but with reluctant heart', as the poet says,[4] welcomed quiet. (7) And so the ambassador reported in detail to the emperor all that had occurred, but his

---

[1] The date of these events is unknown. Theophylact has connected them with the Balkan campaign of 598, but his Balkan chronology is so confused that this synchronism is worthless. A date towards the end of Maurice's reign is probable.

[2] For the functions of the praetorian prefect, which included the assessment, collection, and disbursal of taxes, see Jones, *LRE* 448-62. This embassy by George may well be that on which John of Epiphania served: John (§ 1) states that his embassy occurred 'at a later time, after the end of the war', and that the ambassador George's purpose was to achieve 'the concord for what had happened', an objective that is not dissimilar to that described in Theophylact. M. J. Higgins, 'Chronology of Theophyl. Sim. 8. 1. 1-8', *Orientalia Christiana Periodica* 13 (1947), 219-32, tried to establish the date of George's embassy as spring/summer 592, but his arguments are not conclusive. George was an experienced administrator and diplomat, and may have conducted several embassies to Persia during the 590s.

[3] The strife probably denotes the revolt of Bestam, which continued in the eastern provinces for about a decade (see book v n. 77).

[4] Homer, *Iliad* iv. 43 (also quoted at iv. 15. 11, again with reference to Chosroes).

exposition of the conversation did not gain a beneficial outcome, because in addressing the emperor George said: 'The king of the Persians spoke as follows in the hearing of the satraps: "On account of the ambassador's excellence, I am putting a stop to the war." ' (8) On hearing this the emperor grew angry with the ambassador, and the success of his mission was perilous for George. For, in truth, speech that is not regulated by moderation can provide great misfortunes for its practitioners.

(9) But when the Chagan (for let us return to events in Europe) had crossed the Ister while returning home because of the peace, the Roman forces in Thrace sent ambassadors to the emperor Maurice with accusations of treachery against Comentiolus the general.[5] (10) Then fierce dissension arose in the royal city, and the emperor appointed arbitrators for Comentiolus and the ambassadors; in fact, when the judicial assembly took place, and the emperor pleaded with the ambassadors, the indictment received a check and Comentiolus again became general. (11) When summer came round, he left the city;[6] since the Romans had resolved their grievance with the general, Comentiolus collected the army, came to the river Ister, and united with Priscus at Singidunum.(2. 1) On the fourth day, an assembly of the armies was held, and after Priscus had made a speech the peace between Avars and Romans was severed: for the emperor Maurice had ordered the generals by a royal command to contravene the treaty.

(2) Then, since the peace had been publicly broken, the Romans came to Viminacium, which is an island located in the streams of the Ister.[7] On this island Comentiolus appeared to fall sick.[8] (3) While the

---

[5] The embassy is also described by John of Antioch, fr. 218b, who records that the future emperor Phocas was one of the ambassadors.

[6] Although Theophylact has not stated that a new year has now arrived, this cannot be the same year (598) as that in which the Avars routed Comentiolus: in 598, the Avars had besieged Priscus until Easter, 30 Mar. (vii. 13. 1-3); they then routed and pursued the Romans, were struck by plague, and eventually accepted a Roman embassy; after this the Avars had to withdraw beyond the Danube, while the scattered Roman forces in Thrace collected themselves and lodged complaints against Comentiolus. This process must have occupied most of the summer of 598, so that it must be in 599, 'when summer came round', that Comentiolus set out from Constantinople.

[7] Viminacium had in fact been an important city, located near the confluence of the Danube and Morava rivers, which the Avars had captured in 583 (i. 4. 4). It is possible that the inhabitants who survived this capture had subsequently moved to a safer site on a nearby island in the Danube, but there is no evidence to corroborate this.

[8] The contrast in the following narrative (viii. 2. 3-4. 8) between the laudable victories of Priscus and the contemptible inaction and ill-fated stubbornness of Comentiolus is particularly blatant. It is likely that both Priscus' successes and Comentiolus' failures have been exaggerated.

Romans were crossing from the island to the mainland, the Chagan learned of the movements of the Roman camp. And so the barbarian gathered forces and ravaged Roman land, while to the four sons which he possessed he entrusted forces and instructed them to guard the crossings of the Ister. (4) And so the barbarian's sons attempted to guard the crossings of the Ister in accordance with the command, but the Romans fabricated rafts, as they are called, and with one accord traversed the river. Then, in a battle which took place on the river banks, the Romans overcame the opposing forces. (5) But Comentiolus, along with Priscus, made his quarters at Viminacium. His dilatory reluctance to engage was by no means unconvincing: for he slashed the veins in his hand with a doctor's knife, and at the outflow of blood his cowardly non-combatance became respectable, as it were. (6) Then, although the Romans had been ferried across the Ister and constructed the camp, Priscus did not leave the island, for he was reluctant to join battle without Comentiolus; but, since the Roman force was lacking a leader, the barbarians made raids on their camp. (7) The Romans sent messengers to the generals at Viminacium and pointed out their danger: since Priscus refused to deal with the task without Comentiolus, and the barbarians were pressing very strongly, Priscus persuaded Comentiolus to depart and he himself undertook charge of the dangers.[9] (8) Therefore he left Viminacium and came to the Roman camp. On the second day he ordered the ships to leave the banks of the Ister and move their anchorage close to Viminacium; (9) for Priscus feared that, while their boats were stationed by the river banks, the Romans would perhaps make frequent crossings to the island, and that consequently, through the fragmentation of the Roman force, the rampart would be less strongly guarded. (10) Then, since the barbarians were impatient for battle, on the fourth day in the morning Priscus ordered the Romans to arm; having organized his dispositions as best he could in three divisions, he initiated military operations.[10]

[9] Maurice, *Strategicon* xi. 4, 89 ff., recommended that on campaigns beyond the Danube a significant force of cavalry should remain near the river to protect the crossing and to spread terror among the Slavs by threatening attacks in different directions, thereby allowing an advance party to gain easier victories over disorganized opponents; at *Strategicon* xi. 4, 180 ff., the commander is advised when attacking the Slavs to divide his army and to entrust a fast-moving column to a subordinate who would ravage the country ahead of, but in conjunction with, the slower-moving contingent led by the senior general. It is likely that these anti-Slav tactics were being adapted by Comentiolus for use against the Avars, which would help to explain Comentiolus' apparent inaction and would put Priscus' achievements into perspective.

[10] The following campaign began on the banks of the Danube opposite Viminacium

(11) And so the Romans laid aside their bows and combated the barbarians at close quarters with their spears. The Avars had equipped their disposition in fifteen companies; the Romans had arranged their disposition in a single conjunction, both from fear about the camp and so as to fight in square formation; hence they provided security for the camp. The battle continued in progress for many hours; (12) but as the sun sank the battle also sank with it, and this turn of the battle was favourable to the Romans: although three hundred Romans were killed, four thousand of the Avars perished. So when night had come the Romans returned to the camp.

(3. 1) On the third day the barbarian organized another battle. And so Priscus marshalled his army as well as possible, and in the morning moved to the engagement. (2) Then he strictly marshalled three forces for the Romans. Next he firmly committed the wings to split apart at once and thus admit the Avars, so that the barbarians would be cooped up in the middle as the forces surrounded the cavity, and would fall into unexpected disasters. (3) Then in such a manner the barbarians were outgeneralled and nine thousand of the opposing enemy force were slain. As the sun sank the victors returned to the rampart. (4) On the tenth day the general heard that the barbarian had again arrived for an engagement; when day grew light, he equipped the Romans, drew them up in good order, and moved to battle. (5) And so Priscus mobilized his forces in three divisions again, whereas the barbarian moved against Priscus after forming a single division. And so Priscus occupied the advantageous land in the locality and, having the might of the wind as assistant, he clashed with the Avars from a height and with his two wings outfought the enemy. (6) Since a swamp was spread below that locality, he drove the barbarian towards the waters. For this reason the barbarians were beaten back amidst the shallows, had the ill fortune to confront the swamp, and drowned most horribly. (7) Then, after a great multitude had perished in this swamp and the Chagan's sons were drowned there, Priscus procured the most glorious victory. In this battle then, fifteen thousand barbarians were annihilated.

(8) And so the Chagan, who survived at great peril, came to the river Tissus; on the thirtieth day the barbarian assembled a force. When he took the initiative for a fourth battle and the Roman general had heard of this, Priscus encamped at the river Tissus. (9) Accord-

and proceeded in a north, or north-westerly, direction towards the river Tisza (viii. 3. 8, the Tissus). The sites of the individual engagements cannot be located.

ingly, a day for battle between the two forces was determined; when the
appointed time had come, at the first hour Priscus marshalled his forces
in inverse order, placing the left contingent on the right and the centre
on the left.[11] The barbarian deployed for battle in twelve companies.
(10) And so the Romans endured the conflict with greater heroism;
then they outfought the barbarian by their resolution, and a very large
number of the enemy perished in this battle as well. Then the Roman
army won this even more glorious crown of victory. (11) Priscus marshalled four thousand men and ordered these to traverse the Tissus and
investigate the enemies' movements. And so the men dispatched by the
general crossed the nearby river. Accordingly they encountered three
Gepid settlements; the barbarians knew nothing of the previous day's
events, had arranged a drinking session, and were celebrating a local
feast. (12) Then they had entrusted their cares to drink and were passing the night in festivity; but in the twilight, as it is called, when remnants of night still remained, the Romans attacked the drunken
barbarians and wrought extensive slaughter. For thirty thousand barbarians were killed. (13) After securing a very large body of captives,
they recrossed the river and escorted the booty safely to Priscus. On the
twentieth day the barbarian again assembled forces near this particular
river, and for this reason Priscus returned to the vicinity of the river
Tissus. Accordingly, there was in this place a very great and most noteworthy engagement. (14) And so, on this very day, the barbarians were.
mightily outfought, so to speak, and they drowned in the streams of the
river, and a very great portion of the Sclavenes also perished along with
them. (15) After the defeat the barbarians were taken prisoner: three
thousand Avars were captured, a total of six thousand two hundred
other barbarians, and eight thousand Sclavenes. And so the prisoners
were thus consigned to chains, while the general dispatched to the city
of Tomi the barbarians taken as booty. (4. 1) But, before the emperor
came to know anything of these events, the Chagan sent ambassadors
to Maurice in an attempt to regain the captives. (2) Maurice, being
shaken by the barbarian's threats and deceived by his words, ordered
Priscus by courier to give up the captured Avars to the Chagan. And so
the barbarians were thus delivered to the Chagan from Tomi.[12]

[11] Contrast vii. 14. 2, where Comentiolus is harshly criticized for attempting a similar
manœuvre.
[12] For reasons of safety the captives would have been conveyed down the Danube by
boat and not sent overland to Constantinople. This explains why the captives had
reached Tomi on the Black Sea coast, a location that might otherwise appear surprising, since they had been captured in Pannonia.

(3) But Comentiolus, as if he were with difficulty coming round from lengthy dreams, appeared to be released from his illness. Accordingly he reached Novae, assembled some of the inhabitants, and demanded to be given a guide by them so that he might pass across the Track of Trajan, as it is called:[13] for he was hastening to Byzantium to spend the winter season. (4) And so the inhabitants dissuaded Comentiolus from this particular path; enraged at this, he executed two of those who were dissuading him. And so the men of Novae declared to Comentiolus that they did not have anyone to show the way, but that twelve miles distant there was an exceedingly ancient old man, a total of one hundred and twelve years old, whom they guaranteed knew the Track of the emperor Trajan, as it is called. (5) Then the general Comentiolus came to that place, and demanded that the veteran act as guide for the journey. But the old man was perplexed and distressed; he predicted to the general the extreme difficulty of the enterprise, and described in detail the difficult terrain, the wintry conditions, and the wildness of the track: for this track had not been traversed for ninety years.[14] (6) Then the general opposed the old man's words, and after the worse plan had prevailed the Roman troops began their journey. (7) During these very days, there was a visitation of an abnormally severe cold, a heavy frost occurred, and the biting winds pressed strongly, so that many of the force and the greatest portion of the baggage animals perished. (8) So Comentiolus was most thoroughly execrated when he reached Philippopolis. Then he remained there for the whole of the winter season, and at the beginning of spring he came to Byzantium. In the following summer he was again proclaimed general by the emperor Maurice.[15]

(9) In the nineteenth year of the reign of the emperor Maurice, there was no action between Romans and barbarians. In his twentieth year, the emperor Maurice appointed his own brother Peter as

[13] The Trojan pass, which had carried the main Roman road across the Haemus mountains. Comentiolus' determination to traverse this pass in autumn or early winter was probably more sensible than Theophylact's account suggests: he perhaps wished to reopen this important route and to remove the danger of Slav ambushes, an operation that could best be carried out in winter when the trees afforded less cover to the Slavs (cf. Maurice, *Strategicon* xi. 4, 82 ff.).

[14] It is difficult to believe that this pass had not been traversed for ninety years, i.e. since the reign of Anastasius. Justinian had constructed numerous refuge-forts in the Haemus mountains, and it would be surprising if some had not been located near the route across the Trojan pass.

[15] Summer 600.

general in Europe.[16] (10) Before this year the emperor's son Theodosius was escorted as bridegroom,[17] and his father gave to him in
lawful marriage the daughter of Germanus, an exceedingly distinguished man, who was a most illustrious member of the senate.[18]
(11) Then, some days after the marriage, in the season of winter, a
shortage of food afflicted the Byzantines; this in fact turned into
famine and, when the fortieth day came round following the birthday
festival of the great God Jesus, whom the nations in the inhabited
world honour as Christ, the masses rioted against the emperor.[19]
(12) It is the custom for the emperor to celebrate the feast with the
people; then while the emperor was making supplication in company
with the throng, some of the multitude revolted, cursed Maurice, and
dispatched stones against the emperor. (13) And so Maurice commanded his bodyguards to make threats against his assailants with
their iron maces (these are in fact called *distria* in the Roman tongue),
and commanded them to put on a display of pretended aggression.

[16] The insertion of these two regnal-year dates into the military narrative is a surprise, and might indicate that this section was derived from the chronicle which provided the subsequent account of Theodosius' marriage and the rioting in
Constantinople at Candlemas (viii. 4. 10-5. 4). The two dates refer to 600 and 601 respectively (since there has to be time for one further campaign before Maurice's overthrow
in 602), and were thus calculated by counting calendar years inclusively from Maurice's
accession in 582; strictly Maurice's nineteenth year ran from 14 Aug. 600.
[17] Theophanes 283. 35-284. 3 dates the marriage to Nov., Indiction 5, i.e. Nov. 601;
Chron. Pasch. 693. 3-5 dates it to Feb. 602, and notes that the celebrations lasted seven
days, 9-15 Feb. It may be correct to combine this information, by placing the marriage
itself in Nov. 601: in Feb. 602 there followed public festivities which sought to regain
popular goodwill after the rioting at Candlemas (viii. 4. 11-5. 4). Theophylact has
inserted this Constantinopolitan information in his military narrative at the wrong
place, since he still had the campaigns of 601 (viii. 5. 5-7) and 602 (viii. 5. 8 ff.) to record.
[18] This Germanus was probably the man who had been governor of Africa under
Tiberius, been proclaimed by Tiberius as Caesar in a joint ceremony with Maurice, and
been betrothed to one of Tiberius' daughters (Theophanes 252. 2-4).
[19] i.e. the Feast of Candlemas, celebrated on 2 Feb. in honour of the Purification of
the Virgin Mary. The rioting is also described by Theophanes, 283. 12-24, but is placed
in the *annus mundi* before the marriage of Theodosius, i.e. Feb. 601. Theophylact's
description of how Germanus protected Theodosius (viii. 4. 13) suggests that Theodosius was already married to Germanus' daughter, which would place the rioting in
602. If this is correct, the rioting was followed almost immediately by a week-long festival (*Chron. Pasch.* 693. 3-5), which would have been an obvious method for the emperor
to recapture popular favour. The ceremonial associated with the Candlemas feast is
described by Constantine Porphyrogenitus, *de Caer.* i. 36 (27): the standard ceremony was
for the emperor to spend the eve of the feast in vigil in the church of the Virgin at Blachernae and then to proceed back to St Sophia in the centre of Constantinople, but a variant is
also recorded in which the emperor proceeded on the feast-day from the Great Palace to
the church at Blachernae. Maurice must have been observing the latter form of the
ceremony, since the imperial procession was directed towards Blachernae (viii. 5. 1).

But Germanus hid Theodosius under his cloak and secretly withdrew him from the litanies and escorted him to safety through the Hilaras, as they are called: this is a place in the city.[20] (5. 1) Therefore the emperor, without making an interruption to the litany, was kept safe by his bodyguards. Next they came to the church of the Mother of God, which Byzantines honour with the name Lachernae.[21] (2) This precinct is one of the most venerated, and is especially revered by the city: for it is said that the Robe of the Virgin Mary, whom we Romans honour supremely and alone as Mother of God, is deposited in a gold-inlaid casket here.[22] (3) Accordingly, after the emperor had performed the entire celebration of holy mysteries in this very church in accordance with custom, he returned to the palace. On the following day he disciplined the more eminent of the rioters with minor punishments, and banished them from the city. (4) But the banishment was of brief duration: for the emperor soon reversed his anger and gave those banished authority to enter the city.

(5) Now indeed the general Peter collected his forces, moved to the Ister, and arrived at Palastolon; he made a camp and thus passed the summer season. At the start of autumn, the general took up position in the Dardanian province, for he had heard that the Avar hordes were assembled at the place called Cataracts, and that Apsich was encamped here.[23] (6) Then, after the Romans had arrived there, the general Peter exchanged discourse with Apsich, the second-in-command of the Avar force. Apsich was attempting to win control from the Romans of the place called Cataracts. (7) After the general

---

[20] Theophanes 283. 13 records that the riot occurred while the imperial procession passed through the area known as Τὰ Καρπιανοῦ, which is to be located on the Golden Horn near Blachernae (Janin, *Constantinople* 368). The only other reference to the Hilaras (John of Ephesus v. 18) describes it as a house in the Zeugma district of the city, which Maurice gave to his sister and her husband Philippicus.

[21] i.e. Blachernae, a suburb located just outside the walls at the north-west corner of the city.

[22] The Virgin's Robe was one of the most important relics at Constantinople: see N. H.Baynes, 'The Finding of the Virgin's Robe', *Byzantine Studies and Other Essays* (London, 1955), 240-7, and 'The Supernatural Defenders of Constantinople', ibid. 248-60, at 257-8.

[23] Summer and autumn 601. Peter's campaign along the middle Danube was intended to secure Roman control of the Cataracts, the turbulent stretch of the Danube about 80 miles long (also known as the Iron Gates), where the river forces a passage through the Carpathian-Balkan mountain ranges. It was very difficult to sail upstream through the Cataracts because of the strength of the current, and ships were towed from a special path constructed along the south bank of the river. Thus if the Avars could dominate the river banks at the Cataracts, they could seriously hinder the operations of the Roman fleet further upstream.

had angrily refused to kindle the spark of peace on such terms, the two forces separated. The Chagan moved to the place called Constantiola, while the Romans returned to their stations in Thrace.

(8) As summer was hastening on,[24] word reached the emperor Maurice that the Chagan was cunningly providing a respite for warfare, so that when the Roman troops were wandering at random, he might in a surprise move assault the vicinity of Byzantium. (9) Therefore he ordered the general to leave Adrianopolis, and commanded him to make the crossing of the Ister. (10) And so Peter prepared to move camp against the Sclavene horde, and wrote to Bonosus: this man was a distinguished member of the imperial body-guard, whom the masses are accustomed to call *scribo*.[25] (11) At that time this man was under obligation to assist the general Peter. The purport of the letter was that he should furnish the Roman ferry-boats for the forces, so that they might cross the river. (12) Peter appointed Godwin as second-in-command of the army. Then Godwin crossed the river, destroyed hordes of enemies in the jaws of the sword, secured a large body of captives, and acquired great glory. And so the Romans tried to return to their own territory across the river, but Godwin for a time prevented them from doing this. (13) But the Chagan, when he had learned of the Roman incursions, dispatched Apsich with soldiers to destroy the nation of the Antes, which was in fact allied to the Romans.[26] (6. 1) In the course of these very events, large numbers defected from the Avars and hastened to desert to the emperor. So the Chagan was thrown into confusion at the news; he became greatly terrified, imploring and devising many schemes to win back the force which had defected.

[24] This must be summer 602. Theophylact has already referred to the start of autumn 601 (viii. 5. 5), and the Romans' subsequent retreat to their stations in Thrace (viii. 5. 7) should probably be interpreted as a move into winter quarters; the narrative reaches autumn 602 at viii. 6. 2.

[25] For the *scribones*, cf. vii. 3. 8 with n. Bonosus, an eminent official attached to the Balkan army, should probably be identified with the man who was subsequently a notorious supporter of Phocas (see, for example, John of Nikiu cv. 3; cvii. 19); if so, Theophylact was unaware of Bonosus' identity, since he accords the hated man a complimentary description. Cf. viii. 10. 11 with n. for the parallel case of Alexander, who is praised for his exploits with the Balkan army and cursed for his association with Phocas.

[26] Relatively little is known about the Antes, a nation which was broadly similar to the Slavs (see Bury, *HLRE* (1) ii. 21-2); they lived to the north or north-east of the Slavs. They had suffered severely from Avar ravaging during Justinian's reign (Menander, fr. 6), and in about 587 they had reached an agreement with Maurice to ravage Slav territory in an (unsuccessful) attempt to persuade the Slavs to terminate their raids into the empire (Michael the Syrian x. 21).

(2) Then, when the autumn season was present, the emperor Maurice insisted to Peter that the Roman forces should pass the period of winter in the territory of the Sclavenes; but the Romans were troubled by the emperor's purpose, both because of the booty itself, and because of the exhaustion of the horses, and in addition because hordes of barbarians were surging around the land on the opposite bank of the Ister.[27] When the general confirmed the royal command, a serious mutiny arose among the soldiers. (3) And so with frequent missives Maurice instructed Peter that the Romans should do this, whereas the Romans resisted with an intensified refusal. Wherefore they crossed the river on their march; when this had happened, they reached Palastolon with their spirits intoxicated by extreme rage.[28] (4) Peter was camped about ten miles distant from the rampart; the general, therefore, in indignation at the forces, turned to senseless folly and resolved not to camp with the army. (5) On the third day he spoke to Godwin, and what he said was this, that it had seemed in a dream that royal missives had been sent to him, and that the salutation of the letter was this, word for word: (6) 'Our Lord Jesus the Christ, the true God, the divine grace, the leader of the churches, accomplishes what is lacking for the advantage of everyone, and for the present promotes this master of the revolt.'[29] Then Peter was perplexed and distressed; in his anguish, he was utterly distracted and confounded as to what would be the results of the dreams which had appeared. (7) And so Godwin continued in silence, dismayed by the confusion among the troops and by the pronouncements of the dreams. But on the following day the forces moved camp and, bypassing Asemus (which is a fort), they came to Curisca, from where they were intending to ferry themselves across to the encampments of

---

[27] For the purpose of winter campaigns against the Slavs, cf. vi. 10. 2 with n.

[28] According to John of Nikiu cii. 10-11, the mutiny began as an attempt by the army to force Maurice to concede improvements in conditions of service, and only subsequently became an attempt to replace him as emperor. Such a development is plausible, and would help to explain why the mutineers, at first somewhat indecisive, made preparations to cross back to the north bank of the Danube (viii. 6. 7-8, an incident in Theophylact's narrative that might otherwise appear surprising). Theophylact's account seems to be intended to justify the mutiny: it is in accordance with God's will (viii. 6. 6), natural phenomena intervene to rekindle the mutiny when it appeared to have subsided (viii. 6. 8), and Maurice's motives for insisting that the army spend the winter north of the Danube are misrepresented (viii. 6. 10-7. 3 with n. 30). This must reflect the bias of Theophylact's source, since he himself had no desire to justify Phocas' coup.

[29] Although this prophecy suggests that the mutiny already had a recognized leader ('this master'), according to Theophylact (viii. 7. 7) Phocas was only acclaimed as leader rather later.

the barbarians: for they had altered their arrogance a little. (8) So, during these days, they constructed vessels; but, while this was in fact happening, they were beset by furious storms and also assailed by an onset of cold. For this precise reason the troops mutinied again in their unwillingness to cross the river. (9) Then the Romans sent eight ambassadors to Peter, who was located twenty miles distant from the camp; one of the ambassadors was in fact the most cruel tyrant Phocas. Their request was that the force should be dismissed homewards to endure the winter season. (10) The emperor insisted to Peter by courier that he lead the forces across the river and attack the land of the barbarians; and that the Romans derive from there the provisions for the camp, and thereby provide for the treasury an interruption of public maintenance.[30]

(7. 1) And so the general summoned the ambassadors, and promised that he would come to them on the morrow and provide a solution to their grievance. Accordingly, he sent for Godwin and addressed to him the sentiments of men in despair: (2) 'Precipices of dangers surround me; the emperor's command is hard to escape; it is both impossible to oppose and even harder to obey. An avaricious manner brings forth nothing good; avarice is a citadel of evils. (3) By such affliction is the emperor stricken that "he may perhaps soon lose his life", so that I may also spice my speech with a phrase from the Homeric tragedy.[31] This day will be the start of many evils for Romans; I know and am convinced.' (4) Then Peter became tearful, and interrupting his speech on account of his tears, he approached the camp. So, on the following day he assembled the brigadiers of the entire force and revealed to them the emperor's letter. (5) But the leaders of the army contingents told the general that the soldiery were unwilling to make the crossing to the further side, and they presented the causes in the form of an exposition. (6) When Peter confronted the masses with his speech, a massive squall of rage assailed the army. For this reason the forces retired from the camp, and convened an assembly by themselves. When the army officers observed this, they retired in flight and came to the general Peter. (7) The troops also

[30] Theophylact was unaware of the main reason for Maurice's insistence upon the army's wintering north of the Danube, which was that this was considered to be the best time of year for campaigns against the Slavs (see book vi. n. 54). The portrayal of Maurice as avaricious, and only concerned with public funds, serves to justify the mutiny. For Maurice's reputation for greed, cf. iii. 2. 8 with n.

[31] *Iliad* i. 205, etc. This conversation, in which even Maurice's brother accuses the emperor of avarice, provides further excuse for the mutiny.

held another assembly on the day after, appointed the centurion Phocas as commander and, raising him aloft on a shield, irregularly acclaimed his proclamation.[32] When Peter had heard this, he turned his thoughts to flight and made the events known to the emperor Maurice.

(8) And so Maurice summoned the ill-omened messenger into the palace, and in seclusion made enquiries about the sequence of events. Then he was distraught by anxieties and engulfed in great helplessness. Nevertheless, he concealed the arrival of the news, in dissemblance held a series of chariot-races as if he were dismissing the worries of the revolution, and informed the people in the stadium through heralds that they should not be distressed by the senseless disorder of the soldiers. (9) And so the supporters of the blue-gleaming colour cried out in rhythm to the emperor as follows (for indeed, let us make a record of the actual composition, word for word): 'O emperor, the God who ordered you to rule will subjugate to you everyone who wars against your kingdom. But if, my benefactor, it is a Roman who offends you, he will subjugate him to your service without bloodshed.'[33] (10) On the fourth day the emperor summoned to the palace the faction-leaders, whom the multitude is accustomed to call controllers of the factions;[34] these men were called Sergius and Cosmas; he enquired the precise number of the faction-members. (11) And so Sergius inscribed on a scroll the arrangement of the supporters of the verdant colour, who were in fact a total of one thousand five hundred, while Cosmas drew up the nine hundred members of the opposite persuasion;[35] for the Roman masses had sunk into passions for the two colours, and thereby extreme troubles came upon our world, since as this raging madness gradually increased the Roman fortunes perished.[36]

[32] This shield-raising ceremony suggests that Phocas was already being proclaimed emperor; Phocas was subsequently also raised on a shield by the factions at the Hebdomon (John of Antioch, fr. 218d. 4).

[33] This chant and the reciprocal chant from the Green faction are recorded by Theophanes 287. 12-21; the Greens complained about the activities of Constantine and Domentziolus, as well as chanting their support for Maurice.

[34] This is the earliest reference to formal faction-leaders; see Cameron, *Circus Factions* 258.

[35] This is our only evidence for the relative size of the faction partisans; the numbers seem small, but they only relate to an official category of registered partisans and exclude the broader populace who supported the factions more loosely.

[36] This judgement on the increasing menace of the factions probably refers to their role in the civil disturbances during the reign of Phocas, when their violence helped to distract the Romans from serious external threats posed by the Avars and Persians. In

(8. 1) And so, when the emperor heard that the tyrant had arrived,[37] he dispatched ambassadors in an attempt to make the disaster wither away, as it were. But the tyrant acted haughtily at these moves, grew frenzied for revolution, and dispatched the ambassadors unsuccessful. (2) But Maurice ordered the factions to guard the Theodosian walls,[38] which ancient report says were built by Theodosius, the son of the emperor Arcadius. (3) Now, a few days earlier, Germanus (this man was father-in-law of Theodosius, the emperor's son) took with him the son of the Caesar Maurice for riding and chariot-driving at Callicrateia; this is a place outside the city which is exceedingly, so to speak, luxuriant.[39] (4) And so Maurice provided a royal equipage for his son Theodosius. While the young man was engaged in hunting, free from care and exceedingly absorbed, a messenger came to him from the Roman fighting force, and presented a letter addressed by the army to Theodosius, the son of the emperor Maurice. (5) Its purport was that either Theodosius himself should assume the authority of power, or that the imperial might should be fastened upon Germanus: for the Roman forces would no longer tolerate the direction of the emperor Maurice. (6) Then this was revealed to the emperor Maurice; and so, when he had learned this, the emperor at once recalled his son to him by letter. (7) On the following day, in great distress, the emperor ordered Comentiolus to take charge of the guards of the city walls;. then on the morrow, at the first hour, Maurice had Germanus brought into the palace and, with much weeping, said that Germanus was responsible for these troubles. (8) As proof of this suspicion there was the fact that the forces, by means of a courier, wished to make Germanus emperor, and second, that when the mutinous mob was plundering all the horses grazing outside the city, Germanus' horses alone had been preserved unmolested. (9) Then, after Germanus had made sufficient defence to the emperor and failed to assuage the royal grievance, Maurice is said to have declared by way of conclusion: 'Refrain from extending your speech, Germanus. There is nothing sweeter than death by the sword.' At

the overthrow of Maurice, their major contribution was that the Greens ensured that Germanus was not proclaimed emperor (viii. 9. 14-16).

[37] It is not clear where Phocas has now arrived; the most likely places are Heracleia or the Long Walls, since shortly afterwards he is welcomed at Rhegium (viii. 10. 1).

[38] The defence of the walls of Constantinople was the main military task performed by the factions; see Cameron, *Circus Factions*, ch. 5.

[39] The precise location is unknown.

this the emperor strode forth and departed from the *secretum*, as it is called by Romans.[40] (10) The emperor's son Theodosius had been standing beside the irate emperor and pitied his father-in-law's peril; deviating a little from his proper station, he secretly whispered to the departing Germanus and said: 'Flee this man, my friend; death is the punishment for you.'

(11) And so Germanus came to his own house by means of the highway which the masses call Mese;[41] but in the afternoon he collected his personal bodyguard and approached the holy precinct of the Mother of God, which unerring report has established was built by the Cyrus who lived under the emperor Theodosius.[42] (12) At that time this man had ascended to the rank of consul; he is said to have been an exceedingly good man, and he had innate a prudent madness in his passion for words. (13) When the sun had set, Maurice heard that Germanus had taken firm hold of the altar-rails; for this reason he ordered Stephen, his own sons' tutor[43] (this man was one of the most distinguished of the imperial eunuchs, and was exceedingly illustrious in the palace) to approach Germanus, in order to lead him from the holy precincts by persuasion. (14) And so, when Germanus' companions saw the imperial eunuch seeking to lead Germanus from the sanctuary of the Mother of God, they opposed Stephen and thrust him away, clothing him with abusive insults. (15) When night had come, Germanus withdrew from the precinct and moved to the great shrine of the city, which had been founded with extreme munificence and expenditure by the emperor Justinian; the Byzantines call this the Great Church.[44] And so Maurice thrashed his own son Theodosius with a staff, because he claimed that the latter had conveyed the secret to Germanus. (9. 1) During these very events, the Romans continued their march and intensified their rush towards Byzantium; Germanus with a guard of soldiers kept tight hold on the shrine, but the emperor dispatched a number of bodyguards in his eagerness to bring Germanus from the church. Hence great rage beset the city. (2) Then Germanus was persuaded to withdraw from the precinct. Then the

[40] i.e. an audience chamber; Theophanes, 288. 1-6, quotes Maurice's words to Germanus at greater length.

[41] The main street of Constantinople, which led from the palace through the imperial fora towards the west of the city.

[42] This church was located in the district of Cyrus in the western quarter of Constantinople; see Janin, *Constantinople* 378. On Cyrus, see *PLRE* ii. 336-9, Cyrus (7).

[43] John of Antioch, fr. 218d uses the official Latin term *baiulus* to describe Stephen's position as royal tutor.

[44] i.e. St Sophia.

city populace gathered at the forecourt of the shrine, and a certain man, Andrew by name, who was one of those employed in the holy litany, shouted at the top of his voice: 'Run back to the shrine, Germanus; save your own life; death is the thing devised for you.' (3) And he persuaded Germanus to pass back again into the inner recesses of the church. But the assembled masses reviled the emperor, hurling the greatest insults at Maurice and arraying him in the register of the Marcianites; this heresy is absurd and ridiculous with a foolish reverence.[45] (4) Accordingly, as the commotion swelled, the faction members who were guarding the walls heard this and, abandoning the watch, mingled with the rioting people. (5) Accordingly, the trouble surged around the city on all sides, and on a senseless impulse the masses madly burnt down with all-consuming fire the house of Constantine, who was called Lardys. (6) This man was in fact a very distinguished member of the senate, who was invested with the patrician rank, and who some time before had received from the emperor the control of the taxes of the east, the position which Romans are accustomed to call praetorian prefect. This man Maurice had retained among the foremost men of power.[46]

(7) Accordingly, in the middle of the night, Maurice divested himself of the royal apparel and donned the garb of a commoner; he brought up the dispatch-boat (which the masses are accustomed to call a *dromon*), placed money in it, embarked on it together with his wife and children and, taking Constantine with him, looked to flight.[47] (8) But the masses lapsed towards tyranny, and spent the night revelling in wickedness and declaiming insulting chants against Maurice; they also mocked the chief priest of that time, whom Romans are accustomed to call Patriarch; this man's name was Cyriacus.[48] (9) For in truth, the multitude is uneducated and is frenzied by changes for the worse, being difficult to correct and utterly uninitiated in expediency. Accordingly, since a tremendous squall arose and an abnormal south wind blew up, with difficulty Maurice reached safety at the church of

---

[45] Theophanes, 288. 17-18, quotes the chant: 'May the man who loves you, Marcianite Maurice, not have a skin.' The attribution to Maurice of Marcianite sympathies was merely abuse, with no serious religious significance, and 'Marcianite' was probably chosen because of the assonance with Maurice's name; cf. H. Grégoire, 'Maurice le marcioniste', *Byzantion* 13 (1938), 395-6.

[46] On the praetorian prefect, cf. viii. 1. 3 and n.; Constantine was unpopular with the Green faction, who had included chants against him in their affirmation of loyalty to Maurice (Theophanes 287. 12-16).

[47] Maurice fled on the night of 22 Nov. 602 (*Chron. Pasch.* 693. 15).

[48] Patriarch of Constantinople 595-606.

the martyr Autonomus, about one hundred and fifty stades from the city of the emperor Constantine.[49] (10) The disease of gout assailed him: an ill-fated abundance of this disease is constantly established among the inhabitants of the royal city. But I will not describe the reasons, lest I should deform my narrative. (11) Then Maurice dispatched Theodosius to go to Chosroes, beg the barbarian for an alliance, remind him of everything that Maurice had discharged for him in his misfortune, and request that the reciprocal favour be weighed out in return, since his whole house together had fallen into greatest danger. (12) Maurice also showed him his ring, and committed him not to effect his return on any account unless perchance he should again behold the ring. And so Theodosius thus came to Nicaea; but Constantine, whom the masses call Lardys, was also his travelling-companion.

(13) During this night[50] an eminent faction member, whose surname was Hebdomites, together with other supporters of the verdant colour, opened the gates in the wall and came to the tyrant. (14) But Germanus had sunk into passion for monarchy: he sent Theodore (this man had been arrayed in the corps of silentiaries)[51] to Sergius (at that time, this particular Sergius was in fact faction-leader of the green mob), and asked the faction to fasten on him the royal crown upon certain conditions and written agreements. (15) And so in the morning, Sergius conveyed Germanus' words to the senior members of the faction; then the men called Greens were enraged, and rejected his request with these words: 'Germanus would never make a change of preference, nor alter his opinion, because of his exceedingly passionate commitment to partisanship for those called Blues.' (16) And so the Greens thus vetoed Germanus' hopes.[52] But Germanus, once his plan had failed, changed to goodwill for the tyrant, and paid homage to the man to whom fortune had, so to speak, migrated. (10. 1) But the Greens came to the place called Rhegium, extolled the

---

[49] The church of Autonomus was located at Praenetus (modern Karamürsel) on the south shore of the Gulf of Nicomedia (*Chron. Pasch.* 694. 2-3; R. Janin, *Les Églises et les monastères des grands centres byzantins* (Paris, 1975), 86-7); the distance from Constantinople is about 45 miles, not 150 stades (19 miles).

[50] The same night as that of Maurice's flight, 22 Nov. 602.

[51] The silentiaries were a corps of imperial ushers, whose ceremonial functions in proximity to the emperor gave them high official standing; see Jones, *LRE* 571-2.

[52] This incident clearly illustrates the important role that the circus factions might play in political affairs in the later Roman empire; the Greens' refusal to accept Germanus as emperor because of his favouritism for the Blues suggests that in some cases partisanship went beyond mere sporting enthusiasm.

tyrant with acclamations, and persuaded Phocas to approach the Hebdomon, as it is called (this is a place seven miles from the city). (2) On that day the tyrant had dispatched the *a secretis* Theodore, a distinguished member of the royal stenographers,[53] to the Church called Great, in order that the Byzantine people should bring the chief priest and senate and come to him. (3) And so Theodore arrived at the city's great precinct, which was erected by the emperor Justinian, ascended the lofty pulpit (the masses call this the *ambo*), and communicated the tyrant's order to the people. (4) Accordingly, when everyone had come before the Calydonian tyrant, the Centaur who most brutally ravaged the chaste purple (for it is fitting that Phocas be so named), the mongrel barbarian tyrant[54] feigned a pretence of wanting to proclaim Germanus. (5) Then, as the factions were applauding the tyrant and everyone was eager for change, the evil was proclaimed, the tyrant was appointed lord of the sceptres, disaster overcame prosperity, and the great and, so to speak, distinguished misfortunes of the Romans took their origin. (6) Then that murderous man donned the royal crown in the church of the Prophet and Baptist John.[55] On the following day he entered the city, seated in the royal carriage.[56] (7) And so the tyrant, drawn by four white horses, thus made his famous and glorious entry into the palace, and he showered those he met with a disbursement from the royal treasuries that rained down like a golden cloud. (8) Loud applause, prayers, and acclama-. tions from the factions flowed around the tyrant's ears. When he had entered the palace, the masses were entertained with chariot races in celebration of this ill-fated proclamation. On the following day he gave the soldiers gifts to mark his accession to the sceptres.

(9) The tyrant also had a wife whose name was Leontia; he placed a royal crown on her. Since it is customary for emperors to proclaim their consorts with processions as well, the tyrant openly honoured the custom and decided to lead the queen Leontia in triumph. (10) On

---

[53] On the stenographers (*tachygraphoi*), see John Lydus, *de Mag.* iii. 9; the *a secretis* was a senior member of the stenographers (see ibid. iii. 27).

[54] Cf. the description of Phocas at Dialogue 4.

[55] *Chron. Pasch.* 693. 16-19 records that the ceremony was performed by the Patriarch Cyriacus on 23 Nov.; on the church of the Baptist at the Hebdomon, a famous shrine that had been used during the proclamation-ceremonies of some emperors in the 5th c., see Janin, *La Géographie ecclésiastique de l'empire byzantin* i. 3 (2nd edn., Paris, 1969), 413-15.

[56] On Sunday 25 Nov., according to *Chron. Pasch.* 693. 19-24; the *Chronicon Paschale*'s account of these events, although brief, provides precise information that is lacking in Theophylact.

this day then,[57] there was a conflict between the factions about their station, since they contested the arrangement of places: for the Greens wanted to take up station in the Ampelion, as it is called (this is a fore-court of the emperor's dwelling),[58] and to serenade the queen with the customary applause, but the Blue faction objected, for they regarded this as contrary to custom and alien. (11) Accordingly, since very great commotion arose, the tyrant sent in Alexander to quell the strife of the disputants. This Alexander was a wicked man, and was extremely prominent among the rebels against the emperor Maurice.[59] (12) And so Cosmas, who was invested with the authority of demarch, resisted Alexander's words. But Alexander, who possessed a proud and tyran-nical daring, assailed Cosmas with insults; next he even placed his hands on this man's chest, and thrust him aside. Cosmas was knocked over by the push. (13) At this, the Blues were enraged, and broke out in factional shouts against Alexander; what they said was this, for it is right that we should make record of the common utterance: 'Go back, learn the position. Maurice is not dead.'[60] (11. 1) When the tyrant heard this, he checked the masses' howling about inopportune matters and, on the morrow, was roused to frenzy for the murder of the emperor. Now Maurice in repentance philosophically accepted the danger, sent his ring to his son Theodosius, who had reached the city of Nicaea, and commanded his speedy return to him. (2) And so Theodosius thus became obedient to his father, volunteered for the disaster, became intent on return, and arrived for slaughter. Then the tyrant dispatched soldiers to the coast opposite the queen of cities,

[57] According to Theophanes 289. 24, this occurred two days after the entry into the city, i.e. 27 Nov.

[58] Ampelion, a name that is not otherwise attested, was probably a synonym for the Augustaeum, which was the location for the coronation of an Augusta; see Constantine Porphyrogenitus, *de Caer.* i. 49 (40) for the ceremonial and acclamations.

[59] This Alexander is very probably the same man as the officer in the Balkan army whose exploits had earlier been recorded (vi. 8. 9 ff.; vii. 2. 6) with some approval: Phocas was an officer in the Balkan army, and his closest associates are likely to have been fellow officers (cf. viii. 5. 10, with n., for Bonosus). John of Nikiu ciii. 10 alleges that Alexander was a popular man who had married one of Maurice's daughters.

[60] This dispute at Leontia's coronation, which provides important evidence for the development of the ceremonial role of the factions, is discussed by Cameron, *Circus Factions* 251-3. The Blues' chant is recorded, with minor variants (which are not in fact correctly recorded by Cameron), by John of Antioch, fr. 218d, Georgius Monachus 662. 15-16, and Leo Grammaticus 143. 20. Cameron suggested that κατάστασις should be translated 'ceremonial'; although this is a possible rendering, we have preferred the less specific translation 'position', since one purpose of the chanting was to remind Phocas of the general state of affairs, that his position was not yet secured beyond challenge, since Maurice was still alive.

where the city of Chalcedon is also located, and slew Maurice at the harbour called that of Eutropius.[61] (3) Accordingly, the male children were slaughtered first before the emperor's eyes; hence, by putting his kin to the sword, by the slaughter of his sons,[62] the murderers inflicted advance punishment on Maurice. And so Maurice, accepting the misfortune philosophically, called on the supreme God and repeatedly uttered: 'Thou art just, O Lord, and thy judgement is just.'[63] (4) So he too became a victim of the sword, by undergoing severance of the head, and was allotted his own subsequent slaughter as if it were an epitaph for his children, after he had first demonstrated his courage in the magnitude of the disaster. (5) For, after the nurse had secretly stolen one of the royal infants and provided her own suckling for slaughter, true report proclaims that Maurice declared the secret to the murderers, revealed the concealment of the child, and asseverated that it was not right to pervert the murder by the secret theft of his son.[64] (6) And so the emperor thus became superior even to natural laws, and exchanged his life. It is said that, some time before his slaughter, the emperor Maurice had by letter supplicated in the more venerable churches of the inhabited world that the Lord Christ, One of the supramundane Trinity, might exact repayment for his misdeeds in this present mortal and perishable world.[65]

(7) But we will not omit to include in our narrative as well the contents of his testament, as it is called. For at the beginning of the.

[61] On 27 Nov., according to *Chron. Pasch.* 694. 3. Maurice and his family had been captured at the Church of Autonomus (*Chron. Pasch.* 694. 1-3), which suggests that Phocas had acted quickly to seize the deposed emperor, and was then having Maurice brought back towards Constantinople while he decided what action should be taken. The factions' disturbance at Leontia's coronation on 27 Nov. persuaded Phocas that Maurice must be killed at once. On the harbour of Eutropius at Chalcedon, see Janin, *Constantinople* 238-9.

[62] *Chron. Pasch.* 694. 4-5 records their names: Tiberius, Peter, Justin, Justinian. The name of Maurice's fourth son Paul (cf. *Chron. Pasch.* 693. 13) is omitted from the list.

[63] This is adapted from Ps. 118 (119): 137 and Job 3: 2.

[64] This act of supreme honesty is also recorded by the Syriac hagiography of Maurice (ed. and tr. L. Leroy and F. Nau, *PO* 5 (1910), 773-8), and was probably included in the corpus of stories that aimed to portray Maurice as a saint; cf. *Byzantion* 53 (1983), 337-44.

[65] For a longer account of this act of repentance, see Theophanes 284. 21-285. 16, 286. 9-14: after dispatching his letter and donations to the patriarchal sees, all cities, and the monasteries in the desert and in Jerusalem, Maurice had a dream in which he was given the opportunity to choose whether he would be punished for his misdeeds in this world or in the next; Maurice chose punishment in the present world and so the vision handed him and his family over to the soldier Phocas; on the following day the desert fathers to whom Maurice's letter had been sent announced that God had accepted Maurice's repentance. This repentance was an integral part of the hagiographic portrayal of Maurice.

reign of the emperor Heraclius, a document enclosed by the seals of the emperor Maurice was discovered, in which he had in fact set out his provisions for procedures after his death. (8) For Maurice, after encountering serious illness, had, in the fifteenth year of his imperial authority, disposed his power in writing.[66] (9) His eldest son Theodosius he established as lord of Constantinople, and invested him with charge of the east; but Tiberius he appointed as emperor of old Rome, and gave him Italy and the islands in the Tyrrhenian Sea.[67] (10) The rest of the Roman state he sliced up among his other sons,[68] and as guardian of the immature youth of his sons he appointed Domitianus, who was connected to Maurice by birth. (11) This man had been accorded the honour of chief priest of the famous church of Melitene; he was a man skilful in action, but more skilful in planning; therefore on account of the loftiness of his intellect, he had been entrusted by the emperor with the more distinguished actions of the Roman state.[69] (12) And so, concerning this man's excellence, it is not now the moment to construct the account more completely; but, lest by expanding the account of this man we cast an incongruous delay on matters more seasonable for description, come, let us steer our history towards the continuation of the narrative.

(12. 1) And so the bodies of the dead were hurled to the waves of the sea as a pitiful toy, and one could behold the marine current, so to speak, now bestowing the newly slain bodies upon the dry land, now enfolding them with eagerly returning counter-thrusts towards the receptive sea. (2) Then the royal disasters, or, to put it more appropriately, the calamities for the inhabited world, were exhibited to the crowds; the shores of Chalcedon were filled with the crowds, who received the narrative of their own folly, as they gazed at the sea-waves' naked exhibition of the emperors' bodies like depictions of misfortunes. (3) When, after the tyranny had ended, these very events were recited in the pulpit by the historian, the assembly was filled with tears as the royal disasters seemed virtually to be before

---

[66] i.e. in AD 596/7.

[67] i.e. Sicily, Sardinia, and Corsica. There are no other references to this proposed partition of the empire.

[68] It is not known how many other sons Maurice had in 597, and it is not clear how he might have divided up the empire: Africa could have constituted a separate unit, and Byzantine possessions in Spain might have been placed under their own imperial commander.

[69] Cf. the brief eulogy of Domitianus at iv. 14. 5.

the eyes of all.[70] (4) For this reason, when the father of the narrative saw that the whole audience was bathed in tears because of their lamentation, he interposed in his descriptions an interruption, and with impromptu mourning presented the following words to the gathering: (5) 'Let theatre and rostrum and free speech join me in mourning this day. Let tragedy and weeping hold festival. Let lamentation leap forth and dance, in reverence and honour for a festival of such gloom. (6) Let speech be shorn of applause, the Muses of praise, Athens of the white cloak; for the virtues are widowed and are searching for their own charioteer, since some furious envy has shattered that man's axle. (7) Spectators, but would that you had not been witnesses of such ills. An *Iliad* of woes is my subject, Erinyes are chorus for my speech. As setting for the drama I have a distinguished tomb. . . .'[71]

(8) And so Lilius (for this man had been entrusted by the tyrant with the emperor's murder) ferried across to the tyrant the heads of the slain. Then, on the plain which extends at the place called Hebdomon, and which Romans name *Campus*,[72] he publicly displayed the emperor's slaughter to the tyrant's armies. (9) For it was necessary that the inhumane army also share in the pollution through observation, so that the evil-hating and impartial judgement of God might also net in the toils of retribution all those who had raged in this cause: for all members of those murderous camps departed this life after falling into manifold grave troubles. (10) For, when the Persian war gained free rein, they received their allotted retribution for those wicked enterprises by divinely ordained threats, now being struck down by fire from heaven at the hour of the engagement, at other times being wasted by famine and ravaging; (11) but the majority perished as they surrendered this sinful life in the jaws of cutlass and sword, and victory did not desert the Persians until that tyrant-loving and most impious mob had been utterly destroyed. (12) The following statement is sufficient proof for anyone: for to confirm our account,

[70] The precise occasion on which Theophylact delivered his speech is unknown. It is possible that Heraclius organized a state funeral for Maurice, and that this provided an opportunity for ambitious orators to offer grandiloquent eulogies.

[71] The rest of the speech is lost in a lacuna of uncertain length. For the origin of the white cloaks of Athens, see Philostratus, *Lives of the Sophists* ii. 1, 550 (Athenian youths had worn black cloaks at public meetings as a sign of mourning for a crime in the distant past, until Herodes Atticus introduced white; we owe this reference to Dr Holford-Strevens). An '*Iliad* of woes' is a cliché for innumerable woes, and the Erinyes are the avenging Furies who form the chorus in Aeschylus' tragedy *Eumenides*.

[72] The *campus tribunalis*, a standard place for marshalling troops; see Janin, *Constantinople* 450.

we will briefly disregard the continuity of successive events. When the emperor Heraclius was making war against Rhazates, he inspected his army in review and discovered that there were two soldiers alone left from the tyrant-loving mob, even though the intervening years had not been numerous.[73] (13) When time had created afresh different forces and the evil had been consumed, success migrated from the Persians, the Babylonian dragon, Chosroes the son of Hormisdas, was slain, and the Persian war was concluded.[74] (14) But let us revert in regular order to the deeds of the tyranny, lest we repeat ourselves by digressions.[75] For from that moment until our present times the Roman realm has had no respite from a variety of extraordinary and intolerably serious misfortunes.

(13. 1) But the tyrant (for I am returning to my account), intoxicated with profanities, was roused to frenzy for other murders, and executed with the sword Maurice's brother, his own general. (2) That Comentiolus whom the narrative has often proclaimed as general in Europe was also slain, as indeed was George as well, the second-in-command to Philippicus, and moreover Praesentinus too, who was entrusted with Peter's affairs and whom the Romans are accustomed to call *domesticus*.[76] (3) And so Theodosius the son of the emperor Maurice fled on his return to the church of the martyr Autonomus.[77] Then, after the tyrant had heard this, he sent Alexander to slaughter the boy. Accordingly Alexander slew Theodosius, and killed with the sword the man called Lardys by the masses, after he had conveyed him to the Diadromoi, as they are called.[78] (4) It was related by some that

---

[73] This was in fact the final battle in Heraclius' campaign against the Persians, and was fought at Nineveh on 12 Dec. 627, twenty-five years after Maurice's overthrow (Theophanes 318-19). In view of the lapse of time and the constant fighting in the intervening period, it is less surprising than Theophylact claims that few troops had survived from the mutiny in 602.

[74] In 628. This is the latest event mentioned by Theophylact.

[75] Cf. viii. 14. 10. These statements indicate that Theophylact intended to continue his *History* beyond its extant terminus and to record the events of Phocas' reign.

[76] *Chron. Pasch.* 694. 11 records that Comentiolus was killed at the Church of Conon. George and Praesentinus are otherwise unknown. The *domesticus* was personal assistant to an officer of state (Jones, *LRE* 602-3); Maurice's brother Peter held the exalted rank of *curopalatus* (*Chron. Pasch.* 694. 6) and naturally had a *domesticus* to administer his affairs. Although Maurice's brother-in-law Philippicus was not killed by Phocas, he entered a monastery in 603 (*Chron. Pasch.* 695. 3).

[77] Cf. viii. 9. 9 with n.

[78] *Chron. Pasch.* 694. 7-8 specifies that the Diadromoi (the name suggests a racetrack or stadium) were near Acritas, a promontory (modern Tuzlaburnu) near the mouth of the Gulf of Nicomedia; see Janin, *Églises et monastères* 53-6. For Alexander, cf. viii. 10. 11 with n.

Alexander received money from Germanus for sparing the perils: on account of this they say that Alexander refrained from the destruction of Theodosius, but slew another who resembled him; this same Theodosius travelled around many places in the east after this unexpected escape from peril; then he subsequently came to Colchis, after that migrated to the deserts of the barbarians, and terminated his life enfeebled in body. (5) And so this story re-echoed throughout the whole inhabited world, but it was some barbarian error that gave it birth.[79] For, after laboriously investigating this matter as far as possible, we discovered that Theodosius also shared in the slaughter. (6) For those who profess that the boy did not die are blustering with meagre evidence: for their story is that, alone of those slain, the head of the emperor Theodosius was not displayed.

(7) But we would not overlook the notable events of the miraculous narrative: for on the day of the slaughter of the emperor Maurice, there took place at Alexandria an act most worthy of record and particularly worthy of the tablets of history. (8) For it was fated that a certain man, one of those who write for adornment, whom the masses in composite utterance call a calligrapher, and who was even known to us, passed the night in revelry at someone's house until the fourth watch of the night. (9) For this particular merchant was holding an all-night celebration, for his wife was observing the seventh day after giving birth to a male child for her husband. Now it is customary for the local inhabitants, in observing the seventh day after the birth of children, to spend the night in festivities of drinking. Then, after the dinner had become subject to satiety, the feasting was terminated, and the man who wrote for adornment left the merchant's house. (10) In the middle of the night then, as he was approaching the city's Tychaeum, as it is called (this is a famous place in Alexandria), he saw the more famous statues stealing down from their pedestals;[80] they emitted to him a very loud utterance, addressing the man by name, and in loud and vehement utterance describing the calamities which had attended the emperor Maurice on that day. (11) And so the man

---

[79] Eastern sources (*Anon. Guidi* 10, and Sebeos, chs. 21, 23) also record the story of Theodosius' escape: he was honourably received by Chosroes, who had him crowned by the Nestorian Catholicus, and who provided him with an army in order to invade the Roman empire. Theophylact returns to the story at viii. 15. 8.

[80] The Tychaeum was a circular shrine in the centre of Alexandria which contained statues of Alexander the Great and Ptolemy Soter, as well as of various gods. It had apparently been turned into a wine-shop after the end of the 4th c. (see P. M. Fraser, *Ptolemaic Alexandria* (Oxford, 1972), i. 242 with n. 417).

reached home, cowering in great fear at this miraculous vision. At daybreak he came to the associates of the Augustalis, as he is called, and detailed these fearful narrations. (12) When the report reached the prefect of Egypt (at that time Peter was guiding the reins of the Egyptian authority, a man who was also connected to us by birth),[81] the man who had heard the statues was summoned in private. (13) The governor, after investigating this man's words and marvelling at the exposition of the narration, adjured the man who wrote for adornment not to impart to anyone else these mysterious and secret descriptions. Then, having registered that day, the governor of Egypt awaited the outcome. (14) On the ninth day a messenger arrived at Alexandria, escorting, so to speak, the slaughter of the emperor Maurice. Then, after Peter had discerned the outcome of the events predicted by the statues, or to speak more appropriately demons, he publicly paraded the prophecy, brought to prominence the man who wrote for adornment, and pointed him out as the authority for the story.[82] (15) Many other miraculous prophecies of the future occurred in the Roman state, but all eternity would fail us if we should try to record these in greater detail.

(16) Now indeed, Maurice is said to have been generous to magnificence of language, and to have honoured exceedingly illustriously those who had striven for the beauties of learning.[83] He is also said to have built at Tarsus the sanctuary of Paul the Cilician, who preached in virtually all of the inhabited world the glad tidings of the wonderful Gospel of salvation of Christ Jesus the only-begotten Son of God.[84] (17) It is reported that the emperor Maurice also remitted for his subjects a third part of the taxes, and bestowed thirty talents on the Byzantines for the renovation of the aqueducts.[85]

[81] This incidental comment that Peter was a relative of Theophylact is evidence for the high social and administrative position that the family occupied in Egypt (cf. vii. 16. 10 for Theophylact's Egyptian origin).

[82] The miraculous announcement of a person's death could be used as proof of his saintliness; cf. the declaration to Sabinus in Alexandria of the death of John the Almsgiver, which had occurred on Cyprus (Leontius of Neapolis, *Life* of John, 46). It is interesting to observe that a relative of Theophylact was involved in the propagation of a story that would help to establish Maurice's holiness.

[83] Evagrius vi. 24, p. 241. 1-5, records that he was granted the rank of consul by Maurice in return for an oration to commemorate the birth of Maurice's son Theodosius.

[84] John of Nikiu c. 2-3 records that, during Maurice's reign, the district of Tarsus known as Antinoaea was submerged by a flood which destroyed many buildings. Maurice perhaps built the church after this disaster.

[85] John of Nikiu xcv. 16-17 records that Aristomachus, the comptroller of the

(14. 1) Let not the wonderful events at that time concerning the martyr Euphemia escape those who love knowledge, but let us extend our account a little. For descriptions which have attained divine illumination bestow their great inherent benefit on the souls of their listeners. (2) Chalcedon is a city situated at the mouth of the Pontus, on the opposite shore from the city of the Byzantines. In it there is situated a church of the martyr Euphemia, where ancient report has established that the most holy body of the martyr is placed in a sepulchre. (3) Now every year on the day of her martyrdom, on account of the superabundance of that divine activity, there appears a most wonderful sign, one which is, in short, most incredible to those who have not witnessed it. (4) For although the body has lain in the tomb for four hundred years or so already, on the aforesaid day, before the eyes of the throngs, the leader of the priestly church of those parts draws up with sponges founts of blood from the dead body. (5) And you may see, as if from a newly slain body, the blood mingled with flux from wounds and blended with certain natural aromatics, and the priest performing the distribution of these to the throngs in little vessels made out of glass. (6) Then there rashly occurred to the emperor Maurice, in the twelfth year of his imperial power,[86] a certain notion concerning the divinity of the soul: he belittled the miracles, rejected the wonder outright, and attributed the mystery to men's crafty devices. (7) Accordingly, the grave was stripped of its silver ornament, and the tomb was guarded by seals, for such was the counsel of bold disbelief. (8) But when the appointed day had arrived, the secret was tested, the mystery examined, the miracles investigated, and through the miracles she became an indubitable witness to her own power: once again rivers of aromatic blood sprang from the tomb, the mystery gushed with the discharges, sponges were enriched with fragrant blood, and the martyr multiplied the effluence. For when God is disbelieved, he is not accustomed to begrudge knowledge. (9) And so in this way the martyr educated the emperor's disbelief. But the emperor sent, in

property of the empress Constantina, constructed aqueducts and a bronze reservoir for Constantinople, whose inhabitants had previously been complaining greatly of the shortage of water.

[86] i.e. Aug. 593-4. Since the martyrdom of Euphemia was commemorated on 16 Sept., the story of Maurice's disbelief is dated to 593. The story is discussed by H. Grégoire, 'Sainte Euphémie et l'empereur Maurice', Le Muséon 59 (1946), 295-302, who suggested that it provided a divine explanation for Maurice's murder at Chalcedon eight years later. This would help to explain its placing in Theophylact's narrative.

return for the gushing forth of blood, an inundation of tears, and repaid the effluences of aromatics with a shower from his eyes, saying: 'God is wonderful in his saints.'[87]

(10) But, now that we have attended most sensibly to this digression, it is time to recollect the return as well, and to record in greater detail the events connected with the tyranny.[88]

(15. 1) Accordingly, the tyrant subjected to confinement Constantina, the daughter of the emperor Tiberius, together with her three daughters, in a private house; the dwelling was called that of Leo.[89] (2) In the fifth month, the tyrant set out his own proclamation in writing, and dispatched Lilius to Chosroes, appointing him the messenger of his tyrannical election: for it was customary for Romans and Persians to do this whenever they ascended to the royal might.[90] (3) Lilius came to Daras, carrying regal gifts. He was received with exceptional splendour by Germanus, who was adorned with the rank of the consuls and had been allotted the charge of the camp arrayed there. (4) For, shortly before the time of the tyranny, when Chosroes king of the Persians was angry with the commander Narses, the emperor Maurice had relieved the leader Narses of custody of Daras and had elevated Germanus instead; Maurice intended thereby to soothe the Babylonian anger.[91] (5) Now, while Germanus and Lilius were out riding, forming a pair, at the third hour a military man struck the mounted Germanus with a sword. (6) And so Germanus dismounted from his horse and arrived home carried on a litter; but since the consequences of the sword-thrust did not gain influence in a vital place, Germanus was cured of the blow in a few days. Then, after he had been made better by medicines, he gave an exceedingly distinguished feast for Lilius, and sent him on to Chosroes. (7) And so Chosroes exploited the tyranny as a pretext for war, and mobilized that world-destroying trumpet: for this became the undoing of the prosperity of Romans and Persians. For Chosroes feigned a pretence of upholding the pious

---

[87] Ps. 67 (68): 36.

[88] Cf. viii. 12. 14 with n.

[89] It is not possible to identify this house of Leo, which was probably a monastery or nunnery. Maurice's three daughters were called Anastasia, Theoctiste, and Cleopatra (*Chron. Pasch.* 693. 15-16).

[90] The fifth month of Phocas' reign was Apr. 603. For the customary messages, cf. iii. 12. 2, 17. 1.

[91] The cause of Chosroes' anger against Narses is not known. One possibility is that he may have been suspected of intriguing with the citizens of Nisibis, who revolted against Chosroes in May 602 (*Chron. Seert* 75).

memory of the emperor Maurice.[92] And so in this way the Persian war was allotted its birth, and Lilius remained among the Persians in great hardship.

(8) In these days, error came upon the inhabited world, and the Romans supposed that Theodosius was not dead.[93] And this became an opportunity for very great evils, and this false supposition contrived an abundance of slaughters. When the rumour spread to the palace, the tyrant was greatly distressed and destroyed Alexander with the sword.[94] (9) For it was necessary for Phocas to destroy his co-partners in the tyranny, and to escort to extraordinary deaths his fellow allies in the evil. For collaboration in evil is incapable of establishing the firm friendship of like minds.

[92] Cf. *Anon. Guidi* 10, which records that Chosroes first gave military support to the supposed Theodosius, the son of Maurice, and then invaded in person after Theodosius had been defeated.

[93] Cf. viii. 13. 4-5 with n.

[94] For Alexander, cf. viii. 10. 11 with n. John of Nikiu ciii. 10-12 records that Alexander was accused of plotting to kill Phocas.

Chronological Table

572		Start of Persian war; Marcian appointed general (iii. 10. 1).
	autumn	Raid into Arzanene (iii. 10. 2-3).
573	spring	Marcian's victory at Sargathon; sieges of Thebothon and Nisibis; flight of Roman army from Nisibis on approach of Chosroes (iii. 10. 4-7, 11. 1-2).
	summer	Chosroes besieges Dara; Adormaanes ravages Syria (iii. 11. 2, 10. 8-9).
	winter	Capture of Dara; Justin II goes mad (iii. 11. 3).
574	spring	One-year truce arranged (iii. 11. 3).
	December	Appointment of Tiberius as Caesar (iii. 11. 4-12. 1).
575	winter/spring	Tiberius negotiates an extension to truce for a further three years; appointment of Justinian as commander in the east and recruitment of new forces (iii. 12. 2-10).
	summer/autumn	Further negotiations (not recorded by Theophylact).
576	spring	Chosroes invades Armenia (iii. 12. 11).
	summer	Failure of Chosroes' invasion (iii. 12. 12-14. 11).
	autumn	Romans ravage northern Persia; Chosroes initiates peace-negotiations (iii. 15. 1-5).
577	winter/spring	Peace-negotiations (iii. 15. 6-7).
	summer	Tamchosro defeats Justinian in Armenia (iii. 15. 8).
578	winter/spring	Peace-negotiations break down; Maurice appointed commander in the east (iii. 15. 9-10).
	spring	Persians anticipate end of truce and ravage Roman territory (iii. 15. 11-12).
	summer/autumn	Maurice's first campaign (iii. 15. 13-16. 2).
	October	Death of Justin II and accession of Tiberius (iii. 16. 3-6).
579	February/March	Death of Chosroes I and accession of Hormisdas (iii. 16. 7-17. 1).
	spring/summer	Protracted peace-negotiations in Persia (iii. 17. 2).
	autumn/winter	After failure of negotiations, Romans prepare to renew war (not recorded by Theophylact).
580	summer	Maurice's second campaign (iii. 17. 3-4).
581	summer	Maurice and Alamundarus campaign down the Euphrates (iii. 17. 5-11).
582	June	Defeat and death of Tamchosro at Constantina (iii. 18. 1-2; i. 9. 4).

	August	Death of Tiberius and accession of Maurice (iii. 18. 3; i. 1-2).
	autumn	Campaign in Arzanene (i. 9. 4-11).
		Avars send embassies to demand elephant and gold couch (i. 3. 8-12).
		Maurice's marriage (i. 10).
583	April	Fire at Constantinople (i. 11. 1-2).
	May	Avars demand increase in tribute (i. 3. 13).
		Earthquake at Constantinople (i. 12. 8-11).
	summer	Campaign in Arzanene (i. 12. 1-7).
		Avars invade as far as Anchialus (i. 4. 1-5).
	autumn	Embassy of Comentiolus and Elpidius to Avar Chagan (i. 4. 6-6. 3).
	December	Maurice's consulship (i. 12. 12-13).
584	spring	Second embassy of Elpidius; conclusion of peace with Avars (i. 6. 4-6).
	spring/summer	Philippicus replaces John Mystacon as commander in the east and prepares to campaign (i. 13. 1-3).
	summer	Slav invasions reach Long Walls; Comentiolus' victory near river Erginia (i. 7. 1-4).
	autumn	Philippicus ravages Beth Arabaye (i. 13. 4-12).
585		Comentiolus' victory at Ansinon (i. 7. 5-6).
		Military action in vicinity of Martyropolis (i. 14. 1-10).
586	spring	Persians renew peace negotiations (i. 15. 1-13).
		Battle of Solachon (i. 15. 14-ii. 6. 13).
	summer	Philippicus invades Arzanene and besieges Chlomaron (ii. 7. 1-9. 17).
	autumn	Heraclius ravages Persian territory (ii. 10. 1-5).
		Avars invade empire again and sack several cities (i. 8. 1-11).
587	spring	Comentiolus campaigns against Avars (ii. 10. 8-15. 12).
	spring/summer	Avars attack cities in Thrace; Drocton's victory at Adrianople persuades Avars to withdraw (ii. 16. 12-17. 13).
	summer	Romans besiege Persian forts (ii. 18. 1-25).
588	winter/spring	Priscus appointed to replace Philippicus as commander in the east (ii. 18. 26-iii. 1. 2).
	spring	Avars demand an increase in Roman tribute payments and prepare to invade (vi. 3. 9-4. 4).
	Easter	Priscus arrives at Monocarton; mutiny of Roman army (iii. 1. 3-2. 10).
	May	Philippicus replaces Priscus as commander (iii. 2. 11).
		Priscus returns to Constantinople (iii. 3. 6) and is appointed general in the Balkans (vi. 4. 7).
	summer	Germanus' successes against Persians (iii. 3. 8-4. 5).
		Priscus' first Balkan campaign (vi. 4. 7-6. 1).

589	Easter	End of mutiny of Roman eastern army (iii. 5. 9-10).
	spring/summer	Betrayal of Martyropolis; defeat of Philippicus while besieging city (iii. 5. 11-15).
		Slavs ravage Balkans (iii. 4. 7).
	summer/autumn	Campaign in Suania (iii. 6. 6-7. 19).
	autumn	Comentiolus replaces Philippicus as commander in the east; Roman victory at Sisarbanon (iii. 5. 16-6. 5).
		Baram revolts against Hormisdas and marches to Zab (iii. 8. 1-3, 10-11; iv. 1. 1-9).
	winter	Comentiolus captures Akbas (iv. 2. 1).
590	January	Baram and Pherochanes encamp near Zab (iv. 2. 2-3. 1).
	6 February	Deposition of Hormisdas (iv. 3. 2-12).
	15 February	Coronation of Chosroes II (iv. 7. 1).
	20 February	Baram and Chosroes confront each other near Ctesiphon (iv. 9. 3-6).
	28 February	Baram attacks Chosroes by night (iv. 9. 9-10).
	1 March	Flight of Chosroes to Circesium (iv. 9. 11-10. 7).
	9 March	Coronation of Baram (iv. 12. 4-6).
	spring/summer	Chosroes appeals to Maurice for help (iv. 10. 8-11. 11, 13. 2-26).
		Unsuccessful coup against Baram (iv. 14. 10-15. 1).
	summer	Maurice decides to support Chosroes; preparations begin for expedition to reinstall him (iv. 14. 1-7).
		Bindoes arrives in Armenia (iv. 15. 2-6).
	October	Maurice leads expedition to Anchialus to inspect damage caused by Avars (v. 16. 1-6; vi. 3. 5).
	autumn/winter	Chosroes gains more support in Mesopotamia; Martyropolis is returned to Romans (iv. 15. 7-16. 28).
		Baram prepares to resist Chosroes (v. 1. 1-2).
591	January/February	Capture of Zadesprates (v. 1. 3-2. 2, 13. 4-6).
	spring	Chosroes advances to Dara and returns city to Romans (v. 3. 1-11).
	spring/summer	Chosroes advances to Tigris (v. 5. 2-11).
		Mebodes captures Persian royal palaces (v. 6. 1-7. 5).
	summer	Armies manœuvre near Zab rivers (v. 7. 10-8. 4).
		Armies cross to Azerbaijan (v. 8. 5-10).
	late summer	Baram is outmanœuvred and defeated (v. 9. 1-11. 7).
		Roman troops return home (v. 11. 7-8).
593		Priscus' second Balkan campaign (vi. 6. 2-9. 15).
	autumn	Roman army returns to Thrace for winter (vi. 10. 1-2, 11. 2-21).
		Slavs ravage widely in Balkans (vii. 2. 2).
594		Peter's first Balkan campaign (vii. 1. 1-5. 10).
595	January	Appearance of comet (vii. 6. 8-9).
	spring/summer	Priscus' third Balkan campaign (vii. 7. 1-5, 10. 1-11. 9).
		Avars ravage Dalmatia (vii. 12. 1-9).

	autumn	Start of eighteen-month lull in fighting on Danube (vii. 12. 9).
	September	Death of Patriarch John Nesteutes (vii. 6. 1-5).
596		No military action on Danube (vii. 12. 9). Avars attack Franks (not recorded by Theophylact).
596/7		Maurice falls seriously ill and makes a will (viii. 11. 7-10).
597	summer/autumn	Avars invade Moesia (vii. 13. 1).
598	winter/spring	Priscus blockaded at Tomi (vii. 13. 1-2).
	Easter	Truce at Tomi (vii. 13. 3-7).
	spring	Comentiolus' expedition to relieve Priscus; rout of Comentiolus (vii. 13. 8-14. 10).
	spring/summer	Avars advance to Drizipera (vii. 14. 11-15. 3). Maurice leads expedition to Long Walls (vii. 15. 7-8; v. 16. 7-vi. 3. 8).
	summer	Avar-Roman treaty (vii. 15. 9-14).
	summer/autumn	Roman army complains against Comentiolus (viii. 1. 9-10).
599	summer	Joint campaign by Priscus and Comentiolus on upper Danube (viii. 1. 11-4. 2).
	autumn/winter	Comentiolus crosses Trojan Pass (viii. 4. 3-8).
600	summer	Comentiolus in command in Balkans; no action on Danube (viii. 4. 8-9).
601	summer/autumn	Peter's second Balkan campaign (viii. 4. 9, 5. 5-7).
	November	Marriage of Maurice's son Theodosius to a daughter of Germanus (viii. 4. 10).
602	2 February	Rioting against Maurice in Constantinople (viii. 4. 11-5. 4).
	summer	Peter's third Balkan campaign (viii. 5. 8-12). Avars fight Antes; some Avar subjects revolt (viii. 5. 13-6. 1).
	autumn	Maurice orders army to winter north of Danube; mutiny of Roman army (viii. 6. 2-7. 7).
	22 November	Maurice flees from Constantinople by night (viii. 9. 7-9).
	23 November	Phocas is acclaimed emperor at the Hebdomon (viii. 9. 13-10. 6).
	25 November	Phocas enters Constantinople (viii. 10. 6).
	27 November	Coronation of Phocas' wife Leontia (viii. 10. 8). Execution of Maurice and his sons at Chalcedon (viii. 11. 1-6).

Gazetteer

Abbaron: iii. 10. 6; iv. 10. 4; also known as Ambar and Perozshapur, a town on the east bank of the Euphrates, about fifty miles from Ctesiphon.

Aboras: i. 13. 10; iii. 10. 7; the Khabour river in upper Mesopotamia.

Adrabiganon: iv. 3. 13, 9. 1, 12. 10, 15. 1; the area of Azerbaijan in north-west Iran.

Adrianopolis: i. 7. 5; ii. 17. 4-10; viii. 5. 9; the modern Edirne in European Turkey.

Aïsouma: i. 13. 3; ii. 1. 3; the mountain of Karaca Dağ to the north of Constantina.

Akbas: i. 12. 1-3; iv. 2. 1; a fort in Arzanene located on the east bank of the Nymphius river not far from Martyropolis; on this and other locations in Arzanene, see L. M. Whitby, 'Arzanene in the late sixth century', *BAR* Int. Ser. 156 (1983), 205-18.

Alaleisus: ii. 9. 17; a fort in the Bitlis pass over the Taurus.

Albania: iii. 6. 17, 7. 13; a district to the south of the Caucasus mountains.

Alexandria: vii. 16. 4, 17. 46; viii. 13. 7-14; the city in Egypt.

Alexandriana: v. 7. 10; also known as Arbela, the modern Erbel in Iraq.

Amida: i. 15. 1; ii. 3. 8, 9. 16; iii. 12. 11, 15. 12; the modern Diyarbakır in eastern Turkey.

Ammodius: v. 4. 4; a fort five miles south of Dara.

Anathon: iv. 10. 4; v. 1. 2-3; a fortified settlement on the Euphrates, midway between Circesium and Abbaron.

Anchialus: i. 4. 4, 7; ii. 10. 8; v. 16. 1; vi. 3. 5, 5. 2, 10. 4; the modern Pomorie on the Black Sea coast of Bulgaria.

Ansinon: i. 7. 5; a fort in Thrace to the north-west of Adrianopolis.

Antioch: iii. 1. 3, 5. 10, 10. 8; iv. 14. 6; v. 2. 7, 6. 9; the modern Antakya in southeast Turkey.

Antioch in Mygdonia: iii. 6. 1; a synonym for Nisibis.

Antioch in Persia: v. 6. 9, 11, 7. 1-3; a city in Mesopotamia, a short distance to the south of Ctesiphon.

Apamea: iii. 10. 9; a city located at Qalat el-Mudiq on the Orontes river in Syria.

Aphumon: i. 12. 1-3; ii. 9. 4-9; iii. 15. 14; a fort in Arzanene, probably to be located on the west bank of the Redwan river opposite Chlomaron.

Appiaria: ii. 15. 13; the modern Tutrakan, on the south bank of the Danube in Bulgaria.

Aquis: i. 8. 10; vii. 2. 2; probably to be identified with the ruins at Gamzigrad in the Timok valley in Yugoslavia.

Arabia: iii. 16. 1, 17. 6; iv. 15. 7; v. 1. 2, 3. 2; viii. 1. 1; the area of Beth Arabaye to the south and east of Nisibis.

Araxes: iii. 6. 16, 7. 13; the Araş river, which drains into the Caspian Sea.

Armenia: i. 9. 4, *al.*; the area to the north of the Taurus in eastern Turkey.

Arzamon: i. 15. 15; ii. 1. 5-7, 5. 4; iii. 5. 9; the Zergan river, which flows from the Tur Abdin plateau to the south of Mardin.

Arzanene: i. 14. 1; ii. 7. 1-9, 8. 6; iii. 4. 2, 10. 2, 14. 11, 15. 12-13, 16. 1; the frontier district of Persia to the east of the Nymphius river.

Asemus: vii. 3. 1; viii. 6. 7; a town situated near the Osam river in Bulgaria.

Astike: i. 7. 6; ii. 15. 4, 17. 4; vii. 7. 1; the Thracian plain.

Atrapaïca: iv. 10. 1; a synonym for Adrabiganon (Azerbaijan).

Augustae: i. 4. 4; a town near the confluence of the rivers Ogosta and Danube in modern Bulgaria.

Babylon, Babylonia: iii. 6. 16, *al.*; a synonym for Persia, or the royal capital Ctesiphon.

Bakath: vii. 8. 13; the region of Bactria beyond the Persian north-east frontier.

Baktriane: vii. 9. 12; Bactria.

Bearbaës: i. 13. 8; a synonym for Arabia.

Bedamas: iv. 12. 8; a settlement near Hierapolis.

Beïudaes: ii. 18. 7-9; the modern village of Fafi in the Tur Abdin.

Bendosabora: iii. 5. 2; the city of Gundishapur in Huzistan in south-west Iran.

Beroe: ii. 16. 12; the modern Stara Zagora in Bulgaria.

Beroe: ii. 6. 9; the modern Aleppo or Haleb in Syria.

Berthamaïs: v. 14. 3; the region of Beth Aramaye in lower Mesopotamia.

Bibas: i. 15. 15; also known as Bebase or Tel Beş, a place on the Arzamon river a short distance south of Mardin.

Bizaë: iii. 5. 2; the region of Beth Huzaye, or Huzistan, in south-west Iran.

Blarathos: v. 10. 3; a branch of the Saruk river, which drains into Lake Urmiah.

Bonkeis: vii. 12. 1; a town or fort in Dalmatia that is otherwise unknown; the form of the name may be corrupt.

Bononia: i. 8. 10; vi. 4. 6; the modern Vidin on the south bank of the Danube in Bulgaria.

Bouron: ii. 1. 5, 2. 4; the Dara river.

Caesarea: iii. 17. 5; the modern Kayseri in central Turkey.

Callicrateia: viii. 8. 3; a district near Constantinople (otherwise unknown).

Callinicum: iii. 17. 8-10; a city on the north bank of the Euphrates, near modern Raqqa in Syria.

Calvomuntis: ii. 15. 3; a place in Thrace, probably in the Sredna Gora range (otherwise unknown).

Canzacon: iii. 7. 2; v. 10. 2, 11. 5; a site to be identified with the remains at Takht-i Suleiman in Azerbaijan.

Cappadocia: iii. 17. 5; the province whose metropolis was Caesarea.

Carcharoman: i. 13. 4; a place of uncertain location in the Tur Abdin.

Carduchia: ii. 10. 3; a range of mountains, also known as Qarhe, to be identified with the Hakkari in south-east Turkey.

Cataracts: viii. 5. 5-6; a turbulent eighty-mile stretch of the Danube, downstream from Viminacium.

Caucasus: ii. 1. 4; iv. 10. 1; vii. 7. 6, 17. 41; the mountain-range of the same name.

Chalcedon: v. 15. 8; vii. 15. 5, 6; viii. 11. 2, 12. 2, 14. 2; a suburb of Constantinople on the Asiatic side of the Bosphorus.

Chalcis: v. 11. 4; a city, also known as Kinnesrin, situated near Barad in Syria.

Chalcitis: i. 8. 9; the modern Heybeli, one of the Princes' Islands in the Sea of Marmara.

Charcha: v. 1. 10, 13. 4; a town two days' journey from Nisibis.

Chlomaron: ii. 7. 6-8. 12; the chief town of Arzanene, to be located on the east bank of the Redwan river.

Chnaithas: v. 8. 1; also known as Chamaetha, to be identified with the district of Honita to the east of Arbela in Iraq.

Chubdan: vii. 9. 8-9; also known as Khumdan, a city in China.

Cilicia: iii. 5. 10; viii. 13. 16; the province on the south coast of Turkey.

Circesium: iii. 10. 6-8, 17. 5; iv. 10. 4-5; v. 1. 2; a city at the junction of the Khabour and Euphrates rivers.

Citharizon: iii. 15. 12; a fortress in Armenia, probably to be located in the valley of the Göynük, a tributary of the Murat river.

Colchis: iii. 6. 8-17, 7. 8; viii. 13. 4; the area, known as Lazica in the sixth century, in north-east Turkey/the Georgian SSR.

Constantina: iii. 1. 1, al.; the modern Viranşehir in south-east Turkey.

Constantinople: i. 10. 1, al.; also referred to as Byzantium, or by periphrases such as the 'royal city' or 'queen of cities'.

Constantiola: vii. 10. 3; viii. 5. 7; a fort located on the north bank of the Danube opposite the confluence of the Morava and Danube.

Ctesiphon: iv. 3. 3, 10. 1; v. 6. 3-10, 9. 2, 15. 9; the capital of Persia, on the east bank of the Tigris in lower Mesopotamia.

Curisca: vii. 2. 19; viii. 6. 7; a fort, also known as Securisca, twenty-six miles west of Novae.

Cyprus: iii. 15. 15; the island.

Dalmatia: vii. 12. 1; the Roman province in the north-west of the Balkans.

Damascus: iii. 1. 3; the city in Syria.

Daonion: vi. 1. 2; a place also known as Baunne, half way between Heracleia and Selymbria.

Daras: ii. 4. 10, 5. 7; iii. 5. 4-7, 11. 2, 12. 9, 17. 2, 18. 10; iv. 13. 24; v. 3. 1-4. 14;

viii. 15. 3-4; the Roman frontier fortress of Dara, located at Oğuz köyü, to the south-east of Mardin in eastern Turkey.

Dardania: viii. 5. 5; the Roman province in the central Balkans, south of the Danube Cataracts.

Diadromoi: viii. 13. 3; a place near Cape Acritas, by the entrance to the Gulf of Nicomedia.

Didymoteichon: vi. 5. 9; a fortress on the west bank of the Marica river.

Dinabadon: v. 5. 8; a place between the Tigris and Great Zab rivers (otherwise unknown).

Diocletianopolis: ii. 17. 1; the modern Hisar in Bulgaria.

Dorostolon: i. 8. 10; vi. 6. 5; the modern Silistra, on the south bank of the Danube in Bulgaria.

Draos: vii. 11. 7; the Drava river in Yugoslavia.

Drizipera: vi. 5. 4, 6. 5, 11. 21; vii. 1. 3, 14. 10-11, 15. 9; a fort located near the modern Büyük Kariştiran in European Turkey.

Edessa: iii. 1. 3 ff.; the modern Urfa in eastern Turkey.

Emesa: ii. 3. 1; the modern Homs in Syria.

Enaton: vi. 2. 1; a place probably located nine miles from Heracleia (otherwise unknown).

Eras: iii. 6. 16; the Araxes river.

Erginia: i. 7. 3; the Ergene river in European Turkey.

Euphrates: iii. 10. 2, al.; the river.

Eutropius, harbour of: viii. 11. 2; a harbour at Chalcedon.

Giligerdon: iii. 5. 2; a fortress near Susan in south-west Iran.

Haemus: ii. 10. 10, 11. 4, 12. 9, 15. 3; the Stara Planina mountain range in Bulgaria.

Hebdomon: v. 16. 4, 9; viii. 10. 1, 12. 8; a suburb of Constantinople seven miles from the centre of the city.

Helibacia: vi. 8. 9; vii. 5. 6; a river to the north of the Danube, probably opposite Dorostolon (otherwise unknown).

Heracleia: i. 11. 6; vi. 1. 1-3, 2. 16, 5. 8, 6. 3; a city, also known as Perinthus, situated on the Sea of Marmara at Marmaraeğlisi.

Hierapolis: iii. 4. 5; iv. 10. 9, 12. 8, 14. 5; v. 12. 1, 8; the modern Membij in Syria.

Hyrcanian Sea: iii. 15. 2; the Caspian Sea.

Iatrus: vii. 2. 16, 13. 9, 14. 7; a city on the east bank of the Yantra river in Bulgaria.

Iberia: vi. 3. 6; a synonym for Gaul.

Ikar: vii. 8. 10-11; the river Guma in central Asia.

Illyricum: i. 4. 4; the Roman administrative region that comprised the western half of the Balkans.

Ionian Gulf: vii. 11. 9; the Adriatic.

Ister: i. 3. 2, *al.*; the river Danube.

Italy: viii. 11. 9.

Izala: i. 13. 4, 7; ii. 1. 1-4, 9. 17-10. 2; the Tur Abdin plateau in south-east Turkey.

Koile Syria: iii. 10. 8; the Roman province centred on the Orontes valley in Syria.

Lachernae: viii. 5. 1; Blachernae, a suburb of Constantinople.

Latarkium: vii. 2. 16; a fort located between Iatrus and Novae.

Lazica: iii. 6. 17; the region, also known as Colchis, in north-east Turkey/the Georgian SSR.

Lethe: iii. 5. 2; a prison near Giligerdon in south-west Iran.

Libidina: i. 8. 6; to be identified with the remains at Slava Rusa, near Babadag in Romania.

Libidurgon: ii. 15. 3; a place in Thrace, probably in the Sredna Gora hills (otherwise unknown).

Libya: iii. 4. 8; vii. 6. 6-7, *al.*; the Roman province of Africa, or a synonym for the whole continent.

Maïacariri: i. 13. 4; a place on the route across the Tur Abdin between Mardin‾ and the Tigris.

Mambrathon: i. 15. 14; a place between Amida and Mardin.

Marcianopolis: i. 8. 10; ii. 11. 3; vii. 2. 1; at the modern Devnja in Bulgaria.

Mardes: ii. 2. 5, 3. 8; iii. 11. 2; v. 3. 1; the modern Mardin in south-east Turkey.

Martyropolis: i. 14. 5-7; iii. 4. 1-2, 5. 8-16; iv. 2. 4, 12. 6-15. 13; the modern Silvan in eastern Turkey.

Matzaron: ii. 18. 7; the village of Maserte in the Tur Abdin.

Media: ii. 10. 3, *al.*; a loose synonym for Persia.

Melabason: ii. 10. 2-3; a range of hills on the course of the Tigris, probably near Cizre in south-east Turkey.

Melas: vii. 7. 13, 9. 12; a river, also known as the Til, probably to be identified with the Tarim river in central Asia.

Melitene: iii. 14. 11; iv. 14. 5; v. 3. 1; viii. 11. 11; the modern Malatya in eastern Turkey.

Mesembria: ii. 12. 6; the modern Nesebăr on the Black Sea coast of Bulgaria.

Monocarton: i. 13. 3, 14. 6; iii. 1. 3-13, 3. 7; a Roman camp near Constantina.

Mygdon, Mygdonia: iii. 6. 1, 10. 5; v. 5. 3; a synonym for the vicinity of Nisibis, and the river (the Cağ-Cağ) which flows through it.

Mysia: i. 8. 10; vi. 10. 10; vii. 13. 1, 8; the Roman province of Moesia in the Balkans.

Nanisenes, region of: v. 8. 5, 9; probably to be located near Rowanduz in north-east Iraq.

Nicaea: viii. 9. 12, 11. 1; the modern İznik in Turkey.

Nicopolis: vii. 13. 8; a city located near the village of Nikyup, to the north of Veliko Tărnovo in Bulgaria (to which the city moved in late antiquity).

Nisibis: i. 13. 5, 15. 12; and *passim* in iii-v; the modern Nusaybin in south-east Turkey.

Novae: vii. 2. 16; viii. 4. 3-4; located at the modern Svištov, on the south bank of the Danube in Bulgaria.

Nymphius: i. 9. 5, 12. 1-6, 13. 8; ii. 9. 16; iii. 4. 2; the Batman river in eastern Turkey.

Odessus: vii. 1. 3, 2. 1; the modern Varna in Bulgaria.

Osrhoene: iii. 10. 2; the Roman province whose metropolis was Edessa.

Palastolon: viii. 5. 5, 6. 3; also known as Palation, a fort near the confluence of the Iskăr and Danube rivers in Bulgaria.

Pannasa: i. 8. 10; a town probably located near the Panysus river, the modern Kamčija in Bulgaria.

Pannonia: vii. 7. 9; formerly a Roman province, but now the Avar homeland, in modern Hungary.

Paspirius: vi. 9. 6-12; a river to the north of the Danube (otherwise unknown).

Pege: v. 16. 8; the site of a famous church of the Virgin Mary, just outside the walls of Constantinople.

Perinthus: i. 11. 6; vi. 1. 1, 5. 8; vii. 1. 3; a synonym for Heracleia.

Phasis: iii. 4. 9; the river Rioni in the Georgian SSR.

Phathacon: ii. 9. 17; a fort probably located in Arzanene on one of the passes over the Taurus mountains.

Philippopolis: ii. 17. 2; viii. 4. 8; the modern Plovdiv in Bulgaria.

Pistus: vii. 2. 16; a synonym for Sexantaprista, located at the modern Ruse on the south bank of the Danube in Bulgaria.

Pontus: viii. 14. 2; the Black Sea.

Procliane: vi. 4. 8; probably the Šipka pass in Bulgaria (otherwise unknown).

Rateria: i. 8. 10; Ratiaria, the modern Arčar on the south bank of the Danube in Bulgaria.

Rhabdion: i. 13. 10; a fort near the edge of the Tur Abdin plateau, to the north-east of Nisibis.

Rhamphus: v. 16. 11; a place between Rhegium and Selymbria (otherwise unknown).

Rhazakene: iii. 18. 6; the area around Rai, near modern Tehran.
Rhegium: v. 16. 9; viii. 10. 1; a suburb of Constantinople, located near Büyükçekmece.
Rhesonchosron: v. 14. 7; a Persian royal palace, probably to be located at Zengabad on the north bank of the Diyala river in Iraq.
Romania: v. 13. 4; the Roman empire.
Rome: iii. 4. 8; viii. 11. 9; referred to as 'Old Rome'.

Sabulente Canalion or Canalin: ii. 11. 4; vi. 5. 1; the Valley of the Roses in Bulgaria.
Saos: vi. 4. 4; vii. 11. 7; the Sava river in Yugoslavia.
Sargathon: iii. 10. 4; a Persian fort located at Qasr Serjihan, a few miles west of Nisibis.
Scopi: vii. 2. 2; the modern Skopje in Yugoslavia.
Scythia: i. 8. 10;. vi. 10. 10; the Roman province in the north-east of the Balkans; elsewhere, used by Theophylact as a general synonym for south Russia or central Asia.
Seleucia: v. 6. 3-8; a city on the west bank of the Tigris, opposite Ctesiphon.
Selymbria: vi. 1. 1; the modern Silivri on the Sea of Marmara in Turkey.
Sicily: i. 4. 6; the island.
Singan: vii. 10. 2; an island in the Danube thirty miles downstream from Singidunum.
Singara: iii. 16. 2; v. 4. 1-2, 6. 1; the modern Sinjar in northern Iraq.
Singidunum: i. 4. 1; vi. 4. 1-2; vii. 10. 1-11. 7; viii. 1. 11; on the site of modern Belgrade.
Siraganon: v. 8. 9; probably to be located at Sirgan, near Ushnei on the west shore of Lake Urmiah in Iran.
Sirmium: i. 3. 3; vi. 4. 4; a city located near the modern Sremska Mitrovica in Yugoslavia.
Sisarbanon: i. 13. 10; iii. 6. 1; a Persian fort located at Serwan to the north-east of Nisibis.
Sogdoane: vii. 8. 13, 9. 6, 12; the region of Sogdiana, beyond the Persian north-east frontier.
Solachon: ii. 3. 12; the modern Salah, a village to the east of the Arzamon river.
Suania: iii. 6. 6-16, 18. 13; a region to the south of the Caucasus mountains.
Syria: ii. 6. 9; iii. 5. 10, 10. 8; v. 6. 9; the Roman province.

Tarsus: iii. 1. 1; viii. 13. 16; the city in Cilicia.
Taugast: vii. 7. 11-12, 9. 1-8; China.
Thamanon: ii. 10. 2, 4; a place east of the Tigris, opposite the Tur Abdin.
Thebothon: iii. 10. 5; a fort south-east of Nisibis, on the route towards Singara.
Theodoropolis: vii. 2. 19: a fort located between Securisca and Iatrus.

Theodosiopolis: i. 13. 10-12; ii. 10. 4; iii. 6. 2, 15. 11-12; also known as Resaina, the modern Ras el-Ain on the Khabour river in Syria.

Thrace: i. 4. 1, *al.*; the Roman administrative region that comprised the eastern half of the Balkans; also used, more specifically, for the Roman province to the south of the Haemus mountains.

Tigris: i. 9. 5, *al.*; the river.

Til: vii. 7. 13; a synonym for the Melas river.

Tissus: viii. 3. 8-13; the Tisza river in Hungary/Yugoslavia.

Tomi: ii. 10. 12; vii. 13. 1-2; viii. 3. 15-4. 2; the modern Constanţa on the Black Sea coast of Romania.

Tur Abdin: ii. 10. 6; either the Tur Abdin plateau in south-eastern Turkey, or the fort of Rhabdion that was situated on the plateau.

Trajan's Track: viii. 4. 3-4; the Trojan pass across the Haemus mountains.

Tropaion: i. 8. 10; a city midway between Dorostolon and Tomi, near the modern Adamclisi in Romania.

Tzurullon: vi. 5. 10-14; the modern Çorlu in European Turkey.

Upper Novae: vii. 7. 3; a fort on the north bank of the Danube opposite Novae.

Viminacium: i. 4. 4; viii. 2. 2-8; a city located near the confluence of the Morava and Danube rivers, near modern Kostolac in Yugoslavia.

Xerogypsus: vi. 3. 2; a river near Tzurullon.

Zab: iv. 1. 6, 2. 5, 9. 1; v. 5. 6, 6. 1; the Great Zab river in Iraq.

Zab: v. 8. 1; the Lesser Zab river in Iraq.

Zaldapa: i. 8. 10; ii. 10. 10; vii. 2. 2, 16; Abrit, a town near Loznica, on the Bulgarian-Romanian frontier.

Zikidiba: vii. 13. 8; also known as Sucidava, a fort thirty miles east of Dorostolon.

Zorbandon: i. 14. 9; a place to the north-west of Martyropolis.

Index of Names

Abdeli: vii. 7. 8; a synonym for the Hephthalites.

Acacius: iii. 11. 1; the son of Archelaus; imperial envoy in 573.

Adormaanes: iii. 10. 7-9, 17. 8; Persian commander in 573 and 581.

Alamundarus: iii. 17. 7-9; leader of the Ghassanid Arabs.

Alans: iii. 9. 7; a nation which lived near the Caucasus.

Albuis: vi. 10. 7-11; king of the Lombards.

Alexander: vi. 5. 2; vii. 14. 11, 15. 2; a martyr, whose shrine was located near Drizipera.

Alexander: vi. 8. 9-9. 11; vii. 2. 6; viii. 10. 11-13, 13. 3-4, 15. 8; a brigadier in the Balkan army and a prominent supporter of Phocas.

Andrew: ii. 10. 6, 18. 7-8; a subordinate Roman commander in the east in 587.

Andrew: viii. 9. 2; a priest at Constantinople.

Ansimuth: ii. 12. 7, 17. 5; a Roman brigadier in charge of an army in Thrace in 587.

Antes: viii. 5. 13; a nation similar to the Slavs who lived north of the Danube.

Aphraates: ii. 3. 3; iii. 5. 15, 6. 3, 6; Persian commander in 586 and 589.

Apsich: i. 14. 5; ii. 3. 1; subordinate Roman commander in the east in 585-6.

Apsich: viii. 5. 5-6, 13; Avar commander.

Arcadius: viii. 8. 2; Roman emperor 395-408.

Archelaus: iii. 11. 1; father of Acacius.

Ardagastus: i. 7. 5; vi. 7. 1-5, 9. 1-6; a Slav leader.

Aristobulus: iii. 3. 11; imperial envoy in 588.

Ariulph: i. 9. 7-8; subordinate Roman commander in the east in 582.

Armenians: iii. 8. 4, al.; Christian nation living in north-east Asia Minor.

Asones: iv. 8. 5; unknown.

Aspabedes: iv. 3. 5; father of Bestam and Bindoes.

Autonomus: viii. 9. 9, 13. 3; a martyr, whose shrine was located on the Gulf of Nicomedia.

Avars: i. 3. 1, and *passim*; the nomadic federation based on Pannonia.

Babylonians: iii. 6. 10, al.; a synonym for the Persians.

Bactrians: vii. 9. 6; inhabitants of Central Asia.

Baduarius: vi. 10. 10; son-in-law of Justin II.

Baram, king of Persia 590-1: iii. 18. 5-12, early career; iii. 6. 7-8. 1, defeat in Suania in 589; iii. 8. 10-9. 1, 18. 4; iv. 1. 1-12. 2, rebellion against Hormisdas; iv. 12. 3-7, coronation; v. 1. 1-9. 12, campaign against Romans and Chosroes; v. 10. 1-11. 7, defeat at Blarathos and flight; v. 13. 4, 15. 1.

Bargusnas: v. 13. 4; father of Baram.

Barselt: vii. 8. 3; one of the nations of south-west Asia.

Bestam: iv. 3. 5, 12. 10, 15. 5-6; v. 11. 4, 7; maternal uncle of Chosroes II.

Bettus: vi. 3. 6; Frankish ambassador.

Gennadius: vii. 6. 6; governor of Africa.

Gentzon: vi. 6. 3, 9. 15; vii. 3. 6-8; commander in Roman army in Balkans in 593-4.

George: viii. 1. 3-8; Roman ambassador to Chosroes II.

George: viii. 13. 2; one of those killed on orders of Phocas.

Gepids: i. 8. 4; vi. 2. 4-6, 8. 13-9. 10, 10. 7-14; viii. 3. 11; one of the tribes in the Avar federation.

Germanus: iii. 1. 3, 2. 4-5, 3. 9; Roman commander based at Damascus (not the bishop); elected leader of mutinous army.

Germanus: iii. 12. 6; father of Justinian the general.

Germanus: viii. 4. 10-13, 8. 3-9. 3, 9. 14-10. 4, 13. 4; father-in-law of Maurice's son Theodosius.

Germanus: viii. 15. 3-6; Roman commander at Dara in 602.

Getae: iii. 4. 7; vi. 6. 14; vii. 2. 5; a synonym for the Slavs.

Glyceria: i. 11. 7; vi. 1. 3; a martyr whose shrine was located at Heracleia.

Godwin: vii. 11. 6-12. 8; viii. 5. 12-7. 1; subordinate Roman commander in the Balkans in 595 and 602.

Golinduch: v. 12; a Persian Christian.

Gordia: i. 13. 2; sister of Maurice and wife of Philippicus.

Gregory: iii. 5. 10; iv. 14. 6; v. 2. 7; Patriarch of Antioch 570-92.

Harmaton: vii. 15. 8-9; Roman ambassador to the Avars in 598.

Hebdomites: viii. 9. 13; a leading member of the Green faction.

Hephthalites: iv. 6. 10; vii. 7. 8; a nation which lived on the north-east frontier of Persia.

Heraclius: ii. 3. 2, 5. 10, 6. 4, 7. 11-8. 4, 9. 17, 10. 1-4, 6, 18. 1-4, 26; iii. 1. 1, 6. 2; subordinate Roman commander in the east in 586-9, and father of the emperor Heraclius.

Heraclius: ii. 3. 2, 5. 10; iii. 6. 2; viii. 11. 7, 12. 12; Roman emperor 610-41.

Herodian: vii. 12. 11; a man (monk?) who predicted Maurice's overthrow.

Homerites: iii. 9. 6; a tribe which inhabited Arabia.

Hormisdas, king of Persia 579-90: iii. 16. 7-13, accession and character-sketch; iii. 17. 1-3, rejects peace overtures from Tiberius; iii. 6. 7-8. 3, 8. 10-12, origins of quarrel with Baram; iv. 1. 1-3. 3, attempts to oppose Baram; iv. 3. 5-13, overthrown by Bindoes; iv. 3. 15-6. 1, trial; vi. 2-7. 3, punishment and death; iv. 7. 7, 13. 17-18, 15. 13; viii. 12. 13.

Hormisdas: v. 1. 9; an alternative name for Rhosas.

Huns: i. 3. 2, al.; a synonym for the Avars and other nomadic tribes.

Iberians: iii. 17. 2; inhabitants of a region south of the Caucasus.

Ilibinus: ii. 4. 3; nickname, or ethnic name, for Theodore.

Indians: iii. 9. 6, a synonym for the Homerites; vii. 7. 11, 9. 10, neighbours of Taugast.

John the Faster (Nesteutes): i. 1. 2, 10. 2, 11. 14-20; vii. 6. 1; Patriarch of Constantinople 582-95.

John Mystacon: i. 9. 4-9, 13. 1, Roman commander in east in 582-3; ii. 17. 8, commander in Thrace in 587; iii. 8. 4; iv. 15. 2-5; v. 8. 7-9. 3, 15. 4, commander in Armenia in 589-91, and one of leaders of expedition to restore Chosroes II.

John: i. 1. 3; *quaestor* in 582.
John: iii. 15. 6; Roman negotiator in 576-7.
Jovius: ii. 7. 7; one of the leading men of Arzanene.
Justin II, Roman emperor 565-78: iii. 9. 1-11. 3, conduct of war against Persia in 572-3, iii. 16. 3; death; iii. 5. 4; vi. 10. 9; vii. 3. 4 (possibly Justin I, emperor 518-27).
Justinian: ii. 3. 13; iii. 9. 3, 10; v. 6. 10, 13. 2, 6, 16. 7; vii. 8. 1, 16. 12; viii. 8. 15, 10. 3; Roman emperor 527-65.
Justinian: iii. 12. 6-15. 8; son of Germanus; Roman commander in the east in 575-7.

Kabades: iii. 18. 10; iv. 6. 5-11; v. 6. 9-10, 13. 2, 6 (Koades); king of Persia 488-531.
Kadasenes: iii. 5. 5; a tribe that lived near the Caspian Sea.
Kardarigan: i. 9. 5, 12. 3, 13. 4-7, 14. 6, 15. 11; ii. 2. 1-5. 10, 8. 1, 7; Persian commander against the Romans 582-6.
Koch: vi. 6. 6; Avar ambassador.
Kolch: vii. 8. 6; one of the nations of central Asia.
Kotzager: vii. 8. 16; a subdivision of the Var and Chunni (possibly the Kotrigurs).
Kunaxolan: vii. 8. 9; one of the Turkish Chagans.

Lardys: viii. 9. 5, 12, 13. 3; surname, or nickname, of Constantine the praetorian prefect.
Latins: ii. 1. 6, *al.*; a synonym for the Romans.
Leontia: viii. 10. 9; wife of Phocas.
Lilius: viii. 12. 8, 15. 2-7; prominent supporter of Phocas, and ambassador to Chosroes II in 602-3.
Lombards: ii. 17. 9, *al.*; the Germanic tribe settled in north Italy.
Lydus: vii. 16. 12; John Lydus, the civil servant and writer.

Marcian: iii. 10. 1-11. 2; nephew of Justin II and commander in the east in 572-3.
Margarites: i. 10. 8; one of the imperial eunuchs.
Marinus: v. 11. 7; subordinate Roman commander in the east in 591.
Martin: ii. 10. 9-11. 3, 11. 9-12, 13. 11; iii. 17. 3; subordinate Roman commander in the east in 580, and in the Balkans in 587.
Maruthas: ii. 7. 7; one of the leading men of Arzanene.
Maruzas: iii. 4. 1-2, 5. 8; Persian general in 588.
Maurice, Roman emperor 582-602: iii. 15. 10-17. 9, *comes excubitorum* and general in the east under Tiberius; i. 1, 2. 7, proclamation as emperor and betrothal to Constantina; i. 10, marriage to Constantina; i. 12. 12, consulship; v. 16-vi. 3, expedition against the Avars; viii. 7. 8-11.6, overthrow and murder by Phocas; and *passim*.
Maurusii: iii. 4. 8; vii. 6. 6; the Moorish tribes of north Africa.
Mebodes: i. 15. 1-2. 12; ii. 3. 3; iii. 5. 14-15, 6. 3; Persian ambassador in 586, and commander in 589.
Mebodes: v. 4. 2-3, 6. 1-7. 10, 9. 1-2, 9. 8 (probably corrupt); Persian commander and supporter of Chosroes II.
Medes: i. 12. 1, *al.*; a synonym for Persians.
Menander: i. 3. 5; the historian Menander Protector.
Menas: vii. 16. 1, 17. 46; prefect of Egypt.
Miragdun: iv. 12. 9; envoy of Chosroes II.

emperor; iii. 12-18. 3, conduct of Persian war 574-82; i. 1. 1-23; iii. 18. 3, appoints Maurice as successor; i. 2. 1-3, death; i. 10. 7, 14. 5; viii. 15. 1.

Tiberius: viii. 11. 9; Maurice's second son.

Timostratus: v. 8. 4; father of Rufinus.

Tuldich: vii. 8. 9; one of the Turkish Chagans.

Turks: i. 8. 5, *al.*; the nomadic federation which inhabited central Asia.

Turum: vii. 8. 8; a Turkish usurper.

Var: vii. 7. 14-8. 5, 8. 16-17; a tribe believed by Theophylact to be one of the ancestral subdivisions of the Avars.

Vitalius: ii. 3. 1, 4. 1; subordinate Roman commander in the east in 586.

Zabender: vii. 8. 17; an offshoot of the Var and Chunni.

Zabertas: ii. 8. 7-9; Persian commander at Chlomaron in 586.

Zadespras *or* Zadesprates: iv. 2. 3-5; v. 1. 2-3, 13-16, 13. 4-6; Persian noble, and one of Baram's generals.

Zamerdes: iv. 9. 2, 14. 11; Persian noble.

Zetonumius: ii. 3. 13; nickname for Theodore, son of Peter the Patrician.

Zoanambes: iv. 14. 11; Persian noble.

Zoarab: iv. 3. 1; Persian officer (possibly identical with Zoanambes).

Zogomus: ii. 2. 5; leader of the Arab tribes allied to the Romans in 586.

Bibliography

Primary sources

Agapetus Diaconus, *Ecthesis*, ed. A. Banduri (*PG* 86. 1, Paris, 1865, 1163-86).

Agathias, *History*, ed. R. Keydell (Berlin, 1967); tr. J. D. Frendo (Berlin, 1975).

Agnellus, *Chronicle*, ed. O. Holder-Egger (*MGH Script. rerum Langobard. et Ital. saec. VI-IX*, Hanover, 1878).

Anon. Guidi = *Chronicon anonymum de ultimis regibus Persarum*, ed. and tr. I. Guidi, *Chronica minora* (*CSCO* Scr. Syri 3, 4, Paris, 1903).

Chronicon anon. ad an. 1234 pertinens, tr. J. B. Chabot (*CSCO* 109, Scr. Syri 56, Louvain, 1937).

Chronicon Paschale, ed. L. Dindorf (*CSHB*, Bonn, 1832).

Chronicle of Seert, Histoire nestorienne pt. ii, tr. A. Scher (*PO* 13, 1919).

Constantine Porphyrogenitus, *de Caerimoniis*, ed. and tr. A. Vogt (Paris, 1935-40).

Evagrius, *Ecclesiastical History*, ed. J. Bidez and L. Parmentier (London, 1898); tr. A. J. Festugière, *Byzantion* 45 (2) (1975).

Fragmenta Historicorum Graecorum, vols. iv and v, ed. C. Müller (Paris, 1851-70). [*FHG*]

Fredegarius, *Chronicle*, ed. B. Krusch (*MGH Scriptores rerum Merovingicarum* II, Hanover, 1889).

George of Pisidia, *Poems*, ed. J. M. Quercius (*PG* 92, Paris, 1865, 1197 *ad fin.*); ed. A. Pertusi, *Giorgio di Pisidia, poemi. i panegirici epici* (Ettal, 1960).

Georgius Monachus, *Chronicle*, ed. C. de Boor (Leipzig, 1905).

Gregory, Pope of Rome, *Register of Letters*, ed. P. Ewald and L. Hartmann (*MGH Epistolae*, vols. 1, 2, Berlin, 1887-9).

John of Antioch, fragments (*FHG* v. 27-38).

John of Ephesus, *Ecclesiastical History*, ed. and tr. E. W. Brooks (*CSCO* 106, Scr. Syri 55, Louvain, 1952).

John of Epiphania, fragments (*FHG* iv. 272-6).

John Lydus, *de Magistratibus*, ed. and tr. A. C. Bandy (Philadelphia, 1983).

—— *de Mensibus*, ed. R. Wuensch (Leipzig, 1898).

John of Nikiu, *Chronicle*, tr. R. H. Charles (London, 1916).

Leo Grammaticus, *Chronicle*, ed. I. Bekker (*CSHB*, Bonn, 1842).

Life of John the Almsgiver, ed. H. Gelzer (Leipzig, 1893); tr. E. Dawes and N. H. Baynes, *Three Byzantine Saints* (London and Oxford, 1948), 195-270.

Life of Theodore of Syceon, ed. and tr. A. J. Festugière (Subsidia hagiographica 48, Brussels, 1970); tr. E. Dawes and N. H. Baynes, *Three Byzantine Saints* (London and Oxford, 1948), 87-192.

Malalas, *Chronicle*, ed. L. Dindorf (*CSHB*, Bonn, 1831).

Marcellinus Comes, *Chronicle*, ed. T. Mommsen (*MGH Auct. Ant.* XI, *Chron. min.* ii, Berlin, 1893-4).

BIBLIOGRAPHY

Maurice, *Strategicon*, ed. G. T. Dennis, with German tr. by E. Gamillscheg (Vienna, 1981); English tr. by G. T. Dennis (Philadelphia, 1984).

Menander Protector, fragments (*FHG* iv. 200-69).

Michael the Syrian, *Chronique*, ed. and tr. J. B. Chabot (Paris, 1899-1910).

Miracula S. Demetrii, ed. P. Lemerle (Paris, 1979).

Notitia Dignitatum, ed. O. Seeck (Berlin, 1876).

Passio S. Golindouch by Eustratius, ed. A. Papadopoulos-Kerameus, Ἀνάλεκτα Ἰεροσολυμιτικῆς Σταχνολογίας 4 (St Petersburg, 1897), 149-74; 'La Passion géorgienne de sainte Golinduch', tr. G. Garitte, *AB* 74 (1956), 405-40.

Paul the Deacon, *History of the Lombards*, ed. L. Bethmann and G. Waitz (*MGH Scriptores rerum Langobard. et Ital. saec. VI-IX*, Hanover, 1878).

Peter the Patrician, fragments (*FHG* iv. 181-91).

Photius, *Bibliotheca*, ed. R. Henry (Paris, 1959-77).

Priscus of Panium, ed. and tr. R. C. Blockley, *The Fragmentary Classicising Historians of the Later Roman Empire* ii (ARCA 10, Liverpool, 1983).

Procopius, *Works*, ed. J. Haury (Leipzig, 1963-4); tr. H. B. Dewing (Loeb, 7 vols., 1940).

Sebeos, *Histoire de Héraclius*, tr. F. Macler (Paris, 1904).

Tabari, *Geschichte der Perser und Araber zur Zeit der Sassaniden aus der arabischen Chronik des Tabari*, ed. and tr. T. Nöldeke (Leiden, 1879).

Theophanes, *Chronicle*, ed. C. de Boor (Leipzig, 1883-5).

Theophanes Byzantinus, summary (*FHG* iv. 270-1).

Theophylact Simocatta, *Quaestiones Physicae et Epistolae*, ed. J. F. Boissonade (Paris, 1835).

—— *Questioni naturali*, ed. L. Massa Positano (Naples, 1965).

—— *On Predestined Terms of Life*, ed. and tr. C. Garton and L. G. Westerink (Arethusa Monographs VI, Buffalo, NY, 1978).

—— *History*, ed. C. de Boor, re-ed. P. Wirth (Stuttgart, 1972).

Select secondary works

Adamek, O., *Beiträge zur Geschichte des byzantinischen Kaisers Mauricius (582-602)* (2 parts, *Jahresbericht des Staats-Gymnasiums in Graz*, 1890-1).

Allen, P., *Evagrius Scholasticus the Church Historian* (Spicilegium Sacrum Lovaniense, études et documents, fasc. 41, 1981).

Blockley, R. C., *The Fragmentary Classicising Historians of the Later Roman Empire* (ARCA 6, Liverpool, 1981).

Bury, J. B., *A History of the Later Roman Empire from Arcadius to Irene* (London, 1889). [*HLRE (1)*]

—— *A History of the Later Roman Empire from the death of Theodosius to the death of Justinian* (London, 1923). [*HLRE (2)*]

Cambridge History of Iran iii, ed. E. Yarshater (Cambridge, 1983).

Cameron, Alan, *Circus Factions* (Oxford, 1976).

Cameron, Averil, *Agathias* (Oxford, 1970).

Dillemann, L., *Haute Mésopotamie et pays adjacents* (Paris, 1962).

Goubert, P., *Byzance avant l'Islam* i, ii (1), ii (2) (Paris, 1951-65).

BIBLIOGRAPHY

Haussig, H. W., 'Theophylakts Exkurs über die skythischen Völker', *Byzantion* 23 (1953), 275-462.

Higgins, M. J., *The Persian War of the Emperor Maurice (582-602)*, i: *The Chronology* (Washington, 1939). [*Persian War*]

Hoddinott, R. F., *Bulgaria in Antiquity* (London, 1975).

Janin, R., *Constantinople byzantine* (2nd edn., Paris, 1964). [*Constantinople*]

Jones, A. H. M., *The Later Roman Empire, 284-602. A Social, Economic, and Administrative Survey* (Oxford, 1964). [*LRE*]

Justi, F., *Iranisches Namenbuch* (Marburg, 1895).

Leanza, S., 'Motivi cristiani nelle storie di Teofilatto Simocatta', in *Umanità e storia, scritti in onore di Adelchi Attisani* (Messina, 1971), ii. 553-74.

—— 'Citazioni e reminiscenze di autori classici nelle opere di Teofilatto Simocatta', in *Studi classici in onore di Quintino Cataudella* (Catania, 1972), ii. 573-90.

Mango, C. A., *The Brazen House. A study of the vestibule of the Imperial Palace of Constantinople* (Arkæol. Kunsthist. Medd. Dan. Vid. Selsk. 4, no. 4, Copenhagen, 1959). [*Brazen House*]

Olajos, T., 'Données et hypothèses concernant la carrière de Théophylacte Simocatta', *Acta Classica Universitatis Scientiarum Debreceniensis* 17-18 (1981-2), 39-47.

Popović, V., 'Les témoins archéologiques des invasions avaro-slaves dans l'Illyricum byzantin', *Mélanges de l'école française de Rome, Antiquité* 87 (1975), 445-504.

Rawlinson, H. C., 'The Site of Atropatenian Ecbatana', *JRGS* 10 (1840), 1-158.

Stein, E., *Studien zur Geschichte des byzantinischen Reiches, vornehmlich unter den Kaisern Justinus II. und Tiberius Constantinus* (Stuttgart, 1919).

Veh, O., *Untersuchungen zu dem byzantinischen Historiker Theophylaktos Simokattes* (Jahresbericht 1956/7 des Human. Gymnas. Furth i. Bay.).

Whitby, L. M., 'The *Historiae* of Theophylact Simocatta', unpublished Oxford D.Phil. thesis (1981).

—— 'Theophylact's Knowledge of Languages', *Byzantion* 52 (1982), 425-8.

—— 'Theophanes' Chronicle Source for the Reigns of Justin II, Tiberius and Maurice (A.D. 565-602)', *Byzantion* 53 (1983), 312-45.

—— 'The Great Chronographer and Theophanes', *BMGS* 8 (1982/3), 1-20.

Maps

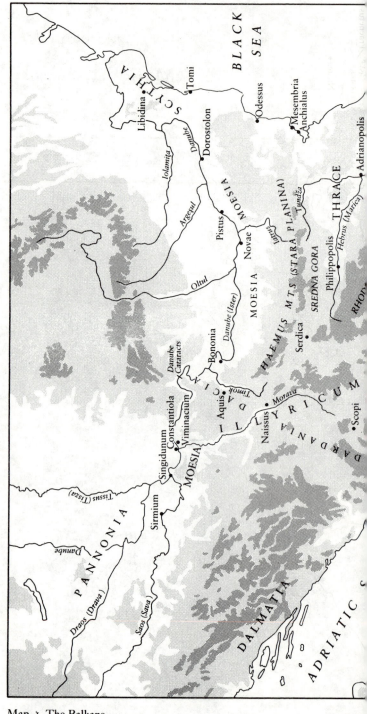

Map. 1. The Balkans

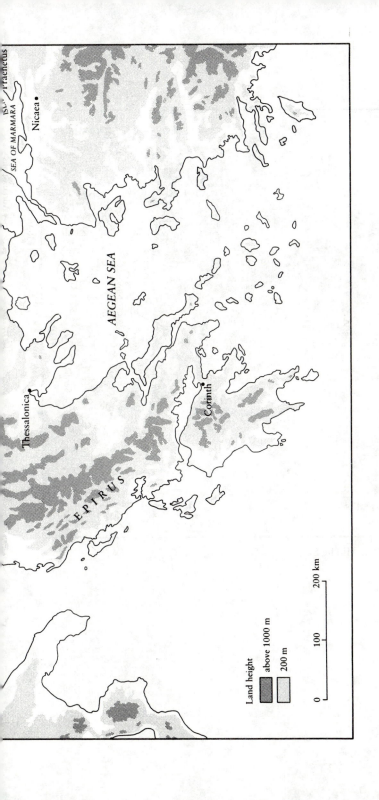

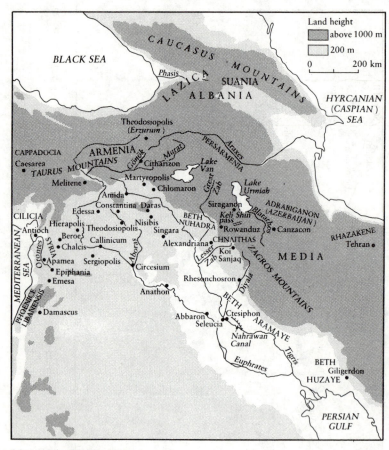

Map 2. The Middle East

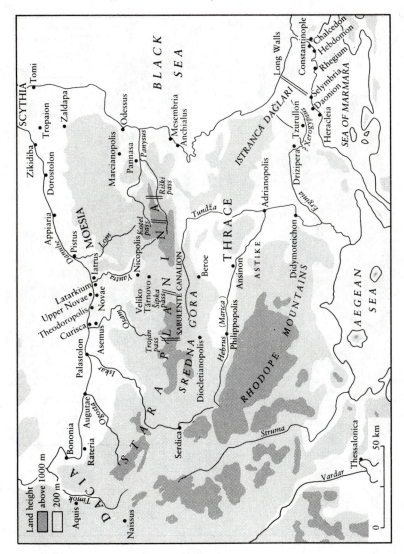

Map 3: Thrace

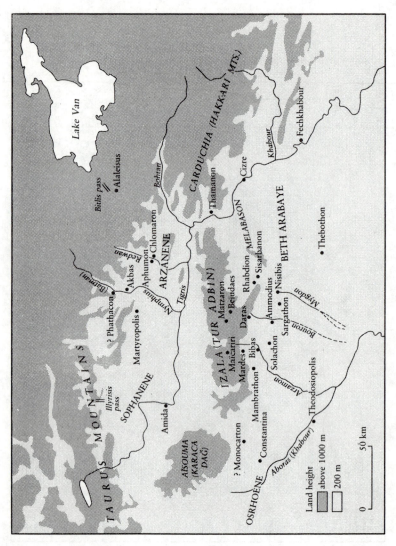

Map 4. Upper Mesopotamia